HOMICIDE

FOUNDATIONS OF HUMAN BEHAVIOR

An Aldine de Gruyter Series of Texts and Monographs

Edited by
Sarah Blaffer Hrdy, *University of California, Davis*
Richard W. Wrangham, *University of Michigan*

Homicide. 1988
Martin Daly and Margo Wilson

The Biology of Moral Systems. 1987
Richard D. Alexander

Child Abuse and Neglect: Biosocial Dimensions. 1987
Richard J. Gelles and Jane B. Lancaster, Editors

Parenting Across the Life Span: Biosocial Dimensions. 1987
Jane B. Lancaster, Jeanne Altmann, Alice S. Rossi, and Lonnie R. Sherrod, Editors

Primate Evolution and Human Origins. 1987
Russell L. Ciochon and John G. Fleagle, Editors

Human Birth: An Evolutionary Perspective. 1987
Wenda R. Trevathan

School-Age Pregnancy and Parenthood: Biosocial Dimensions. 1986
Jane B. Lancaster and Beatrix A. Hamburg, Editors

Despotism and Differential Reproduction: A Darwinian View of History. 1986
Laura L. Betzig

Sex and Friendship in Baboons. 1985
Barbara Boardman Smuts

Infanticide: Comparative and Evolutionary Perspectives. 1984
Glenn Hausfater and Sarah Blaffer Hrdy, Editors

Navajo Infancy: An Ethological Study of Child Development. 1983
James S. Chisholm

In Preparation

Human Ethology
Irenäus Eibl-Eibesfeldt

Brain and Behavior: Biosocial Dimensions
Kathleen Gibson and Anne Petersen, Editors

Early Hominid Activities at Olduvai
Richard B. Potts

Evolutionary History of the Robust Australopithecines
Frederick E. Grine, Editor

Inujjuamiut Foraging Strategies
Eric Alden Smith

Human Reproductive Ecology
James W. Wood

HOMICIDE

Martin Daly
Margo Wilson

ALDINE DE GRUYTER
New York

About the Authors

Martin Daly is Professor of Psychology and Biology, and **Margo Wilson** is Research Associate in Psychology at McMaster University. They have published results of their research, jointly and separately, in more than 40 scientific journals ranging from *The American Anthropologist* to the *Zeitschrift für Tierpsychologie* and in edited volumes ranging from "The Masculine Gender" (1973) to "Child Abuse and Neglect" (1987). Their first coauthored work, "Sex, Evolution and Behavior" appeared in 1978.

ALDINE DE GRUYTER
A Division of Walter de Gruyter, Inc.
200 Saw Mill River Road
Hawthorne, New York 10532

Library of Congress Cataloging-in-Publication Data

Daly, Martin, 1944–
  Homicide.

  Bibliography: p.
  Includes index.
  1. Homicide—Psychological aspects.   2. Behavior evolution. I. Wilson, Margo, 194?–   . II. Title.
HV6515.D35   1988   364.1'523   87-26908
ISBN 0-202-01177-1
ISBN 0-202-01178-X (pbk.)

Printed in the United States of America
10 9 8 7 6 5 4 3 2 1

Contents

v

Preface

Killing one's antagonist is the ultimate conflict resolution technique, and our ancestors discovered it long before they were people. Homicide is a life-and-death issue to the protagonists, of course, but it is also profoundly interesting to those not immediately involved. We invest what is arguably a disproportionate amount of attention, money and expertise in solving, trying and reporting homicides, as compared to other social problems. The public avidly consumes accounts of real-life homicide cases, and murder fiction is more popular still. Nevertheless, we have only the most rudimentary scientific understanding of who is likely to kill whom and why.

Psychiatrists and psychologists have tried to characterize the mind of "the murderer," but he has remained a shadowy—indeed an illusory—figure: Most killers turn out to be ordinary folks, and much more progress has been made toward explaining their actions in terms of culture and circumstance than in terms of personality and psychopathology. But the fact that homicide is a behavioral potentiality of "normal" people does not mean that a psychological account is superfluous, any more than the normalcy of sexuality obviates a psychological understanding thereof. How do normal people weigh the interests of others against their own? In defense of whom or what might a normal person kill? How do mutual valuations arise and how do they influence our willingness to inflict harm? When are normal people in conflict prepared to contemplate violence and why?

This book is an exercise in "evolutionary psychology": the attempt to understand normal social motives as products of the process of evolution by natural selection. There is simply no question that this is the process that created the human psyche, and yet psychologists seldom ask what implications this fact might have for their discipline. We think that the implications are many and profound, touching on such matters as parental affection and rejection, sibling rivalry, sex differences in interests and inclinations, social comparison and achievement motives, our sense of justice, lifespan developmental changes in attitudes, and the phenomenology of the self.

We weren't specifically interested in homicide when we started this project eight years ago. We were interested in the applicability of contemporary evolutionary theory to the analysis of human motives and perceptions of self-interest, and we were interested in where and why individual interests conflict. We doubted the utility of the usual psychological research methods (questionnaires, contrived social psychological experiments, and so forth); we wanted to know about conflicts that were both genuine and severe. Murders obviously filled the bill on both counts, and they also seemed likely to be exceptionally well documented. So we began reading the homicide literature, seeking answers to such questions as "What demographic factors are associated with risk of filicide, parricide and fratricide?" or "Under what circumstances do men kill their wives?" To our surprise, the answers simply weren't there.

Gradually we came to realize that whereas aggregate homicide data have been studied by sociologists seeking social structural explanations for variable rates, and individual homicide cases have been studied by psychiatrists seeking syndromes, hardly anyone had yet approached the analysis of homicides in the light of *any* sort of theory of interpersonal conflict, evolutionary or otherwise. No-one had compared an observed distribution of victim-killer relationships to any sort of "expected" distribution, nor asked about patterns of killer-victim age disparities in familial killings, nor carried out any of a dozen other kinds of analyses that you will encounter in this book. We believe that an evolutionary psychological approach affords a deeper view and deeper understanding of homicidal violence.

Martin Daly
Margo Wilson

Acknowledgments

We are grateful to Craig McKie, J.A. Norland, Gordon Priest, Bryan Reingold, and especially Joanne Lacroix at Statistics Canada, for a great deal of generous assistance. Joanne has repeatedly cleared up ambiguities and anomalies, sometimes pursuing cases back to the reporting police department; we apologize for burdening her with so many questions. We admire and appreciate her consistent concern that the Statistics Canada homicide data file be as complete and accurate as possible. The analyses in this book are based upon the information in that file as of the spring of 1986.

We are grateful, too, to James Bannon, the deputy chief of the Detroit police at the time of our studies there, and Robert Hislop, then head of homicide investigations; both were more than generous in permitting and facilitating our studies of data from their files.

Several people have helped this venture with information. We especially thank Marie Wilt Swanson for her exceptional collegial generosity in giving us, two strangers, all the raw coding forms from her thesis research on Detroit homicides. Alison Wallace sent us useful data on Australian homicides before her monograph was published, and Gisli Gudjonsson related the details of Iceland's only two homicides in forty years. Sarah Hrdy donated an obscure Belgian monograph full of data, which we would otherwise have missed.

Our research and thinking about human psychology and behavior in an evolutionary perspective have been influenced by many friends and colleagues. Outstanding among them has been Richard Alexander, whose criticism and support have been invaluable; his thoughts about society and history surely inform this book more than even we realize. We've profited greatly from discussions with colleagues too numerous to list, at the informal meetings of the Michigan-Northwestern evolution group. Don Symons, Leda Cosmides, and John Tooby have impressed upon us the need to focus upon the evolution of the human psyche, and Randy and Nancy Thornhill have been unfailing sources of encouragement, critical discussion, and insights. Several students have helped out with our homicide research over the years; Suzanne Weghorst and Catherine Carlson are especially deserving of acknowledgment for their intellectual contributions to the final product. Valuable critical comments on the manuscript itself have been provided by Irv DeVore, Mildred Dickemann, Sarah Hrdy, James Wright, and James Q. Wilson. Much of the work on this book was completed during a sabbatical in the anthropology department at Harvard University. Our thanks to Irv DeVore for his many contributions to our enjoyment of that year; and to Leda, John, Irv and the other participants in the "Darwinian psychology and anthropology table" at North House, for lively critical discussion of evolutionary psychology, in general, and of many of the ideas and analyses in this book, in particular. Thanks, too, to the librarians at Harvard, especially at the Tozzer Library.

Our research on homicide would never have been undertaken without the generous support of the Harry Frank Guggenheim Foundation. Some of the research reported in this book has also derived support from Health & Welfare Canada, from the Natural Sciences & Engineering Research Council of Canada, and from the Social Sciences & Humanities Research Council of Canada. Thanks to all of these agencies, and to all the helpful people in our home department of psychology at McMaster University, especially Bev Platt and Wendy Selbie.

Homicide and Human Nature

— 1 —

Why do people kill one another? Many previous writers have hoped to illuminate the murky subject of human violence by theorizing about human nature. Their theories seem to have been more successful at provoking hostility than explaining it. Thinkers from St. Paul to Konrad Lorenz have been taken to task, with considerable justice, for misanthropic moralizing, for logical circularity, and for defending the interests of the privileged. We think the conceptual tools are available to do a better job.

The very distastefulness of violence obstructs objective analysis by inspiring "explanations" that are really just value judgments. Readiness to resort to violence, for example, is regularly interpreted as "primitive" or "immature." Each of these labels seems at first to imply a coherent theory of the origins of violence. Yet even if one accepts, for the sake of argument, the dubious concept of "primitiveness," there turns out to be no empirical support for the assertion that violence is more characteristic of the "primitive"—whether cultures, species or whatever—than of more "advanced" forms. As for "immaturity," potentially lethal violence—in *Homo sapiens* as in most familiar creatures—is the virtually exclusive province of adults, not juveniles, and there is not a shred of evidence that violent people are the products of some sort of developmental arrest. These labels masquerade as theories, although they are really little more than facile disparagements. They reveal more about the prejudices of their proponents than about the causes of violence, and they are worse than no theories at all.

The manifest inadequacy of such simplistic explanations has led most scientific students of violence to shy away from general theories. Why do people kill one another? A hundred answers spring to mind, each limited in its domain but tractable to investigation. Because violent people were themselves abused in childhood. Because of envy engendered by social inequities. Because the penalties are not severe enough. Because of brain tumors, hormone imbalances, and alcohol-induced

1

psychoses. Because modern weapons bypass our natural face-to-face inhibitions and empathies. Because of the violence on TV.

Every one of these answers can be used to generate testable hypotheses. Thus, some investigators compare convicted killers with nonviolent control groups, seeking objectively measurable differences in physiology or personality or upbringing. Others predict that particular cultural or demographic measures will be associated with differential rates of violence in comparisons among nations or cities. Research proliferates. The researchers stake out careers as the leading advocates of one or another hypothesis or "model." And indeed, there is evidently some truth to all of them, for they are seldom formulated as alternatives. Any of the above hypotheses, for example, might be supported or refuted by empirical test and we would remain none the wiser about the validity of the others. One answer tries to characterize the emotions motivating homicidal action; another addresses developmental antecedents. One theorist explains human action in terms of anticipated rewards and punishments, while another invokes androgens or endorphins. Each addresses one small part of what we want to know when we ask "why."

We believe that there is still a place—indeed, a need—for a more encompassing perspective, one that will account for violence within the framework of a well-founded general theory of human nature. We believe, moreover, that the basis for such a theory of human nature is already available in an existing general theory of the nature of all life. This general theory was first proposed well over a hundred years ago and is today about as legitimately controversial as, say, the atomic theory (still, after all, "just a theory" of the nature of matter). In other words, we know with as much certainty as science knows anything that the theory in question is basically correct. It is the bedrock of all life sciences from molecular biology to community ecology, and yet its relevance to the social sciences remains shamefully unappreciated. We refer, of course, to Darwin's theory of evolution by natural selection.

A Brief Introduction to "Selection Thinking"

Organisms are complex adaptive systems. How can such order have come into being? Only two coherent answers have been proposed, and only one turns out to be worth considering. The older theory is that organisms are adaptively constructed because someone made them that way. This is an enormously popular theory which has been invented many times in many lands, but it is scientifically worthless. The problem with creationism as a scientific theory is not its transparent anthropomorphism, nor even that its advocates always seem sure which one of the numerous creation stories is the true one. The more serious problem is that creationism is simply devoid of empirical implications. Whatever turns up must be the will of the creator(s). Implications for the practical investigation of the natural world are nil.

The adaptive construction of organisms once constituted the most powerful argument for the existence of god(s). Charles Darwin and Alfred Russel Wallace destroyed that argument in 1858, when they described a natural process that creates adaptation automatically. Darwin called it "natural selection." According to Darwin and Wallace, adaptation arises because the continual generation of random variation is continually followed by differential survival and proliferation that is nonrandom, the more adaptive forms persisting while their alternatives perish. This is a theory with endless implications about what we are likely to encounter in the natural world, and about how we should go about investigating it. If anyone has come up with a third alternative to explain why organisms are adaptively constructed, it has not been made generally known.

When we say that organisms are complex adaptive systems, we mean that their attributes appear to have been shaped to their purposes. This is perhaps clearest with respect to morphology. We find a fossil jaw full of molars, which are evidently grinding teeth, and we infer that an extinct creature with such teeth must have partaken of grindables. We are reasonably confident that particular tooth structures served particular functions, partly from observation of the diets of living creatures, but also partly from considerations of efficient "design": Molars aren't built to puncture and saber-teeth are not built to grind grain.

If we are good scientists, we do not merely infer the uses of some structure and sit back satisfied. Rather, we treat such inferences as hypotheses, and we try to derive further implications that will subject these hypotheses to potential disconfirmation. We predict, for example, that an apparent grinding tooth will articulate in a certain way with another; we predict muscle attachments appropriate to the hypothesized grinding action; we predict certain patterns of wear. And as each predicted detail—improbable under competing hypotheses—is confirmed, we become increasingly confident that we have attributed the correct adaptive function to the tooth. This sort of attempt to identify the functions of the various attributes of an organism is lately referred to by the ugly label "adaptationism."

The adaptationist approach is just as applicable to living creatures as to extinct ones, and just as applicable to dynamic physiological characteristics as to static morphological ones. The heart, we say, is a pump,

pump, and the movement of fluid is its function. Eyes are organs for seeing, and the adjustable lens and iris are precisely what is needed for resolving images under variable conditions. The evidence that these functions are indeed correctly identified is diverse, but the most essential point is evident design for the function in question (Williams, 1966). The lens must be transparent, the retinal cells must be photoexcitable, and many other improbable things must be true if the eye is going to see. Those who study organismic adaptations are so regularly confronted by the power of natural selection, that apparent failures of design seem themselves to demand explanation in adaptationist terms. Were the heart, for example, a terribly inefficient pump which could be improved by some change in its proportions, we should probably be justified in doubting that its primary function *is* pumping and in hypothesizing that its efficiency as a pump is compromised by the contrary demands of another function, as yet unknown.

It may not at first be obvious just what purpose some structure or physiological process serves. Various hypothetical functions, including cognition, were attributed to the heart before its role in circulating the blood was understood. But progress in understanding has generally followed from the scientist's assuming that the structure under study has *some* utility for its possessor, and attempting to establish what that utility might be. This is an important point because the adaptationist program has recently been criticized from within evolutionary biology, and while the critique has merit, it has been overstated. Palaeontologist Stephen Jay Gould and population geneticist Richard Lewontin have been the main critics of adaptationism. Their pet example is the human chin, and it will suffice to make their point. Our chin is a peculiar structure among the primates, and one might wonder what good it is. Gould and Lewontin (1979) assert that the chin is itself functionless, but can be understood as the epiphenomenal byproduct of other naturally selected changes in growth and structure. Whether they are right in this particular case or not, the general point is well taken: One may indeed slice the pie the wrong way, abstract out meaningless traits, and waste much effort in blind alleys. But what is one to conclude? That Harvey should *not* have wondered what hearts are for? The caveat is useful, but it is hardly a general indictment of adaptationism; as Ernst Mayr (1983) has noted in response to Gould and Lewontin, essentially all the major advances in biological research have been predicated upon the assumption of adaptive function.

In the study of behavior, as in morphology and physiology, researchers assume that the properties of organisms are adaptively constructed as a result of selection, and inquire how behavior is organized to serve the interests of the actors. Predators, for example, exhibit search strategies adapted to the dispersion of their prey, searching the vicinity of the last capture if the prey species is a gregarious one, but moving on if it is solitary (e.g., Smith, 1974). Small mammals that are usually timid become fierce when they have pups to defend (e.g., Svare, 1981). A behavior pattern of unknown utility presents a puzzle to the researcher, who tries to formulate and test hypotheses that would explain why the animal should act thus and not otherwise.

Herbert Spencer epitomized the theory of natural selection as "survival of the fittest." Wallace and Darwin thought the phrase to be apt (see Dawkins, 1982, pp. 179–180), but it has produced a lot of misunderstanding, because both "survival" and "fittest" turn out to mean something other than one might at first imagine. When we speak of the "survival value" of adaptive characteristics, we naturally think of those devices that help the individual find food, conserve energy, dodge predators, and fend off disease. But personal survival is not the bottom line on the natural selective ledger. Over generations, it is successful *traits* that "survive," not individuals, and this sort of long-term survival depends not only or even primarily upon the longevity of those carrying the trait, but upon the abundance of their progeny. Should a more aggressive type of male appear in a population of long-lived pacifists, for example, and should the new type tend to fertilize more females but die younger than the old, then that new type will supplant the old by natural selection, and male life span will decline. It is reproductive success, not bodily condition, that the evolutionist refers to as "fitness."

It is commonly asserted that people and other creatures look to their survival needs first, and that only when these are satisfied do they turn to the gratification of sexual and other "inessential" drives. Many observations seem to affirm such a hierarchy of needs, and it is easy to see why that should be so. Death terminates one's capacity to promote one's fitness; if inclinations have been shaped by natural selection, life should almost always be preferred to death. In other words, life is valued *because* of its historical contribution to fitness, and not as an end in itself. Without this insight, we cannot understand why animals ever take risks. A stickleback fish guarding a nest full of eggs, for example, will stand his ground against an approaching predator longer and dart at the predator more bravely, the more eggs he has in the nest (Pressley, 1981). In effect, the greater fitness value of a larger brood elevates the statistical probability of death that the little fish is prepared to incur. What "selection thinking" suggests is that the evolved motivational mechanisms of all creatures, including ourselves, have been designed to expend the organism's very life in the pursuit of genetic posterity.

Evolutionary Psychology

A Darwinian view of life suggests that the ultimate currency of adaptation is expected fitness. But fitness is a distal end, and we can often analyze the adaptive logic of behavioral control mechanisms quite thoroughly in terms of more proximal goals. Efficiency in gathering food, for example, is obviously useful both for staying alive and for building babies. A student of the adaptive organization of foraging decisions might therefore ignore fitness altogether, and simply test whether the forager acts as if to maximize the number of grams of protein collected per hour or the number of calories ingested per unit of predation risk incurred.

Physiologists and psychologists routinely assume efficient design when they study thirst or respiration or the processing of sensory information, and yet they rarely give a thought to the details of the natural selective process that has sculpted their subject matter. For the most part, this neglect of the natural selective process really does not matter (Symons, 1987). The question of what would be an effective design for an image-analyzing organ, for example, is unaffected by the question of whether the organism's ultimate goal is fitness, survival, or beatitude. However, the concept of the organism as a mere "survival machine" does not always work; sometimes we have to consider the animal's traits as means to the end of genetic posterity in order to understand them. When fathers are seen to evaluate risks differently from bachelors, for example, or mothers are seen to sacrifice their skeletal calcium to maintain their milk quality—when one treats relatives differently from strangers, or age-mates differently from elders—then selection thinking becomes essential if we are ever going to make sense of the actors' motives.

Our theoretical approach in this book is to use Darwin's discovery that the properties of organisms have been shaped by a history of selection as an heuristic for the generation of models and hypotheses about the sorts of psychological mechanisms that an animal like *Homo sapiens* might be expected to have evolved. We then use these psychological models and hypotheses to predict and explain patterned variation in the risk of interpersonal conflict and homicide. What to call the paradigm within which we are working is slightly problematic. Symons (1987) refers to it as "Darwinian psychology," but in our experience the use of this term (and of "Darwinism") sidetracks many readers into fruitless discussion of what Darwin himself did or did not believe. Tooby and Cosmides (1988) use the term "evolutionary psychology" and so shall we, although it can mislead by seeming to imply explicit phylogenetic reconstruction; consider the phrase a shorthand for "psychological theorizing informed by modern evolutionary theory." We shall also use Charnov's (1982) phrase "selection thinking," awkward, perhaps, but refreshingly lacking in distracting connotations. Terminology aside, the important point is this: We are not trying to "test Darwinian theory," but rather to use modern evolutionary ideas to generate new ideas about human social psychology and behavior. The proposition that the human psyche has been shaped by a history of selection cannot reasonably be doubted, but just what this proposition implies has barely begun to be explored.

Evolutionary psychology is not a theory of motivation. No one imagines that genetic posterity (fitness) is a superordinate "goal" in any direct sense. Fitness plays a quite different role in evolutionary theory from the role that self-esteem or a target level of blood glucose plays in a psychological theory. Fitness consequences are invoked not as goals in themselves, but rather to explain why certain goals have come to control behavior at all, and why they are calibrated in one particular way rather than another. This distinction between fitness consequences and proximal objectives is consistently misunderstood by those social scientists who point to vasectomies or adoptions as evidence against selectionist models. Selection shapes the minds and bodies of organisms to the particular conditions within which selection has been operating. Adaptation is not prospective. The apparent purpose in organismic design depends upon the persistence of essential features of historical environments.

The concept of natural selection explains behavior at a distinct level complementary to the explanations afforded by motivational theories. A psychologist might be satisfied to explain the behavior of two men fighting a duel in terms of self-esteem or status or face. An evolutionary psychologist will also want to clarify why the human psyche should be such as to value intangible social resources enough to risk death over them. For although psychology typically focuses upon a different level of explanation from that offered by evolutionary theory, it does not follow that motivational theorists can safely ignore evolutionary biology. Had Freud, for example, better understood Darwin's theory, we might all have been spared his fruitless postulation of the death instinct. Many other theories that are still debated by social scientists implicitly deny the action of natural selection, and are therefore surely wrong. Moreover, what Symons (1987) calls an "imagination informed by Darwinism" is likely to arrive at productive motivational hypotheses that would not otherwise arise. Selection thinking leads us, for example, to a set of detailed predictions about variations in the strength of maternal love as a function of the mother's age, the child's age and several other variables, and there is impressive evidence, as we shall see in Chapters 3 and 4, that this theory of maternal motivation, inspired by evolutionary theory, is correct.

Several critics of "sociobiology" have complained that the application of selection thinking to the explanation of behavior is inappropriately "deterministic." This accusation is philosophically naive. If it is indeed meaningful to complain about "determinism," then the charge must be leveled against all scientific approaches to the study of behavior. Biologist and sociologist alike are committed to the belief that the phenomena under study have knowable causes. We chip away at "unexplained variance" within our various paradigms, trying to better understand what makes the creatures we study do what they do. The entire enterprise is predicated upon "determinism." As our science progresses, we may become concerned about its implications. How, for example, can we retain our belief in free will and personal responsibility as our knowledge and predictive powers grow? But if this is indeed a dilemma, then it is a dilemma for us all. Consider, for example, the writings of the leading behaviorist, B.F. Skinner. His insistence upon the paramount importance and unified nature of experiential learning is generally viewed as the antithesis of "biological determinism," and yet Skinner's faith in the power of reward and punishment compelled him (1971) to reject "freedom and dignity" as illusory. Those who accuse evolutionists of determinism commonly go on to attribute behavioral causation to social and economic factors; ironically, these are the most popular proximal causes in evolutionary theories too. Unfortunately, these critics do not explain how their preferred theories are able to impute causality and yet avoid determinism.

Although "determinism" is a phony issue, there is a genuine disagreement between "imaginations informed by Darwinism" and those social scientists who do not see its relevance to their disciplines. The difference is in conceptions of *human nature*. The very phrase will make some readers recoil, evoking a despised "nativism" antithetical to prevalent emphases upon experiential and circumstantial influences. Yet those who assert that man has no nature would be greatly distressed should their theories of "social comparison processes" or "self-actualization" or whatever prove applicable to Americans but not Papuans. All social theorists, including the staunchest antinativists, seek to describe human nature at some cross-culturally general level of abstraction.

The genuine disagreement is not about the relative importance of "nature vs. nurture" in development (an inane formulation that has spectacularly impeded progress; one might as well ask whether hemoglobin or air is more essential to human survival). The difference is simply this: Those who derive explicit inspiration from selection thinking commonly expect the evolved mechanisms of the human mind to be numerous and specialized, whereas most psychologists and social theorists seem to believe that relatively few general-purpose mechanisms will do the job. As Symons (1987) has argued, much of the dreary "sociobiology debate " of the 1970's can be reduced to this. Evolutionists tend to be impressed by the range of adaptive problems confronting organisms, and to postulate complex evolved strategies to deal with them. Psychologists tend to be suspicious of theories that sound "instinctivist," and invoke the principle of parsimony to justify postulating a simple, unstructured psyche.

Fortunately, there is nothing really fundamental about this division. On the one side, evolutionists have themselves begun to call for parsimony in the postulation of adaptive specializations, citing G.C. Williams (1966) rather than Lloyd Morgan (1894). Meanwhile, in psychology, behaviorist theoretical austerity peaked in 1957 with Skinner's programmatic *reductio ad absurdum:* He insisted that even processes as complex as language acquisition can and should be analyzed only in terms of the few concepts necessary to understand how a rat learns to press a bar for food, whereupon psychologists studying perception, cognition, and language at last called a halt (see, e.g., Chomsky, 1980; Fodor, 1984). Impelled more by their data than by evolutionary ideas, psychologists have taken to positing complex, specialized processes that embed implicit information about the natural world. Even learning theorists have discovered adaptive specialization.

We are both psychologists by training, and we are inspired by the potential of selection thinking as metatheory for psychology. The entire social scientific enterprise is concerned with the characterization of human nature. How could Darwin's more encompassing theory of *organismic* nature—so heuristic in so many areas of the life sciences and unquestionably correct in its basics—how could it *not* be relevant to the task? The development of an evolutionary psychology is inevitable and to be welcomed. It will use selection thinking to generate testable hypotheses about motives and emotions and cognition and child development. It will link psychological processes both to their behavioral outcomes and to the selective pressures that have shaped them. This book is an effort in these directions.

Self-Interest and Conflict

Thinking about the world in terms of natural selection leads to a nonintuitive view of the "interests" of its inhabitants. The ultimate objective of our conspicuously purposive physiology and psychology is not longevity or pleasure or self-actualization or health or wealth or peace of mind. It is fitness. Our appetites and ambitions and intellects and revulsions exist because of their historical contributions to this end. Our perceptions of self-interest have evolved as proximal tokens of expected gains and losses of fitness, "expected" being used here in its statistical sense of what would be anticipated on average from the cumulative evidence of the past.

Such a theory of the origins of perceptions of self-interest suggests, in turn, a theory of the essence of commonalities and conflicts of interest. You and I are likely to perceive our interests to be harmonious insofar as the exigencies that raise or lower my expected fitness have a like effect on yours, and to be in conflict insofar as either's expected fitness can be enhanced at the other's expense. If this theory is sound and nontrivial, then it ought to shed some light on that most drastic of conflict resolution techniques, killing.

In subsequent chapters, we shall explore some implications of the above theory of conflict and apply it to data on homicide. Here, a brief example will illustrate the possible uses of the theory. Selection thinking suggests that genetic relationship should be highly relevant to solidarity and social conflict, because the fitnesses of relatives covary, and do so increasingly the closer the relationship. Siblings, for example, each have a stake in the others' survival and reproductive success, because nieces and nephews are vehicles of fitness, although less valuable in that capacity than one's own offspring. (The power of the idea that collateral as well as descendant kin are valued fitness vehicles was not grasped until 1964, when W.D. Hamilton published his theory of "inclusive fitness," launching a conceptual revolution in ethology.) It follows that animals competing over a resource are likely to be sensitive to the degree of relatedness between their competitors and themselves. They should prove to be less willing to inflict damage, for example, on a related competitor than on a nonrelative, and they should also perceive as less important the difference between gaining the resource and ceding it to the competitor when the latter is kin. Kinship, in other words, should be seen to mitigate conflict, all else being equal, and to do so in proportion to its closeness.

Recent studies of animal behavior abundantly confirm the above theory. A particularly interesting example is that of female ground squirrels who discriminate between those of their littermates who are their full sisters and those who have a different father, their mother having mated with more than one male during her annual estrus (Holmes & Sherman, 1982). When occupying adjacent territories as adults, half sisters exhibit more territorial aggression against one another than do full sisters; a female is moreover less likely to help a littermate half sister than a full sister in defending her burrow against the nonrelatives of both sexes who occasionally invade a female's territory to kill her young. Presumably, a squirrel is able to make this discrimination on the basis of her sister's phenotypic (and hence genetic) similarity to herself, since there is no circumstantial cue that would enable her to differentiate among littermates.

Now, this sort of phenomenon raises an interesting caveat about the likelihood of particular psychological mechanisms having evolved. One might theorize, correctly, that the fitness interests of human identical twins covary perfectly, unlike fraternal twins who are no more closely related than other full siblings. One might then deduce that identicals should act with perfect harmony, each being prepared even to die if the net benefit to the pair were thus enhanced. But is there reason to suppose that identical twins have been born and successfully reared so regularly in our evolutionary history that such a specialized psychology could have evolved? There is not. In the case of the squirrels, mixed paternity of litters and the occupancy of adjacent territories by littermate sisters are both typical; under these conditions, the capacity to discriminate has a sustained and significant selective advantage. No such natural selective scenario seems plausible in the case of people distinguishing their identical from their fraternal twins, because hardly any surviving individuals are likely to have had a twin at all. A much more plausible hypothesis of the same sort, however, is that the paternity of *successive* children has been different with sufficient frequency that we might have evolved specialized psychological mechanisms whose function is to assess the likelihood of common paternity and to adjust the intensity of sibling competition accordingly. Some psychologist should check it out.

Why Homicide?

For the scientist wishing to test theoretically derived propositions about human conflicts, homicides afford a uniquely valuable kind of data. Self-report methods, so often adopted out of expediency, are of dubious validity at the best of times, and perhaps especially so for studying conflict. People may or may not be prepared to discuss their hostilities and affections, and they may or may not be willing to predict their own behavior in various hypothetical situations, but even if we could be sure that our subjects were being forthcoming, we would not have much reason to trust their introspections. Homicide, by contrast, is drastic action, with a resultant validity that all self-report lacks.

One may protest that homicides are too infrequent and extreme to illuminate conflict generally, but there is advantage in focusing upon acts so dire. People who kill in spite of the inhibitions and penalties that confront them are people moved by strong passions. The issues over which people are prepared to kill must surely be those about which they care most profoundly. Moreover, since homicide is viewed so seriously, there is less reporting bias in police files and government statistics on homicide than in the records of any lesser manifestation of conflict.

Homicide is, of course, a heterogeneous class of acts, and the analyses to follow fully acknowledge that fact. Homicides culminating a history of conflict between acquaintances, for example, clearly constitute a different class from those committed by strangers during robberies. As it happens, there are interesting similarities as well as differences between these two sorts of cases, and we shall explore both. Some homicides are premeditated and instrumental while others are impulsive and reckless, but both sorts reflect human passions that are effectively self-interested and therefore prove amenable to our theoretical approach.

It is important to note that our evolutionary psychological approach in no way depends upon homicide *per se* being "an adaptation." It may or may not be the case that actual killing was a regular component of the selective events that shaped the human passions we shall discuss; in either case, adaptation is more appropriately sought at a more psychological level. Suppose, for example, that selection has favored those sexually jealous males who so effectively intimidated their rivals and bullied their wives as to guarantee their paternity of their putative offspring. We might then expect to find male sexual jealousy a prevalent motive in interpersonal violence, including homicide. Moreover, we might predict certain variations in the intensity of jealousy, and hence in the rates of such homicides, as a function of circumstances, societal differences, and demographic variables. This sort of exercise in no way depends upon sexual jealousy *homicides* enhancing their perpetrators' fitness, or indeed having ever done so. It does depend upon sexual jealousy—and, as the argument is here stated, an attendant threat of violence—having enhanced fitness during some selective past. Whether homicide has been a significant selective force in human evolution, and whether selection has shaped the specific intent to kill, are two interesting (and distinct) questions, but our treatment of homicide is not predicated upon an affirmative answer to either one.

We reiterate that in using selection thinking as an heuristic for generating psychological hypotheses and predictions about homicide, we do not pretend to be "testing" some monolithic "Darwinian theory." On the contrary, imaginations informed by evolutionary theory often generate *alternative* hypotheses about how selection might have shaped mind and behavior. At what age would you expect wives to be maximally at risk of homicide by their husbands? Selection thinking suggests the hypothesis that postmenopausal women will be least valued by men and therefore most at risk, but it also suggests an alternative, namely that wife-murder is the tip of the iceberg of the coercive violence that men employ to control the *most* reproductively valuable women. As we shall see in Chapter 9, the data match the latter hypothesis better than the former. There is nothing embarrassing or "unscientific" about the fact that imaginations informed by evolutionary theory can generate alternative scenarios. Selection thinking is not merely "a theory," but a paradigm, and it suggests fresh lines of inquiry. (To the best of our knowledge, no previous student of homicide had ever thought to inquire whether the risk of spouse-murder might be systematically related to the parties' ages.)

What's A Homicide?

Recent Australian government statistics report between two and four "homicides" per 100,000 persons per annum (Biles, 1982). Reading on, one may be startled to find that this figure includes all "murders, attempted murders, and manslaughters." What are "attempted murders" doing in there?

The Australian definition is not unique. The official statistics of several countries treat successful and failed murders as a single category, and it must be conceded that such record-keeping has a certain logic. Why, after all, should a particular act of violence be included or excluded from the statistics on the basis of such fortuitous considerations as the distance to the nearest hospital? If our concern is with motives, surely the appropriate cases to be considered are assaults with *intent* to kill.

Problems immediately arise. The distinction between "murder" and "manslaughter," for example, is in principle defined in terms of the intent to kill, but in practice is made on various other criteria including frank plea-bargaining. So should we include the manslaughters and, like the Australians, define homicides as those assaults intended to be fatal regardless of outcome plus those assaults that were fatal regardless of intent? Unfortunately, if we do that, we lose the conceptual unity of intention that was the rationale for including attempted murders. Moreover, intent is a matter of rank speculation, so that it seems certain that there will be a great deal more reporting bias in a sample of "attempted murders" than in a sample of bodies. Finally, one suspects that "attempted" murders may be systematically different from those successfully consummated, as is the case with "attempted" versus actual suicides. Back to square one: We shall consider as homicides only the fatal cases.

But the issue of intent is not so easily swept away. What do we make of the drunken driver who inadvertently kills a pedestrian? Several jurisdictions have recently adopted the charge of "vehicular homicide," and may or may not include such events in their homicide statistics. But this extends the word more widely than seems useful for our purposes, the culpability of the driver notwithstanding. Accidents may be "acts of god" or they may be such that blame can be apportioned; in either case, most people would wish to distinguish accidents from assaults, and so do we. By "homicides," we shall refer to *those interpersonal assaults and other acts directed against another person (for example, poisonings) that occur outside the context of warfare, and that prove fatal.* In our analyses, a "case" will generally equal one body. It is slightly embarrassing that intent, dismissed only a paragraph ago as "rank speculation," has crept back into our definition in the phrase "directed against" and in the discrimination of "assault" from "accident." We plead pragmatism. Definitions are tricky.

One virtue of the definition stated above is that it identifies a set of cases corresponding almost perfectly with those that are investigated by the homicide division of the Detroit police, and with those that are included in the comprehensive homicide data files assembled by Statistics Canada. These happen to be the archival sources for most of our own original research, and we shall present many analyses of data from these two sources. However, we have also utilized any available data that would permit novel analyses of interest, whatever the source, and wherever possible we introduce evidence from a variety of human societies. We believe that we have avoided the ethnocentric error of equating human nature with the cultural peculiarities of North America.

When we are engaged in analyses of the characteristics of homicide offenders, we confront another problem that is just as tricky as that of defining a case. Who are to be considered confirmed offenders? An obvious answer would seem to be those convicted after trial. However, this would be a hopelessly biasing criterion. In a sample of homicides committed in Detroit in 1972, for example, 20 men were convicted for killing their wives and 9 women were convicted for killing their husbands. Were these the only cases considered, one would never suspect that more women in fact killed their spouses in Detroit in 1972 than did men. It so happens that 75% of homicidal wives had their cases dismissed without a trial, compared to just 20% of homicidal husbands (see p. 200).

We are just as interested in those homicides judged to be "justifiable" as in those judged to be "criminal," and we shall have a good deal to say about what distinguishes them. The exclusion of "justifiable" homicides could have a major impact on one's conclusions, for such cases are far more frequent than is generally known. In the single city of Miami, Florida, for example, more than 100 of the solved homicides that occurred in 1980 were deemed to be either "justifiable" or "excusable"— whether at the prosecutor's discretion or on the decision of a grand jury—and were therefore not prosecuted (Wilbanks, 1984). Some of these cases involved self-defense, but in many others the victim was neither armed nor threatening. (With respect to the question of what justifies homicide, the written law and actual practice may be very different, as we shall see in subsequent chapters.)

So if our aim is to understand the behavior of killers, not prosecutors, our offender populations will have to include those identified by the police but not convicted. Such a criterion must of course admit some number of falsely accused innocents, but fear that the number will be significant is probably unfounded. The whodunits notwithstanding, a homicide detective's life contains a good deal more paperwork than mystery. When solved cases are not prosecuted, it is usually either because the victim is an unsympathetic character who is believed to have "deserved" his demise (making a jury conviction unlikely), or else because the killer acted in self-defense or cannot be proved *not* to have done so. Even in the case of acquittals after trial, the offender's identity is less often in doubt than are the circumstances surrounding the death.

Most of the analyses of North American homicides in the criminological literature define the subject matter essentially as do we, and several have exploited similar archival materials. But selection thinking has inspired us to analyze the data in a number of novel ways, and we believe that the results will engage any reader with an interest in murder.

Killing
Kinfolks

— 2 —

In the mythology of many cultures, the primordial homicide was a fratricide. The antagonists are often portrayed as the first pair of brothers in the history of the world. According to one such tale, still recounted and enjoyed in our society, the killer Cain resented his younger brother Abel's greater success in currying favor with their god; their conflict is furthermore portrayed as one between pastoralist and crop farmer, as befits the near eastern etiology of this particular variant. In similar stories from other cultures, the quarrel concerns inheritance or women or envy of the brother's skills.

It really does not matter whether these tales of fraternal violence have a factual basis, nor is it of great import to what degree they have been separately invented as opposed to having spread from one society to another. Whatever their origins, their persistent appeal is revealing. They strike a chord of human experience. Brothers can indeed be fierce competitors, and if they are important men, their conflicts may prove woefully consequential for others within their social sphere.

Potentially homicidal conflicts within the family extend far beyond sibling rivalries. According to Freud's enormously influential theory of the Oedipus complex, the urge to kill one's father is a normal, perhaps universal, element of the male psyche. Women need not feel slighted: Various writers have insisted that normal girls are equally eager to kill their mothers. And of course, parents are widely alleged to reciprocate with murderous inclinations of their own. Little wonder, then, that the "central preoccupation of childhood," according to the child psychoanalyst Dorothy Bloch (1978), turns out to be our fear that our parents will decide to do us in!

If social scientists are to be believed, these murderous impulses within the family are not merely the stuff of our fantasies, but are manifest in action as well. According to Richard Gelles and Murray Straus (1979), probably the best-known investigators of family violence in contemporary America:

17

> The family is the most frequent single locus of all types of violence ranging from slaps, to beatings, to torture, to murder. Students of homicide are well aware that more murder victims are members of the same family than any other category of murder-victim relationship . . . . In fact, violence is so common in the family that we have said it is at least as typical of family relations as is love. (p. 188)

This is all rather puzzling from the perspective of evolutionary theory. The ultimate "objective" of the evolved psychological mechanisms of any creature is hypothesized to be the enhancement of the individual's "inclusive fitness" (Hamilton, 1964), a quantity which refers to the focal individual's contribution to the proliferation of copies of his or her genes. Selection—both "natural" and "sexual"—favors only those characteristics that contribute to fitness, because selection *is* differential success in gene replication. One's inclusive fitness can be promoted both by personal reproduction and by the promotion of the reproductive prospects of genetic relatives. Ego's daughter, for example, carries half of Ego's genes by direct descent; Ego's sister also carries half of Ego's genes (on average) by virtue of descent from the same parents. From Ego's perspective, then, reproduction by a daughter will have identical inclusive fitness consequences as reproduction by a sister, each replicating a like proportion of Ego's genotype. The two relatives are equally "valuable" to Ego as vehicles of fitness, and one may therefore anticipate that Ego's evolved motivational mechanisms should be such as to cherish both. (Though perhaps not equally. The precise equation is complicated by changes in fitness value with age and by the fact that paternity is mistakable, so that the "sister" might be only a half sister. These are matters to which we shall return.)

In other words, natural selection creates "nepotism": inclinations to discriminate in favor of blood relatives. Indeed, it is sometimes convenient to divide *all* adaptive action into the two categories of resource accrual and nepotism, the latter referring to the expenditure of one's resources in order to create genetic relatives and promote their fitness. So if the motivational mechanisms of all creatures have evolved to generate behavior that is effectively nepotistic, then what on earth are we doing killing relatives?

Who Kills Whom? Some American Data

In the summer of 1979, we contacted the Detroit, Michigan, police department, seeking a sample of homicide cases for analysis. Detroit is a city well-known for a substantial incidence of homicide, and it happened to be handy to our home in southern Ontario. But Detroit had an even more important advantage. The deputy chief of police, Dr. James Bannon, was a sociologist by training, and was sympathetic to the general idea of research from police archives. Indeed, he had himself published statistical studies of assaults, based on his department's records.

We chose as our sample all cases that had occurred in 1972, partly because this was a year far enough in the past that the information on offenders and dispositions was likely to be as complete as ever it would be, and partly because we could utilize some prior codings of the same year's cases that had been undertaken several years earlier by a doctoral student in sociology, Marie Wilt (1974).

In 1972, 690 nonaccidental homicides occurred in Detroit and were investigated by the city police department's homicide bureau. By October 1980, 512 of these cases were "closed," which means that the police had identified a perpetrator to their own satisfaction, regardless of whether there had been a prosecution. In 508 closed cases, the relationship between victim and offender was known. These included 243 unrelated acquaintances (47.8%), 138 strangers (27.2%), and 127 "relatives" (25.0%).

One murder victim in four was related to the killer, then, at least among the solved cases. (There are several reasons to believe that the unsolved cases include a much higher proportion of homicides by strangers and a much lower proportion by relatives.)

Those 127 victims related to their killers included only 32 consanguineal relatives, however (Daly & Wilson, 1982). Of the other 95, 80 were spouses (36 women killed by their husbands and 44 men killed by their wives), while 10 were in-laws, and 5 were steprelations. The 32 victims of genealogical relatives included 8 who were children of their killers, 11 who were the killers' parents, 9 brothers, and 1 sister. One 18-year-old boy killed his 14-year-old female cousin. A 65-year-old man killed his 52-year-old nephew. A 12-year-old boy killed his infant nephew.

So most murdered "relatives" turned out to be spouses, a very special kind of "kinship" that will warrant a chapter of its own, and many of the remainder were also relatives by marriage. Blood kin accounted for only 25.2% of the 127 "relatives" or 6.3% of the total of 508 homicides.

Are these Detroit data typical of American homicide? Unfortunately, previous studies of the cases in one or another city have not fully distinguished *genealogical* (blood) relationship from *affinal* (marital) relationship, and the same goes for the widely publicized national murder statistics compiled by the Federal Bureau of Investigation (FBI). However, the proportions of victim–killer relationships in previous studies that fall into the broad categories of strangers, "relatives," acquaintances, and so forth indicate that the Detroit data are indeed typical. The classic study of a police department's homicide archives is Marvin Wolfgang's (1958) analysis of cases occurring in Philadelphia between 1948 and 1952. He found that 136 of 550 people killed by known assailants, 24.7%, were the victims of "relatives," a result almost identical to the 25.0% in our Detroit study. And as in Detroit, most of these "relatives" were in fact spouses. Among the remainder, Wolfgang did not distinguish affines from genealogical kin more distant than siblings, but the total number of blood relatives lay somewhere between 26 (4.7% of the entire sample of solved cases) and 36 (6.5%).

In a recent study of "Murder in Miami," criminologist William Wilbanks (1984) appended a brief case summary for each of the 574 homicides occurring in that city in 1980. Out of 494 cases in which the relationship between the victim and the offender or primary suspect could be surmised, we counted just 59 cases of "relatives" (11.9%). These included 43 victims of a spouse or ex-spouse. (Wilbanks's own count is slightly different; his characterization of "common-law marriage" as opposed to a "boyfriend–girlfriend" relationship is undefined and apparently inconsistent, as some of the latter clearly lived together.) Four people were killed by in-laws and three by stepfathers. Only nine of the Miami victims, hence 15.3% of "relatives" and a mere 1.8% of solved cases, died at the hands of blood kin, an even lower proportion than in the Detroit and Philadelphia data.

Do Relatives Pose a Lesser Risk?

So the proportion of blood relatives among American killers turns out to be about 6% in a couple of studies and less than 2% in another, much lower than seems to be widely believed. That's all very well, but what about it? After all, whether there's a-lot-of-familial-homicide-going-on-out-there or not-so-much-really-after-all is a rather pointless debate, the answer being a matter of emphasis and prior expectation. What we should like to assess is whether and to what extent kinship promotes solidarity and mitigates conflict within relationships.

Most people interact with relatives frequently and intensely throughout their lives. Some criminologists and social theorists write about family relationships as if they were distinguished from other relationships *only* by that high frequency and intensity of interaction, and as if genealogical versus affinal kinship were a variable of no particular importance. Wolfgang, for example, has used a triple classification of victim–offender relationships in most of his writings: "primary group relations" versus "acquaintances" versus "strangers." The first of these categories incorporates family, lovers, and friends. In some finer analyses, Wolfgang has distinguished 11 categories of relationship, and yet "family" remained a single category, incorporating all manner of genealogical and affinal relatives.

When U.S. president Lyndon Johnson appointed a commission to investigate the "Causes and Prevention of Violence" in 1968, sociologist William Goode of Columbia University presented expert testimony on the relationship between violent offenders and their victims. Categorizing even more broadly than Wolfgang, Goode conflated relatives, spouses, lovers, and close friends into the single category of "intimates," in order to pose the question, "Why do intimates commit violence against one another?" His answer (Goode, 1969):

> Perhaps the most powerful if crude answer is that they are *there*. Most automobile accidents occur within 25 miles of the home because that is where the cars *are* at the time. Home may not be as dangerous as mines or ski slopes, but more injuries occur there because people are there more of the time. It cannot be surprising that more violence is directed against those with whom we are in more intimate contact. We are all within easy striking distance of our friends and spouses, for a goodly part of the time. Moreover, again crudely but reasonably, we are violent toward our intimates—friends, lovers, spouses—because few others can anger us so much. As they are a main source of our pleasure, they are equally a main source of frustration and hurt. What they do affects us more directly and painfully than what most strangers do. (p. 941)

No doubt this is all perfectly true, and it seems to be a point that needed making. Too many writers have implied—whether because of faulty reasoning or faulty expression—that a large number of homicides in situation X constitutes evidence that situation X is especially dangerous, regardless of whether situation X is itself common or rare. In a recent paper, for example, Franklin Zimring, the director of the University of Chicago Law School's Center for Studies in Criminal Justice, has written (Zimring, Mukherjee, & Van Winkle, 1983):

> It is a criminological cliché that a person is safer in Central Park at three o'clock in the morning than in his or her own bedroom. This chestnut is based on a large body of research. (p. 910)

What Zimring *et al.* do not remark is that this "chestnut" is patent nonsense, confounding frequency with rate. At three o'clock in the morning, two hundred million Americans are in their bedrooms and a handful are in Central Park. If there were only one murder in the park per century, the bedroom would still be far the safer place.

So Goode's point to the effect that the risk of violence is partly a matter of mutual access is well taken. But it still begs all the interesting questions. Of course we do not have violent conflicts with people with whom we do not interact, but neither do we have violent conflicts with all the people with whom we *do* interact. The interesting thing about the distribution of relationships between killers and their victims is that some categories of "intimates" are evidently at higher risk than others. If 6% of homicides in Detroit or 2% in Miami involve blood kin, that is arguably a remarkably *low* percentage considering the probable frequency and intensity of familial interactions. But how are we to analyze the matter further? If we wish to quantify the risks in one type of relationship as opposed to another, it appears that we must somehow measure the "availability" of different categories of potential victims to each potential killer, and that seems an almost insuperable task.

There is, however, a simpler approach to the question of differential risk: We can confine attention to cases involving members of the same household. While we cannot describe the "victim pool" available to a potential killer within the community at large, we can at least describe the lesser pool of *potential victims living in the same household.* This is the approach we adopted in analyzing the risk of familial homicide in Detroit. For the analysis in question, we considered only those 98 homicides for which victim and offender were residents of the same household, and the offender was an "adult" 14 years of age or older. The age of 14 was dictated by available census information, but it is an appropriate cutoff point on other grounds: 14 is about the age at which people begin to kill one another at an appreciable rate. (In Detroit in 1972, less than 1% of all homicide offenders were under 14, whereas over 12% were older teenagers.) We then used United States Census information for the city of Detroit for 1970 to estimate the average household composition of all such adults, our "potential homicide offenders," and hence to describe the pool of potential cohabitant victims. The results are shown in Table 2.1.

The average potential homicide offender had three potential victims available at home, as indicated in the first column of the table. ("0.6 spouses" means than 60% of adults resided with a husband or wife. The category of "other relatives" consists mainly of siblings—recall that our "adults" are as young as 14, and hence often resident in the parental home.) The column labeled "expected" indicates how many victims there would be in each relationship category if victims were distributed in proportion to their availability as indicated in the first column. Clearly, they were not so distributed. There were many more spouses and nonrelatives than one would expect from sheer availability, and

Table 2.1. Risk of Homicide by Relationship (Cohabitants)[a]

The average Detroiter ≥ 14 years old in 1972 lived with 3.0 people	Number of victims		Relative risk (obs./exp.)
	Observed	Expected	
0.6 Spouses	65	(20)	3.32
0.1 Nonrelatives	11	(3)	3.33
0.9 "Offspring"	8	(29)	0.27
0.4 "Parents"	9	(13)	0.69
1.0 Other "relatives"	5	(33)	0.15

[a]Risk of homicide by relationships, considering only those cases where victim and offender were cohabitants, for Detroit 1972. Risk estimates for "offspring", "parents", and other "relatives" are inflated because these categories include step and in-law as well as natural relationships. "Other relatives" are mostly siblings, but census information is not adequate to separate these from more distant relatives. From Daly and Wilson (1982).

many fewer kin. The effect is highly significant ($p < .00001$ by binomial test). Cohabitants who are not blood relatives of the killer are more than eleven times as likely to be murdered as cohabitant kin. Spouses are clearly the principal victims, but if spouses are removed from the analysis, the result is little changed: Unrelated cohabitants still endure more than eleven times the risk experienced by blood kin, and the effect is still highly significant ($p < .00001$ by binomial test).

The difference in risk between blood kin and other cohabitants must in fact be even greater than the data in Table 2.1 suggest. The United States Bureau of the Census does not distinguish steprelationships from their biological counterparts, with the result, for example, that the "0.9 offspring" residing with the average adult Detroiter includes some very small fraction of a stepchild. Since we were obliged to lump step- and natural children in the census data for the reference population, we have done likewise for the homicide sample. Now, as it happens, the eight victims who were "offspring" of their killers include two 5-year-old children killed by stepfathers, as well as two infants whose beating deaths were charged solely against their mothers even though a stepfather was present. (The much greater risk endured by stepchildren in comparison to natural children is a topic to which we shall return in Chapter 4.) The effect of these cases is to exaggerate the risk to "offspring" of the killer. Similarly, both the "parent" and "other relative" categories include homicide victims who were not in fact blood kin of their killers, but were instead relatives by marriage, even though

American adults rarely dwell with such affines. So if all these "fictive kin" categories could be distinguished from blood relationships, the risk differential would surely be seen to be even greater than the elevenfold difference documented in Table 2.1.

This analysis of Detroit data makes it clear that different categories of "intimates" differ dramatically in the likelihood of a homicide between them, and, in particular, that blood relationships are much less lethal than other intimate relationships. Some other analyses of data from other times and places reinforce this conclusion.

Collaborative Killing in 13th-Century England

As part of the centralization of power under the Norman monarchy, a system of itinerant courts, the *eyres,* was established in England in the 12th century. The "justices in eyre," agents of the crown, visited a county at intervals of a few years, and heard and judged the criminal cases that had occurred since their last visit, district by district. Each district was represented by a *jury* of twelve local men, who, unlike a modern jury, were assumed to be familiar with the parties and the facts of each case, so as to present the case fairly to the king's justices. In the event of a homicide, an *appeal* might have been lodged against the killer by a relative of the victim, and again, this had a very different significance from that of a modern appeal. Only in the event of an appeal was the killer arrested and held for trial at the next visit of the eyre. If he evaded arrest, he was *outlawed:* stripped of all property and placed under sentence of death. Any able-bodied man who lodged an appeal might be obliged to duel with the accused if the latter denied the charge.

The eyres pursued their mandate zealously. In the event of a conviction, the felon's chattels were confiscated by the king. By the 13th century, the crown had gained a virtual monopoly of the right to try criminal homicide. In principal, all homicides were to be reported and tried, whether appealed or not; the members of the jury were held responsible if a killing in their district was not made known to the eyre, and the whole district was then fined. If a homicide victim was of Norman descent, an additional *murdrum* fine was levied, again against the entire district in which the death had taken place.

The rolls on which 13th-century court clerks recorded the proceedings in eyre survive today in the Public Record Office in London. These rolls remain a superb archive, from which, in 1977, historian James Given published a detailed analysis of "Society and Homicide in Thirteenth Century England."

In Given's sample of several thousand cases, more than one-third of all homicides were collaborative affairs, in which two or more people were identified as co-offenders. This peculiarity of 13th-century English homicide affords an opportunity for a quite different sort of analysis of kinship effects, complementing that which we conducted in the Detroit data. The logic is as follows. If conflict and cooperation were to arise in proportion to "intimacy"—that is in proportion to the frequency and intensity of social interactions—then we might expect that the more intimate types of relationship would provide more opportunities for *both* conflict *and* cooperation. It should then follow that those relatively intimate links that are prevalent among victim–offender relationships will turn out to be similarly prevalent within a sample of persons collaborating in homicide. In other words, if conflicts and alliances tend to arise among "intimates" merely because, as Goode put it, "they are *there*," then the distribution of victim–offender relationships should look like the distribution of co-offender relationships. Insofar as relatedness promotes cooperation and mitigates conflict, however, these two distributions should look different.

The distributions of victim–offender and co-offender relationships within Given's sample are portrayed in Figure 2.1, and they are dramatically different. Co-offenders were more than three times as likely to be related to one another as were victim and offender (20.2 vs. 6.5%). On closer examination, this difference is much greater still, for the so-called "relatives" are not the same: 75% of "related" co-offenders were blood kin, compared to just 35% of "related" victims. So if we confine attention to *blood* relatives, the co-offenders were more than *six* times as likely to be related to one another as were victim and offender (15.2 vs. 2.3%).

As in the Detroit analysis, spouses are numerically important in these English data, amounting to more than half of the "related" victims but less than a quarter of the "related" co-offenders. If spouses are removed from consideration, however, the affinal versus blood kin contrast remains striking: Affines represent 23.4% of "related" victims, but only 3.2% of "related" co-offenders. A 13th-century Englishman was far less likely to kill his brother than to unite with that brother in the killing of a nonrelative, but the same could certainly not be said about his brother-*in-law*.

Collaborative homicide perpetrated by close relatives is not some eccentricity of mediaeval Englishmen. Relatives conspire in violence the world 'round, most notably in the context of feuds between rival lineages. According to Given (1977), "although the formal, institutionalized blood feud had ceased to be a feature of English society by the

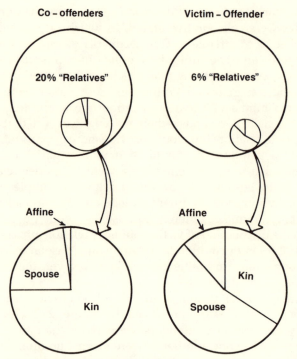

Figure 2.1. Kinship and homicidal conflict in 13th-century England. 2434
homicides form the data base. (After Given, 1977, Tables 5, 6, and
21.)

13th century, kinsmen on occasion still exacted revenge for the death of
one of their relatives." (p. 44). We shall return to the subjects of blood
revenge and family feuds in Chapter 10.

Some Other Studies with Higher Proportions of Blood Kin

In the homicide samples we have discussed thus far, the slayer and
the slain proved to be genetic relatives in some 2–6% of solved cases.
With a little effort, one can find samples within which this proportion is
substantially higher.

Canada

We have analyzed data on all the homicides known to Canadian
police departments between 1974 and 1983. During that decade, 863
Canadians died at the hands of blood relatives, amounting to 15.9% of
5444 solved cases.

This does *not* mean that the rate of familial homicide is higher in Canada than in the United States or in 13th-century England. What it means is that the much higher overall rates of homicide in those two countries were due mainly to much higher rates among nonrelatives. The homicide rate for the city of Detroit in 1972 was about 450 deaths per million citizens. That is approximately 15 times the annual rate for Canada between 1974 and 1983, whereas the rate of homicides by blood relatives is "only" 5 times higher in the Detroit sample.

Denmark

The highest percentage of blood relationships that we have found in any substantial sample of homicide cases comes from Denmark. According to the Italian criminologist Siciliano's (1965) analysis of Danish records, solved cases between 1933 and 1961 included 678 people killed by identified assailants. Of those people, 50.6% were killed by close relatives (parents, offspring, and siblings) and another 2.9% by more distant relatives, including in-laws. A very large proportion of these cases were either infanticides or cases in which a depressed mother killed her children and then herself. The killing of one's own offspring is perhaps the most surprising sort of homicide from a selectionist perspective, and it is the subject of the next two chapters.

It should be noted that Denmark (like the other Scandinavian countries) has an exceptionally low homicide rate. Siciliano's 678 solved cases amount to less than 6 killings per million citizens per annum, and there were very few additional cases remaining unsolved. In comparisons among modern western nations, we find enormous variation in such overall rates (Archer & Gartner, 1984), and wherever the homicide rate is relatively low, the proportion of cases that occur within the family is relatively high. The implication is that intrafamilial homicides are less variable in their incidence, from one country to another, than are some other types of homicide. Thousands of Americans, for example, are murdered annually by strangers during the course of robberies, a variety of homicide that has virtually disappeared in several western European countries.

The point here, as before, is not that Danes are unusually inclined to killings of blood relatives. On the contrary, their rate of killing blood kin—the number of such cases per million citizens per annum—is slightly below the rate in Canada and far below that in Detroit. The point is that the Danish rate of killing nonrelatives is even farther below the corresponding North American rates.

We are sorry to have to keep hammering on an elementary statistical matter, but confusion about the interpretation of rates versus propor-

tions abounds in the professional literature on homicide. Many criminologists—especially those with a fondness for psychobabble about
"national character"—have waxed eloquent on such questions as why
"the Danish murderer" should be the sort to "choose as his victim" an
offspring, while "the American murderer" is likely to pick on a
nonrelative instead. Such speculations are misguided for several reasons, one of which is that they are predicated upon the false assumption
that murderousness resides solely within the killer—that the motive to
kill is initially impersonal and precedes the choice of victim. To the
contrary, all evidence indicates that the urge to kill derives largely from
situations and from the tensions of specific, individual victim–offender
interactions. But the still more basic flaw in such speculation—in this
and many similar instances—is that the whole phenomenon under
discussion is misapprehended. Danes are not more likely to kill their
children than Americans, just as bedrooms are not more dangerous than
Central Park at night.

The Bison-Horn Maria of India

Here and there in the anthropological literature, someone has assembled a sample of homicide cases from some culture very different from
our own. These should provide some of our most valuable materials, but
unfortunately, most such samples consist of a set of the more "interesting" cases, selected on some unspecified criterion, or else they have
been chosen to represent a gamut of "types." As soon as the larger
number of cases is thus sifted, the remaining sample becomes useless
for most purposes, such as the assessment of sex differences or age
effects or the distribution of victim–offender relationships. Happily, a
few samples are relatively uncontaminated by biased inclusion. One
such is Verrier Elwin's (1950) account of 107 cases occurring among the
Bison-Horn Maria of India between 1920 and 1941.

The Bison-Horn Maria, in Elwin's time, were an "aboriginal" group
retaining much of their traditional life style. Their agricultural practices
were still largely "slash-and-burn"—that is, the cutting of some forest,
burning the brush *in situ*, and raising a few crops before the soil gave
out. Some fortunate families, however, had more settled and productive
agricultural holdings, with irrigation works. Hunting and gathering
were also important subsistence activities. Descent reckoning was
primarily patrilineal, although the mother's–brother/sister's–son relationship, so important in matrilineal societies, had ritual and perhaps
practical significance.

Maria men, with the help of their fathers and other agnatic
(patrilineal) kinsmen, purchased wives from those women's patriclans.

A man without the means to purchase a wife could acquire one by working for her father for 3–5 years, after which he was entitled to take her away to his own family's holdings. Successful men might have two or more wives simultaneously, to the great disgruntlement of any agnatic kinsmen still consigned to bachelorhood. Marriage by abduction was alleged to have occurred in the past, but was probably never typical. In all these features, the Bison-Horn Maria resemble many other horticulturalists, whether in South America, Africa or New Guinea.

Though the Maria and other aboriginals were largely left to their traditional devices, the British Raj intruded in the matter of homicide, and it is from the records of British courts that Elwin assembled his materials. His study, therefore, has the virtue of being based upon rather thorough investigative materials, and there is much rich detail; a possible limitation derives from the fact that Elwin included only convictions.

Elwin estimates 69 homicides per million Maria per annum, somewhere between the rates for Canada and Detroit. But of special interest is the very high proportion of cases that involved relatives of one sort of another: Out of 107 murder victims, only 1 was killed by a stranger and 37 more by nonrelatives. Thirty-five people were killed by affines—23 spouses, 10 in-laws, and 2 stepparents; 34 (31.8% of the 107) were killed by their blood kin, and (unlike the Danish sample) only 6 of these were by parents.

Why do Maria homicides so often involve kinsmen? Goode's point about differential access to relatives and nonrelatives (p. 21) is obviously relevant here: In a traditional agricultural society with patrilocal residence patterns and cooperative labor organized along lines of agnatic kinship, men interact with hardly anyone *but* their relatives. The ten victims who were in-laws surely represent a much greater risk in such relationships than the more numerous blood-kin cases, since men live briefly if at all among their in-laws, whereas they pass most of their lives with their agnates. However, there are additional reasons besides mere access for the unusually large number of blood-kin killings. In societies such as the Maria, fierce rivalry among agnates is an ironic consequence of familial solidarity: It is precisely because land and other essential resources are familially held that a man's principal competitors are his brothers and other agnatic kinsmen.

By far the most common issue in fatal disputes between genetic relatives was rivalry among agnates over familial property. An exemplary case is that in which Marvi Chule killed his paternal half-brother Marvi Buti (Elwin's case No. 49). Upon their father's death, the elder Buti had inherited the family farm. Like many a disenfranchised younger brother throughout human history, Chule left home to seek his fortune. He did not find it, and so, after several years, the prodigal Chule returned to his father's land, there to rent a plot from his brother and farm it. So he did, but only for one year. When the lease came up for renewal, Buti at first doubled the rent, and then reneged on the agreement altogether, in order to bestow the land on a third brother. Defeated, Chule again moved away, but on a return visit to collect his possessions, he was confronted by Buti brandishing a knife. To be thus run off his natal farm was too much for the propertyless Chule, whose resentment at last exploded. Close at hand was an axe.

Several other disputes between agnates were similarly concerned with family landholdings, and most of those that were not over land were still about property of one sort or another. A half-brother, a cousin, a second cousin, and an uncle were killed in four separate cases, for example, each the result of a quarrel over a man's unauthorized disposal of his kinsman's animals. One man killed his father for refusing him a loan, and another killed his uncle for refusing to contribute to his bridewealth. One murdered father had purchased wives for his sons, but then decided to keep them—and all the family lands as well—for himself.

Fraternal Strife

Intense sibling rivalry is an ironic consequence of kin solidarity. It is precisely because property is held familially that brothers are likely to be one another's foremost rivals. Conflict between brothers and other agnatic kinsmen is particularly severe where property like the family farm is not considered divisible, or where titles and offices with substantial perquisites are part of the patrimony.

In agricultural societies like the Bison-Horn Maria, where one son gets the farm and the others hit the road, it is hardly surprising that fratricides may constitute a substantial proportion of all homicides: 7.5% of Elwin's 107 cases, for example. Studies of other aboriginal horticultural Indian peoples indicate similar levels of fraternal strife. Six of 100 Bhil homicides summarized by Varma (1978) were fratricides; all 6 were property disputes, which may be contrasted with 8 killings of brothers-in-law, only 1 of which concerned a property or financial issue. A sample of 90 solved homicides among the Munda and Oraon included 9 slayings of brothers. Eight of these arose from property disputes, the ninth from a challenge to an elder brother's authority (Saran, 1974). The inheritance practices of the Bhil, Munda, and Oraon sound like a virtual prescription for fratricide: Ideally, half of the patrimony goes to the *youngest* son and the other half is divided among his elders.

In our urban, industrial society, the patrilineal descent of property is less crucial to a young man's prospects than in agricultural society, and fratricides are accordingly rarer. They still tend to revolve around familial property, however. The 508 solved homicides in Detroit in 1972, for example, included 7 brother–brother cases (1.4% of the total). At least 5 of these resulted from disputes over property or money; in the other 2 cases, the nature of the dispute could not be discerned from the information in the police files.

In foraging (hunting-and-gathering) societies, there is little familial property for brothers to contest, and agnatic kinsmen are themselves a man's most valuable assets, by constituting a deterrent force against mistreatment by hostile nonrelatives, as we shall consider in Chapter 10. We would therefore expect fratricide to be exceedingly rare in such societies, and so it is. We have read a good deal of ethnographic literature on foraging societies, including information on dozens of homicides, but we have yet to encounter even *one* account of a fratricide among people who own and inherit neither land nor domestic animals. No doubt there are *some* such killings—for one thing, even in foraging societies, brothers may be rivals for brides, and for another, there are insane killers who lack normal perceptions of self-interest. But it would appear that the specter of Cain arose only upon the invention of agriculture.

Where the temptation to fratricide really gets out of hand is in the circumstance where brothers are rivals for a position of enormous value, and yet agnatic kinsmen are not themselves a crucial source of a man's power. In a tribal society in which power blocs are patrilineages (or so-called "fraternal interest groups"), the temptation to kill one's kinsman and thereby succeed to chiefly status is tempered by the knowledge that the slaying will cost you at least the one ally in arms and possibly the good will and essential support of other kinsmen as well. In a feudal society, on the other hand, vassalage at least partially replaces kinship as a basis of loyalty and power, and rivalrous power blocs may line up behind related pretenders to the same throne. Here, surely, is a situation designed to overwhelm brotherly affection, and indeed the history of royal families in feudal empires is a seemingly endless tale of fraternal bloodletting (see, e.g., Hogan, 1932; Goody, 1966).

As we have seen, male–male disputes in a traditional patrilineal society frequently involve brothers and other close agnates. This is so partly because proximity and interaction patterns are structured along kinship lines, and partly because kinsmen are inevitable rivals for limited family property. Selection thinking leads us to expect, however, that even here, blood relationship will be associated with a softening of conflict, other things being equal. Our hypothesis is that natural selection has shaped psychological mechanisms of interpersonal "valuation," such that Ego will ordinarily tend to value other individuals in rough proportion to their expected contribution to Ego's inclusive fitness. One major determinant of such valuations will be consanguinity. If Ego finds himself in competition with his brother, Sib, for example, the situation is not the same as competition with an unrelated rival: Sib is valuable to Ego, and Ego should be aggrieved by any wounds that Sib incurs. It follows that Ego will be relatively disinclined to employ potentially dangerous competitive tactics against Sib, as compared to a less closely related rival. The fact of relatedness mutes the conflict by reducing both the perceived cost of a defeat and the perceived benefit of a victory: Should he lose the competition, Ego can still expect to gain some inclusive fitness benefit from Sib's use of the contested resource, and, on the other hand, Ego will suffer an inclusive fitness cost if he has to damage Sib in order to win the contest.

Is there any evidence that such kinship-modulated valuations apply even in patrilineal societies like the Bison-Horn Maria, where agnatic kinsmen are a man's principal rivals? It is certainly easy to find *assertions* of fraternal solidarity in such societies, but one may reasonably wonder if these are not exhortative responses to an appalling *lack* of brotherly love, rather than a statement of reality. We simply do not have the necessary population-at-large data to assess, for example, whether violence is more likely to erupt in an inheritance dispute between half brothers than in one between full brothers, as we would expect. We have found one set of relevant data, however, in an account of sexual rivalry murders among the Tiv of central Nigeria.

The Tiv are farmers, living along the Benue River. Their staple crops are yams, corn, and millet. In 1952, there were about 800,000 Tiv, divided into several patrilineal clans, each inhabiting a *tar* or clan territory. Like many people, the Tiv learn and recite extensive genealogies. They trace their ancestry through some 17 or 18 generations to a common ancestor "Tiv," a son of god, and they are highly cognizant of the nested hierarchy of patrilineages that unites kinsmen into ever larger units at each earlier generation. According to anthropologists Laura and Paul Bohannan (1953), who studied the Tiv during colonial days, "The greater the distance, genealogically, between two lineages inhabiting adjacent *tar*, the more likely they are to think of each other as potential enemies" (p. 25).

Bridewealth in Tivland is explicitly concerned with the acquisition of the wife's reproductive powers by the husband's patriclan. Only a small initial payment is required for the husband to take his bride home, but future payments are demanded on a per-birth basis. If the father cannot or will not make the payment, then his lineage cannot claim the baby, who is instead designated the son or daughter of its maternal grandfather and hence a member of its mother's patrilineage.

Tiv families live in compounds: clusters of huts containing as many as a hundred people. The men in such a compound are typically close agnates, who work together and fight their enemies side-by-side. A few successful men are highly polygamous; one of the Bohannans' informants, for example, proudly recounted that his grandfather had had 21 wives. This sounds like a situation fraught with possibilities for jealousy and violence, and so it is, but agnatic solidarity is invoked to mitigate the dangers (Bohannan & Bohannan, 1953):

> To strike a close agnate is a moral offense [whereas] to get into a fight with a non-Tiv is sometimes foolhardy, but certainly not immoral . . . Tiv are highly indignant when gaoled for killing a foreigner in a brawl. (p. 26)

What makes the Tiv case a particularly nice illustration is that the Bohannans back it up with numbers. They conducted a survey of living arrangements, and they report that 83% of the men within a compound and within the larger *tar* share the lineage name of that *tar*, which bespeaks a common patrilineal ancestor about four or five generations back. (Imagine a trip to the ancestral McLeod turf, there to find that 83% of the men are still named McLeod.) Then, as Elwin had done with the Bison-Horn Maria, Paul Bohannan (1960a) assembled data on homicide cases from the British colonial court records.

Despite the preponderance of agnates in a man's immediate environs, well under half of the homicide victims were agnatic relatives of their assailants. The most interesting evidence that kinship mitigates risk comes from Bohannan's analysis of homicides by cuckolded husbands. In homicide among the Tiv—as in homicide everywhere else on the planet—adultery is a major motive category. Bohannan writes (1960b),

> In a community in which 83 percent of the adult males are agnatic kinsmen of one another, the chances that a woman's lover will be a kinsman of her husband are obviously extremely high . . . . In the eight cases in which men killed their wives' lovers, only [two cases] show any kinship relation between the husband and the lover. Any field worker in Tivland realizes that adulteries between women and their husband's kinsmen occur frequently. Tiv do not suggest that such adultery does not occur. They insist, however—and the cases prove them right—that a wife's adulteries must not be allowed to disturb relationships among kinsmen. (p. 42)

Kinship and Collaborative Homicide Revisited

It so happens that the very first case in Bohannan's sample of Tiv homicides concerns not adultery but simple theft. Five young men, the sons of two older brothers, caught a man who had stolen some hoes from their compound, and they beat him to death. As we saw in the case of 13th-century England, so too in other samples: Two or more people often kill collaboratively and the collaborators are often close kinsmen.

It is very rare, however, that the details of a sample of cases are so thoroughly laid out that one can assess the incidences of relationship of varying degrees among co-offenders as we did in Figure 2.1. We have found a few such samples, however, and have used them to test the generality of our conclusion about mediaeval England: that *relatives tend to find common cause in murderous disputes, so that co-offenders are more closely related on average than victim-and-offender.*

To make such comparisons, one needs an index of consanguinity, and we have used the standard one: Sewall Wright's (1922) coefficient of relatedness, r. The most convenient way to conceptualize the value of r between persons A and B is that r represents that fraction of A's genotype that is shared with B by virtue of their having inherited copies of the same genes from recent ancestors. The value of r for parent and offspring is 0.5, and for full siblings the same. For half-siblings (one parent the same and one different), r equals 0.25, as it does for the relationship between uncle or aunt and niece or nephew, and for grandparental relationships too. For first cousins, r equals 0.125.

We collected every sample of homicides we could find that met two criteria: The information necessary to estimate the relationships of interest had to be available, and the sample must not have been selected on some obviously biasing criterion. We then computed the average coefficients of relatedness across all victim–offender pairs and all co-offender pairs. The results are presented in Table 2.2.

It is clear from the table that the degree to which the average homicide victim is related to his or her killer is highly variable from one society to another. But what is even clearer is that co-offender relatedness surpasses victim–offender relatedness by a wide margin in every case.

Evolutionary theory does not deny the reality of conflict between relatives. On the contrary, the existence of such conflict is *guaranteed* by genetic nonidentity. (The only creatures with a perfect commonality of interest are the genetically identical members of a clone.) What selection thinking *does* in fact suggest is subtler and more interesting: In homicide, as in human affairs generally, otherwise equivalent conflicts will tend to be increasingly severe and dangerous the more distantly related are the

Table 2.2. Estimated Average Relatedness of Victim-and-Offender versus Co-offenders[a]

	Relationship			
	Victim-offender		Co-offender	
	r	(N)	r	(N)
Detroit	.03	(508)	.09	(43)
Miami	.01	(494)	.09	(27)
Bison-Horn Maria	.09	(130)	.16	(17)
Bhil	.05	(100)	.27	(22)
Munda	.07	(47)	.33	(9)
Oraon	.06	(43)	.23	(7)
Tzeltal Mayans	.08	(26)	.35	(6)
Gros Ventre	.01	(14)	.50	(1)
13th-Century England	.01	(2434)	.08	(2372)

[a]The Bhil (Varma, 1978), Munda, and Oraon (Saran, 1974) are all "aboriginals" of the Indian subcontinent, resembling in some ways the Bison-Horn Maria; these three samples were all selected on unspecified criteria, and might therefore be biased. The Tzeltal are Mayan-speaking Mexican Indians, and the sample consists of all the cases recalled by three informants in a village (Nash, 1967). The Gros Ventre lived in Montana, and the sample consists of "all the murders that were known to have occurred in the period from about 1850 to 1885" (Flannery, 1953). The Detroit data (Daly & Wilson, 1982) represent all cases known to the police in 1972, and the Miami data (Wilbanks, 1984) represent all those in 1980.

principals. The other side of the coin is that people will be likelier to find common cause as consanguinity increases. All the evidence in this chapter—and indeed all the evidence of which we are aware—confirms this fundamental prediction of a pervasive nepotism tempering interpersonal conflict.

Killing
Children

I. Infanticide in the Ethnographic Record

— 3 —

Desperate Decisions

> We lived with the Ayoreo for 6 months before we began interviewing women. We were accustomed to seeing them walking from their gardens laboring under loads of bananas or sitting in front of their mud houses weaving and chatting. Like mothers everywhere they anguish when their babies are sick and beam with joy when told their babies are beautiful.
>
> Some of the women in the sample became our good friends. Soon after we moved into her village, Eho welcomed us with a gift of a chicken. She often visited us and more than once lamented that we had no children and told us when we did they would surely be beautiful. We were somewhat incredulous when we first heard of Eho's infanticides from another woman. Even when trained as an anthropologist, it is difficult to believe that someone one knows as a charming friend, devoted wife, and doting mother could do something that one's own culture deems repugnant. Yet even the most intolerant missionary understands that there was mercy involved in the burying of infants. (Bugos and McCarthy, 1984, p. 512)

The Ayoreo occupy the border area of Bolivia and Paraguay, where they are slash-and-burn gardeners for about half the year and become nomadic foragers during the dry season. Perhaps it is because of this nomadic opportunism that Ayoreo society is less patriarchal than that of many other tribal horticulturalists. There are named patrilineal descent groups, but these lack the spatial cohesion and unity of political purpose that typify patrilineages among the Tiv, say, or the Bison-Horn Maria. The politically autonomous territorial band is instead based on matrilineal and sororal links, for an Ayoreo man typically goes to live with his wife's family, thus falling under the authority of her father, rather than taking her away to live among his relatives. According to Paul Bugos and Lorraine McCarthy (1984), "From the 18th century until the 1950s, contact between the Ayoreo and other peoples—both indigenous and European—was rare and usually violent" (p. 504).

An unusual feature of Ayoreo life, again related to the relatively weak patrilineal organization, is that marriages are not negotiated by elders but by the principals themselves. Women play a very active role in courtship. Simultaneous polygamy is rare, but a typical marital career may include a number of brief cohabitations and affairs before a stable marriage. Couples with living children seldom divorce, not simply because children promote marital stability, but also because such stability may be a prerequisite to the decision to keep and rear a baby (Bugos & McCarthy, 1984).

> When labor begins, the expectant mother moves to the nearby forest, accompanied by a party of close kinswomen. The attending women prepare the spot of earth upon which the infant will fall by softening it with water. They dig a hole near this spot to bury the afterbirth and the newborn if it is not kept. While in labor, a woman sits on or hangs from a tree branch. The attending women comfort the mother and chant therapeutic songs to ease the delivery. Ayoreo newborns are not eased into the world by human hands. The Ayoreo verb "to be born" *(basui)* also means "to fall." The women inspect the newborn for signs of deformity. If the infant is unwanted, it is pushed into the hole with a stick and buried, never touched by human hands.
>
> If the newborn is wanted, the senior attending woman—ideally the maternal grandmother—cuts the umbilicus, applies hot ashes to the stub, bathes the infant in water warmed in her mouth, and then hands it to the mother. There is a special bond in Ayoreo society between the child and the woman who washes it—the *upurigado*—who also is responsible for naming the newborn. Once the newborn has been accepted, the relationship between infant and mother is close and prolonged. Ayoreo mothers carry infants in a sling that permits the infant to nurse on demand. Children nurse for as long as 3 or 4 years. (p. 508)

The news about their friend Eho that startled Bugos and McCarthy was this: Between the ages of 17 and 22, during the course of six brief unions, she had buried her first three children, two sons and a daughter. When at last, at age 24, she settled into a permanent marriage, Eho lovingly raised four daughters.

Ayoreo women are reluctant to recall the tragic experiences of their own infanticides, but they can recount more dispassionately those of their close friends and relatives. Through sensitive interviewing and cross-checking of details, McCarthy discovered that Eho's maternal career was not exceptional. One woman had buried her first *six* children before raising three sons and a daughter, the last of which was born in her 45th year.

It is impossible to be sure whether such phenomenal wastage has been endemic in Ayoreo life or is a response to recent stresses. In the 1930's, life was disrupted by the Chaco War between Bolivia and

Paraguay; a railway, missionaries, and white men's diseases have followed. However, early accounts suggest that infanticide was extremely prevalent among Chaco Indians even before the destructive effects of contact. In any case, at least from the 1930's to the 1970's, it has not been unusual for a new Ayoreo mother to bury her baby, with the intention of trying again later when circumstances have improved. The principal reason for such a drastic decision, according to the mothers themselves, is a lack of assured paternal support. Other reasons that mothers offer are deformities, the birth of twins, or the arrival of the new baby so soon after an older sibling as to overburden the mother and imperil the older child's survival.

Women's Life Histories

Homo sapiens is one of the most intensively parental animal species on the planet Earth. A mouse or a gerbil will produce a whole litter of babies after a pregnancy of a few weeks' duration, will copulate again on the day of birth so that she can gestate the next brood while nursing the present one, and may bid her weaned young a final farewell before they are a month old. Most large mammals take things more slowly, producing a single offspring annually and conceiving next year's only after this year's is weaned. But there are just a handful of mammals— the elephants, some whales perhaps, the anthropoid apes, and ourselves—who, in a state of nature, produce young not annually or even every second year but at longer intervals still, nursing each offspring for years and maintaining a nurturant maternal bond literally for decades.

It is a common misapprehension that prehistoric women must have been prolific breeders. When our parents tell of a great-grandmother who raised 14 children, we may imagine that today's low fertility represents a radical departure from the human experience of times past. But in fact, it was those 19th-century broods of a dozen or more that were exceptional. High fertility in historic times is the evolutionarily unanticipated result of a relatively recent invention: animal husbandry and the consequent availability of substitutes for mother's milk. We can get a much better idea of what ancestral maternal careers must have been like from recent anthropological studies of the few peoples who make a living in something like our ancestral life-style, which was one of mixed foraging (hunting and gathering).

Herding and farming are developments of the last few thousand years. We discovered them long after we had evolved the distinctive characteristics of modern *Homo*, and there is no evidence of any major

evolutionary change in postagricultural people. The adaptations of the
human species—all the distinctive aspects of our morphology and
physiology and psychology—have been shaped by at least a hundred
thousand generations of differential survival and reproduction in a
preagricultural ecological niche. If we wish to understand human
characteristics, then, we should study the hunting and gathering
life-style in which and for which those characteristics have been shaped
by natural selection. That, at least, is the argument behind the special
urgency with which modern anthropologists have been endeavoring to
document the vanishing cultures of remnant hunter-gatherers. The
best-studied such people—and one whose way of life is probably as
close as any to that of early human history—is the famous !Kung San of
southwest Africa's Kalahari Desert (see especially Lee & DeVore, 1976;
Howell, 1979; Lee, 1979; Shostak, 1981).

The !Kung San are wandering foragers who camp in groups of
perhaps 20 to 40 people, always ready to move on—within the constraints of access to waterholes—when the food supply looks better
elsewhere. As is the case in most peoples lacking agriculture, the
women gather mainly plant foods and thereby contribute most of the
calories, while the men hunt and thus contribute most of the protein.
Group composition changes as the more stable units that are nuclear
families come and go somewhat independently of one another, banding
together with one set of relatives for awhile, perhaps, and then with
another.

In a !Kung San population studied by Nancy Howell of the
University of Toronto, women experience their first menstruation at an
average age of 16 years, 7 months, and it is at about that age that they
first marry. The husband is likely to be at least 5 years older than his
wife, and may not be the man she would have chosen for herself.
Adolescent fertility is low, and the first child is born at an average
maternal age of $19\frac{1}{2}$. Nursing commonly continues until age 4 and
exceptionally until age 6. The child is typically weaned only when the
mother discovers that she is again pregnant and informs her
disgruntled toddler that her milk and energy are henceforth required by
a younger sibling-to-be.

Well-nourished but thin, !Kung San women seldom conceive within
the first couple of years of nursing. Like the Ayoreo, !Kung San mothers
carry their babies in slings, allowing them to suckle essentially at will
throughout the day and night. The resultant feeding schedule—dictated
by the baby itself rather than by the latest pediatric theories—is not one
you will find in Dr. Spock: The baby nurses for a couple of minutes
about once every quarter hour throughout the daylight hours. (If this

rate persists through the night—and at least at first it may well do so—then that is about a hundred feedings a day.) This demand nursing schedule does not seem to vary much for at least the first $2\frac{1}{2}$ years of the baby's life (Konner & Worthman, 1980).

Such frequent suckling has hormonal consequences for the mother that tend to inhibit ovulation and hence delay her next conception. In the rare event that a baby is born before the mother feels she can safely wean its older sibling, then she may feel compelled to abandon the newborn. Howell reported 6 infanticides in 500 live births, but there is probably some under-reporting, since !Kung San women, like the Ayoreo, consider infanticide a major personal tragedy and would sooner not dwell on such painful memories.

Although neither contraception nor abortion was evidently practiced, a healthy fertile !Kung San woman—if she had the good fortune to survive until menopause—was likely to produce only about five children. Despite her best efforts, one of these five, on average, would die before its first birthday, of malaria, perhaps, or some other disease. Even more heartbreaking would be the deaths of two older children, nurtured through several years only to succumb to disease or accident or violence while still unmarried and childless. A girl who lived to reproduce—and only 48% of female babies did so—could expect to raise successfully one son and one daughter who would marry and produce children of their own. These, of course, are approximate averages, and individual experiences varied. The eloquent !Kung San autobiographer Nisa, for example, lost all of her children, at various ages and in various ways, and thus suffered the grief of a middle age without descendants (Shostak, 1981). Other women were luckier.

Howell has cautioned against romanticizing the !Kung San as if they constituted some sort of prototype of pure, natural humankind, and her point is well taken. The !Kung San are, after all, a single human culture—unique, as is every culture—and they have been relegated to a marginal habitat by several centuries of competition from other African peoples with domestic animals. Nevertheless, all available evidence suggests that the general features of a !Kung San woman's reproductive career as described above—the wide birthspacing, the prolonged demand nursing, low fertility, high childhood mortality, and the other demographic details—are indeed representative of hunter-gatherers, and of the life history that has characterized *Homo* for thousands of millenia (see, e.g., Lozoff *et al.*, 1977). Raising 2 or 3 children to competent maturity—the life's work of a successful woman—has typically required hard decisions about priorities, attentive management of social relations, ingenuity, luck, and decades of hard labor.

Discriminative Parental Solicitude

What could be more startling to an imagination informed by evolutionary theory than the killing of one's own children? Parental care makes a clear, direct contribution to parental fitness. It would seem that infanticide by the mother could only be interpreted as pathology—as the complete collapse of the normal adaptive functioning of evolved mechanisms of parental psychology.

The circumstances of Ayoreo and !Kung San infanticides should be sufficient to show that maternal psychopathology is not the answer. Infanticide can be the desperate decision of a rational strategist allocating scarce resources. There is no reason to suppose that an evolved parental psychology should be such as to value every offspring equally and indiscriminately, and there are many good reasons to doubt it (Daly & Wilson, 1987c).

Every offspring that a parent commits herself to rearing represents an investment of the parent's limited means, and that investment might have earned better fitness returns elsewhere. It would be an ill-designed organism indeed that delayed or jeopardized her future reproduction in order to nurture present offspring whose own reproductive prospects were nil. A newly parturient hamster tests the vitality of her newborn pups as she licks them clean for the first time, and she rejects any that are born dead; we should think it bizarre if she were to persist in mothering the stillborn. But efforts to rear a *live* pup who had absolutely no prospects of living to maturity would be equally bizarre, and for the same reason: Natural selection would be expected to favor those individuals whose parental efforts are allocated in such a way as to best promote their own fitness. As Richard Alexander (1979) has written,

> According to an inclusive-fitness model, selection should refine parental altruism as if in response to three hypothetical cost-benefit questions: (1) What is the relationship of the putative offspring to its parents? (Is the juvenile really my own offspring?) (2) What is the need of the offspring? (More properly, what is its ability to translate parental assistance into reproduction?) (3) What alternative uses might a parent make of the resources it can invest in the offspring? (p. 109)

In any particular species under study, the mechanisms of parental assessment and discrimination may prove to be few and imperfect, or they may prove to be remarkably fine-tuned. Birds abandon nests with cracked eggs, as well they should, and hamsters recycle dead babies, but discrimination often goes no further; sometimes predictors of the offspring's eventual fitness may be so imperfect that selection has devised no more subtle a strategy than simply abandoning the moribund. But there are also well-studied cases in which discrimination is much more sophisticated, as for example when it is important that a parent discriminate its own offspring from unrelated little beggars. Guillemots, marine birds whose nests are typically situated only a few centimeters apart, recognize their newly hatched chicks and even their eggs, rejecting any unrelated chicks or eggs that somehow turn up in the nest uninvited (Birkhead, 1978). The closely related razorbill, by contrast, nests more dispersedly, and therefore incurs no risk of parental mixups in nature. And as it happens, the razorbill simply lacks the specialized discriminative ability of the guillemot, and is oblivious to experimental cross-fosterings of eggs and hatchlings. (Parental recognition of one's own babies commonly develops in the animal world shortly before the age when the young become so mobile as to place the parents at imminent risk of misdirecting parental care to nonrelatives; see, for example, Holmes & Sherman, 1983).

Detailed mechanisms of parental psychology cannot be deduced from evolutionary theory, but must be discovered by empirical research. Theory *can*, however, suggest what adaptations would be useful under one or another set of conditions, and thus help us decide what sort of mechanisms we ought to be looking for. Fitness benefits would obviously accrue to the parent who could assess available predictors of an offspring's eventual contribution to parental fitness, and adjust parental inclinations accordingly. Such parental predictive skills would be especially valuable for an animal such as *Homo sapiens* with its prolonged, intensive parental care: Every child that is reared represents a significant fraction of its mother's life span and labor, so that bad decisions are penalized especially severely. The "predictors" of a child's eventual fitness that might influence a mother could be characteristics of the child—whether robust or sickly, for example—but they might also be characteristics of the circumstance, such as the season, or the size of one's larder, or one's present mate's skills as a hunter.

A Cross-Cultural Review

People of most cultures recognize that parents will sometimes choose not to raise a child. The factors that they consider relevant to such a decision vary, to some degree, from one society to another. The topic has interested many travellers, missionaries, and anthropologists, so that an enormous amount of information has been recorded concerning the circumstances in which infanticide is alleged to be common, acceptable, or in some cases even obligatory, in various parts of the world.

If parental psychology has been shaped by selection to make adaptive decisions about the magnitude of parental commitments, then there are at least three classes of circumstances in which we might anticipate some reluctance to invest wholeheartedly in a particular child. The first such class consists of circumstances in which there is some doubt that the offspring in question is indeed the putative parent's own. The second class encompasses indications that the offspring itself may be of dubious quality, and hence a poor prospect to contribute to parental fitness even if carefully nurtured. We have already discussed examples showing that other animals are sensitive to these issues. The third class of reasons why we might encounter a dampened parental enthusiasm includes all those extrinsic circumstances that might bode ill for a particular child-rearing effort: food scarcities, a lack of social support, overburdening from the demands of older offspring, and so forth.

These considerations of adaptive parental decision-making provide a framework for the analysis of the ethnographic record on infanticide: If parental psychology has been shaped by natural selection, then we may expect that the typologically described circumstances of infanticide will reflect parental sensitivity to each of these issues. In fact, we should be surprised to discover any case in which parentally instigated infanticide is alleged to be common in a set of circumstances that can*not* be interpreted within this framework. Although some extreme cultural relativists seem to believe that mores are arbitrarily reversible from one culture to another, an imagination informed by selection thinking must be skeptical of such claims. Surely psychological processes that power-fully influence fitness—things like parental motives—must be con-strained, as a result of our selective history, to arrive at adaptive rather than arbitrary ends.

In order to test the adequacy of these ideas, it is necessary that we go beyond anecdote and the mustering of examples that seem supportive. What we have to do is take some sort of sample of ethnographies, unselected for the information they contain about infanticide, and then record and summarize *all* such information, whether it be readily interpretable within our framework or seemingly anomalous. This we have done, using a standard sample of sixty ethnographies, assembled by anthropologists for just such cross-cultural surveys and analyses.

The cross-cultural survey can be an extremely valuable method for testing theories in the social sciences. Suppose, for example, that we have the idea that the "double standard"—according to which adultery by the wife is a graver offense than adultery by the husband—is a consequence of the fact that paternity is mistakable while maternity is not. A cross-cultural review of the phenomenon is immediately called for: If we were to find that double standards in the opposite direction are just as common as the more familiar variety, we could hardly attribute one of the other type of double standard to a universal human circumstance, and we could therefore discard the hypothesis. As it happens, there do not seem to be *any* cases of a reversed double standard of adultery (see Chapter 9) and so the hypothesis remains viable.

More complex cross-cultural tests involve assessing the associations among phenomena that vary between societies. Suppose, for example, we were to entertain the theory that tribal warfare is provoked by competition for scarce game animals. We could then assign to various tribal societies some sort of prevalence-of-warfare score, and we could generate another score reflecting the scarcity of game animals, such as the grams of protein ingested per capita per day. We would then assess by correlational means—or, if the scales were coarse, by a simple 2×2 cross-tabulation and contingency assessment—whether a society's score on either of these measures carried any predictive information about its score on the other. If not, good-bye theory.

The assumption behind such tests—especially when we employ statistical methods to quantify the probability of obtaining our results under one or another hypothesis—is that each individual society in our tabulation constitutes an "independent instance." Suppose, for example, that we were to propose this hypothesis: Some fundamental constraint leads children to associate the syllable "ma" with their mothers. If we were to offer as evidence the fact that "mama" has a common meaning in New Zealand, England, and the United States, you might be unimpressed, and you should be little more impressed if we were to add Italy, France, and Spain. But if we were to test the idea in Amazonia, New Guinea, and Finland and still not reject it, you might begin to show some interest, since we would now be sampling from language families so distantly related that they are almost bereft of such lexical parallels. Human cultures are not, of course, truly "independent instances" in the strict statistical sense. There is a transmission of elements between cultures ("diffusion") in the present and in the recent past, and—somewhere in the past, however distant two cultures may be at present—there is common ancestry as well. These problems can be largely but not entirely obviated if one samples cultures not randomly but in a systematic "overdispersed" manner, so that two cultures with recent common ancestry or a history of contact are not both included.

The sample of ethnographies that we used is one that was designed to sample the language families and geographic regions of the world as thoroughly as possible: the "Probability Sample" of 60 societies devised by the Human Relations Area Files (HRAF), an American organization dedicated to the assembling of anthropological materials into indexed compendia facilitating cross-cultural studies (Lagacé, 1974). The sample includes one randomly selected society from each of the sixty major culture clusters proposed by the dean of ethnographic encyclopedists, George Peter Murdock.

Hundreds of topics are indexed in the HRAF, and the relevant pages of the original ethnographic materials are duplicated on microfiche under an index number for each topic. Each society is represented by a packet of microfiches in a file drawer. "Infanticide and abortion" is subject No. 847. To find out what has been recorded about infanticide in a particular society of interest, one simply has to pull the microfiches for that society and read everything coded under "847"; this may amount to a line or two, or to several pages of detailed text from each of several ethnographies.

We examined the HRAF materials under code "847," for each of the 60 societies in the "Probability Sample" (Daly & Wilson, 1984). Infanticide was mentioned in 39 of the 60, and some description of the circumstances in which it occurs was offered in 35. This does not, of course, mean that infanticide is not practiced—nor even that it is not legitimized—in the other 21. The ethnographic record is far from complete, and any anthropologist necessarily studies only certain spheres of activity, while ignoring many others. Furthermore, an unfortunate consequence of the random element in the selection of the Probability Sample is that a number of the societies in that sample are poorly documented.

Very few ethnographies contain accounts of particular infanticide cases, perhaps because of that same reticence to discuss the matter that we have already noted in the case of the Ayoreo and !Kung San. Almost all the material consists instead of typological descriptions of circumstances or rationales surrounding the practice. In the case of the Probability Sample's randomly chosen tribe of Australian aborigines, for example, we read (Spencer & Gillen, 1927), "The Arunta native does not hesitate to kill a child—always directly it is born—if there be an older one still in need of nourishment from the mother" (p. 221). Of the Aymara Indians of South America, we are informed (Buechler & Beuchler, 1971) that "Cases of infanticide were known to all. They occur in cases of infants born out of wedlock, incestuous unions and in large families" (p. 23).

Our research strategy was to enumerate each distinct circumstance of infanticide that was noted in each society. The brief passage by Spencer and Gillen indicates a single circumstance: birth at too brief an interval.

The Aymara quotation warrants three entries: unwed mother, incestuous conception, and too many children. In this fashion, we enumerated 112 stated circumstances of infanticide from those 35 societies for which the topic was discussed at all. A small number of themes predominated (Table 3.1), themes corresponding precisely to the three issues that we have already suggested should be relevant to adaptive parental decision-making.

Issue 1. Is the Infant the Putative Parent's Own?

Twenty of the 112 infanticidal circumstances that we noted were clearly related to this question, each being an explicit matter of nonpaternity. In 15 societies, adulterous conception was offered as grounds for infanticide. In three cases, tribal males were said to insist upon the death of any child whose features provoked suspicion of a nontribal sire. And in two societies—Yanomamö (South America) and Tikopia (Oceania)—men who acquired wives with dependent children from a previous union were reported to demand that those children be put to death.

In several ethnographies, a category of infanticide was described in which there was no direct male coercion, and yet the mother's decision seemed clearly related to men's reluctance to invest in other men's children. In the Ojibwa, for instance (Dunning, 1959),

> It would appear that the ideal of not marrying a woman with someone else's child is strongly held. As marriage seems to be the *sine qua non* for every woman, this then could account for the need to abort or do away with an illegitimate child. (p. 148)

Classifying such cases under the rubrics of "no male support" or "unwed mother," we have chosen (somewhat arbitrarily perhaps) to count them up under Issue 3, where we discuss mothers' limited resources and capabilities, rather than including them here under Issue 1.

Issue 2. What is the Infant's Quality, and Hence Its Ability to Convert Parental Assistance into Eventual Fitness?

Recall the point that we made earlier with the example of a mother hamster: Persistent nurture of a dead baby would represent a pathological manifestation of parental urges, and the persistent nurture of a baby who is certain to die in spite of that nurture would be no more adaptive. When Richard Alexander writes (as quoted above), that parents should

Table 3.1. Circumstances of Alleged Infanticide in a Representative Cross-Cultural Sample of Societies[a]

			Number of societies
Issue 1.	Is the infant the putative parent's own?		**20**
	Adulterous conception	15	
	Nontribal sire	3	
	Sired by mother's first husband	2	
Issue 2.	What is the infant's quality, and hence its ability to convert parental assistance into eventual fitness?		**21**
	Infant deformed or very ill	21	
Issue 3.	Are present circumstances favorable for child rearing?		**56**
	Twins	14	
	Birth too soon or too many children	11	
	No male support	6	
	Quarrel with husband	1	
	Mother died	6	
	Mother unwed	14	
	Economic hardship	3	
	Wrong season	1	
Other circumstances not obviously subsumed under the above three categories:			**15**
	Female infant	4	
	Eliminating claimants to throne	2	
	Ritual purposes	3	
	Conceived in incest	3	
	By maternal grandfather out of enmity with son-in-law	1	
	By matrilateral male kin to avoid obligation to "sister's sons"	1	
	To avoid lactational sex taboo	1	

[a]Modified from Daly and Wilson (1984).

have evolved to be sensitive to offspring "need," it is important to note the technical and nonintuitive meaning that he then attaches to the word "need," namely the offspring's capacity to transform parental investment into personal fitness. A hopelessly deformed infant, for example, is desperately "in need" in ordinary parlance, but not in Alexander's special sense. This is because parental care is of no utility to such an infant, since "utility" is here equated with the potential to promote one's fitness. Whatever our moral sympathies in the matter, we should recognize that the rejection of an unhealthy newborn could be an adaptive (fitness-promoting) parental response.

The killing or abandonment of children who are deformed or severely ill was noted for 21 of the 35 societies. In only one of these cases—Blackfoot (North America)—was there any suggestion that such a practice on the part of mothers might be disapproved by the larger society.

Among various peoples from various parts of the world, it is reported that deformed children are considered to be ghosts or demons (or the progeny thereof), so that the rationale for infanticide is expressed in terms of a struggle with hostile supernatural forces. Rafael Karsten (1932), for example, generalizes about several South American Indian tribes as follows:

> It is superstitious fear that induces the Indian to kill his children. According to the Indian idea monstrous or in some way deformed children, or children which in general are born very sickly, cannot have been conceived in a natural way; they must have come into being through the operation of a demon. Indian myths, to which I shall refer later on, have much to tell about women who became pregnant in a supernatural way, during bathing or otherwise, and in consequence gave birth, not to a human child, but to a monster. Such a monster is looked upon with horror and regarded as a most ominous thing not only for the family concerned but for the whole village. (p. 77)

It is interesting that Karsten goes on to remark the pragmatic element in such cases, although he does so in order to assert its relative unimportance:

> We may of course also assume that practical considerations have led the Indians to infanticide. The Indians understand that a sickly or deformed child has scarcely any chance of developing into a strong man and a useful member of society. In the hard struggle for existence under which the Indian lives it may even be merciful to destroy him. I believe however that such considerations play only a subordinate part in the custom of infanticide, which must first of all be explained by superstition. (p. 78)

Just why this author "believes" that superstition is more important than practicality he does not say, and the question bears on the entire agenda of cultural and social anthropology. Many anthropologists evidently feel that the proper subject matter of their discipline is the *meaning* that people attach to their actions, rather than the causes of those actions, or even the characterization of the actions themselves. This sort of "idealism" has been sharply criticized by Marxists and other "cultural materialists," but the criticism seems only to have stiffened the resistance. Marshall Sahlins (1976), for example, begins a lengthy attack on Marxism as follows: "This book amounts to an anthropological critique of the idea that human cultures are formulated out of practical activity and, behind that, utilitarian interest" (p. vii).

Other eminent anthropologists have gone further, explicitly repudiating the quest for causal understanding altogether. Clifford Geertz (1983) advocates an "interpretative anthropology," its ambition being, "To turn from trying to explain social phenomena by weaving them into grand textures of cause and effect to trying to explain them by placing them in local frames of awareness" (p. 6). Edmund Leach (1982) proposes that "Social anthropology is not, and should not aim to be, a 'science' in the natural science sense. If anything it is a form of art. . . . Social anthropologists should not see themselves as seekers after objective truth . . ." (p. 52).

This seems to us an unnecessarily narrow agenda. Meaning and expressed rationales for action are highly interesting data to be sure, but they are not the *only* interesting data. We have known at least since Freud that people may have little insight into their own motives. What people actually do is a question of great interest, and why they do what they do is another. How they interpret and explain their own actions is a third.

Widespread human motives assume different garb in different societies, and the cross-culturally general features can be every bit as interesting as the culturally particular ones. Karsten attributed the "horror" evoked by deformed babies to beliefs about demons. This attribution loses its force when we observe an identical horror in similarly unfortunate mothers in our own society. North Americans are not devoid of superstitious beliefs, but a demonic sneak fertilizer in the bathtub is not usually among them. As it happens, people dispose "superstitiously" of deformed or sickly babies in many societies, even though the expressed rationales and associated ideologies vary from place to place. Somehow, as we shall see shortly, it is hardly ever reported that people dispose "superstitiously" of well-formed, healthy babies, and when they do, they kill other people's babies, not their own. What explanatory force can we then grant to the concept of superstition?

Issue 3. Are Present Circumstances Favorable for Child Rearing?

We have already discussed 41 of the 112 infanticidal circumstances that we recorded in our HRAF review: 20 having to do with inappropriate paternity, and 21 with poor quality of the child itself. Another 56—exactly half of the total list—have to do with circumstances that limit the mother's present capacity to cope with the demands of child rearing. These fall into several subcategories.

The first type, accounting for 14 of the 56, is the birth of twins. Where this is a situation calling for infanticide, the prescribed victim may be the second born, the weaker, the female. As in the case of deformed children, much mythology about demons and unnatural conception surrounds twin births. If infanticide is the prescribed remedy, the western observer is again likely to invoke "superstition" to explain it. It should be noted, however, that *both* twins were reported to be killed in only 2 of the 14 societies presently under consideration—Aranda (Oceania) and Lozi (Africa)—and in the latter case, different ethnographers contradicted one another on this point.

Gary Granzberg (1973) has used a cross-cultural test to provide evidence of a pragmatic element in twin infanticide. He categorized 70 societies—all those for which the HRAF materials specifically indicated the presence *or absence* of twin infanticide—with respect to the availability of female relatives or other mother's helpers, and the extent to which new mothers are free of arduous work. These variables he combined into a summary measure of the burden of maternity, which was then cross-tabulated against the practice of twin infanticide. The relationship was striking: Twins were killed in 16 of 37 societies in which mothers have relatively little relief, but in only 2 of 33 in which social supports make the burden of maternity lighter.

Another circumstance in which infanticide represents a decision about the allocation of scarce maternal resources is that in which lactational suppression of ovulation fails, so that a baby is born too soon after the last one. Napoleon Chagnon (1983) writes of a Yanomamö headman's wife, for example:

Bahimi was pregnant when I began my fieldwork, but she destroyed the infant when it was born—a boy in this case—explaining tearfully that she had no choice. The new baby would have competed with Ariwari, her youngest child, who was still nursing. Rather than expose Ariwari to the dangers and uncertainty of an early weaning, she chose to terminate the newborn instead. (p. 27)

In 11 societies in our sample, it was noted that infanticide might result either from this problem of a short birth interval or simply because the mother had too many dependent children already. A different problem of timing confronted Copper Eskimo women, whose children born at the wrong time of year could not conveniently be carried on the arduous seasonal migration and therefore had to be abandoned. In three further cases, infanticide was attributed simply to poverty or hard times.

In other cases, the new mother's difficulty is that she lacks the paternal support that is characteristic of the society. In six cases, for example, infants were said to be killed when no man would acknowledge paternity or accept an obligation to provide for the child. The same uncertainty about male assistance can probably be invoked in connection with a slightly different characterization of an infanticidal circumstance: Baganda (Africa) women were reported to kill infants if the couple had quarreled severely. In addition, the mother's unwed status was offered as grounds for infanticide in 14 societies. Unwed mothers presumably lack reliable paternal support for the children, besides finding the child an impediment to future matches. Finally, there were six societies for which it was reported that an infant is killed when the mother has died in childbirth.

The decision that present circumstances are not favorable for child rearing is an implicitly relative one. Some more promising alternative must, at the least, be a possibility in the future, or else the present decision would be futile. In general, a new mother can be expected to exhibit some reluctance to rear a particular child if that rearing will require her to neglect alternative vehicles of parental investment promising better fitness returns. The "alternatives" in question might be older children still dependent upon her, or they might be future marital and reproductive prospects compromised by the present child. Earlier in this chapter, we quoted ethnographic materials that illustrate both sorts of dilemmas.

The alternatives to a present reproductive venture shrink with time. The younger a new mother, the greater her future reproductive prospects, or, in the jargon of evolutionary biology, her "residual reproductive value." So if selection has shaped maternal psychology, we would expect a woman to be less and less inclined, as her reproductive years slip away, to devalue a present offspring in terms of its compromising effects upon her future. It follows that her willingness to jettison a present infant should decline with her age. Bugos and McCarthy have provided strong evidence that this is so among the Ayoreo (Figure 3.1). As we shall see in the next chapter, the risk of infanticide is strongly related to maternal age in our own society too.

Figure 3.1. The proportion of births leading to infanticide, as a function of the mother's age, for a sample of Ayoreo women all of whom were known to have buried at least one baby. The figure is based on 141 births, 54 of them followed by infanticide. Modified from Bugos and McCarthy (1984).

Female-Selective Infanticide

As we have just seen, 97 of the infanticidal circumstances on our list of 112 are readily interpreted within the framework of selectionist psychology: Parents are reluctant to commit their efforts where they are unlikely to reap eventual fitness benefits, whether because of non-relatedness, poor offspring quality, or poor circumstances. But there is a fourth determinant of discriminative parental solicitude and infanticide that is more puzzling: the child's sex.

In four societies in our sample (Yanomamö, Mataco, Trobriand Islanders, Tikopia), the fact that the baby is a girl was offered as distinct grounds for infanticide. In an additional four (Copper Eskimo, Tlingit, Aranda, Tucano), the same consideration was offered as relevant to the infanticidal decision in the event of twins or births in too rapid succession. Selective infanticide of daughters has provoked more theorizing than any of the more prevalent rationales discussed above, but fully satisfactory explanations remain elusive.

From a selectionist perspective, widespread parental preference for *either* sex presents a conundrum. As Ronald Fisher pointed out more than 50 years ago, each sex contributes half of the ancestry of all future generations, with the result that daughters and sons have an identical value as vehicles of parental fitness. Imagine, for simplicity, a population divided into discrete generations, and imagine further that sons outnumber daughters 2 to 1. Since every child in the next generation will have both a mother and a father, it follows that the average daughter will have twice as many children as the average son. If a member of the parental generation were attempting to maximize his expected number of grandchildren, he should therefore invest preferentially in the rarer sex, in this case daughters. Selection, by Fisher's argument, should always incline parents to prefer the rarer sex (more exactly, the sex of offspring that has been receiving less parental investment in the population as a whole), with the result that the equilibrial parental strategy—that which, if typical, cannot be bettered—is to invest equal effort in daughters and sons. (Fisher's theory is the prototype for what have come to be known as "Evolutionarily Stable Strategy" models, as well as being the foundation of an elegant body of theory and research on "sex allocation" in plants and animals; see Charnov, 1982). In any population in which female-selective infanticide has produced a male-biased sex ratio, the fitness-promoting response of an adaptive parental psychology should be to reverse the former practice and favor daughters over sons. How then can female-selective infanticide persist?

Part of the answer might be that such infanticide is a feature only of certain cultural settings—perhaps primarily recent ones—and has not been a sufficiently consistent selective force to produce adaptive parental counterinclinations. But this idea cannot really solve the problem. Human parents have been confronted since time immemorial with the task of assessing their children's life prospects; the child's sex and local sex ratios have surely always been relevant to such assessments. Part of the answer may be that female-selective infanticide serves other people's interests rather than the parents' and is coerced; to this we shall return. But first we must situate female-selective infanticide within the larger phenomenon of which it is only the most extreme manifestation: the preference for sons.

Actually killing daughters is relatively infrequent, but lesser manifestations of a preference for sons seem to be remarkably widespread. Where daughters are not killed, they are still commonly discriminated against: in the duration of nursing, for example, or in the size of the food bowl or the provision of expensive medical care (see, for example, McKee, 1984). Under Fisher's theory, these acts of discrimination pose the same theoretical problem as outright infanticide: How can parental preference for *either* sex be widespread and stable within a population?

One possible explanation for such biases is that a son's reproductive *potential* is greater than a daughter's so that his expected fitness can profit more than hers from increments in parental investment beyond some minimum necessary to ensure survival. This hypothesis provides an explanation for male-preferential inheritance, as has been developed especially by John Hartung (1982, 1985). It may also provide an explanation for at least some cases of female-selective infanticide. Anthropologist Mildred Dickemann (1979b, 1981), following arguments by Trivers and Willard (1973) and Alexander (1974), has pointed out that consideration of the male's greater reproductive potential leads to the nonintuitive prediction that infanticide of daughters will be especially prevalent among the *upper* classes of highly stratified societies. This is because the reproductive potential of well-endowed sons is enormous—as a result of polygamous marriage or concubinage or both—and because families pay crippling dowries to marry their daughters upward, and thus to acquire high-ranking grandsons. This dowry competition makes daughters a financial burden and sons a financial asset to the affluent, exacerbating the favoring of sons.

Dickemann has assembled evidence that female-selective infanticide really is status-graded, in the way the theory suggests it should be, in the highly stratified societies of India, China, Japan, and mediaeval Europe. However, a strict application of Fisher's sex ratio theory to this case would seem to demand that a preference for sons in the upper strata should be offset by a preference for daughters in the lower. We have not seen any report of a switch to direct male-selective infanticide in the lower echelons of a stratified society, but of course the behavior of the lower classes is generally less well documented than that of the upper classes. There *is* some evidence of sex-differential nurture and neglect that may amount to the same thing. Voland (1984) has analyzed an outstanding archive of genealogical data from the mainly rural German parish of Leezen between 1720 and 1869, with respect to this question. He reports that daughters (especially the first-born) suffered higher infant mortality than sons among the landholding classes, but that this sex-differential mortality was reversed among the landless. Moreover, the sons of landholders were more marriageable than their daughters, whereas daughters of the landless were more marriageable than sons. Voland interprets these patterns as evidence that parents indeed invested preferentially in the sex of greater reproductive value, and sometimes practiced the indirect infanticide of severe neglect upon the less desirable sex.

In the case of less stratified (so-called "primitive") societies, the best-known explanation for female-selective infanticide is William Divale and Marvin Harris's (1976) notorious theory of the "male supremacist complex." They argued that warfare (eliminating males) and infanticide (eliminating females) are complementary elements of a "response to the need to regulate population growth" in horticultural societies. This theory is a textbook example of the fallacy that biologists refer to as *naive group-selectionism:* the uncritical supposition that complex "adaptations" will somehow arise such that individuals will sacrifice their own fitness interests to improve the survival prospects of entire populations (see Williams, 1971).

Divale and Harris's theory collapsed under the weight of this and other failings, both theoretical and factual (see Bates & Lees, 1979; Chagnon, 1983). However, there may yet be an element of truth to their idea that warfare and female infanticide are causally linked in certain settings. Where chronic hostility and fragile balances of power exist between small, neighboring patrilineal kin groups—as in the Yanomamö, for example, or in certain New Guinea tribes—female-selective infanticide occurs, and may be more prevalent than elsewhere. The men in these societies articulate their preference for sons as a need for warriors, and indeed, the fact that there are periodic annihilations of vulnerable patrilineages—with theft of their women—suggests that this expressed rationale is a genuine one. Little wonder that a new father and other men might sometimes pressure the new mother to dispose of her infant daughter and get on with the production of males. One consequence of such infanticide is then a shortage of women, which exacerbates the conflict, since the theft of women is much of the point of fighting in the first place! If this vicious circle is an accurate portrayal of the situation among certain horticulturalists, then Divale and Harris were surely right to ask why some societies have fallen into the trap and not others. Moreover, they were probably right to seek an ecological answer, even though their own proposal—protein shortage—was a failure (Chagnon, 1983).

Other Interests

Just 11 out of our original list of 112 circumstances of infanticide remain to be discussed. Most of these apparently reflect intervention or coercion by parties other than the parents. A clear example is that in which Baganda (Africa) chiefs ordered the death of collateral male kin at birth, with the express purpose of eliminating rival claimants to the succession. In this example, parental interests are simply overruled by those of someone more powerful.

In another example, the Tiv autobiographer Akiga (1939) alludes darkly to ritual sacrifices when crops fail: "Some say that a man is killed, but those who know best say that it is not a man that is used to set it right, but a baby, or the foetus procured from a woman who has aborted" (p. 227). Unfortunately, Akiga says little about how the victims were selected, but his account implies that they were not related to their slayers. In ethnographic accounts of ritual head-hunting or other human sacrifice in other societies, it is generally explicit that the victims were kidnapped nonrelatives: either complete strangers or persons with whom the kidnappers had some lasting enmity.

Two more cases of infanticide for purely magical reasons occur on our list, but both are so lacking in detail and credibility that they must at best be labeled hearsay and at worst slander. One is the claim by a Muslim writer that the Somalis used to kill babies born under inauspicious astrological signs in the bad old days before their conversion to Islam. Similarly, infanticide of healthy children superstitiously believed to be ghosts is said by the Trukese (Oceania) to have been practiced in some unspecified past before modern morality took hold. Such myths about a distant evil past are widespread, and have little bearing on the reality of infanticide; we included these 2 accounts among our 112 circumstances simply to uphold the aim of recording all the HRAF infanticide materials without prejudicial sifting.

A possibly surprising grounds for infanticide is that the child was conceived in incest, as was noted in three societies (Tarahumara, Aymara, Cuna). Such a rule might be interpreted as reflecting an apprehension of poor offspring quality, but if this were the rationale, the decision would probably rest on overt defects. In each of these cases, there was some hint that the infanticide may be coerced upon the mother. Moreover, in all three cases, the scanty accounts could be read to mean that the problem was more the infant's illegitimacy than its incestuous conception.

Ultimately, there are just 4 circumstances, out of the initial 112, for which the accounts suggest that the infanticidal person might damage his own fitness. It is interesting that males are protagonists in all four. The first of these again concerns the Baganda chiefs, who reportedly killed not just collateral kin but even one's own first child if it was a son, stating that the birth of a boy indicated that the father would die. This may be that rare case in which superstition really does overrule nepotistic self-interest, but even here a: more pragmatic rationale is almost certain, namely that the chief's concern was again to delay a successional bid (Southwold, 1966). The second is Karsten's assertion that "a Toba man may kill the newborn child of his married daughter if his son-in-law has incurred his dislike"; regrettably, no more is said, but it seems clear that this is at best an occasional event rather than a category of prescribed infanticides. The third is Hocart's account of the Lau Islanders: "the people of Wathiwathi used to destroy the children of all their women who married into Tombou so that they should have no *vasu*, that is sister's sons to be a burden upon them"; this refers to a dispute between two particular villages among many, and the ethnography makes clear that the so-called "sister's sons" in question could be genealogically distant relatives.

Of all the expressed rationales for infanticide in this ethnographic sample, the only one that seems clearly and explicitly contrary to the killer's fitness interest comes from the Yanomamö (Chagnon, 1967):

> Young couples do not relish the prospect of a long period of celibacy that pregnancy and lactation taboos impose on them. From the time a woman discovers she is pregnant until the time she weans her child, she is not allowed to have sexual relations. Faced with this prospect, young couples may decide to kill their child, irrespective of its sex. (pp. 53–55)

This last rationale for infanticide stands alone in contravening the hypothesis we stated at the beginning of this review. We proposed that any circumstance in which parentally instigated infanticide is allegedly prevalent should be interpretable within the framework of adaptive allocation of parental effort. In this one remarkable case, Yanomamö parents reputedly sacrifice the realized fitness of a child for the hedonic goal of mere copulation. It is ironic that this single "least sociobiological" rationale should have been recorded by Napoleon Chagnon, who happens to be the cultural anthropologist who has most enthusiastically and effectively applied inclusive fitness theory in his research. If this motive is genuine, then one must ask how Yanomamö society has come to be one in which the ordinary fitness-promoting human motives of sexual desire and parental love are so at odds. Who enforces such unpopular taboos and are the interests of the powerful in any way served?

In general, then, the circumstances in which infanticide occurs and is legitimized correspond remarkably well with circumstances in which such infanticide is likely to enhance the fitness of the actors. Reading a large sample of ethnographic literature, we found no descriptions of infanticide according to arbitrary cultural rules and superstitions, nor did we read of parents willingly suffering fitness costs by sacrificing their children to some higher good. In those few cases where the parent's interests seemed not to be served by the practice, it was usually clear that infanticide was coerced by self-interested third parties. Puzzles remain, especially regarding female-selective infanticide, and precise data on the incidence of infanticide are seldom available; nevertheless, the risk factors suggested by selection thinking are demonstrably relevant.

Early European accounts of infanticidal savages bristled with ethnocentric moralizing. Even the recent literature is not entirely devoid of it. And yet as we read the tragic accounts of this desperate deed from one society after another, it is not the inhumanity of the unfortunate perpetrators that confronts us, but rather their humanity.

Killing
Children

II. Parental Homicide in the Modern West

— 4 —

The situation in our own society provides an interesting counterpoint to the anthropological materials reviewed in the last chapter. The ethnographies present us with many typological descriptions of the circumstances that legitimize infanticide in one society or another, but there are seldom any quantitative data on the actual frequency of the act or its correlates. (Bugos and McCarthy's Ayoreo study described in the last chapter is the outstanding exception.) Ironically, it is from societies in which infanticide is criminalized—modern western nations—that the greatest body of quantitative data is forthcoming. Despite the law's threats, some people kill children anyway, and when they do, the feature of our society that endears it to social scientists comes into play: the passion for record-keeping. Coroners investigate suspicious deaths and file their reports, police of course do likewise, and whole departments of civil servants exist to collect and collate the information. In consequence, we can lay hands on large files of data on homicide, including infanticide, and these data permit altogether different sorts of analyses from what we were able to do with the terse and often idealized descriptions in the Human Relations Area Files.

Every time a homicide is discovered in Canada, the investigating police force is obliged to file a report with the federal information agency, Statistics Canada. Police record the time, the place, and the method of killing on a standard form, and tick off one from a list of 12 "apparent motive" categories. Other details are entered on the same form, including the age, sex, and marital status of the victim and of any identified suspect, and the nature of their relationship. Subsequent reporting forms follow the accused's progress through the criminal justice system. Ultimately, all this information finds its way into a computerized data bank in Ottawa, whence researchers such as we can commission particular tabulations.

61

During the decade 1974–1983, 6559 homicides were investigated in Canada; 5444 were solved. In 367 solved cases, the offender (or one of two co-offenders) was a natural parent of the victim. One hundred fifty homicide victims were infants under 1 year of age, and of these infanticides, 141 were solved; the natural mother was the accused killer in 88 cases.

The Statistics Canada "motive" categories are regrettably few, and apply mainly to conflicts between adults. Neither "euthanasia" nor "despair," for example, occurs among them. We cannot tot up the numbers of infanticides provoked by some deformity in the child, nor those attributable to dubious paternity, short birth intervals, or whatever. What we can do, however, is examine in detail how the risk of parental homicide is related to certain variables that theory suggests might be relevant.

Infanticide and Maternal Age

In Chapter 3, we proposed that the risk of maternal infanticide should prove to be a declining function of maternal age. The prediction follows, in brief, from the fact that a woman's "residual reproductive value" wanes over time. The psychological trade-off is between the woman's valuation of the baby and her valuation of herself; the latter quantity should have evolved to be a token of her remaining reproductive potential. As her potential future reproduction diminishes, that future may be expected to weigh less and less heavily upon her present reproductive decisions.

This hypothesis was strongly upheld by data from the Ayoreo Indians (Figure 3.1, p. 53). Do infanticides in a modern western nation also match the predicted pattern? By and large, they do (Figure 4.1): The risk to an infant is greatest by far in the case of a teenaged mother, and declines through her 20's and into her 30's. The little increase in risk with older mothers (at the right of Figure 4.1) may or may not prove reliable, as it represents infanticides by just three women, aged 38, 41, and 41. It is certainly possible that there really is a renewed elevation of risk for infants born to older mothers who already have large numbers of children, and who are more likely than younger mothers to produce a baby with certain defects. Ideally, the prediction about maternal age should be tested with the confounded variables of birth order and infant quality controlled, but we do not presently have the data to do that; our strongest expectation is that older mothers would be less and less likely to dispose of a *healthy, first-born* child.

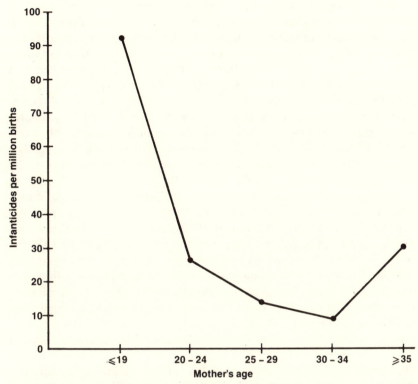

Figure 4.1. Risk of infanticide (homicide at the hands of the natural mother within the first year of life) as a function of maternal age. Canada, 1974–1983.

Infanticide and Maternal Marital Status

As we saw in Chapter 3, illegitimacy or a lack of paternal support may be grounds for infanticide in many cultures. Fatherless children suffer disadvantages in modern North America too, largely though not entirely because single mothers are so often poor and overextended. It follows that a single mother would be more likely than her married counterpart to feel despair and a disinclination to embark on the possibly lost cause of child-rearing.

Infanticidal mothers in Canada are indeed more often unmarried than one would expect by chance. Between 1977 and 1983, single women delivered only 12% of the two million babies born in Canada ("Vital Statistics: Births and Deaths," as published annually by Statistics

Canada), and yet single mothers were responsible for just over half of the 64 maternal infanticides known to the police (Daly & Wilson, 1987b).

An important question is whether the observed tendencies for infanticidal mothers to be relatively young and to be relatively often unmarried are truly distinct. On the evidence thus far, one might remain skeptical of the effect in Figure 4.1, arguing that a new mother's age is not in *itself* relevant to her maternal inclination or lack thereof, but is incidentally correlated with another variable that *is* directly relevant, namely marital status. In other words, teenagers might be over-represented among infanticide offenders simply by virtue of the fact that they are overrepresented among unwed mothers and not directly by virtue of their youth. Data from France for the period 1945–1954 seem to support this argument (Leauté, 1968): As in Canada, infanticidal moth-ers were both younger and more often unwed than new mothers generally, but within the categories of single versus married mothers, the risk of infanticide did not appear to be systematically related to age. These French results must be viewed with caution, however, since they were based only on those women who were convicted of the killing and imprisoned. This was by no means the fate of all detected infanticides, and we do not know what caused these unfortunates to be singled out for harsh punishment.

The Canadian data on this point are presented in Figure 4.2, and in this case it is clear that the two factors—age and marital status—indeed make separate contributions to the risk of infanticide, as theoretical considerations suggested they would. When married women and single women are considered separately, the probability of infanticide is seen to decline with maternal age in both groups. When maternal age categories are considered separately, single women are generally more likely to dispose of a new baby than married women of the same age.

A Brief History of Infanticide in England

Poor, unwed mothers have certainly disposed of unwanted infants during the entire history of the English-speaking world, as they have done elsewhere. The prevalence of infanticide, however, appears to have undergone some dramatic fluctuations over the centuries. Histor-ical records reveal a great deal about the economic and other circum-stances conducive to high rates of child-killing, as well as providing a chronicle of changes in judicial reaction and public sentiment (Seaborne Davies, 1945; Hoffer & Hull, 1981).

The information on infanticide in mediaeval England is sparse, despite a large volume of coroners' and courts' records of homicide.

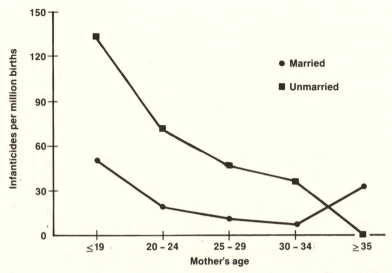

Figure 4.2. Risk of infanticide as a function of the mother's age and marital status. Canada, 1974–1983.

The historian Barbara Hanawalt (1979) reports, for example, that 2933 homicide cases were recorded in the counties of Norfolk, Northamptonshire, and Yorkshire between 1300 and 1348, but only one of these was an infanticide. No doubt, infanticide was more frequent than such records attest but was typically ignored by officialdom.

One reason why a blind eye has often been turned to infanticides, in England and elsewhere, is that infanticides, unlike most homicides, leave no aggrieved party to encourage the legal authorities to press the matter. In any criminal justice system beset with a heavy case load, those matters will be preferentially pursued that have the most insistent suitors. This may be especially so in the case of homicide. We are used to thinking of murder as an offense against the state, but in most legal systems, homicide cases have *plaintiffs,* namely the aggrieved relatives of the victim, who are entitled to compensation from the offender or his relatives for the loss of their kinsman. It follows that homicides within the family are often not a matter for legal action at all, since those entitled to compensation would be the same people as those obliged to pay it. The logic and workings of such homicide laws will be examined in Chapter 10. Our own legal system is descended in part from Roman law, under which the father's right *(potestas patriae)* included the freedom to dispose of all his descendants as he pleased. Infanticide by the mother only constituted an offense if it had been carried out against the wishes of the father, and even then it was *his* business and not the state's, since his rights extended also over his wife (see, for example, Jolowicz, 1932).

The crown's assumption of the role of plaintiff in homicides and other criminal cases occurred gradually in mediaeval England, as one part of a larger process of centralization of power. By making "society" rather than the victim's kinsmen the wronged party in homicide, the crown was able to usurp the right to compensation, and so it did, confiscating the chattels of convicted killers. The eyres—the itinerant king's courts that we discussed in Chapter 2—were therefore not only dispensers of justice but collectors of revenue as well, and a drain on the resources of the communities that were obliged to welcome them. Although entire communities were threatened with reprisal if crimes were concealed from the eyres, it is easy to imagine that an infanticide that had not aroused local outrage might be overlooked. Besides, the women responsible usually had no chattels worth confiscating anyway.

It was the economic impact of those bastard children who were *not* eliminated that eventually led to infanticide laws in England (British Parliamentary Papers, 1871). Throughout the mediaeval period, the gradual replacement of the ties of kinship by those of vassalage entailed an increasing marital and reproductive disenfranchisement of the poor. Servants and indentured laborers often had no chance to establish a stable family life, but of course that did not render them asexual, nor infertile. The Poor Law of 1576 was instituted to penalize those who imposed their bastard offspring upon the local charity and thus "defrauded" the parish of its capacity to relieve the "true poor." But the Poor Law did not solve the problem of illegitimacy.

As bastard children became an increasing burden to local authorities, unwed mothers were increasingly subjected to interrogation about paternity, and hence to abuse and repudiation by fathers who had been ordered to pay for the children's support. Domestic servants who became pregnant—often by their masters—were liable to dismissal by their mistresses. Unwed women who kept their children were often driven into virtual penal servitude in workhouses. The situation provided obvious incentives to hide one's pregnancy and dispose of the child at birth, and such behavior evidently became epidemic. In the absence of witnesses it could not be proved that a baby found dead in a ditch had been born alive, and hence no crime was demonstrable even if the mother could be found.

Official displeasure seems to have been directed at the illicit conception almost more than the infanticide. In 1624, parliament passed "An

Act to prevent the destroying and murdering of bastard children . . .'',
which began:

> Whereas many lewd Women that have been delivered of Bastard Children,
> to avoid their shame and to escape punishment, doe secretlie bury, or
> conceal the Death of their Children. . . . (21 James I, ch. 27, 1624)

This remarkable piece of legislation made Concealment of Birth a capital
crime, regardless of whether evidence could be adduced that the child
had actually been murdered; the concealment was proof enough of evil
intent. Moreover, it was a crime of which *only* an *unmarried* woman
could be convicted.

Over the next 200 years, hangings of infanticidal mothers declined
almost to nil, not, it seems, because of any decline in the rate of
infanticide itself, but because of a growing disinclination to convict.
Juries were sympathetic to destitute mothers, and began acquitting
them by reason of "insanity," with little regard for medical testimony. In
1803, "Concealment" was extended to apply to legitimate as well as
illegitimate births and the penalties were greatly reduced, but conviction
rates continued downward.

The industrial revolution increased the incentives to infanticide by
exacerbating the isolation from family of those young people who went
into domestic service or apprenticeship. According to Behlmer (1979),
domestic servants comprised 11% of the entire female population of
England in the late 19th century, and 78% of the unwed mothers. By the
1860's, London newspapers were reporting up to five dead babies found
in city parks in a single day. According to the *Daily Telegraph* of February
26, 1862, there were 3901 coroners' inquests held into suspicious deaths
of infants less than 2 years of age in London alone in the 5 years from
1856 to 1860. Two hundred ninety-eight verdicts of "wilful murder"
were returned. Another item from the same year reminds us of the sort
of fate awaiting those women who chose *not* to dispose of their infants.

> THE FEMALE INMATES OF OUR WORKHOUSES.—A return to an order of the
> House of Commons, obtained by Mr. Kekewich, just issued, throws some
> light on the class of characters the ratepayers have to support under the
> denomination of "Female Adult Paupers," in the workhouses of the unions
> and parishes in England and Wales. The paupers are classified "according
> to character," and the list is as follows: Single women pregnant with their
> first child, 569; single women who have had one bastard child, 2,847; single
> women who have had one bastard child, and are pregnant again, 292;
> single women who have had two bastard children, 1711; single women
> who have had three bastard children, 877; single women who have had
> four or more bastard children, 782; idiotic or weak-minded single women
> with one or more bastard children, 470; women whose out-relief has been

taken off on account of misconduct, 327; women incapable, from syphilis, of getting their own living, 543; prostitutes, 790; girls who have been out at service, but do not keep their places on account of misconduct, 383; girls brought up in the workhouse, and who have been out at service, but have returned on account of misconduct, 373; widows who have had one or more bastard children during their widowhood, 680; married women with husbands in the workhouse, 1,698; married women with husbands transported or in gaol, 258; married women deserted by their husbands, 2,131; imbecile, idiotic, or weak-minded women and girls, 5,160; respectable women and girls incapable of getting their living on account of illness or other bodily defect or infirmity, 5,300; respectable able-bodied women and girls, 2,267; respectable aged women, 11,615. Total, 39,673. (cited from "Eagle Eye," 1861–1863).

Reformers decried the hypocrisy of laws that punished the "victims of cruel seduction" but not their seducers. Psychiatrists debated the possible duration of "puerperal insanity" and "lactational psychosis." Judges decried the "mockery of law" represented by frequent acquittals. Doctors debated the precise moment at which a child could be said to have been "born alive." A burst of publicity surrounded the arrests and trials of several "baby farmers," women who made a profession of "adopting" babies, charging the mothers a one-time fee, ostensibly for the baby's food, and then letting the babies die. Parliament appointed a commission, which was to look into the infanticide problem and recommend new laws. Certain leading jurists argued before the commission that the acknowledged provocations to infanticide by poor women constituted grounds not for mercy, but for stiffer penalties, on the theory that greater temptations demand greater deterrence. Others argued the opposite, more humane, view. And while the arguments raged, desperate women continued to dispose of babies.

It is impossible to say even approximately how many babies were killed. No mother was hanged for the offense after 1849 (Wilson, 1971). Concealment of Birth proceedings declined from over 200 a year during the 1860's to less than 100 by the 1880's, but a good deal of suspicious infant mortality persisted. In 1912, for example, 1176 coroners' inquests were held in England and Wales "upon the bodies of children suffocated whilst in bed with their parents or others." The juries returned 1086 verdicts of accidental death, 87 open verdicts, and 3 of manslaughter. In the next year, 1080 such inquests produced no criminal charges at all (Judicial Statistics, 1912, 1913).

Gradually, the terrible toll declined. Birth control information and technology began to be disseminated, in spite of fanatical opposition. Social welfare programs at last began to afford single mothers some choice other than concealment or the workhouse. By the mid 1930's, the law had so proliferated that a mother who killed her newborn might be guilty of any one of five distinct offenses (murder, manslaughter, infanticide, child destruction, or concealment of birth), but the total proceedings under these charges amounted to fewer than 100 cases annually. More than 100 coroner's inquests to investigate suffocations in the parental bed were still being conducted every year, but none of them led to homicide charges (Judicial Statistics, annually 1856–1938). There were a lot of deaths to be sure, but it was a far cry from the numbers even 20 years earlier.

With improvements in government-financed social services, access to contraception and to safe legal abortions, and a continuing relaxation of the dire social consequences of unwed motherhood, infanticides have continued to decline. Yet there are still medical practitioners who consider childbirth to be a sort of disease, and parturient women to be dangerously unbalanced. "Lactational psychosis" remains in psychiatric dictionaries, and the modern doctor who smiles at this anachronism is still apt to consider "postpartum depression" to be purely an endocrine problem. If the history of English infanticide reveals anything, however, it is surely that acts of desperation are principally the products of desperate circumstances.

On Maternal "Bonding"

The nature of the bond between a mother and her offspring has long been a subject of controversy. Pregnancy, birth, and lactation are associated with enormous changes in hormone levels and other physiological phenomena. A great deal of research, most of it on rats, has explored how these changes interact with experiences to affect "maternal responsiveness." Students of certain other mammals, such as goats, have been primarily impressed with the mother's discriminative solicitude for her own baby and simultaneous hostility to others, and thus have been less inclined to postulate a motivational state of generalized maternalness.

Many writers (most of them men) have speculated on the possible relevance of these and other animal studies for our own species. Feminists have bristled, interpreting these speculations as sexist propaganda, new versions of tired old arguments to the effect that women are creatures of lowly nature rather than lofty reason and are hence deservedly subordinate to men. In this politicized arena, it has somehow become the "progressive" view that women and men are identically equipped for child care (well, except for mammary function!), and that there is no such thing as a specialized psychology of parenthood—

or of anything—in either sex. Needless to say, this dogma has not promoted our understanding of maternal affection in *Homo sapiens*. What it *has* promoted is the medicalization and dehumanization of the birth experience: If people are unspecialized, general-purpose devices, then there is nothing special about particular life events such as birth, and there is no reason why we should not place them in the efficient hands of technocrats.

In the early 1970's, the question of the nature of maternal love was given a fresh empirical footing by the pioneering studies of Marshall Klaus, John Kennell, and their associates. Klaus and Kennell (1976) proposed that the routine practices of maternity wards, by whisking babies away from their mothers and allowing them only brief contacts at feeding times, interfered with the natural course of maternal–infant bonding, with repercussions that extended long after departure from the hospital. Moreover, they did experiments that seemed to prove the point. All previous research on the sequelae of early mother–infant contact had been inconclusive because the mothers chose the degree of contact themselves. This meant that the mothers who chose "rooming-in" probably differed from those who did not, right from square one, and any subsequent differences probably reflected the prior differences rather than effects of rooming-in *per se*. But Klaus and Kennell *assigned women at random* to one of two groups: a "hospital-routine group"— which would ordinarily have been the fate of *all* the women on the maternity ward—or an "extra-contact group," in which mothers spent just a few hours more with their babies in the couple of days before hospital discharge.

Effects of this minor intervention were detectable months and even years later! In a number of studies carried out in several countries (e.g., Ali & Lowry, 1981; Carlsson *et al.*, 1978; de Chateau & Wiberg, 1977; Hales *et al.*, 1977; Kennell *et al.*, 1974; Klaus *et al.*, 1972; Sosa *et al.*, 1976), researchers found that "extra-contact" mothers breastfed their children longer, looked at them more, spoke to them in longer sentences, and so forth. Most dramatically, the "hospital-routine" babies were found to be significantly more likely to be abused (O'Connor *et al.*, 1980).

These "bonding" studies provided important ammunition for the proponents of more natural birth practices during the 1970's. Routine postpartum mother–infant separation was eliminated in many hospitals; rooming-in was heralded as a necessity and a woman's right. The conventional wisdom turned around so abruptly, in fact, that the early postpartum period acquired an inflated importance in both public and professional eyes. Mothers who had to deliver by caesarian section began expressing fears that their bonds to their babies would be stunted.

Maternity room staff became suspicious of those women who were simply too tired or too sore to interact enthusiastically with their newborns.

Around 1980, the reaction to these events provoked a hard critical look at the "bonding" evidence (Herbert *et al.*, 1982; Lamb & Hwang, 1982). Several much-cited studies purporting to demonstrate dramatic effects of early contact were shown to have methodological flaws. The particular measures of later behavior that were supposedly affected by the hospital experience were inconsistent from one study to another, and many measures had often been scanned to uncover a few significant effects. As concern about the reliability of the early studies grew, other studies that had obtained *no* significant differences—and were therefore evidence of nothing at all by the usual rules of scientific research—now became publishable as "failures to replicate" and hence disconfirmations (e.g., Svejda *et al.*, 1980). Expert opinion made its second abrupt about-face within a decade: The "bonding hypothesis" had been "found not to hold up."

In this latest turn of opinion, the baby has been thrown out with the bathwater (Daly & Wilson, 1987a). Attributing the sporadic effects of extra contact to chance cannot explain their directional consistency. Some of the early studies may have had certain methodological flaws, but others avoided them. The child abuse data are meager, but they are strongly in the direction of an ameliorative effect of early contact; at worst, the hypothesis deserves a more thorough test rather than a rejection. Critics of the "bonding hypothesis" cite evidence that various factors—the mother's economic circumstance, the involvement of the father, whether the pregnancy was planned—are related to the quality of infant care. Somehow these complications are supposed to represent counterevidence against the existence of mother–infant bonding. But this attack is directed against a straw man: that the new mother is a simple, hormonally primed automaton ready to "attach" maternally to the first suitable stimulus she encounters and oblivious to all else.

Selection thinking inspires a compromise view of the mother–infant bond which is entirely consistent with present evidence: Maternal bonding is likely to entail at least three distinct processes proceeding over different time courses, and is likely to be influenced by both situational factors and the quality of the mother–infant interaction.

The first process to be expected is an *assessment*, in the immediate postpartum period, of the quality of the child and the quality of present circumstances. As we have seen in abundant detail, the new mother is not invariably eager to raise her baby, and it would be curious if she were. The emotional flatness or "indifference" that is experienced by some new mothers—and is often alarming to hospital staff—seems to reflect such an assessment phase.

Even if initially indifferent, mothers commonly report developing, over the course of about a week, a feeling that their baby is uniquely wonderful. This change seems to reflect the second aspect of bonding suggested by an evolutionary view, namely *the establishment of an individualized love* for the child, guaranteeing that maternal effort will not be parasitized by unrelated young. Women are highly sensitive to their babies' distinctive features, recognizing them by voice and by smell within a day or two of birth. Some mothers find their own babies' feces unexceptionable, and yet are nauseated by those of other babies. These discriminative reactions can be powerful and involuntary, making the simulation of genuine parental attachment by substitute parents an emotional impossibility, as we shall see shortly.

The third and most prolonged bonding process that we would expect is *the gradual deepening of maternal love* over the course of years. This process is predictable from a consideration of the increasing reproductive value of the growing child (and the simultaneous decrease of the mother's own). This growing love is manifested in the growing disinclination of the parent to abandon or damage the child in times of duress, as we shall consider shortly.

When a Defective Child Is Born

As we noted above, the Statistics Canada data do not permit us to say whether defective children are likely victims of infanticide in modern Western society. There is, however, a great deal of evidence that they are likely victims of neglect and abuse (reviewed by Daly & Wilson, 1981). It has been demonstrated repeatedly that retarded children are subject to exceptionally high rates of parental violence, but the child's symptoms may often be a consequence rather than a cause of ill treatment. It is clear, however, that the defect antedates the abuse in the case of such congenital handicaps as spina bifida, cystic fibrosis, talipes, cleft palate, and Down's syndrome. Various studies have shown that those children who are severely abused include anywhere from two to ten times as many of these congenital problems as one would expect on the basis of their incidence in the population-at-large.

When defective children are placed in institutions, the parents' concern and active involvement are apt to wane rapidly. In 1976, according to the United States Bureau of the Census, American institutions were homes to more than 16,000 children whose families had ceased to visit them altogether. About 30,000—some 22% of all institutionalized children—were visited once a year or less (U.S. Bureau of the Census, 1978).

Although some mitigation of parental feeling toward defectives is a likely result of natural selection, it need not follow that parental feeling is directly inhibited by overt signs of abnormality. A new mother and her baby interact intensively. Within the first few hours after birth, healthy human infants exhibit a precocious social responsiveness—eye contact and selective attention to maternal speech—that may be a specialized attempt to advertise quality and elicit maternal commitment during the mother's assessment phase. If circumstances are dicey and the mother is in any way ambivalent, then the poor responsiveness of a defective baby might tip the scales toward a maternal decision to abandon. In our own society, defective children are separated from the mother at birth, treated elsewhere in the hospital, and sent home after some weeks or months. When such children are subsequently abused—and they frequently are—the failure of maternal solicitude could be as much the result of the postnatal separation as of the defect *per se*. Nevertheless, there is good evidence that the birth of a child with major defects commonly evokes an immediate shocked rejection in the parents, a rejection that would undoubtedly lead to quick abandonment in historical settings. (See Weir, 1984 for exemplary discussion of the ethical problems caused by improving medical capacity to "save" defective babies.)

The Child's Changing Risk of Homicide at Parental Hands

If natural selection has shaped the psychological mechanisms by which we value one another, then one might expect that A's love of B will tend to be a positive function of B's expected contribution to A's fitness. In the case of the parent–offspring relationship, the child's expected contribution to parental fitness is more or less directly related to the child's own expected fitness or "reproductive value." We thus expect *child-specific parental love* to be variable in its strength, and we expect that strength to be influenced by any variable that both affects the child's reproductive value and is accessible to parental assessment. This, of course, is the same argument that we used to identify the common denominator of the various circumstances—deformity, lack of male support, twins, and so forth—that are regularly cited as provoking or legitimizing infanticide.

In the absence of mishap, one's reproductive value increases steadily from birth until at least puberty. This is so primarily because surviving to maturity cannot be taken for granted: The average 12-year-old girl will

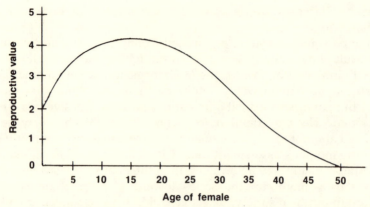

Figure 4.3. Reproductive value (expected future live births) as a function of
female age, in a natural-fertility foraging society (after data in
Howell, 1979).

bear more children in her remaining lifetime than will the average
female infant, because those who die childless before age 12 count
toward the latter average but not the former. In the modern West, this
early increase in reproductive value is muted by recent declines in infant
and juvenile mortality, but where life-historical mortality and fertility
are closer to the levels that must have prevailed for most of human
history, the prepubertal increase in reproductive value is not trivial
(Figure 4.3).

Evolutionary psychologists thus expect parental feeling to have
evolved such that parents will seem to value offspring increasingly with
age. Several studies of nonhuman parents have confirmed this expectation (e.g., Andersson *et al.*, 1980; Barash, 1975; Greig-Smith, 1980;
Patterson *et al.*, 1980; Pressley, 1981). The basic test situation is one in
which an experimenter assesses the extent to which parents will tolerate
risks to their own lives in order to defend helpless young in the nest.
Most of this research has been conducted with birds, and the typical
result is that the parent becomes increasingly likely to attack rather than
to flee from a predator that endangers both its own life and the life of the
offspring, as the eggs, and later the chicks, grow older and hence closer
to mature independence. We would expect people, like other creatures,
to value older dependent children more highly than younger ones.

The hypothesis that human parents "prefer" their elder children may
appear improbable: The lastborn child seems often to be the most
indulged, and parents often intervene in sibling disputes on behalf of
the younger. But these are not really counterexamples. The genetic

nonidentity of nuclear family members guarantees that there will be competition between siblings. If parental motives are such as to promote the parent's own fitness, then we should expect that parents will often be inclined to act so that neither sibling's interests prevail completely. Typically, parental imposition of equity will involve supporting the younger, weaker competitor, even when the parent would favor the older if forced to choose between the two. It is this latter sort of situation—"Which do you save when one must be sacrificed?"—in which parents' differential valuation of their children really comes to the fore. Recall that there were 11 societies in the ethnographic review of Chapter 3 for which it was reported that a newborn might be killed if the birth interval were too short or the brood too numerous. It should come as no surprise that there were *no* societies in which the prescribed solution to such a dilemma was said to be the death of an *older* child. Indeed, such a report would be hardly credible, and we think it enlightening to contemplate why: Dramatic cultural variability notwithstanding, the feelings of people in exotic societies are not alien to us. If one says "of course" when told that the mother sacrifices the infant to save the toddler rather than vice versa, this reaction merely illustrates that one takes for granted the phenomenon under discussion, namely the gradual deepening of parental commitment and love.

The child's growing value to the parent may be expected to produce an increasing parental inhibition against the use of dangerous tactics in conflict with the child. If parental homicides—especially those occurring beyond the child's infancy—result largely from temporary, angry lapses of parental solicitude, then the variable magnitude of child-specific parental love is likely to influence the risk of such lapses (Daly & Wilson, 1987b). Putting the point more plainly: Children annoy adults frequently, and the risk that the adult might react so angrily as to damage the child must surely be influenced by the particular adult's degree of concern for the particular child's welfare.

Figure 4.4 shows that the risk of parental homicide is indeed a declining function of the child's age. As we would anticipate, the most dramatic decrease occurs between infants and 1-year-old children. One reason for expecting this is that the lion's share of the prepubertal increase in reproductive value in natural environments occurs within the first year. Moreover, if parental disinclination reflects any sort of assessment of the child's quality or the mother's situation, then an evolved assessment mechanism should be such as to terminate any hopeless reproductive episode as early as possible, rather than to squander parental effort in an enterprise that will eventually be abandoned. Among the "infant" victims, the Statistics Canada data discrim-

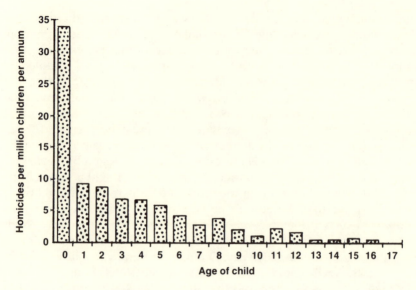

Figure 4.4. Risk of homicide by a natural parent in relation to the child's age. Canada, 1974–1983.

inate those killed within the first 6 months of life *vs.* those killed within the second 6 months. Mothers killed 61 in the first 6 months compared to just 27 in the second 6 months. For fathers, the corresponding numbers are 24 versus 14. Moreover, Figure 4.4 demonstrates that there is a prolonged decline in parental homicides beyond age 1. This pattern of victimization contrasts dramatically with the risk of homicide at the hands of *non*relatives (Figure 4.5), whose "valuation" of the child is not expected to parallel the parent's.

The differences between Figures 4.4 and 4.5 are of course multifarious. In part, the contrasts must reflect increasing access of nonrelatives to older children. Yet the two histograms are dramatically different even if one attends only to infants versus 1-year-old children, parents being far more likely to kill the infant while nonrelatives actually killed more 1-year-olds. One could argue that the parental decline simply reflects the increasing self-defensive capabilities of the child, and to some degree it must. Yet this factor does not prevent a huge increase in the overall victimization rate for adolescents; as we shall see in Chapter 8, the risk of becoming a homicide victim is in fact *greatest* for those age-sex classes that are most formidable in violent conflict. Teenagers are highly conflictual creatures, and the rate at which *non*relatives kill them explodes after puberty. When we consider the conspicuous, tempestu-

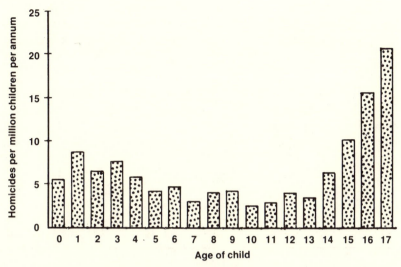

Figure 4.5. Risk that a child will be killed by a nonrelative, as a function of age. Canada 1974–1983.

ous conflicts that occur between teenagers and their parents—conflicts that apparently dwarf those of the preadolescent period—it is all the more remarkable that the risk of parental homicide continues its relentless decline to near zero.

Mothers Who Kill Older Children

Although mothers seldom kill children beyond their infancy, these rare cases still warrant scrutiny from the perspective of evolutionary psychology. We have proposed, for example, that child-specific maternal love is a variable, determined in part by the mother's residual reproductive value and hence her age. Moreover, we have proposed that this variable influences the probability that the mother would resort to violence when in conflict with the child. If this argument is sound, then we should expect not only infanticides but later maternal homicides as well to be less and less likely the later the child was born in the mother's life.

This prediction is upheld by the Canadian data, although the effect of the mother's age is weaker in the case of older victims than in the case of infanticides (Table 4.1). When mothers killed infants, the victims had been born to them at a mean age of 22.7 years, whereas older victims had been born at a mean maternal age of 24.5. This is a significant

Table 4.1. Age Distributions of Homicidal Mothers at the Birth of
Children They Killed, in Comparison to the Distribution
that Would Be Expected If the Risk of Such Homicide were
Unrelated to Maternal Age (Canada, 1974–1983).

Mother's age at birth of victim (years)	Proportion of mothers in population-at-large	Infanticidal mothers		Mothers who killed children > 1 year old	
		Actual	Expected	Actual	Expected
< 21	.141	39	12.3	30	16.2
21–25	.353	27	30.7	38	40.6
26–30	.338	13	29.4	32	38.8
31–35	.133	5	11.6	12	15.3
> 35	.035	3	3.0	3	4.0

$$\chi^2_{4df} = 71.3 \qquad\qquad \chi^2_{4df} = 14.1$$
$$p < .001 \qquad\qquad\qquad p < .01$$

difference, but both means are significantly below the 25.8 years that
was the average age of all new Canadian mothers during the same
period, according to Canadian Vital Statistics.

We find a similar result with respect to marital status: Mothers who
killed older children are again intermediate between infanticidal women
and the population-at-large. Whereas 51% of mothers committing
infanticide were unmarried, the same was true of just 34% of those
killing older children. This is still substantially above the 12% of
Canadian births in which the new mother was unmarried, and we have
some grounds to estimate that the unmarried percentage is no higher
among women residing with their older children (Daly & Wilson, 1985).
In sum, it appears that the causes of maternal homicide of older children
overlap the causes of infanticide, but only in part.

Killing of an older child is often associated with maternal depression.
Of the 95 mothers who killed a child beyond its infancy, 15.8% also
committed suicide. Fifteen of those 95 mothers killed 2 or more children in
a single incident, and a still higher proportion of these (33%) committed
suicide. By contrast, only 2 of 88 infanticidal mothers committed suicide
(and even this meager 2.3% probably overestimates the association of
infanticide with suicide, since infanticides are the only category of
homicides in which a significant incidence of undetected cases is likely).
The two infanticidal mothers who killed themselves were significantly

older (mean age = 29.5 years) than the 86 who did not (mean age = 22.5), and one of these 2 killed three older children as well.

Infanticide is primarily the recourse of young women who want to live but cannot cope with the present baby, whereas mothers who kill older children are frequently in a quite different state of depression. Such suicidal women occasionally leave notes indicating that the homicide is perceived as an act of love. Having decided that life is unbearable, the mother has resolved to save her child from living through misery like her own. Here, for example, is the text of a note left by a divorced American mother who shot her two young sons and took a drug overdose on October 3, 1974 (Alabama Court of Appeals, 370 So. 2d 749):

> Dear Mother & Daddy,
> I'm sorry to do this to you'all but I can't take this life any more. I'm taking my boys with me. Please put one on my right and one on my left side. I love my boys and hope God forgives me and lets me be with them. I know in my heart that my boys will be with God. God please forgive me for I have sined.
> I love you Mother & Daddy
Eileen
>
> Please dress the boys in blue they look good in it.
> Please put me between them I love them and want them
> to be in heven Gods heven. Please put with Monty
> Jay his night night & blanket one that Mom made.
> Please put with Jeff his little tiger that he got on
> his first Christmas on my bed.
> Read later
> Mother & Daddy
> Please let Gail have my side board and something
> else two.
> Please let Diane have something and also some
> clothes.
> Mother & Daddy let Jimmy & Camille have something if
> they want it.
> Renea will help you'all two.
> Im Sorry
I love you all
Eileen

The author of this note was found in a drug-induced coma, and was revived by heroic medical intervention, only to be tried and sentenced to life in prison.

In the Canadian data, it is also noteworthy that 35% of maternal infanticides were attributed by the investigating police force to the Statistics Canada motive category with the clumsy label of "mentally ill or mentally retarded (insane)," versus 58% of maternal homicides of older children. Here and elsewhere, it seems that the sorts of cases that are simultaneously rare and seemingly contrary to the actor's interests—in both the Darwinian and the commonsense meaning of interest—also happen to be the sorts of cases most likely to be attributed to some sort of mental incompetence. The validity of such attributions is of course questionable, and one may reasonably wonder whether the label "insane" tells us more about the labeler than the labeled. But either way, the state that is called "insanity" invites an evolutionary theoretical interpretation: We identify as mad those people who lack a species-typical nepotistic perception of their interests or who no longer care to pursue them. In Chapter 11, we shall examine more closely the application of concepts of mental incompetence in the explanation and judicial treatment of homicide. For the moment, we merely emphasize that a class of homicide that is relatively difficult to reconcile with an adaptive parental psyche—killing an older child in comparison to an infanticide—is not only relatively rare, but is also relatively often associated with suicide, alleged insanity, or both. We shall see those attributes in association again.

Fathers Who Kill

We would expect that many of the variables that are relevant to the risk of maternal homicide should be similarly relevant for fathers. The paternal case presents some complications, however.

The reproductive value of men reaches its peak somewhat later in young adulthood than does that of women, and it declines more gradually into old age. We would thus expect that infanticide by fathers will exhibit an age trend somewhat like the maternal age trend in Figures 3.1 and 4.1, but less steep. Unfortunately, we lack good data on the age-specific fertilities of men, so we cannot plot a figure equivalent to Figure 4.1. We do at least know the ages of the 38 men who killed their infant children: The mean was 26.3 years. Moreover, we know that fathers averaged 4 years older than mothers for that substantial majority of Canadian births that occurred within marriages (Canadian Vital Statistics, as published annually by Statistics Canada). Since the mean age for all new Canadian mothers during the relevant period, married or not, was 25.8, it seems clear that infanticidal fathers are indeed relatively young. And as was the case with mothers, infanticidal fathers were

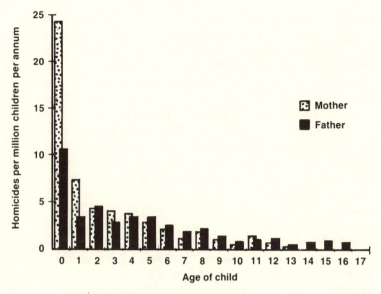

Figure 4.6. A child's risk of homicide at the hands of mother versus father as a function of the child's age. Canada 1974–1983.

significantly younger than those fathers who killed older offspring (mean age at the victim's birth = 29.2 years).

Fathers are also like mothers in being decreasingly likely to kill older children. Again the effect is less striking in men (Figure 4.6).

"Father" is an attribution. We safely assume that the relationship of homicidal mothers to their victims has been identified correctly, but we cannot be so certain about fatherhood. Nor can the putative fathers themselves. Descriptions of homicide cases occasionally point to a suspicion or revelation of nonpaternity as a stimulus to violence. Since information contributing to paternity doubt may be forthcoming at any time—and the evidence of relationship is often clearer in older children than in infants—the uncertainty of paternity may be one factor contributing to the relatively sustained risk from fathers as compared with mothers.

The probability of suicide by homicidal fathers is related to the same variables as in the case of mothers. The overall suicide rate is much higher in fathers, but of course men are much more likely than women to commit suicide in any case (e.g., deCatanzaro, 1981). As with mothers, fathers who killed older children killed themselves as well significantly more often (43.6% of 101) than did those who killed their infant children (10.5% of 38). Also like mothers is the fact that those infanticidal fathers who did commit suicide were significantly older (mean age = 30.5 years) than those who did not (mean = 25.8). Likewise, the paternal age at which older victims had been born was also significantly greater for suicidal (mean = 31.1 years; $N = 71$) than for nonsuicidal (mean = 27.5; $N = 67$) homicidal fathers. And men who killed their older children were a little more likely to be deemed mentally incompetent (20.8%) than those who killed their infants (15.8%).

Not all patterns are similar in mothers and fathers, however. If we further divide parental homicides after the first birthday into the killing of "children" aged 1–17 versus "adults" 18 or older, some interesting distinctions emerge. Mothers were significantly more likely to commit suicide after killing an adult offspring (100% of 4 women) than after killing a child (11% of 91 women), continuing the trend we saw in comparing infanticides to older victim cases. Fathers, however, were significantly *less* likely to commit suicide after killing an adult offspring (19% of 21 men) than a child (50% of 80 men). It is probably relevant to the interpretation of this difference that 20 of the 22 adult victims of their fathers were sons and only two were daughters.

Whereas these fathers killed mostly sons, three of the four adult victims of mothers were daughters. There is thus a same-sex bias in parental homicides of adult offspring (Fisher exact test, $p = .014$). There is no hint of such a same-sex bias in the killings of either infants (51% male victims if killed by mother, 55% if by father) or older children (55% male if by mother, 54% if by father). Violent conflict between parents and adult offspring may exhibit a same-sex bias because the relationship has become more peerlike and competitive; competition, as we shall consider in Chapter 7, occurs predominantly within sexes regardless of relationship. The conflicts between parents and adult offspring will be examined more closely in Chapter 5 when we consider parricides.

The most dramatic difference between homicidal fathers and mothers is illustrated in Table 4.2. An infrequent but regular variety of homicide is that in which a man destroys his wife and children. A corresponding act of familicide by the wife is almost unheard of. The table covers a 10-year period for which we have evidence on all homicides. Before 1974, some infanticide-by-mother cases were omitted from the records, but the information on cases of familicide is complete back to 1961. Beginning in that year, we find 61 cases in which a Canadian man killed his wife and one or more children, over a 23-year period, and not a single such massacre by a wife. Some women kill their children. Other women, for other reasons, kill their husbands. But familicide—often but by no means always followed by suicide—is a peculiarly male crime. We suggest that the psychology of familicide must be understood in terms

Table 4.2. Parental and Spousal Homicides in Canada, 1974–1983[a]

Sex of offender	Victims		
	Spouse and one or more children	One or more children but not spouse	Spouse but no children
Female	0	175	248
Male	26	89	786

[a]Table entries are numbers of offenders.

of men's proprietary attitude toward women and their reproductive capacity. This is a topic that we shall examine further in Chapter 9, when we focus on violence between husbands and wives.

Substitute Parents

Perhaps the most obvious prediction from a Darwinian view of parental motives is this: Substitute parents will generally tend to care less profoundly for children than natural parents, with the result that children reared by people other than their natural parents will be more often exploited and otherwise at risk. Parental investment is a precious resource, and selection must favor those parental psyches that do not squander it on nonrelatives.

In most relationships between two people, reciprocity is carefully monitored by both parties. If either seems regularly to take more than he or she gives, the imbalance is resented as exploitative. Parental altruism is different—unique in fact—in that the flow of benefits is prolongedly, cumulatively, and ungrudgingly unbalanced. Why this should be so is evident: Organisms have evolved to expend their very lives enhancing the fitness prospects of their descendants. That is the ultimate "self-interest" of which our more immediate perceptions of personal welfare are tokens.

What, then, of the party who steps into a "parental" relationship with a child not his or her own? With all the good will in the world, the substitute parent is likely to find the situation difficult. Child-specific parental love is the emotional mechanism that permits people to tolerate—even to rejoice in—those long years of expensive, unreciprocated parental investment. Substitute parents are less likely than natural parents to experience the emotional rewards that make the costs of parenthood tolerable. In an interview study of stepparents in Cleveland,

Ohio, for example—a study of a predominantly middle-class group suffering no particular distress or dysfunction—Louise Duberman (1975) found that only 53% of stepfathers and 25% of stepmothers could claim to have "parental feeling" toward their stepchildren, and still fewer to "love" them. In an observational study of Trinidadian villagers, Mark Flinn (1988) found that stepfathers interacted less with "their" children than did natural fathers; that interactions were more likely to be aggressive within steprelationships than within the corresponding natural relationships; and that stepchildren left home at a younger age.

Pop psychology and how-to manuals for stepfamilies have become a growth industry. Serious study of "reconstituted" families is also burgeoning. Virtually all this literature is dominated by a single theme: coping with the antagonisms (see Wilson & Daly, 1987, for references). Indeed, many professionals have concluded that steprelationships are inevitably conflictual, and that the best advice to the warring parties is that they abandon the ideal of becoming a nuclear family. This is not to deny that the psychology of parental love can sometimes be activated (more or less fully) within an artificial parent–offspring bond. It can, after all, be activated with surprising intensity toward a nonhuman pet! But whether a successful approximation of parental love will be established in any given case is no sure thing.

One relevant consideration in predicting the success of artificial parent–offspring relations must surely be the initial strength of the substitute parent's *wish* to simulate a genuine parental love. And therein lies an important reason to discriminate step- from adoptive relationships. Adoptions by "strangers"—that is to say by unrelated couples, as distinct from adoptions by stepparents or by biological relatives—are primarily the recourse of childless couples, who are strongly motivated to simulate a natural family experience and who have been carefully screened by adoption agencies. While the adoptive couple may not be in perfect agreement about the desirability of adopting, there is at least no exploitation of one partner's efforts for the other's fitness benefit. Furthermore, those who adopt are much more affluent than parents generally, so that the pressures of poverty—so powerfully relevant to the risks of infanticide and child maltreatment—do not apply. And finally, if the adoption proves unsatisfactory, or if the marriage fails, the couple can return the child, which happens more often than is generally realized (see, e.g., Festinger, 1986). For all these reasons, we would not especially anticipate elevated risks to adopted children. It is interesting, however, that such children have sometimes been found to suffer when natural children are subsequently born to the adopting couple, a result that has led some professionals to counsel against adoption by childless couples until infertility is definitely established (e.g., Kraus, 1978).

Stepparenthood presents itself, *a priori*, as a much more dangerous circumstance. Whereas the adoptive couple specifically desires to establish a fictive parent–offspring relationship, the stepparent will usually have entered into the relationship incidentally to the establishment of a desired mateship. The child must often enter into the prospective stepparent's marital decision as a cost, not a benefit.

Risks to Children Living with Stepparents

Stepparents have rather a poor reputation. Webster's unabridged dictionary defines "stepmother" as follows:

1. The wife of one's father by a subsequent marriage.
2. One that fails to give proper care or attention.

The "step" root comes from an Old English word meaning "to deprive or bereave." The negative characterization of stepparents is by no means peculiar to our culture. The folklorist who consults Stith Thompson's (1955) massive *Motif-Index of Folk Literature* will encounter such pithy synopses as "Evil stepmother orders stepdaughter to be killed" (Irish myth), and "Evil stepmother works stepdaughter to death in absence of merchant husband" (India). For convenience, Thompson divided stepfather tales into two categories: "cruel stepfathers" and "lustful stepfathers." From Eskimos to Indonesians, through dozens of tales, the stepparent is the villain of every piece.

The ubiquity of Cinderella stories (e.g., Cox, 1892) is surely a reflection of certain basic, recurring tensions in human society. Women must often have been forsaken with dependent children throughout human history, and both fathers and mothers were often prematurely widowed. If the survivor wished to forge a new marital career, then the fate of the children became problematic. We have already encountered the Tikopia or Yanomamö husband who demands the death of his new wife's prior children. Other solutions have included leaving the children with postmenopausal matrilineal relatives, and the *levirate*, a widespread custom by which a widow and her children are inherited by the dead man's brother or other near relative. In the absence of such arrangements, children were obliged to tag along as stepchildren under the care of nonrelatives with no particular benevolent interest in their welfare. They surely had genuine cause for alarm (see, for example, Hill & Kaplan, 1988).

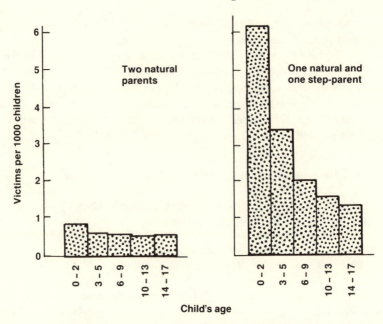

Figure 4.7. Per capita rates of validated child abuse reports to the American Humane Association, under a compulsory reporting scheme. United States, 1976. (Modified from Wilson *et al.*, 1980.)

Social scientists have turned this scenario on its head. The difficulties attending steprelationships—insofar as they are acknowledged at all— are presumed to be *caused by* the "myth of the cruel stepparent" and the child's fears. But if the cruel stepparent is alleged to be mythical, then we must surely inquire *why* stepparents should be the victims of this particular slander—and in so many cultures at that. Those who consider the cruel stepparent a mythical beast typically ignore this question altogether or else explain the slander psychoanalytically, by appeal to the "defenses" of the slanderers. Why this bizarrely counterintuitive view is the conventional wisdom would be a topic for a longer book than this; suffice to say that the answer surely has more to do with ideology than with evidence. In any event, social scientists have staunchly ignored the question of the factual basis for the negative "stereotyping" of stepparents. Where there's so much smoke, one might do well to inspect the fire.

So are children at risk in stepparent homes in contemporary North America? Well, their chances of becoming reported victims of child abuse are certainly elevated (Figures 4.7 and 4.8).

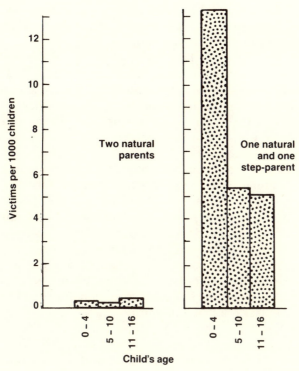

Figure 4.8. Per capita rates of child abuse cases known to children's aid societies and reported to a provincial registry. Hamilton, Ontario, Canada, 1983. (Modified from Daly & Wilson, 1985.)

Before we accept the enormous differences in Figures 4.7 and 4.8 at face value, however, there are several possibly confounding factors that must be considered. Both child abuse and familial breakdown are associated with poverty, for example, so that the association between abuse and stepparenthood might be an incidental consequence of poverty. This appealing idea fails: Poverty is associated with a high incidence of *single*-parent families, but within two-parent homes—which are the only ones considered here—the proportion of children living with a stepparent is virtually identical across socioeconomic classes, in both Canada and the United States (Wilson & Daly, 1987). There is, in other words, no appreciable statistical confound between steprelationships and poverty in North America. Other possible confounded factors, such as the mother's age and the size of the family, do not account for the differences either (Daly & Wilson, 1985). Stepparenthood *per se* remains the single most powerful risk factor for child abuse that has yet been identified. (Here and throughout this discussion "stepparents" include both legal and common-law spouses of the natural parent.)

Still, stepparents may be the victims of myth and slander. Suppose that you were suspicious about the treatment of a child next door. Is it not possible that your suspicions would be increased—and the chances that you would place a call to child welfare authorities increased as well—if you knew that the man of the house was not the child's natural father? In other words, the detection or reporting of abuse may be biased against stepparents.

Such biases surely exist, and it is almost impossible to estimate their magnitude, but they cannot begin to account for the facts. The reasoning behind this assertion is as follows. If reporting or detection biases were responsible for the overrepresentation of stepparents among child abusers, then we would expect the bias, and hence the overrepresentation, to diminish as we focused upon increasingly severe and unequivocal maltreatment up to the extreme of fatal batterings. But the actual trend is precisely the opposite. Of the 87,789 maltreatment victims identified by the American Humane Association in 1976, 15% lived with substitute parents. Less than one-third of these victims exhibited overt nonaccidental injuries, and when we consider only this subset, the percentage living with substitute parents rises to 25%. Finally, we can confine attention to the most extremely and unequivocally abused children: the 279 fatalities. Not only should reporting bias be minimal for this group, but their relative youth (median age = 3.6 years) is an additional reason to expect fewer stepparents; nevertheless, the fraction dwelling with substitute parents rises again to 43%. Whatever the degree of reporting bias that may operate against stepparents, then, it is surely the case that the risk of fatal abuse is hugely elevated in their presence.

Just how great an elevation of risk are we talking about? Our efforts to answer that question have been bedevilled by a lack of good information on the living arrangements of children in the general population. Astonishingly, census bureaus in the United States, Canada, and elsewhere have never attempted to distinguish natural parents from substitutes, with the result that there are no official statistics on the numbers of children of each age who live in each household type. There is no question that the 43% of murdered American child abuse victims who dwelt with substitute parents is far more than would be expected by chance, but estimates of that expected percentage can only be derived from surveys that were designed to answer other questions. For a random sample of American children in 1976, with an age distribution corresponding to that of the 279 fatal abuse victims, the best available national survey (Bachrach, 1983) indicates that only about 1% or fewer would be expected to have dwelt with a substitute parent. An American child living with one or more substitute parents in 1976 was therefore approximately 100 times as likely to be fatally abused as a child living with natural parents only (see also Kaplun & Reich, 1976).

Results for Canada are similar. In Hamilton, Ontario in 1983, for example, 16% of child abuse victims under 5 years of age lived with a natural parent and a stepparent (Daly & Wilson, 1985). Since small children very rarely *have* stepparents—less than 1% of preschoolers in Hamilton in 1983, for example—that 16% represents *forty times* the abuse rate for children of the same age living with both natural parents. And again, as in the United States, the overrepresentation of stepparents is even more extreme among homicides than among nonfatal abuse cases. One hundred forty-seven Canadian children between the ages of 1 and 4 were killed by someone *in loco parentis* between 1974 and 1983; 37 of those children (25.2%) were the victims of their stepparents, and another 5 (3.4%) were killed by unrelated foster parents.

In 1984, Statistics Canada conducted a "Family History Survey" on a national probability sample of 16,103 Canadians in the "labour force" (ages 18–65 years). This survey (Burch, 1985) provides the best information yet available on the living arrangements of North American children. The survey shows, for example, that 0.4% of 2,852 Canadian children, aged 1–4 in 1984, lived with a stepparent. It should be noted that this survey was conducted just after the end of our decade of homicide data. Since divorce and remarriage rates rose over that decade, it is likely that stepparenthood rates did too, and hence that the 1984 survey estimates a higher incidence of steprelationships than that which prevailed over our homicide sampling period.

The population-at-large information provided by the 1984 survey permits the calculation of age-specific risks of homicide at the hands of stepparents versus natural parents (Figure 4.9). As we would anticipate from the discussion above, the difference is even larger than in the case of nonfatal abuse (Figure 4.8); note again that this difference is almost certainly underestimated due to the late date of the population-at-large survey. For the youngest age group in Figure 4.9, those 2 years of age or younger, the risk from a stepparent is approximately 70 times that from a natural parent (even though the latter category includes all infanticides by natural mothers).

The English experience is similar. Forensic psychiatrist P.D. Scott (1973b) reported on a sample of 29 "fatal battered baby cases" in which the father or substitute father had killed out of "exasperation or loss of

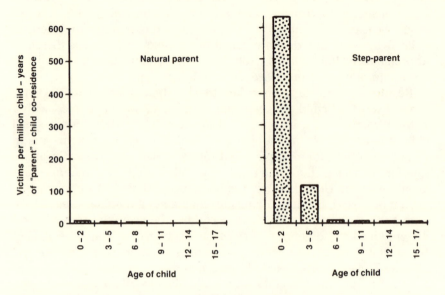

Figure 4.9. The risk of being killed by a stepparent versus a natural parent in relation to the child's age. Canada 1974–1983.

temper." Fifteen of the men (52%) were stepfathers, a remarkably high proportion considering that the victims averaged only 15 months of age. By comparison, a major study of an English cohort born in 1970 showed that just 3% lived in stepfamilies at 5 years of age (Wadsworth *et al.*, 1983). Since the probability of living in such a family increases roughly linearly, we may infer that fewer than 1% of 15-month-old English babies dwelt with stepfathers.

Stepparents and Offspring Age

Much of the popular literature on stepfamilies takes it for granted that conflict derives principally from the children's rejection of the substitute parent, rather than the reverse. From the perspective of selection thinking, this interpretation rings false. Surely it is the stepparent who is likely to resent the pseudoparental obligation thrust upon him, and any rejection by the child may be interpreted as reflecting a well-founded apprehension of that lack of genuine parental solicitude.

These alternative hypotheses lead to contrasting predictions about the effects of age upon the risk of violence. If it is the child who refuses

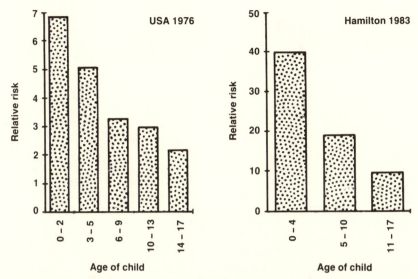

Figure 4.10. The ratio of child abuse risk in a stepparent-plus-natural-parent home over the risk in a two natural-parent home, in relation to the child's age. (a) United States, 1976. (b) Hamilton, Ontario, 1983.

the new parent, then any problems that are peculiar to steprelationships may be most severe with adolescents. At the least, such problems should be absent in the very youngest infants. If, on the other hand, the problem resides primarily in the substitute parent's resentment and disinclination, then the elevation of risk should be worst when the anticipated dependency and obligation is maximal. We would then see the greatest difference between stepparent and natural-parent homes in the maltreatment not of adolescents, but of infants.

The facts support the latter view. The elevation of child abuse risk in stepparent as opposed to natural-parent homes is maximal with the youngest infants, and declines monotonically with the child's age (Figure 4.10). The homicide data are similar to the abuse data (Figure 4.11).

A baby's chance of being abused or murdered is greatly elevated by the presence of a stepparent (which almost invariably means a stepfather, since mothers rather than fathers typically have custody of infants). The natural mother is often implicated in—or at least turns a blind eye to—the violence and neglect. Just as in several of the ethnographic examples discussed earlier, the baby is a resented impediment to the new relationship, and the mother has to make a choice.

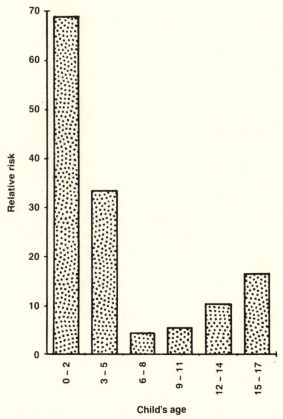

Figure 4.11. The ratio of the risk of being killed by a person *in loco parentis* to the
victim in a stepparent-plus-natural-parent home over the risk in a
two natural-parent home, in relation to the child's age. Canada,
1974–1983.

When the child is older, the natural parent is much less likely to forsake
it, and some other compromise must be found. Although conflicts
between adolescents and their stepparents may be spectacular, both
parties can at least look forward to the youngster's imminent departure
from the home.

The view of parental behavior that is currently prevalent in the social
sciences is altogether different from the model espoused here. Parenthood is typically considered a "role." This metaphor (sometimes inflated to the status of a "theory") nicely captures the abrupt behavioral
changes that occur as one switches between parental and other social

interactions, and it is also useful in directing attention to the social learning necessary for competent parenting. It is positively misleading, however, in its implication of arbitrary substitutability. A role is something that any competent actor who has studied the part can step into, whereas parent–offspring bonds are individualized, and cannot be established at will. Indeed, the concept of "roles" utterly fails to capture the motivational and emotional aspects of parenthood. Parents care profoundly, often selflessly, about their children, a fact with immense behavioral consequences about which "role theory" is mute.

The prevalent view of stepparenthood within the social sciences is that it too is a "role," only partly overlapping that of natural parenthood. The undeniable tensions of steprelationships are then attributed to role "ambiguity" and "newness" (e.g., Cherlin, 1978; Kompara, 1980; Giles-Sims, 1984). Stress is alleged to be the product of uncertain and conflicting expectations about what a stepparent can and should do; stepparenthood will remain stressful until "society" defines the role more clearly. We doubt that this view would survive empirical tests of its implications, but its proponents have attempted none. One clear implication is that there is a greater societal consensus about what fathers ought to do around the house than there is about what stepfathers ought to do. Another implication must be that the difficulties attending steprelationships will fade away as the subject is more widely discussed and the "ill-defined new role" becomes better articulated.

There is a commonsense alternative hypothesis about why some "roles" seem easy and "well-defined" while others are difficult and "ambiguous." It is simply that the former match our inclinations while the latter defy them. Stepparents do not find their roles less satisfying and more conflictual than natural parents because they don't *know* what they are supposed to do. Their problem is that they don't *want* to do what they feel obliged to do, namely to make a substantial investment of "parental" effort without receiving the usual emotional rewards. The "ambiguity" of the stepparent's situation does not reside in society's failure to define his role, but in genuine conflicts of interest within the stepfamily.

Mainstream social science views of social life, such as "role theory," ignore the most basic distinguishing characteristics of different kinds of relationships, and therefore offer little or no insight into the particular relationship between parent and offspring. Without recourse to the concept of evolutionary adaptation, we could not hope to understand why parental love and altruism even *exist*, let alone why they sometimes fail.

Parricide

Killing Parents

— 5 —

In a profound sense, the bearing and rearing of children is the meaning of life and the point of all striving. A child is a ticket in the natural selective lottery. The most basic human qualities have arisen and persist only by virtue of their contributions to success in that lottery. And yet, as must be evident from the last two chapters, children are by no means invariably perceived as blessings.

In any sexually reproducing species such as ourselves, parents and their offspring are not genetically identical, with the result that the ideal course of action for the advancement of one party's fitness interests is often suboptimal for the other. In this regard, the parent–offspring relationship is like any other blood link: The two parties have a fundamental commonality of interest by virtue of relatedness, but they have a potential for conflict as well. The primary arena of parent–offspring conflict concerns the allocation of parental efforts and resources, since the ideal allocation from an offspring's point of view nearly always differs from that suiting the parent. ·

The Logic of Parent–Offspring Conflict

A simple, artificial numerical example can be used to convey the logic of the conflict. Suppose that you and a sibling have been reared by an even-handed mother, with the result that you presently have the same "fitness value" (expected future reproductive output). Suppose further that your mother comes home with two items of food, and that you (like your sibling) could enhance your present fitness value by consuming them. Now comes a crucial assumption: Your gains from consuming parental resources exhibit diminishing returns. (This may seem an arbitrary assumption, but it is in fact realized under a wide range of realistic conditions, such as when your first priority is to avert starvation, or when your capacity to store energy or nutrients is limited.) So let us say that by consuming the first item you would raise your present fitness value by 4 units, and that by consuming the second you would raise it an additional 3. Your sibling has the same capacity to utilize the goodies. Who, then, should get them?

If your mother has her way, the spoils will be divided equally. Should you and your sibling consume one item each, the total fitness value of mother's brood will increase by 8 units, whereas if either party monopolizes both items, the gain will be only 7. But *your* perspective should have evolved to be slightly different. Your sibling is a potential replicator of your genes, but not so efficient a one as you yourself; you perceive a fitness unit that *you* gain to be twice as valuable as one gained by your sibling. The net gain to your inclusive fitness is 6 units if mother imposes equity, and 7 if you can grab the lot. Unfortunately, your sibling's view of the matter is as selfish as your own. (This argument assumes common paternity and a relatedness between siblings of $r = 0.5$. If you are actually just maternal half-siblings, then your view of equity should be all the more jaundiced.)

For the sake of clarity, the above example is ploddingly specific. However, the implications of the argument—unappreciated before Robert Trivers's (1974) analysis of "parent–offspring conflict"—are breathtakingly general. The first is that each offspring will routinely desire a larger share of parental investment than would be ideal from the parent's perspective. In the example above, we imagined an equal contest between sibling rivals, but the point also stands when the young differ in age and present value to the parent, and even when the rearing of one does not overlap the next at all; by acceding to offspring's demands, a parent would in effect still be withdrawing resources from other avenues of fitness, and the parent's ideal allocation will never match the child's (except in the exceptional limiting case where both parties agree that the child should get nothing). One expected consequence of this analysis is that parent and child will disagree about the time at which the child should be weaned, an expectation that is clearly fulfilled. But, more generally, the magnitude of parental investment in a particular child is expected to be a point of contention at all life stages.

In the numerical example, each child values itself above its sibling, while the parent values the two equally. While such precisely equal parental valuations are not generally to be expected, it *will* generally be the case that the parent's interest would be served by encouraging the children to value their siblings to a greater degree than they are spontaneously inclined to do. Thus, parents may be expected to suppress and punish overt sibling conflict, and to reward solidarity and altruism within the brood. Moreover, as Trivers (1985) has elaborated the issue, the parent's and child's views of other relatives are similarly distinct. To the parent P, for example, its child C is twice as valuable

($r = .5$) as its niece or nephew N ($r = .25$). From C's perspective, however, N is a cousin ($r = .125$) and only one-eighth as valuable as self ($r = 1.0$). A similar calculus applies to other collateral kin. We may therefore expect that parents will consider their children too self-centered, and will encourage them to take a benevolent interest in collateral kin that the children are relatively inclined to disdain.

Since parental assistance to the young is largely a cooperative venture that advances the fitness of both parties, it follows that young will have evolved means of communicating their needs to responsive parents. But the nonidentity of fitness interests suggests that selection will incline offspring to exaggerate their needs (and their quality). When confronted with the threat of a withdrawal of parental investment on behalf of a younger sibling, children may exaggerate their own dependency and need by "regressing." In a study (Dunn & Kendrick, 1982) of 40 English children just after the births of younger siblings, for example,

> Signs of regression were noted by 28 mothers. For 15 children these were mild—occasional baby talk, demands to be carried around, or requests to be fed. For an additional 13 children there was a definite regressive step over toilet training, or an insistence on being fed by a child who had previously fed himself, and so on. (p. 30)

This sort of psychological warfare on the part of children in turn sets up selection pressures for any parental counterstrategies that effectively discount propaganda and contribute to a correct assessment of the offspring's true needs and quality. More generally, each party may be expected to use whatever means are available to manipulate the other's behavior in the direction of one's own optimum, whether by deceit, by coercion, or by sheer nagging. Children, for example, can impose costs on parents who are reluctant or slow to respond by resorting to aversive pleading and temper tantrums. But for the most part, it is the parents who, by virtue of their greater size and experience, possess the greater arsenal of sticks and carrots. As Richard Alexander (1974) has pointed out, pressing a losing battle of wills profits neither party, and one might therefore expect that children will have evolved "tendencies to accede to parental discipline." Trivers (1985) concedes the point (see also Slavin, 1985), and adds this interesting rider:

> We expect adolescence to be a time of identity reorganization. Since adolescence signals impending offspring independence, the offspring no longer has to submit to parental demands; were it to continue to act out parental wishes that were not in harmony with its own self-interest, it would continue to lower its own inclusive fitness. Thus, we expect

individuals at this time to reorganize their personalities in such a way as to reflect their own self-interest more exactly. (p. 164)

Killing Parents

> On Sunday afternoon, January 2nd, the victim (male, age 46) was killed in his home by a single shotgun blast at close range. The killer (male, 15) was the victim's son, and the circumstance was familiar to the investigating police.
>
> The victim, employed as a sandblaster, had a criminal record that included two convictions for assault. The home was a scene of recurring violence, in which the victim had assaulted his wife and sons, had threatened them with the same weapon he eventually died by, had even shot at his wife in the past. On the fatal Sunday, the victim was drunk, berating his wife as a "bitch" and a "whore," and beating her, when their son acted to terminate the long history of abuse.
>
> Detroit, 1972, case 6

Our 1-year sample of Detroit homicides includes four cases in which teenagers killed their fathers. Three were committed by sons and one by a 13-year-old daughter. All four were much the same. In each case, the eventual victim was beating his wife, not for the first time, when the teenager fetched the family gun and demanded that the beating stop.

Limited evidence suggests that adolescent patricide typically follows the Detroit pattern. Corder *et al.* (1976), for example, reviewed the psychiatric examination records for a sample of adolescents charged with murder in North Carolina, and reported, "All 6 patients charged with murdering their fathers came from homes in which the father was a chronic alcoholic who was severely abusive to both the patient and his or her mother" (p. 960). Russell (1984) describes four "patricides" (one of which actually involved a stepfather) in a similar study of juvenile murderers in Massachusetts. Again, in all four cases, "the fathers were most brutal characters" (p. 186).

Adolescent matricides appear to be an altogether different matter. Murdered mothers have not typically been physically abusive to their eventual killers, although they may have been psychologically abusive. In the single Detroit case, the offender (female, age 18) was found insane, a verdict that was not returned for any of the four patricides.

Parricide (the killing of one's father or mother) is concentrated upon fathers rather than mothers, and this is especially true when the killer is an adolescent, as opposed to an adult. In Canada between 1974 and 1983, for example, fathers outnumbered mothers by 41 to 13 as homicide victims of their teenage children (hence comprising 76% of adolescent parricide victims), and by 69 to 49 as victims of their offspring aged 20 or more (hence comprising 58% of such victims). In view of the abusive provocation of many patricide victims, the greater number of adolescent patricides than matricides is not surprising. It might also have been anticipated from considerations of the uncertainty of paternity, which may be a factor both in the eventual victim's hostility and abuse, and also in the patricidal adolescent's readiness to resort to violence in defense of mother, the more certain parent. The difference is all the more striking in view of adolescents' greater access to their mothers than their fathers and in view of men's greater self-defensive and intimidating capabilities.

An Asymmetry of Valuation

Parent and child are equally related each to the other, but it does not follow that each should have evolved to be equally concerned for the other's welfare. As we discussed in Chapter 4, a parent's valuation of an offspring is theoretically expected to increase over time, at least until the latter's maturity. The fact that reproductive value varies over time means that mutual valuations between individuals are similarly unstable. From A's point of view, B's value as a potential vehicle of A's fitness is the product of B's relatedness (r) to A times B's reproductive value (RV), i.e. ($r_{AB} \times RV_B$). From B's perspective, A's value is the product of the same coefficient of relatedness times A's reproductive value ($r_{AB} \times RV_A$). If A's reproductive value exceeds B's, and the two are close kin, it follows that B may be more willing to incur costs—risk to own life, for example—on behalf of A than vice versa. (The effects of such asymmetrical solicitude are likely to increase A's advantage, possibly even to the point that B's best course of action is to forsake personal reproduction altogether and become a celibate "helper." When bridewealth or some other threshold resource for reproductive status is hard to come by, parents may manipulate one or more children to subordinate their interests to those of siblings. In certain circumstances, the parents may be able to so effectively tip the scales at an early stage that the helper role becomes the manipulated child's best course of action, and remains so even after parental pressures are removed.)

By virtue of greater reproductive value, an adult offspring will typically be more valuable to its aging parent than vice versa. We have previously suggested that such interindividual valuations constitute one determinant of the probability that dangerous tactics will be employed when two people find themselves in conflict. In particular, we would expect the individual less valued to be more at risk. An obvious

Table 5.1. Homicides in which Killer and Victim Were Both Adults
(≥ 16 years), and Were Related as Parent-to-Offspring,
Broken Down by Gender Combinations and by Generation
of Killer (Canada, 1974–1983)

	Father–son	Mother–son	Father–daughter	Mother–daughter
Parent kills offspring	20	1	5	3
Offspring kills parent	91	45	7	12

prediction, then, is that offspring will kill their parents more often than
the reverse. However, we must immediately exclude young children
from this proposition, mainly because their relative defenselessness
makes them much more likely to be victims than offenders regardless of
any relationship with the adult involved, and also because the parent's
reproductive value may well still exceed the child's at this stage. Turning
to our 1-year sample of homicides in Detroit, we find this prediction
clearly supported: Only 2 parents killed an adult offspring (at least 16
years old), whereas 9 parents were killed *by* one.

The 10-year Canadian sample permits a more elaborate analysis.
Again, we shall define an "adult" as someone at least 16 years old.
Parent–offspring cases in which both parties were adults are broken
down in Table 5.1. The differences are emphatically in the expected
direction. In each column of Table 5.1 except for father–daughter (where
the generally greater violence of males acts against the prediction) the
difference is statistically significant (by sign test).

Before we accept these results as evidence of the predicted asymmetry in mutual valuation, however, there is a confounding variable to be
considered. As we shall see in Chapter 8, young adults are the most
homicidal of age classes. Are the asymmetries in Table 5.1 anything
more than what we would expect simply on the basis of the ages of the
antagonists, regardless of any relationship between them?

A particularly apt comparison for answering this question is that
between natural parent–child relationships and the corresponding
steprelationships. Only in the former case would we expect the
antagonists to show much sensitivity to one another's reproductive
value, so that the proportion of deaths in which the "parent" is the
killer should be higher in the case of steprelationships. This indeed
seems to be the case, but the data are too few to make the point

Table 5.2. Homicides in which Both Parties were Adults (≥ 16 Years), and One Was the Other's Father or Stepfather (Canada, 1974-1983)

	Father–son	Stepfather–stepson	Father–daughter	Stepfather–stepdaughter
"Father" is the killer	20	10	5	4
"Father" is the victim	91	25	7	3
Percentage in which "father" is the killer	18.0	28.6	41.7	57.1
Fisher exact test		$p = .11$		$p = .43$

convincingly. In Table 5.2, we see that the elder party was indeed more often the offender in cases involving stepfathers than in those involving natural fathers, but the differences are not statistically significant. (Only three cases involved step*mothers* as either offender *or* victim.)

Another possible control comparison for our father–son cases is to take all the male–male social conflict homicides in which victim and offender were not related at all. Using this larger sample of cases, we can then generate, for each father–son pair, the probability that one or the other party would have become the victim, on the basis of their ages alone. To reduce meaningless variation, we shall consider 5-year age categories. Take, for example, those social conflict homicides involving two men aged 25–29 and 45–49, respectively. There were 25 such cases involving nonrelatives, and the younger man killed the older in 19 (76%). (The relevance of age to homicidal violence between unrelated men will be considered in Chapter 8.) We then take that 76% estimate, and apply it to the 3 father–son cases involving the same age brackets, leading us to expected values of 2.28 fathers as victims and 0.72 sons. (As it happens, son killed father in all 3 cases in this age class.) Applying the same method to the entire sample of 111 homicides involving adult sons and fathers, we find that the killer would have been expected to be the son, on the basis of the two men's ages alone, in 88 cases and the father in 23. This is not very different from the 91–20 split actually recorded in Table 5.1. The difference is again in the direction predicted by the hypothesis of parent–offspring valuation asymmetry, but it falls far short of providing significant support for that hypothesis.

The weakness of the evidence suggests that the hypothesis is inadequate as stated. The inadequacy may lie in the use of "reproductive value" as our conceptualization of what should ideally be construed as "fitness-promoting value." Although a postmenopausal woman, for example, has *no* residual reproductive value in the usual limited meaning of that term, her capacity to promote the welfare of her relatives and hence the replication of her genotype is obviously not exhausted, even if her children are mature and self-sufficient. Similarly, a father can be an important promoter of his children's material, political, and reproductive ambitions. So it is not mere "reproductive value"—expected future reproduction—that should be expected to influence one's perceived value to relatives, but something more like one's *"residual nepotistic value"*: that is, one's expected future inclusive fitness effect, however achieved. (It might, therefore, be interesting to investigate whether asymmetries in parent–offspring homicides vary with socioeconomic class.)

If the psychology of mutual and self-valuation is indeed tuned to nepotistic value in the manner suggested, then the net value of aging parents may gradually decline from the perspective of adult offspring, perhaps even becoming negative. Eventually, old people's capacities to advance their own interests may be so reduced that their expected impact upon even their *own* inclusive fitness is negative. We might then expect them to manifest a concern to "not be a burden." "Altruistic suicide" in such circumstances is not unknown.

A sinister element in this situation derives from the fact that the adult offspring is apt to view the aging parent as a net liability before the latter's own calculus would concur. This conflict of interests may inspire the adult offspring to hasten the old parent's unwilling demise, or to manipulate the parent to concur that he or she is useless. One can also envision a risk of homicide in which the killer self-righteously maintains—both to others and to self—that the act was euthanasia, refusing to acknowledge a self-interested, conflictual motive. (It should also be noted that even where residual nepotistic value *is* negative, the aging individual is "useless" only in a particular, technical sense. It does not follow that the individual in question will *feel* useless, since the capacity to advance one's fitness interests in particular circumstances or life stages may or may not have had specific selective effects on the human psyche. When discussing what sort of feelings and evaluations one would expect people to have, there is a risk of being taken to imply that certain actions would be justified, which of course we do not intend.)

Factors Associated with the Risk of Parricide

In the above analyses of Canadian homicide data, we found only slight evidence for an asymmetry of mutual valuation between parent and child. Nevertheless, the same data set contains clear evidence that *greater parental age is associated with a greater risk of parricide.* The mean age of all new Canadian mothers was 27.3 years in 1961 and had fallen to 25.6 years by 1971 (Canadian Vital Statistics). But 11 women killed by their daughters averaged 27.9 years of age, and 50 women killed by their sons averaged 30.0, at the time when they gave birth to their eventual murderers. This difference between the parturient ages of eventual matricide victims and those of all new mothers greatly exceeds what would be expected by chance: The proportion of Canadian births in which the mother was past the age of 30 has consistently been less than 30% (and has recently fallen below 20%), and yet 27 of 50 matricidal sons were born to women older than 30.

Murdered fathers also tend to be somewhat older than would be expected by chance, given their killers' ages. We do not have complete father's age data for the population-at-large comparable to that for mothers, but we know that the mean age of the fathers of new babies born *within marriages* was 30.9 in 1961, and 28.6 in 1970 (Canadian Vital Statistics). Since unwed mothers are on average much younger than married mothers, we can probably assume that the inclusion of births out of wedlock would lower the average age for new fathers too. Yet those men who were killed by their sons averaged 32.7 years of age at the time of their eventual killers' births, and the comparable figure for men killed by their daughters is 32.4.

In Chapter 4, we saw—for all four gender combinations—that children who are killed by their parents tend to have been born at an *earlier* parental age than average. The same is true of nonfatal child abuse (Daly & Wilson, 1985). We now find—again for all four gender combinations— that children who grow up to kill their parents tend to have been born at a *later* parental age than average. This difference is anomalous from several traditional theoretical points of view. It is contrary, for example, to what one would expect from psychoanalytic "Oedipal theory," since sexual interest in the mother and rivalry with the father would surely be reduced, not exacerbated, by an increased age disparity between parent and child.

Some other popular theories of the etiology of family violence do not anticipate the present results any better. In particular, we might assume that parricidal resentments arise as the consequence of prolonged parental mistreatment. We would then expect that the risks of parricide, filicide, and child abuse would be related to demographic variables in directionally similar ways. Moreover, this expectation would appear to follow from *any* theory that treats parricide and filicide as alternative products of a common set of stressors. And yet we find that the effect of parental age upon the risk of parricide is precisely the opposite of its effect upon the risk of filicide and child abuse. This is not to deny that these various kinds of family violence may share common causal factors as well. The risk of all sorts of violence may be exacerbated by poverty, for example. Nor does this analysis deny the possible relevance of abuse by the parent to later parricide. It suggests, however, that violence between parent and offspring is not merely reciprocal (nor merely "transmitted" by parental "models"), but instead manifests asymmetries related to the life stages and life history strategies of the antagonists.

It is possible that an effect of birth order contributes to the fact that children who grow up to commit parricide tend to have been born relatively late in their parents' lives. In other words, children with older siblings may be especially likely to kill their parents. Unfortunately, we have no information on birth order for our Canadian sample. The possibility is especially intriguing because of an apparent syndrome in parricides (especially matricides), as described in psychiatric case histories. Parricide often presents the appearance of an emotionally explosive escape from a pressure cooker of ambivalence, a love/hate relationship that might be attributable to a history of parental manipulations contrary to the child's interests. Many psychiatric writers have noted that excessive violence is often seen in parricides, multiple stab wounds being inflicted, for example, long after the victim is dead. It is also commonly reported that some proportion of matricidal sons exhibit an excessive idealization of and devotion to their victims, that parricides have had little sexual experience for their age, that they are disproportionately single, and that most have never left the parental home (e.g., Green, 1981; Mohr & McKnight, 1971; Campion *et al.*, 1985). These considerations suggest that at least some parricides terminate a festering resentment of long-term parental manipulation, perhaps associated with the grooming of older siblings for career and marriage while the eventual killer is retained as a parental helper.

Christopher Green, a forensic psychiatrist, has reported on a study of 58 Englishmen who killed their "mothers" and were detained in Broadmoor psychiatric hospital. (Regrettably, this figure includes two stepmothers and two adoptive mothers, who cannot be distinguished in the data that follow.) Forty-three of the killers (74%) were diagnosed as "schizophrenic." The men had killed at a mean age of 31.2 years (range 18–51 years). Their mothers averaged 31.9 years of age at the homicidal son's birth, hence much older than the average new mother, just as in the Canadian sample. Forty-nine (84%) of the killers had never married, while 8 were divorced or separated; only 1 of the 58 was married at the time of the matricide. (In this one case, the killer initially assaulted his wife, and killed his mother when she intervened.) Twenty-six of the killers were adjudged to be suffering from "paranoid delusions of persecution by the mother" (and the lone married man had similar delusions about his wife); an additional 14 "claimed altruistic motivations;" in a further 11 cases "the patients could not explain their actions, apart from describing an inexplicable impulse or outbreak of rage;" the remaining 6 presented "a diversity of motives."

This is, of course, a psychiatric population, and it may not be representative of all English matricides; however, data cited by Green suggest that the great majority of English matricides are committed to psychiatric hospitals, and that the Broadmoor patients were representative of that majority. Many of Green's results seem to reflect a junior son's resentment of parental manipulation, as we suggested above, but some additional facts suggest a more complex etiology. It is particularly noteworthy that the fathers were dead in 33 cases and absent in an additional 8; many of the killers had lived alone with their mothers for more than a decade. Nineteen of the killers (31%) were their mothers' only children and 9 more their only sons. Among the 30 who had brothers, we should like to know the killers' birth order and the brothers' marital status, but Green does not report them.

In Canada, as in the British psychiatric sample, a remarkable proportion of adults who kill their parents have never married (Table 5.3). Eighty-five percent of parricidal sons were still single, including 78% of those at least 20 years old and 69% of those at least 30. Of the remainder, exactly as many were formerly married as presently married. All ten sons who killed both parents were single. Fifty-five percent of parricidal daughters were single, a significantly lower proportion than in the case of parricidal sons. (Thirty-six percent of the victims of daughters were more than 70 years old, compared to 15% of the victims of sons. Perhaps parricides committed by daughters are relatively more often "euthanasias" than those committed by sons.)

In Chapter 4, we observed that homicides by parents—and especially those in which the victim was beyond infancy—were more likely to be followed by suicide than most other homicides, and also more likely to be attributed to insanity. We then suggested that those categories of homicide that are relatively difficult to reconcile with the rational pursuit

Table 5.3. Marital Status and Age of Canadian Parricides, 1974–1983[a]

	Killer's age	Killer's marital status			
		Single	Presently married	Formerly married	Not reported
Son killed father	<20	37	1	0	0
	20–29	33	4	3	1
	≥30	14	3	4	0
Son killed mother	<20	12	0	1	0
	20–29	17	1	1	1
	≥30	13	2	2	0
Daughter killed father	<20	3	0	0	0
	20–29	0	2	1	0
	≥30	1	1	2	0
Daughter killed mother	<20	0	0	0	0
	20–29	4	1	0	0
	≥30	3	2	1	0

[a]"Presently married" includes common law. "Formerly married" includes separated, divorced, and widowed. Ten sons (all single) killed both parents and are included under both "son killed father" and "son killed mother."

of the killer's fitness interests are in general relatively rare, relatively often followed by suicide, and relatively often attributed to insanity. The data on parricides are for the most part supportive of these generalizations. Parricide presents itself, *a priori*, as a crime more damaging to the perpetrator's fitness than the killing of a nonrelative, but less clearly maladaptive than filicide of a child beyond its infancy. As expected, then, parricides exhibited an intermediate likelihood of being adjudged by the reporting police to have acted out of mental incompetence: 25% of parricides (35 of 140 sons and 6 of 22 daughters), compared to 41% of filicides, and just 2% of those who killed nonrelatives. As for suicide, only 3.1% of parricides killed themselves: 3 of 140 sons and 2 of 22 daughters. This is far below the 31% of filicides who killed themselves, as expected, but it does not exceed the 4.8% among killers of nonrelatives (i.e., persons related to the offender neither by blood nor marriage). Almost all of these suicidal killers of nonrelatives were men who killed women in whom their interest was sexual; of this, more will be said in Chapter 9.)

The proportion of Canadian parricides that were considered mad is at first sight surprisingly low in view of Green's British study and other psychiatric literature. Psychiatry claims a special expertise in such judgments, and we think it worthwhile to digress at this point to consider a particular psychiatric theory of parricide that has easily been the most influential analysis of the phenomenon ever proposed. We refer, of course, to Freud's theory of the Oedipus complex.

Oedipal Conflict and the Primal Parricide

It is hard for educated citizens of the present to recapture the world view of our counterparts just a century ago. Although the philosophers' "age of reason" was long since over, utilitarian views of both the psyche and the state were alive and well. Although warfare had attained new depths of destructiveness, Europeans remained confident of their higher level of culture and their colonial mission. Although Darwin had rocked our serenity, anthropocentric arrogance survived: Evolutionism was equated with progress, and the challenge it posed was considered to be that of explicating the transition from brute instinct to human rationality. Any constraints on that rationality were assumed to be constraints of our sense organs and memories; an experimental psychology was established to study them by the method of introspection. Somehow, despite many blows and disillusionments, western man staggered through the 19th century still clinging to his conviction that the essence of human action is the rational pursuit of conscious goals. Then, in 1900, Sigmund Freud published *The Interpretation of Dreams*.

What follows is highly critical both of Freudian theory and of his methods of argument, so let us acknowledge now that Freud was one of the giants of intellectual history. He dealt the naive rationalism of the 19th century its death blow, opening a door to the unconscious mind that can never again be shut. But that does not mean that his specific theories are correct, and Freud himself would undoubtedly be appalled at the way his ideas have become more the dogma of a cult than the preliminary hypotheses of a science.

One of the many provocative arguments advanced in the 1900 book was an interpretation of Sophocles' play *Oedipus Rex*. As Freud (1900) summarized the plot for his own purposes:

> Oedipus, son of Laius, King of Thebes, and of Jocasta, was exposed as an infant because an oracle had warned Laius that the still unborn child would be his father's murderer. The child was rescued, and grew up as a prince in an alien court, until, in doubts as to his origin, he too questioned the oracle and was warned to avoid his home since he was destined to murder his father and take his mother in marriage. On the road leading away from what he believed was his home, he met King Laius and slew him in a sudden

quarrel. He came next to Thebes and solved the riddle set him by the Sphinx who barred his way. Out of gratitude the Thebans made him their king and gave him Jocasta's hand in marriage. He reigned long in peace and honour, and she who, unknown to him, was his mother bore him two sons and two daughters. Then at last a plague broke out and the Thebans made enquiry once more of the oracle. It is at this point that Sophocles' tragedy opens. The messengers bring back the reply that the plague will cease when the murderer of Laius has been driven from the land.

But he, where is he? Where shall now be read
The fading record of this ancient guilt?

The action of the play consists in nothing other than the process of revealing, with cunning delays and ever-mounting excitement—a process that can be likened to the work of a psychoanalysis—that Oedipus himself is the murderer of Laius, but further that he is the son of the murdered man and of Jocasta. Appalled at the abomination which he has unwittingly perpetrated, Oedipus blinds himself and forsakes his home. The oracle has been fulfilled. (pp. 261–262)

Freud conceded that the play's tragedy resides in Oedipus's inability to escape his fate, but he insisted that the play's *power* resides elsewhere.

If *Oedipus Rex* moves a modern audience no less than it did the contemporary Greek one, the explanation can only be that its effect does not lie in the contrast between destiny and human will, but is to be looked for in the particular nature of the material on which that contrast is exemplified. . . . His destiny moves us only because it might have been ours—because the oracle laid the same curse upon us before our birth as upon him. It is the fate of all of us, perhaps, to direct our first sexual impulse towards our mother and our first hatred and our first murderous wish against our father. Our dreams convince us that this is so. King Oedipus, who slew his father Laius and married his mother Jocasta, merely shows us the fulfillment of our own childhood wishes. But, more fortunate than he, we have meanwhile succeeded, in so far as we have not become psychoneurotics, in detaching our sexual impulses from our mothers and in forgetting our jealousy of our fathers. Here is one in whom these primaeval wishes of our childhood have been fulfilled, and we shrink back from him with the whole force of the repression by which those wishes have since that time been held down within us. (p. 223)

In 1913, Freud elaborated his theory in *Totem and Taboo*. The urge to kill one's father and copulate with one's mother, he now maintained, was more than merely an immature stage of male psychological development. Instead, it was alleged to be an urge that our ancestors had retained into adulthood, and had acted upon. Moreover, this act of primal parricide lay at the origin of the incest prohibition, of religion, and indeed of all social contracts! Freud was not altogether clear about whether he imagined the primal parricide to have been a unique event or a recurring drama during some prolonged phase of our evolutionary history; he implied the former in his narrative reconstruction, but seemed to suggest the latter in a footnote. He was utterly clear, however, in proposing that the primal parricide was fact rather than parable. Without the historical reality of "the Deed," he believed that one could account for neither the evolution of society nor "the discoveries of psychoanalysis."

The "discoveries" that Freud's theory was invented to explain were, first, that a boy's earliest sexual impulses are directed to his mother, and, second, that he simultaneously wishes for the death of his father. Are these "discoveries" to be credited? Alas, we still do not know. Freud's method of arguing for their veracity was weak and transparently self-serving, and most of his successors have argued similarly. When a patient accepts the psychoanalyst's interpretation, that acceptance is treated as evidence that the interpretation is correct; if the same patient rejects the interpretation, the rejection is construed as evidence of "repression." Criticisms by third parties are similarly outflanked. In a footnote in *The Interpretation of Dreams*, for example, Freud (1900) wrote,

> None of the findings of psycho-analytic research has provoked such embittered denials, such fierce opposition—or such amusing contortions—on the part of critics as this indication of the childhood impulses towards incest which persist in the unconscious. (p. 263)

Such debating tactics do little to substantiate the alleged psychological phenomena.

The positive evidence that Freud mustered for the existence of these infantile urges was not impressive, consisting entirely of anecdotes. Clinical notes, already recorded selectively in accordance with the theoretical prejudices of the analyst, were winnowed for mental associations (hence symbols) that seemed to support the theory. In the most famous example, little Hans's fear that a horse would fall down was asserted to represent his repressed wish (and hence fear) that his father would die (Freud, 1909). Some of the things that this boy said seem clearly to support Freud's symbolic interpretation and it may well be correct. But for all we know, Hans could have volunteered associations between the horse of his fears and every individual in his social universe, while Freud and the father (whom Freud had deputized as informant in this case, and who was an enthusiastic convert to the psychiatrist's theories) waited impatiently for the "truth" that they already knew. (*Any* two anxieties have enough in common that one might associatively call up the other. If that were not the case, we would not call them both by the common label "anxiety.") Such unfettered clinical impressions may suggest hypotheses, but can hardly be offered as proof of them.

Freud can be excused for failing to collect and present his data in an unbiased fashion. He was writing at the turn of the century, when the methods of psychological inquiry were in their infancy. The unfortunate thing is that Freud's psychoanalytic successors have continued to scorn scientific methodologies, with the result that their theories are dismissed as mysticism by some people and embraced as dogma by others, but are seldom restated as testable hypotheses. The upshot is that we still do not know whether Freud's theory is an accurate description of ontogeny (development within the individual life span), that is to say whether mature sexual desires really do develop out of a childish lust for mother. But for the sake of argument, suppose we were to accept the "Oedipus complex" as established. As Freud himself was well aware, even if his description of ontogeny were accurate, he could still be in error in the evolutionary scenario proposed in *Totem and Taboo*. And indeed, while we may still hesitate either to accept or to dismiss Freud's ontogenetic theory, we can reject his evolutionary tale with confidence.

In developing his primal parricide theory, Freud endeavored to take account of contemporary knowledge and theory in cultural anthropology, motivational psychology, and animal behavior. All of these fields have come a long way since 1913, and it is hardly surprising that the theory now seems hopelessly naive. Freud accepted, for example, prevalent "evolutionary" views of culture, according to which "matriarchy" had preceded "patriarchy" and "group marriage" had preceded individualized pairings. He conceived of "instinctual drives" as things that had to be "discharged" in action. He imagined that the "classificatory" kinship systems of Australian aborigines and other "savages" bespoke a less precise differentiation of their relatives than the simple ego-centered kindred terminologies of Europeans. He assumed that nonhuman animals lack psychological disinclinations to mate with close kin. He accepted Frazer's allegation of a "universal horror of incest," and assumed further that "the horror of incest . . . must be recognized as the root of exogamy." He believed that male anthropoid apes are driven out of their natal groups at maturity. Every one of these assumptions has turned out to be wrong.

Besides these numerous errors of fact, Freud's evolutionary imagination was hobbled by a major error of conception. Despite his respectful citations of Darwin, he never really grasped the fundamental implication of the concept of natural selection: that the organismic attributes that survive and proliferate are those that contribute to *fitness*. One consequence of this failure was a misconception of the adaptive functions of evolved psychological mechanisms: Freud supposed that they had evolved merely to achieve "mental relief." Now, such relief might well be the proximal goal in an evolved motivational mechanism—the "off-switch" as it were—but such a mechanism could not arise by natural selection unless the means of achieving mental relief happened also to be means to the end of fitness. Freud, by contrast, imagined again and again that such mental quiescence would be reason enough for a trait to evolve, regardless of any costs that the trait's carrier might incur in time, energy, or risk. Thus, for example, he proposed (1913) that

> Totemic religion arose from the filial sense of guilt, in an attempt to allay that feeling and to appease the father by deferred obedience to him. All later religions are seen to be attempts at solving the same problem. (p. 145)

It apparently did not occur to Freud that a "filial sense of guilt" would be unlikely to evolve at all unless it were reproductively useful to those individuals who harbored it.

Oedipus Overextended

Why pick on Freud? *Totem and Taboo* was written more than 70 years ago, and he would undoubtedly have propounded a very different theory in the light of present knowledge. He can be faulted, perhaps, for his failure to grasp the implications of Darwin's theory, but most professional biologists grasped them little better for the next 50 years. Hundreds of authors have propounded evolutionary scenarios that are untenable in retrospect, and Freud's "primal parricide" story is by no means the silliest. So why pick on Freud? The answer is that this one theory remains influential while the others are deservedly buried.

It is disappointing that Freud read Darwin and came away with no appreciation of selection thinking. But it is more than just disappointing that the psychoanalytic writers of today are still in the same boat. That is scientific illiteracy.

Melford Spiro's *Oedipus in the Trobriands* was published in 1982. The book is a spirited and ingenious refutation of Bronislaw Malinowski's famous claim that the Oedipus complex was absent among the Trobriand Islanders, a matrilineal Pacific island society. The significant adult male in a Trobriand boy's life was not his father, but his mother's brother. No matter, says Spiro: The manifestations of Oedipal conflict are rampant. As one "prediction" from "Oedipal theory," Spiro proposes "that men would wish to possess women attached to other men and would be jealously possessive of the women to whom they themselves are attached." His argument is that "the son's wish for an exclusive relationship with his mother is frustrated by his powerful father," leading to "a repressed Oedipus complex" that "promotes attempts to undo this defeat, by reconstituting such a triangle in adulthood" (Spiro, 1982, pp. 101–102). Needless to say, this prediction of male sexual rivalry is upheld. What Spiro does not understand is that the same prediction is just as well fulfilled in a bull seal, a bison, or a billy goat! These are all animals in which father and mother part company before their son is born, so that the latter has his mother all to himself. Mammalian males are sexual competitors for reasons that have nothing to do with the relationship between immature son and mature father. It is therefore absurd to treat evidence of male sexual rivalry as evidence of "Oedipal conflict."

In attempting to interpret conflict within the family, Freud was conceptually at sea. Having no theoretically based view of the essential nature of individual self-interests, he postulated arbitrary psychological needs in an *ad hoc* manner. The anchor that eluded him, and continues to elude virtually all of his followers, is the insight that the ultimate function of evolved psychological mechanisms is the promotion of fitness.

Lacking this insight, psychoanalytic writers regularly misinterpret genuine conflicts of interest as nonadaptive symbolic manifestations of "primal" conflicts. Take this example from a recent review of Oedipal and related themes in India (Ramanujan, 1983):

> *Relations of Mother and Daughter*
> I have not yet found striking and explicit tales of a mother's rivalry with her own daughter, but one could cite numerous tales of stepmothers tormenting or exiling their stepdaughters, and cruel mothers- in-law trying to kill or harm daughters-in-law. Demonic mother-goddesses, ogresses, stepmothers and mothers-in-law are mother-figures specializing in the terrible aspects of mothers toward daughters. (p. 251)

But steprelations and in-laws have genuine conflicts of interest that far surpass those between mothers and daughters. When we are assured that a straightforward tale about the greater of two conflicts is "really" symbolic of the lesser, we may wonder whether we have joined Alice in Wonderland.

Or consider this example from *Oedipus in the Trobriands* (Spiro, 1982):

> In this tale, the younger of two brothers seduces the wife of a chief of a distant place. Her husband captures the adulterer and places him on a high platform to die, but his elder brother rescues him, and subsequently causes all the men of that village to disappear (by magic). Following their victory, the two brothers take all the women of these men in marriage. In short,

every boy's Oedipal fantasy—the killing of the father(s) and the marrying of the mother(s)—is carried out with a vengeance! (p. 103)

Like Ramanujan, Spiro is so immersed in symbolic interpretations that he appears not even to notice the explicit content of the story. The tale is about reproductive competition between unrelated males, a conflict that—as we shall consider at length in the next three chapters—is far more serious and dangerous than any disagreement between fathers and sons. Once again, we are asked to believe that a story about a universal, profound conflict between unrelated rivals "really" symbolizes a *lesser* conflict between relatives. In fact, Spiro interprets not only the above tale of fraternal solidarity as evidence of the Oedipus complex, but numerous tales of fraternal conflict in the same light. One must wonder whether any tale could be concocted that would *not* constitute such evidence.

Thus blinkered, psychoanalytic writers have thoroughly misapprehended the manipulative uses of taboo and symbolism by which individuals promote their own interests at others' expense. Freud, for example, interpreted the fact that incest prohibitions are extended to distant relatives and affines as a nonadaptive vestige of "group marriage," never realizing that manipulative elaborations of primary incest avoidance serve the interests of the rule-makers (Thornhill & Thornhill, 1987). A young man's natural sexual interest in his father's junior wife, for example, is proclaimed the equivalent of that unnatural abomination "incest with the mother," in a transparent attempt to exploit the repugnance of real mother–son incest in the father's reproductive interest.

Similarly, Freud turned the metaphor of king as "father" on its head. Instead of perceiving that powerful people exploit metaphors of familial relatedness in order to claim entitlement to respect, obedience, and affection, Freud imagined that the subjects create a symbolic father to satisfy their own (guilty) psychological needs. In 1609, King James I of England proclaimed himself *"parens patriae,* the political father of his people"* (Stone, 1977); the title was not thrust upon him by his "children." The following analysis by sociologist Pierre van den Berghe (1985) is much more insightful than Freud's:

> If power is to be justified (so as to be more readily exercised), the aim of power must be hidden or denied. The best denial of the effect of power is that oppression is in the best interest of the oppressed. . . . Paternalism mimics the genuine *concern* of the parent for the child, which is founded on the real overlap of interest inherent in genetically based nepotism, and thus hides the overwhelmingly conflictual basis of the ruler–subject relationship. Paternalism models itself on a relationship of genuine *dependence* and

incapacity, in which the helpless child's survival and well-being is contingent on adult care, and extends it to a situation in which the dependence is *reversed*. The ruler who parasitizes the subject disguises parasitism as altruism. (p. 262)

We predict that formal analyses of written materials would refute Freud and support van den Berghe, by demonstrating that the case of King James I is typical, that is to say that the paternal metaphor is generally pushed from the top down, and is resisted by the underlings upon whom it is imposed.

The issue here is not merely one of academic interest. By interpreting rebellious behavior as the immature "acting out" of "unresolved" primal conflicts, modern psychoanalysts implicitly assert the rebel's irrationality and deny the legitimacy of his grievances. Oedipal theory has thus become a weapon of authoritarianism. Consider, for example, the following passage from a recent volume; its author—while primarily concerned with elaborating Freud's "monotraumatic" theory of primal parricide into a "polytraumatic" theory— incidentally discovered "the true nature of student and much other protest" (Badcock, 1983):

> It is in fact directed against the protesters' own parents—especially the father—and is intended to take the place of the infantile and adolescent reproaches and criticisms of the parental authority which have now come to be directed at each and any cultural equivalent of the father. This explains why heads of government, the police and the Establishment in general are such popular targets for the protesters' attacks. Fundamentally, such protests against the cultural surrogates of the parents arise from the same origin as the assault on boundaries, standards and restraints—the parricidal resentment against the father's sexual rights over the mother which results from the failure to resolve the Oedipal conflict. (p. 101)

Such polemics are by no means rare in the psychoanalytic literature. As a more enlightened commentator (Sheleff, 1981) has inquired,

> Can it not be that the popularity [of Freud's Oedipus theory] stems from the fact that the theme accords with what adults wish to hear: namely, that it is the evil inherent in the psychological makeup of the young that is primarily responsible for generational conflict? (p. 9)

Conflict Over What?

Oedipal theory warrants our continued skepticism, but obviously Freud must have been on to *some*thing, or his ideas would never have seized so many imaginations. (To concede this much is not to concede that the theory has scientific validity. Even a religious belief system obviously has to make some sort of contact with the realities experienced by the faithful.) Selection thinking can help us find the kernel of truth in Freud's analysis, as well as the errors. There is indeed a conflict between father and son over the wife/mother. There is furthermore a genuine "sexual" conflict between them, or at least a conflict over the timing of the son's accession to a potentially reproductive status, often necessarily subsidized by the father, at a considerable cost to his own continuing reproductive ambitions. But the former conflict is not sexual and the latter is not over the mother. Freud concatenated two distinct father–son conflicts into one.

Young human beings are extremely dependent upon the benevolent attentions of adult caretakers for a very long time; for the most part, that has meant and continues to mean their mothers. Children are not impatient to be weaned, even in societies where nursing continues for several years (see, e.g., Shostak, 1981). The child's attitude to mother's next pregnancy is frequently ambivalent if not downright hostile, despite parental efforts to engender enthusiasm about becoming a sibling. As one "precocious 4-year-old" asked his newly parturient mother, "Why have you ruined my life?" (Dunn & Kendrick, 1982, p. 1).

From the child's point of view, daddy has his own uses for mommy, and they are not necessarily harmonious with the child's. Parental sexuality threatens to produce a younger sibling, and it is not implausible that young children have evolved specific adaptive strategies to delay that event by diminishing mother's sexual interest and thwarting father's access to her. This is the same basic parent–offspring conflict with which we began this chapter. Moreover, besides the child's preference for a longer birth interval than the parental optimum, father himself is a competitor for the fruits of mother's labors, which he may use to the advantage of his own phenotype or to court other mates. Without even considering the additional problems engendered by the uncertainty of paternity and by marital instability, the human infant has good grounds to regard mother's consort with a wary eye! Note that all these sources of potential father–child conflict apply to daughters every bit as much as to sons.

Father-Daughter Conflict

As the child approaches maturity, new bases of competition and conflict with the father become salient, and for these later concerns, the child's sex is no longer irrelevant. In patrilineal societies with bride-wealth, a pubertal daughter is an asset. A well-negotiated marriage will reap her father not only economic benefits but political advantage as well, by creating or cementing alliances with the bridegroom and his kin. The daughter's perception of her own interests may well conflict with father's proposed uses of her. This kind of parent–offspring conflict is a special case of the ubiquitous struggle between women and men over control of female reproductive capacity. In societies with a highly developed ethic of "honor and shame" revolving around female chastity, daughters may be so coerced in this struggle as to be locked away (ostensibly for their own protection) or even mutilated to destroy sexual inclinations (Dickemann, 1981). In the event that these attempts to guarantee a daughter's "purity" fail, she is likely to be transformed in parental eyes from an asset to a liability, and she may even be executed by her father or brothers in order to "rescue familial honor" (e.g., Kressel, 1981).

Feminists have been appalled by the existence of these practices, and by the collusion of mothers and other senior women in perpetrating them. In this regard it is important to note that the mother's view of the matter may be closer to the father's than to the daughter's. The bridewealth gained by marrying off her daughter, for example, may be used to acquire a wife for her son. If, on the other hand, the bride's father has or hopes to acquire other wives—as he may do in most societies with bridewealth—then any gains that the father enjoys from his daughter's marriage may be dispensed without advantage to the girl's mother, and we would expect that the mother in such cases will more often take her daughter's side.

There is another possible sort of father–daughter conflict in which the mother's interests are more clearly in line with her daughter's interests and not her husband's. This is the case in which the father decides to use his daughter sexually himself (Irons, 1986). If close incest entails a risk of defect—and it appears that it does—then daughters might be expected to have evolved a preference for outbreeding. But it is far from clear that the same argument applies with equal force to fathers. Women have historically reared one child at a time, at intervals of several years, so that a child sired by one man in effect precludes a potential child sired by another. For a man, by contrast, an extra offspring borne by an unmarried girl under his control need not detract from alternative avenues of reproduction at all. (This is a version of the standard argument from sexual selection theory that females should be more discriminating than males; see Trivers, 1972). Of course, the father's fitness also suffers if the child is defective, nor should the father, in principle, lack concern for his daughter's eventual fitness. Nevertheless, these considerations suggest that "normal" fathers might at least sometimes be tempted to incest, and the more so if the man's paternity of the girl is at all in doubt. While Freud stretched credulity in postulating the offspring's incestuous desires for the parents, an incestuous impulse in the opposite direction is not altogether implausible in this one dyad, namely father toward daughter. It is noteworthy that father–daughter cases seem indeed to account for virtually all parent–offspring incest (see, e.g., van den Berghe, 1983); furthermore, the evidence is unequivocal that the initiative in such cases resides with the father, the daughter being coerced. (Perhaps the fact that such cases are not more common is ultimately attributable to the fact that in this particular father–daughter conflict, the mother's fitness interests coincide with the daughter's, so that the latter has an ally in the home. If this is true, then a corollary hypothesis is that sexual abuse by natural fathers will be more likely in homes with stepmothers than in those with natural mothers; we know of no relevant data.)

Toppling the Patriarch

Much the more dramatic conflict is that between a father and his maturing son, and here at last we see something akin to Freud's perception of the "primal conflict." By the time a son reaches adolescence, however, it is no longer the mother that is the object of contention.

Human fathers frequently command resources (including status and titles as well as the obvious material resources), that are familially held and patrilineally transmitted. Such resources are limited, and hence impose limitations upon reproductive and other ambitions. A still robust father can therefore be an impediment to the aspirations of a young man. The two may indeed become sexual competitors, as in this sad tale from the Bison-Horn Maria (Elwin, 1950):

> Hemla Gunda was the Dhurwa or clan-priest of the Hemla clan-god. He was also a well-known medicine man and, although he was excommunicated for reasons that will appear immediately, was a person of great influence among the Maria of Bijapur Tahsil.
>
> He was, however, a cruel and unnatural man. About a year before his murder, he seduced the wives of each of his two sons, and not content merely to seduce them drove out of his house his own wife and his two sons, and lived there openly with the two young girls. He refused to do anything to maintain his wife and would not give his sons any share in the family property, although by tribal custom he should have allowed its partition, since he was doing nothing to support his family.
>
> When the sons applied to the panchayat for justice, that body met, but so great was Gunda's influence that they were afraid to take any strong line against him. But they did excommunicate him for his relations with the

wives of his sons and for the even more serious offence of keeping a Ghasia woman.

In May 1928, one of the sons, Hemla Mundra, went to his father's house and attempted to get some share of the property. He failed then, but on the afternoon before the murder, returned and tried to take away two cows from the family herd. His father caught him and abused him, and the boy was so annoyed that he struck the older man on the face with a lathi, a blow that probably fractured the jaw. Gunda prepared to go to the police station to make a report against his son. Mundra, reflecting that his father had not only robbed him of his wife and property, but was now going to deprive him of his liberty as well, decided to kill him and prevent him from going to the police. He managed to get ahead of Gunda on the path, and the moment he appeared broke his skull with several blows of a heavy stick. (pp. 89–90)

Although this father's behavior was extreme, and led to an extreme end, his inclinations hardly deserve to be called "unnatural." In a summary discussion of "Intergenerational Tensions" in a number of polygynous societies of sub-Saharan Africa, Robert LeVine (1965) writes:

> Here the tension often centers about the father's fear that the son, particularly the eldest, will wish to hasten his death in order to gain independence from the old man or replace him as head of the family. In societies where the father is expected to transfer goods to his son for brideprice payment, conflict may arise over the father's delaying the transfer and/or the son's appropriating the goods in advance of formal permission from the father. The sexual rights of father and son also present problems: where the father exercises authoritarian domination over his sons, the danger exists that he will commit adultery with their wives, and this danger is recognized in many African groups. On the other hand, when the father is a senescent polygynist, wealthy enough to acquire numerous young wives but not virile enough to keep them sexually satisfied, the danger exists that the sons will commit adultery with his younger wives. In some groups—where the sons inherit these wives upon the father's death—this may be overlooked when the father is very old, but in others it is a real source of conflict. (p. 193)

When we view intergenerational conflict as an active contest, Oedipal and other folktales acquire a fresh significance: They are *manipulative devices*. Myths and folktales do not persist merely in order to reflect or symbolize themes of psychological significance. They are used. Self-interested individuals are the medium of oral tradition; if a tale is to be recalled and told, it must appeal to the teller's social purposes. The manipulative uses of folktales are especially obvious when they promote "virtues" that serve parental interests. After remarking the rarity of patricidal tales in India, for example, Ramanujan (1983) continues:

> But another pattern is very common: the aggression of the father towards the son. In all these stories the son willingly gives up (often transfers) his

political and sexual potency. In the epic Mahabharata, Bhisma, the first son of Santanu, renounces both kingdom and his reproductive sexual life so that his father may marry a fishergirl and continue his (father's) sexual/ reproductive life. Bhisma, lifelong celibate, lives on to become the most revered old man of the epic, warrior and wise man.

Yayati, a king cursed by a sage to suffer senility, wishes to prolong his life of pleasure and asks his five sons to transfer their youth to him. The elder sons refuse and earn his curses. The youngest son exchanges his youth for Yayati's age for a thousand years. For this sacrifice, the son receives great honor, and inherits the whole kingdom later. (pp. 244–245)

So a father may often delay his son's career in order to prolong his own, and he may furthermore be reluctant to relinquish the patrimony because he wants to maintain his ability to impose an equitable distribution among all his offspring once his younger sons are grown. In either case, the son whose ambitions are thwarted is likely to feel aggrieved, and in the latter case, there may be even more impetus to act *now*, in order to effect a more favorable partition of the patrimony than may be attainable once the brothers are mature. Consider this case synopsis from a society akin to the Maria (Varma, 1978):

Gulab Bhil, 24 years, was a resident of village Lakhankot of Dhar district. He was the eldest son of Tersingh, aged 46 years, whose 2 other sons, Rama and Jamoo, were minors in 1966. Gulab was married in 1960 and had 3 children. On 29 April 1966, Gulab demanded from his father his share of land in the ancestral property. Tersingh declined on the ground that 2 of his sons were still minors and said that there could be no partition till they were grown-up and married. At that time, Tersingh was lying on a cot. Gulab's temper flared up. He dealt one club blow on his father and when the latter got up, Gulab took out his sword and dealt several blows killing him instantaneously. (p. 240)

Intrasexual Rivalry or Parent–Offspring Conflict?

According to Freud's scenario, parent–offspring antagonisms are reducible—*from infancy*—to rivalry with the same-sex parent over the opposite-sex parent. According to the view espoused here, by contrast, conflict between parents and very young children occurs for reasons that have little or nothing to do with the child's sex. The bone of contention between parent and child is instead the allocation of parental investment, and daughters and sons are alike in coveting a larger share than the parents are inclined to give. (And if there *is* some reproductive strategic rationale for differential treatment of sons versus daughters, it will be felt similarly by fathers and mothers, so that there will still be no *contingency* between parent sex and offspring sex in parent–offspring conflict.) Only around the time of maturity does parent–offspring conflict begin to be concerned with same- sex rivalry over reproductive status, and with resources of differential utility to daughters and sons.

If the Freudian view were correct, we would anticipate a same-sex tendency in parent–offspring violence—the victims of males being more often male than the victims of females—*at all ages*. The present analysis, by contrast, suggests that there should be no contingency between the victim's sex and that of the assailant when young children are involved, but that such a contingency should appear—due mainly to a preponderance of male–male rather than female–female cases—after the child reaches maturity.

We can test these alternatives from the Canadian data. Defenders of the Freudian scenario are insistent that it is endemic to human development and is cross-culturally universal, regardless of social structural and ecological variations. If they are correct, the Oedipal theory of same-sex conflict beginning in infancy should certainly apply to present-day Canada. According to our alternative account, there should be no same-sex contingency in cases involving young children, although one may appear later. (A modern western nation is not so strictly patrilineally organized as the tribal societies considered above, but father–son rivalry over the use of family property has not vanished.) So what are the facts? Table 5.4 presents them.

Table 5.4. Parent–Offspring Homicides in Canada, 1974–1983, Broken Down by Sex of Killer and Victim, and by Offspring Age

Offspring's age (years)	Victim's sex	Killer's sex		
		Male	Female	
0–10	Male	72	96	
	Female	61	87	$\chi^2_{1df} = 0.1$
	% Male	54.1	52.5	$p > .9$
11–15	Male	21	8	
	Female	11	5	$\chi^2_{1df} = 0.1$
	% Male	65.6	61.5	$p > .9$
≥ 16	Male	111	8	
	Female	50	15	$\chi^2_{1df} = 10.3$
	% Male	68.9	34.8	$p < .001$

There is no evidence whatever of a same-sex bias in homicides involving infants or prepubertal children: The proportion of victims that are male is virtually identical whether the killer is male or female. (Similarly, we find no evidence of any same-sex bias in the physical abuse of small children by mothers versus fathers, using data sets much larger than the present homicide data; Wilson, Daly, & Weghorst, 1983). It is only after puberty that any same-sex tendency becomes apparent. The data in Table 5.4 are unanticipated and anomalous from the perspective of Oedipal theory, but they are fully in keeping with a selectionist analysis of the temporally shifting conflicts between parent and offspring.

Altercations
and Honor

— 6 —

Friday, September 5th, 1980

On a Friday night in September, 1980, a few blocks west of Morningside Park in downtown Miami, Florida, V. W., age 24, was shot dead with his own gun. It seems that he and R. J., 30, had got into a pushing match that escalated into a fist fight. R. J. was winning—the witnesses were agreed about that—when V. W. pulled his pistol. He never got to use it. R. J. managed to wrestle the gun away and gave his younger adversary a pistol whipping, and then some mutual acquaintances stepped in and got them separated. It looked like the hostilities were over, but R. J., still incensed, suddenly snatched up V. W.'s pistol and fired (Wilbanks, 1984, case 361).

V. W. wasn't the first body of the day for the homicide detectives of Dade County, 1980's "Murder capitol of the USA." There had been a rather similar case at 1:20 that morning, outside a bar a couple of miles away. The quarrel had begun inside, an argument over a woman, and O. C., age 32, had smashed a bottle and waved the jagged weapon at M. L., 36. In this case too, some mutual acquaintances separated the combatants, but tempers didn't cool. When O. C. left the bar with the lady in question, M. L. followed them, called to the woman to stand aside, and shot his rival dead (Wilbanks, 1984, case 360).

A two-murder Friday. Neither an unusually busy day nor an unusually quiet one for Miami's homicide detectives. Saturdays generally tend to be worse, and indeed there would be four new homicides to be investigated on September 6th. In fact, September the 5th was actually quite a *good* Friday in some ways: In both cases, there were witnesses who were willing to talk, and so both cases eventually led to murder convictions. (More than 80% of the homicides in Dade County in 1980 did not.) On Saturday, by contrast, in three separate incidents, two men were shot and a third was beaten to death with a tire iron, and the frustrated police weren't able to make an arrest in *any* of them. The fourth case, at least, was easily closed: A man had shot his wife and then himself. A "platter case": nothing to investigate.

1980 was a bad year for murder in Miami, the worst, in fact, since 1930. But Friday, September the 5th was not unusual, neither in Miami nor in the United States as a whole. It was a typical Friday: People killed people all over the country. The next day's *Denver Post*, for example, filled a little space on the bottom of page 36, by reporting that a 33-year-old man from Iowa had been shot in a parking lot after a fight in a city bar. Murders, especially such run-of-the-mill murders, are not big news.

On Sunday, September 7th, the *Detroit News* reported that city's five Friday night homicides in a single brief story in Section B. Headlined was the stabbing death of a woman in her home. Four men who had been shot dead in four unrelated incidents around town got a few lines each.

It is not that murders lack human interest. It depends on the murder. On that same Sunday, for example, the *Chicago Tribune* gave a lot of space in Section 1 to homicide. There was a big story about a woman in jail for killing her parents. There was a full-page piece on crime statistics. And there was a lurid story of a homicidal plot in California, the principal characters including a rich Buddhist monk's wife and a doctor. But the several men who had been killed in Chicago over the weekend were briefly enumerated on page 10 of Section 3.

Under what circumstances do Americans kill one another? Most people would probably guess that robberies by strangers or family disputes constitute the most prevalent varieties of murder. Both types indeed occur, and they often get a lot of press. But the ugly little dramas of a Miami Friday night represent a variety of homicidal conflict that is more frequent still, and may not be reported by the media at all. Criminologists like to refer to such cases as having arisen from "altercations."

If that Friday in 1980 was a typical Friday, then about 100 Americans died at the hands of their fellow citizens. Most of the victims were men, and almost all were killed by men. Most of the victims, like most of the offenders, were nobodies: unpropertied and unmarried, little educated, often unemployed. Most of the homicides were not committed in the course of robbery, but instead arose out of arguments or insults or rivalries. Most of the victims were acquainted with their killers. Only a handful were related to them.

Trivial Altercations

The classic study of American homicide was published by sociologist Marvin Wolfgang in 1958, and was based on the files of the Philadelphia police department. Wolfgang read the investigative and judicial materials for 588 criminal homicides that had occurred in that city between 1948 and 1952, classifying them this way and that. His aim was a statistical summary of killings: "patterns" according to sex, age, race, weapon, locale—whatever the police recorded.

"Motive" is a tricky thing to classify, but it is, of course, a primary concern of police investigations because of its relevance to the question of what charge should be brought, or even whether the case should be prosecuted at all. Accepting the police's conclusions, Wolfgang was able to classify 560 cases into one or another of 12 motive categories. By far the most frequent, accounting for 37% of the cases, was a sort of dispute that Wolfgang labeled an *"Altercation of relatively trivial origin; insult, curse, jostling, etc."* Subsequent studies in other American cities have regularly replicated this aspect of Wolfgang's results: Such altercations constitute the most prevalent variety of urban homicide in the United States.

One might suppose that homicidal altercations in America are a sign of the times, a modern scourge. People seem almost to relish an apocalyptic vision of the present as an era of collapsing social order, when traditional morality has been undermined, leading to an epidemic of "senseless violence." But people—especially members of the Establishment, who have the most to lose from violence—have espoused such grim visions for as long as human history has been recorded, regardless of the actual levels of violence within their societies. In England, for example, the homicide rate has declined more or less continuously for at least 700 years (see Figure 12.1, p. 276), until the modern Englishman is only about one-twentieth as likely to be murdered as his 13th-century counterpart, and yet, throughout those centuries, commentators have decried the rising tide of violence (Beattie, 1974). As for modern America, Miami's rate of 350 homicides per million citizens in 1980 made that city the nation's homicide leader, but it did not come close to Miami's peak rate of 1101 per million in 1926 (Wilbanks, 1984).

Homicide is no latecomer to the American scene, and neither is today's most prevalent variety, the "altercation of relatively trivial origin." A hundred years and more before Wolfgang began his analyses of Philadelphia police records, the same scenes of contest and braggadocio were being played out in that city's bars and alleys. Social historian Roger Lane (1979) writes,

> The modal homicide in nineteenth-century Philadelphia resulted from a brawl or quarrel originating in a saloon but reaching a climax in the street. Drink was an important part of the culture of the city, enormously so among those subgroups in which most killings occurred; as in Western

cultures generally, drunkenness was closely associated with assault. Other than the alcohol itself, whatever allegedly precipitated the trouble—a spilled drink, a careless remark, an argument about the merits of different steam engines—almost always seemed tragically out of proportion to the aftermath. (pp. 59–60)

Nor are such altercations peculiarly American. An example comes from an Israeli study, modeled upon Wolfgang's (Landau & Drapkin, 1968). Certain motives that are virtually unknown in America account for a significant proportion of cases in Israel, namely blood feuds (to which we shall return in Chapter 10) and "honor killings" of unchaste female relatives. But despite such cultural differences, and despite the fact that modern Israel has a homicide rate only a fraction of that in America, the most frequent motive category in Israel still proved to be the same one as in Philadelphia: "personal conflict or altercation (insult, curse, jostling)."

Altercations are not the leading variety of homicide in *all* cultures, and we shall consider some possible reasons for their varying prevalence in later chapters. In general, however, altercations assume a proportionally greater importance wherever homicide rates are high, with the result that altercations surely constitute a very large proportion of all the world's killings. This is not a postindustrial phenomenon, as both anthropological and historical materials amply testify. Of 13th- and 14th-century Oxford, England, for example, a university town with a homicide rate about equal to that of Miami in 1926, historian Carl Hammer (1978) writes,

> When all of the evidence is considered, one is left with the overwhelming impression that most homicides were not premeditated but were, rather, spontaneous, arising on the spot. The question then is whether they were provoked. Often the jurors provide information on this point. For example, in September 1272 Walter de Eure, a local smith, knifed John Attenhalle of Wallingford who seems to have been visiting his mother in Oxford; this took place in the evening after there had been, in the jurors' phrase, a "strife of words" between them. Likewise, a year later an Irish clerk [i.e., a student], John Burel, was killed in a tavern brawl after a dispute arose between two groups of students. Thus, sharp tongues, quick tempers and strong drink often seem to have been a fatal combination. . . ." (p. 20)

Status, Reputation, and the Capacity for Violence

On June 10, 1968, in a climate of public alarm over recent political assassinations, United States President Lyndon Johnson established a National Commission on the Causes and Prevention of Violence, under the chairmanship of Dr. Milton Eisenhower. Seven investigative task forces, each made up of lawyers and social scientists, were created to analyze the problem of violence and to suggest solutions. In 1969, this gaggle of expertise presented the commission with a 13-volume *Staff Report on Crimes of Violence.* Having analyzed homicide data from 17 American cities, the authors of the report (Mulvihill, Tumin, & Curtis, 1969) concluded that:

> Altercations appeared to be the primary motivating forces both here and in previous studies. Ostensible reasons for disagreements are usually trivial, indicating that many homicides are spontaneous acts of passion, not products of a single determination to kill. (vol. 11, p. 230)

The report continued by quoting a Dallas homicide detective:

> "Murders result from little ol' arguments over nothing at all. Tempers flare. A fight starts, and somebody gets stabbed or shot. I've worked on cases where the principals had been arguing over a 10 cent record on a juke box, or over a one dollar gambling debt from a dice game." (p. 230)

The authors of this report then went on to describe a series of petty but fatal disputes, choosing their words in such a way as to invite their readers' astonishment ("Believe it or not, here's the police summary of another killing . . .").

It is easy to see the fascination of playing "top this tale if you can," and many commentators have done just that. But to marvel at the "triviality" of the circumstances precipitating such altercations is subtly patronizing, and is ultimately unenlightening. By accepting the detective's characterization—"little ol' arguments over nothing at all"— the commentator dismisses the homicidal motive as inadequate, without trying to understand it. An implicit contrast is drawn between the foolishness of violent men and the more rational motives that move sensible people like ourselves. The combatants are in effect denigrated as creatures of some lower order of mental functioning, evidently governed by immediate stimuli rather than by foresightful contemplation.

The participants in these "trivial altercations" behave as if a great deal more is at issue than small change or access to a pool table, and their evaluations of what is at stake deserve our respectful consideration. If one wishes to argue that those men who participate in the brinksmanship of barroom altercations are exceptionally irrational, the argument cannot be made convincing simply by pointing to some number of homicides. Who knows how many thousands of altercations are dissipated in mutual threats and face-saving verbiage, how many hundreds in nonlethal violence, for every one that becomes an addition to the homicide statistics? And the emphasis on "triviality" obscures a still more important point. A seemingly minor affront is not merely a "stimulus" to action, isolated in time and space. It must be understood within a larger social context of reputations, face, relative social status, and enduring relationships. Men are known by their fellows as "the sort who can be pushed around" or "the sort who won't take any shit," as people whose word means action and people who are full of hot air, as guys whose girlfriends you can chat up with impunity or guys you don't want to mess with.

In most social milieus, a man's reputation depends in part upon the maintenance of a credible threat of violence. Conflicts of interest are endemic to society, and one's interests are likely to be violated by competitors unless those competitors are *deterred*. Effective deterrence is a matter of convincing our rivals that any attempt to advance their interests at our expense will lead to such severe penalties that the competitive gambit will end up a net loss which should never have been undertaken.

The utility of a credible threat of violence has been mitigated and obscured in modern mass society because the state has assumed a monopoly on the legitimate use of force. But wherever that monopoly is relaxed—whether in an entire society or in a neglected underclass—then the utility of that credible threat becomes apparent. That which is threatened may be punitive action by one's self, by one's allies, or by one's relatives. The last of these—blood revenge—has been enormously important in human history, as we shall examine at length in Chapter 10, but both personal prowess and the capacity to forge political alliances are also crucial to personal success in any society, including even those in which corporate kin groups remain strong.

Roger Lane (1979) conveys a hint of the utility of a man's capacity for violence, when he illustrates the barroom altercations that constituted the "modal homicide" in 19th-century Philadelphia as follows:

> Perhaps, as in the case of Big John Rox, fighting for its own sake served a recreational function, or, cumulatively, an instrumental one, to the extent that a reputation for toughness was a social or even economic asset. But the price was high. Rox was a figure out of the heroic age of Irish immigration, before the Great Famine, a powerful man who had apparently parlayed his brute strength into a position as labor contractor and owner of a small string of taverns. Convicted of manslaughter in May 1839 for killing his old friend "Pat" Kelly with an ax handle, he was pardoned by the governor in time to get involved in a similar episode just twelve months later. He and Barney Browning, his closest surviving companion, were quarrelling in Gunn's Tavern about who had been the toughest man in Donegal, where both had grown up, when Rox confirmed his claim by beating the smaller man onto

the floor with his fists. At the bar just afterward, much subdued, he turned occasionally to the dying Browning and urged him to stop "playing possum. . . ." (p. 60)

In a well-policed society, going so far as to kill may of course be going *too* far in the defense of status and honor—overstepping the limits of utility by bringing down the penalty of law upon oneself. Yet even in a modern state like the United States, the lethal exercise of violence need not be disadvantageous to the killer; in fact, it is not altogether implausible that the eventual consequences of homicidal altercations in America are *typically* positive for the killer, as we shall discuss further in Chapter 8. In any case, whether homicide in an American tavern is ultimately damaging to the killer's interests or not, having killed is a decided social asset in many, perhaps most, prestate societies. The classic examples are such practices as head-hunting and coup-counting, customs whereby a young man might attain full adult status only by notching his first kill, and experienced killers might add to their honors by running up the list of their victims. Such practices are known from warring tribal societies in all parts of the world.

Consider the following declaration, uttered by Obaharok, an ambitious (and still rather youthful) warrior chieftain among the Dani of highland New Guinea, in introducing himself to foreign visitors (Sargent, 1974):

I knew I was meant to be a *kain*. My father told me. But everyone said I couldn't kill because I was too young. I began by stealing a pig. I succeeded and so I stole again and again. Each time I succeeded. The braveness in my heart grew bigger. I felt myself a brave man. Quietly, I tried to kill a man. I returned home with that victory. I wanted to go to war and fight with the others, but they still considered me to be a child. I felt so angry. I went, anyway. With bows and arrows in my hand, I killed the enemy one by one. I killed and I killed until many enemy were dead. I have killed many, many people. In the end I was accepted by the people as overlord. I am not afraid of anybody. (p. 178)

Obaharok proved not to be merely a blowhard. He had indeed been a leader in bloody intertribal warfare, and he was one of the most prominent leaders of a later unsuccessful rebellion against the Indonesian government.

The list of men who have risen to positions of power by displaying their willingness to kill is a long one. But sheer violence is obviously not the only way to gain high status, and perhaps not even the major one. Expert knowledge and wise decision-making can earn a man respect, for example, and can inspire others to elevate him to leadership status. Such status is a limited resource, however, and others will therefore envy him and attempt to devise ways to challenge him. The challenge is often individualized, and can be difficult to ignore without loss of face and consequent loss of status. This remains true even in highly stratified societies in which the state makes strenuous efforts to enforce its monopoly on the use of force.

The classic example of such challenges is the tradition of dueling between "men of honor." The duel is often portrayed as an absurd convention, entered into for trivial reasons, and the predilection for dueling is then portrayed as self-destructive rather than self-aggrandizing. Certainly one of America's most famous duelists, vice-president Aaron Burr, did not gain prestige or power when he forced a duel on an aging political enemy, Alexander Hamilton, and killed him (see e.g., Vail, 1973). Burr was disgraced, but this outcome was by no means typical. As one historian (Williams, 1980) has written of dueling in the American south, "a number of public figures gained prominence and were pushed ahead in their careers because of prowess in dueling" (p. 16). Certainly the fighting of two duels, and several attempts to provoke others, did not damage the political ambitions of President Andrew Jackson (see, e.g., Davis, 1977).

In some societies, willingness to spill blood is virtually synonymous with honor. Here is a European example (Arlacchi, 1980):

> What does it mean to "behave in the manner of the mafia"? It means "to make oneself respected," "to be a man of honour" capable of revenging by his own force any sort of offence done to his own personality and capable equally of dealing out offence to an enemy. Such behaviour, be it defensive or aggressive, was not only justified but encouraged and even idealized by the society. . . .
>
> Given the importance of honorific conflict in the strategy of mafia values, taking a life, especially killing a fearful enemy, was honorific in the highest degree. "X is an exceptional man; he 'has' five killings." "Y is a man of respect; he has 'stubbed out' four Christians." These sorts of phrases recur in mafia conversation. Among the *mafiosi* of the Plain of Gioia Tauro the act of homicide, if carried out in a competition for supremacy of any sort whatever, indicated (and still does, for these attitudes persist in the flourishing mafia of today) courage and the capacity to impose oneself as a man. It brought an automatic opening of a line of credit for the killer. The more awesome and potent the victim, the more worthy and meritorious the killer. (pp. 111–113)

The complex ideal of "machismo" is occasionally discussed in the social science literature, generally under the rubric of "sex roles" or cultural conventions. The implications of such an interpretive framework are that the ideal is as arbitrary in its details as a dress code, and that a shortfall of machismo is a social failing like poor table manners.

But there is nothing arbitrary about a social ideal that is equivalent to effective deterrence! Here is how 32-year-old Manuel Sánchez of Mexico City explains machismo in Oscar Lewis's (1961) famous urban ethnography *The Children of Sánchez:*

> I have learned to hide my fear and to show only courage because from what I have observed, a person is treated according to the impression he makes. That's why when I am really very afraid inside, outwardly I am calm. It has helped me too, because I didn't suffer as much as some of my friends who trembled when they were grabbed by the police. If a guy shows weakness and has tears in his eyes, and begs for mercy, that is when the others pile on him. In my neighborhood, you are either a *picudo,* a tough guy, or a *pendejo,* a fool.
>
> Mexicans, and I think everyone in the world, admire the person "with balls," as we say. The character who throws punches and kicks, without stopping to think, is the one who comes out on top. The one who has guts enough to stand up against an older, stronger guy, is more respected. If someone shouts, you've got to shout louder. If any so-and-so comes to me and says, "Fuck your mother," I answer, "Fuck your mother a thousand times." And if he gives one step forward and I take one step back, I lose prestige. But if I go forward too, and pile on and make a fool out of him, then the others will treat me with respect. In a fight, I would never give up or say, "Enough," even though the other was killing me. I would try to go to my death, smiling. That is what we mean by being *"macho"* by being manly. (p 38)

A Question of Variance

Why do men's minds work this way? Why would *any* creature place so much value on intangible social resources—on status, face, and honor—that he would risk his life pursuing them? If selection has shaped this aspect of the human psyche, it would appear that the answer must somehow take the following form: Such social resources are (or formerly were) means to the end of fitness.

There is little mystery about the link between honor and status, on the one hand, and fitness, on the other. Consider again, for example, the Dani tribesmen of highland New Guinea (Matthiessen, 1962):

> A man without valor is *kepu*—a worthless man, a man-who-has-not-killed. The kepu men go to the war field with the rest, but they remain well to the rear. Some howl insults and brandish weapons from afar, but most are quiet and unobtrusive, content to lend the deadwood of their weapons to the ranks. The kepu men are never jeered or driven into battle—no one must fight who does not choose to—but their position in the tribe may be determined by their comportment on the field. Unless they have strong friends or family, any wives or pigs they may obtain will be taken from them by other men, in the confidence that they will not resist; few kepu men have more than a single wife, and many of them have none. (p. 15)

Homo sapiens is very clearly a creature for whom differential social status has consistently been associated with variations in reproductive success. Men of high social rank have more wives, more concubines, more access to *other* men's wives than men of low social rank. They have more children and their children survive better. These things have consistently been the case in foraging societies, in pastoral societies, in horticultural societies, in state societies.

Polygynous marriage—the simultaneous union of one man with two or more wives—is legitimate in the great majority of human societies, 83% of 849 in an encyclopedic compendium called the *Ethnographic Atlas* (Murdock, 1967), for example. Polygynous status is invariably the prerogative of men of high social rank, exceptional material means, or both. "Isn't One Wife Enough?" inquires a chronicler of American Mormon life (Young, 1970), recounting the costs that the polygynous husband incurred in money, in time, and in strife. According to men's behavior, the answer is clearly "No"! In some polygynous societies, wives are economic assets, but in others they are economic burdens. In either case, they are invariably sources of competition and contention between men. And yet, wherever polygyny is an option, successful men tend to accumulate as many wives as they can afford and manage.

Consider as one example and by no means an extreme one, the famous Yanomamö Indians of Venezuela, immortalized by anthropologist Napoleon Chagnon as "the fierce people." The Yanomamö are slash-and-burn horticulturalists living in villages of perhaps a hundred people. Warfare between villages is chronic, and many—perhaps most—men die violent deaths at the hands of other men. Chagnon (1983) describes his friend Kaobawa, headman of the village of Bisaasi-teri:

> There are different "styles" of political leadership among the Yanomamö. Some leaders are mild, quiet, inconspicuous most of the time, but intensely competent. They act parsimoniously, but when they do, people listen and conform. Other men are more tyrannical, despotic, pushy, flamboyant, and unpleasant to all around them. They shout orders frequently, are prone to beat their wives, or pick on weaker men. Some are very violent . . . Kaobawa stands at the mild, quietly competent end of the spectrum. He has had six wives thus far—and temporary affairs with as many more, at least one of which resulted in a child that is publicly acknowledged as his child. (p. 26)

How is it that a "mild" man like Kaobawa is the acknowledged headman? Partly by virtue of kin solidarity, partly by political skill, partly by being perceived as wise, partly by personal bravery (Chagnon, 1983).

He leads more by example than by coercion. He can afford to be this way at his age, for he established his reputation for being forthright and as fierce as the situation required when he was younger, and the other men respect him. He also has five mature brothers or half-brothers in his village, men he can count on for support. (p. 27)

The man who has ascended to Yanomamö headman status cannot shirk danger or his status will wither. Chagnon describes incidents in which Kaobawa guaranteed the safe passage of visitors to his village although an angry faction wished to murder them; in which he disarmed an irate husband who had wounded his wife and was still brandishing a machete; in which he disarmed one of his own brothers in a drugged state of randomly directed violence and hid his weapons; in which he refereed and controlled fights within his village (Chagnon, 1983).

Finally, one of Kaobawa's most unpleasant tasks is to scout the village neighborhood when signs of raiders have been found. This he does alone, since it is a dangerous task and one that is avoided by the other men. (p. 124)

The inclination to acquire wives is obviously contributory to fitness. Headmen like Kaobawa leave more descendants than the average Yanomamö man, and a few leave *many* more (Chagnon, 1983):

There was a particularly accomplished man in the Shamatari population several generations back named "Shinbone." Some of his children are still alive today, so he is still well-known to many people who knew him personally. Shinbone had 11 wives, by whom he had 43 children who survived long enough for people to be able to recollect them. (p. 2)

At last count, Shinbone's 20 sons had produced 120 grandchildren and his 23 daughters had produced 111; his great-grandchildren numbered 480 with more still to come.

The reproductive success of a man like Shinbone is predicated upon the reproductive failure of many rivals. It took the reproductive capacities of 11 women to produce Shinbone's 43 children. If one man monopolizes 11 women, and the sexes are about equally numerous, it would appear that about 10 men must be missing out altogether. For every Shinbone with his great cascade of descendants, there are many other men who will be nobody's ancestors. If status has persistently contributed to reproductive success, and a capacity for controlled violence has regularly contributed to status, then the selective advantage of violent skills cannot be gainsaid.

What Do Men Want?

The *Guinness Book of Records* (McWhirter & Greenberg, 1979) credits
one Moulay Ismail the Bloodthirsty (1672–1727), one-time emperor of
Morocco, with the world's record for personal reproduction: 888 acknowledged offspring. This record-setter came by his nickname hon-
estly, being renowned for his uses of arbitrary terror as a social display.
He was wont, for example, to strike off the heads of attending slaves
while entertaining foreign guests, and was said to have killed 30,000
people by his own hand, a figure he was not displeased to have bruited
about his kingdom.

As a pious Muslim, Moulay Ismail was restricted to just 4 wives, but
his religion placed no limit on the number of his concubines. An account
of royal harem procedures has been left us by a French diplomat named
Busnot, who visited the emperor in 1712 to ransom some prisoners, and
wrote a memoir that was translated into English in 1715, under the title,

> The History of the Reign of Muley Ismael, the present King of Morocco,
>   Fez, Tafilet, Sous, &c.
> Of the Revolt and Tragical End of several of his Sons, and of his Wives.
> Of the horrid Executions of many of his Officers and Subjects.
> Of his Genious, policy, and Arbitrary Government.
> Of the cruel Persecution of the Christian Slaves in his Dominions: With an
>   Account of three Voyages to Miquenez and Ceuta, in order to Ransom
>   them.

Busnot's own slaves interviewed the slaves and eunuchs of the
imperial palace, and ferreted out many details about the operation of the
royal seraglio. The emperor maintained a harem of 500, each of whom
dwelt in a separate cell, attended by her personal eunuch, and her
personal female slave. Moulay Ismail's senior wife, the empress
Zeldana, managed the harem for her husband, and she ran a tight ship.
The concubines were not at liberty, for example, to visit even among
themselves; fourteen who had been doing just that at the time of
Busnot's visit had all their teeth pulled as punishment. At 30 years of
age, each woman was shipped out to some provincial underling's
harem, and her place was taken by someone younger.

Dismiss Moulay Ismail as a madman, if you will, but his preoccupations were by no means unique. Enormous harems have arisen in
stratified societies across Asia and the Middle East, in sub-Saharan
Africa and in the New World, in short wherever despotic power has
accumulated (Betzig, 1985). And it is a telling commentary on their
masters' ambitions that harems were invariably guarded, usually by
eunuchs. There are even tales, for several parts of the world, of entire

harems being put to death after a security failure was discovered. The maintenance of *exclusive* sexual access seems always to have been one of the primary goals of those powerful men who have amassed women.

There can be very little doubt that harem holders have often achieved exceptional reproductive success. Darwinian anthropologist Mildred Dickemann has written a lively review of harem polygyny, especially as it was practiced in Asia. She maintains that even royal harems of a thousand women were managed as reproductive resources, and writes (1979a) that the careful management of the Chinese Imperial Harem, "involving copulation of concubines on a rotating basis at appropriate times in their menstrual cycles, all carefully regulated by female supervisors to prevent deception and error, shows what could be achieved with a well-organized bureaucracy" (p. 175). Of an Indian potentate, she notes (1979a), "An early 20th century observer reported that the Nizam of Hyderabad became the father of four children in the space of eight days with nine more expected the following week . . ." (p. 176).

Laura Betzig (1982, 1985) has assembled several accounts of similarly managed and guarded harems, and has documented the world-wide generality of the association between despotic power and extreme polygyny. In the precolonial kingdoms of Africa, harems of the Ashanti, Azande, Baganda, and Zulu kings were all reputed to have exceeded a thousand women, as did the greatest harems in India, China, and the Muslim world.

Imperial harems and the despotism that permits them are relatively modern aberrations in human history. Although their reproductive consequences are dramatic, one may protest that such extreme concentrations of sexual privilege have had little or no selective effects upon the evolution of our species. Indeed that is likely. We do not discuss harems here because of any impact they may have had upon the course of human evolution. Rather, we consider them to be revealing because they are the hypertrophied manifestations of male appetites, released from the usual constraints of limited personal power. A well-guarded harem of nubile women is the realization of a male fantasy. It is a fantasy that has apparently arisen in men's minds repeatedly and independently in a variety of cultures, and has been so appealing as to be implemented again and again, at great expense, when men have somehow amassed the means to do so. It is the fantastic aspiration of a male psyche with a natural selective history.

Great disparities of status and power must be recent phenomena in human evolutionary history, for they are possible only where agricultural technology has permitted large-scale food storage, dense settlement, and extensive role specializations, all of which arose only within the last few thousand years. But even in relatively egalitarian societies where people occupy a preagricultural foraging niche, much like that known to most of our human ancestors, still there is some differentiation of status, and it is still the most respected men who are able to maintain two or three wives (see, for example, Balikci, 1970; Hart & Pilling, 1960; Hiatt, 1965; Howell, 1979). For each such polygynous man, some other male has been consigned to bachelorhood, and so men compete not merely to attain the highest status, but to avoid the lowest. Indeed, competition can sometimes be fiercest near the bottom of the scale, where the man on track for total failure has nothing to lose by the most dangerous competitive tactics, and may therefore throw caution to the winds.

It is in such a social milieu that man's psyche was shaped, a psyche obsessed with social comparisons, with the need for achievement, and with the desire to gain control over the reproductive capacities of women.

Why Men and Not Women?

Why was the last chapter entirely about *men?* We have proposed that dangerous altercations derive from status competition, and that the inclination to compete for status has evolved because high status has been contributory to fitness throughout human history. If this proposal is sound, why should it not apply equally to women?

Recall the Yanomamö headman Shinbone and his 11 wives. As we noted earlier, the fact that one man monopolizes several women means that others are consigned to celibacy. Indeed in any polygynous system, the fact that a few males each have more children than any one female could ever bear, necessarily implies that males are also much more likely than females to leave very few descendants, or none. And that is demonstrably the case. In a demographic survey of the Xavante Indians of Brazil (Salzano, Neel, & Maybury-Lewis, 1967), for example, 40% of the married men were polygynous. Other adult men were thus unmarried, although no woman of fertile age was without a husband. By 20 years of age, only 1 out of 195 women had not yet borne a child. By contrast, 6% of men who reached the age of 40 were still childless. The maximum number of children for a man was 23, for a woman 8.

So we are primarily concerned with reproductive competition among men rather than women, not out of arbitrary sexism, but because the differentials among males are larger, and the competition is therefore more severe. A man has a higher ceiling upon his potential fitness than does a woman, but he also has a greater likelihood of going to his grave with no descendants at all (Ellison, 1985). There is, in other words, a sex difference in *fitness variance,* and this difference is causally linked to a host of other sex differences, the explication of which will require an excursion into basic evolutionary theory.

Sexual Selection and "Parental Investment"

Charles Darwin published his great work on natural selection in 1859. His second greatest contribution, the concept of *sexual selection,* he elaborated 12 years later (Darwin, 1871), but this idea had rather little impact for almost 100 years.

Whereas most adaptive attributes of animals are clearly of service in the struggle to survive, certain features—particularly those used by males in courtship—seem positively to *detract* from survival. The peacock's gaudy tail, for example, may charm the peahen, but it is conspicuous to potential predators too, and it is an impediment to flight. How could such traits persist if the more spectacular males tend to die sooner than their duller rivals? Darwin's answer was that mere longevity was not the same thing as reproductive success. A trait might be penalized by "natural" selection and yet win out by "sexual" selection, a process that occurs whenever some attribute contributes to success either in wooing the opposite sex or in vanquishing members of one's own sex in competition for mates. But just why sexual selection should appear to apply primarily to *males*—that is to say why males generally court and fight over females rather than the reverse—was not clearly elucidated for several decades, until the publication of a laboratory study, not of a spectacular wooer like the peacock nor a battler like the elk, but of the innocuous little fruit fly, *Drosophila*.

In 1948, the British geneticist A.J. Bateman published in the journal *Heredity* the results of his experiments on the reproduction of these tiny animals, when maintained in jars on the laboratory shelf, with each jar containing equal numbers (3, 4, or 5) of each sex. Bateman constituted the groups in such a way that he could attribute offspring to particular parents on the basis of distinct "genetic markers," characteristics analogous to human eye color or birth marks. By observing the behavior of the flies directly, and subsequently counting the progeny of each individual, he was able to relate individual differences in mating behavior to eventual reproductive success.

What Bateman found was that the reproductive success of a male is dependent upon his behavior in a very different way from that of a female. A fly of either sex might be observed to mate with anywhere from 0 to 4 individuals. In the case of females, fitness was unaffected by the precise number of mates: Assuming she mated at all, a female could expect to produce about 60 to 80 offspring, and it did not matter whether she had copulated with one male or with several. In the case of males, however, eventual reproductive success was a linear function of the number of sexual partners: Those who copulated with one female produced about 40 young, those who copulated with two produced about 80, and so forth. Related to this sex difference in the effects of differential mating frequency is a further difference: Whereas one female laid more or less the same number of eggs as another, the maximum being limited by her physiological capacity to produce them, a minority of males did much better than average, and a much greater proportion of males than of females produced no young at all. In other words, the variance in male fitness greatly exceeded the variance in female fitness.

With a little thought these phenomena may seem rather obvious, but Bateman was the first scientist to document such sex differences and to discuss their broader implications. Noting that the "greater dependence of males for their fertility on frequency of insemination" is "an almost universal attribute of sexual reproduction," he suggested that selection would produce tactics of male mating competition, as well as "an undiscriminatory eagerness in the males and a discriminatory passivity in the females." Thus Bateman explained Darwin's observation that in the animal kingdom generally, "the males are almost always the wooers": Male fitness is directly limited by access to fertile females, whereas a female's fitness is limited not by access to males but by access to the material resources necessary for reproduction, or, when resources are abundant, by her limited intrinsic capacities to convert them to babies.

Essentially the same argument applies to *Homo sapiens*. Female reproduction in people (and other mammals) is not, of course, limited simply by *egg* production capacity as in the case of the fruit fly: A woman may produce hundreds of eggs in a lifetime, but that does not mean that she could produce hundreds of children. However, in mammals, as in fruit flies, it is still the case that female productivity has a much lower potential maximum and a much lower variance than male productivity.

As Robert Trivers (1972) has elaborated Bateman's argument, the common denominator in fruit flies and ourselves is that females typically make a greater *parental investment* (PI) in each offspring than do males, with the result that female PI is, in effect, the "resource" that limits male fitness, and hence is a commodity for which males have been selected to compete. In the fly, the sex difference in PI resides in the greater material cost of a batch of eggs as compared to the ejaculate that fertilizes them. In a woman, the investment includes a 9-month gestation, lactation (lasting many months in the environments in which we evolved), and much subsequent nurture. While men *may* supply some of this later PI, women never had many options (at least before the domestication of milk animals). So a man—like a male fruit fly—could always increase his expected fitness by gaining sexual access to one more fertile female, regardless of whether he presently has no mates or fifty, whereas a woman—like a female fruit fly—typically would not enhance her expected fitness by gaining sexual access to every fertile male on the planet.

Her female rivals may limit a woman's fitness, to be sure—it is not our point to disparage the selective consequences of competition among females. And having multiple suitors may often provide material and protective advantages over monogamy (Hrdy, 1981). Nevertheless, male fitness is limited by access to the opposite sex much more directly than is female fitness, with the result that females compete *for mates* much less than do males. Partly for that reason, the competition between females is often less direct and confrontational than that between males. Competition among females for limited food resources, for example, is often a "scramble" in which the competitors do not even encounter one another. But the still more important sex difference is quantitative. Competition among males is more intense than that among females in a simple objective sense: The variance in male fitness is greater than the variance in female fitness. Among men as compared to women, the big winners win bigger, and the losers are more likely to be total losers. As Richard Alexander (1979) has written, "as a general consequence, the entire life history strategy of males is a higher-risk, higher-stakes adventure than that of females" (p. 241).

Polygyny Is a Matter of Degree

Our point in discussing sexual selection and parental investment is not to make a facile comparison between fruit flies and people. Nor is it to claim that "competitiveness" is an attribute of maleness in the animal world generally. On the contrary, there is a sizable minority of animal species—some birds, for example, some frogs, a few insects, and others—in which the sex differences discussed above are reversed. In such species, the males make the greater parental investment and have the lower reproductive potential, and this being so, sexual selection has operated more intensely on the females, who are larger and more combative, have greater fitness variance, and tend to die younger than the males. Such reversals provide some of the strongest evidence for the Bateman-Trivers theory, because they support the idea that it is parental investment disparities that drive the system.

The interesting point for our purposes is comparative: Animal species vary in a large number of correlated traits, all of which turn out to be related to the species-typical magnitude of the sex difference in parental investment, in fitness variance, and in sexual selection. And *Homo sapiens*, it so happens, can be readily situated within this comparative scheme.

A *monogamous breeding system* can be defined for present purposes as one in which individuals breed only with a single member of the opposite sex. If eight children represent the maximum for a female, for example, then under monogamy, eight will be the maximum for a male as well. The frequency distribution of numbers of offspring is identical for females and males, and the fitness variances are equal (if the sexes are about equally numerous). Now, whereas monogamy implies equal fitness variance, the reverse is not true: Both sexes could change partners frequently and still have identical fitness distributions. However, we refer to any case in which female and male variances are equal as "effectively monogamous" because sexual selection is likely to have had approximately equal impact upon the two sexes in any case where the variances are equal, just as in true monogamy.

Where male fitness variance exceeds female fitness variance, we refer to the system as "effectively polygynous." Note that effective polygyny is a matter of degree (see Daly & Wilson, 1983, pp. 151–156). The degree of effective polygamy can be approximated as the ratio of male variance over female variance. A value of 1 is effective monogamy, greater than 1 is effective polygyny, and less than 1 is effective polyandry (a state of affairs that exists in the "sex-reversed" animals alluded to earlier, but probably does not characterize any human society, although a tiny minority practice polyandrous marriage; Murdock, 1967).

The data on animal breeding systems are seldom good enough to permit precise quantification of the degree of effective polygamy. However, we can often get a reasonable estimate from proxy measures such as the number of females in a sexually active male's "harem." By such measures, we find dramatic differences in polygamy among closely related species. Certain species of African antelopes (see, e.g., Jarman, 1974), for example, are monogamous. In some other related species, a successful male may sire the calves of three or four females in a single season, while other males lose out. In still other species, the most successful males may sire dozens, while the majority of males never get to breed at all. (See Clutton-Brock, 1988, for recent studies of lifetime reproductive success and the degree of effective polygamy in animal breeding systems.)

What is most interesting about this variability in the degree of effective polygamy among animal species is that other traits vary along with it. Among monogamous antelope species, for example, female and male are about the same size, are of similar build and markings, and may indeed be virtually indistinguishable. When we then examine other antelope species with increasingly polygynous breeding systems, we find that males are larger and larger relative to the females, and the sexes exhibit increasingly dramatic differences in armament. As the degree of polygyny increases, so too does the fitness prize to the most successful males, and so does the probability of total reproductive failure.

Sexual Success versus Survival?

One might imagine that a polygynous male's large size and armament would contribute to his survival as well as to his competitive success. But that is demonstrably not the case. Within a comparative series such as the antelopes, the trend toward greater polygyny and increasing size difference between the sexes parallels another trend toward a greater and greater sex difference in mortality, and it is the powerful males who are the more vulnerable sex. In highly polygynous species, males die in combat, of course, but they also suffer greater mortality than females in other contexts as well, sometimes because of starvation, sometimes because of greater conspicuousness to predators, sometimes because of relative immobility in hard conditions such as deep snow. Thus sexual selection for intraspecific competitive ability often acts counter to natural selection for ecological efficiency and survival capability. As the intensity of sexual selection in an effectively polygynous breeding system increases, the male's design for survival is more and more compromised by the requirements for success in reproductive competition.

The fact that the males of a polygynous species may expect to die younger than the females means that selection operates differently on the sexes, with respect to any trait that might enhance present fitness at a cost in long-term maintenance of bodily condition or survival capability. If we intervene to remove the normal extrinsic causes of mortality, maintaining the animal in a sheltered captivity, we would typically expect to find that males and females of a monogamous species exhibit similar life spans before senescing and dying, whereas males senesce more rapidly than females in those species that are effectively polygynous. Elevated function of adrenals and gonads, for example, contributes to the competitive success of males of the Australian small mammal genus *Antechinus* during the single breeding season that a male ordinarily lives to see; the same hormonal events contribute to anemia, hemorrhages, and the suppression of the immune system, which guarantee the male's death soon after the mating season ends, while the females live on to raise their litters and perhaps to breed again another year (Lee *et al.*, 1977).

The same arguments of course apply to psychological attributes and behavioral propensities: A more polygynous system selects for riskier behavior by males competing for mating opportunities, whether the risks in question are incurred in combat with rivals or in less directly competitive pursuits, such as exposing oneself to predation in order to visit scattered females. Animals, as we have said before, are not designed to live forever, but to outreproduce their rivals. The more polygamous the breeding system, the greater is the difference between the sexes in how long each *is* designed to live.

The Sexual Selective History of *Homo sapiens*

The relevance of all this to the human case should be obvious. What do the sexually differentiated characteristics of this particular animal reveal about its history of sexual selection? The clear answer is that we are the products of a mild but sustained polygynous competition.

Within the primates generally, the ratio of male body length to female body length is strongly correlated with effective polygyny (Alexander *et al.*, 1979). Moreover, there is some evidence that the females of polygynous primate species are closer than the males to a body size that is optimal for the species' feeding ecology (Gaulin & Sailer, 1985); males, in other words, are "oversized," presumably for the sake of combative prowess. The ratio of male body length to female body length in our own species is greater than in such monogamists as gibbons or marmosets, less than in such extreme polygynists as baboons or gorillas. An independent vestige of our polygynous selective history can be seen in the fact that males senesce more rapidly than females. Still another is that females are sexually mature a little before males; a sex difference in the age at maturity is yet another correlate of the species-characteristic degree of effective polygamy in comparative studies, apparently because whichever sex is the more competitive requires longer to attain sufficient competitive abilities to make a first breeding attempt worthwhile. All the available evidence is consistent in suggesting that our sexual selective history has been one of effective polygyny.

Sexual dimorphism and violent male–male competition are ancient and enduring elements of our evolutionary history. Fifty thousand years ago, there was approximately the same degree of sexual size dimorphism among Neanderthals as we find in modern men and women (Trinkaus, 1980). Indeed, our nearest living relatives, the anthropoid apes, are all sexually dimorphic and effectively polygynous, and the same appears to have been true of the earliest fossil anthropoids (Fleagle *et al.*, 1980).

There can be no doubt that men have killed one another at high rates for as long as there have been men. Twenty years ago, this claim engendered great controversy, but we have learned a lot in the interim.

Where ethologists once believed that intraspecific killing was rare in the animal world in general and among our close kin in particular, we have since found that attacks by conspecifics are a major cause of mortality in many (probably most) mammals, including those most closely related to ourselves. At the same time, novel theoretical work has elucidated the conditions under which intraspecific violence would be adaptive for the aggressor, providing an impetus for researchers to record and study such violence, instead of attributing it to pathology. As a result, careful field studies have demonstrated that male–male combat is a leading cause of death in polygynous, dimorphic mammals. In our closest relatives, the chimpanzees, males form alliances, partly along kinship lines, and conduct prolonged campaigns of intergroup hostility (see Goodall, 1986).

Most importantly, we have discovered in the past 20 years a great deal about the violent history of man himself. The old idea that hunter-gatherers are nonviolent was an ideologically motivated myth that *never* matched the evidence: Old and recent ethnography alike provide ample testimony of murder and prolonged blood feuds among Australian aborigines, Plains Indians, Eskimos, Kalahari San, and other hunter-gatherers. To this we shall return in Chapter 10. Moreover, the evidence of prehistoric violence has accumulated greatly (and paleonto-logical detective work has become much more sophisticated) since Raymond Dart's controversial claim that australopithecines staved in one another's skulls. In some ancient skeletal samples, for example, one can observe and count cranial fractures (evidently by clubbing) and rib fractures (evidently by stabbing), both healed and fatal. Sometimes the wounds still contain fragments of the weapon. It is regularly found that male skeletons exhibit more such wounds than female skeletons, and moreover that men (more than women) are more often wounded on the left than on the right side, evidently by right-handed antagonists (e.g., Walker, 1985). The earliest known victim of human weapons was a Neanderthal man, frontally stabbed in the chest by a right-handed antagonist more than 50,000 years ago (Trinkaus & Zimmerman, 1982).

We still cannot say to what extent human sex differences in size and bodily structure reflect specific sexually selected adaptation to male–male combat. It is possible, for example, that the selective pressure for male body size and power resides primarily in hunting rather than in fighting. What *is* certain is that men have fought and killed one another for tens of thousands of years. It is hard to doubt that the winners in such combat generally outreproduced the losers.

What evidence we have on modern human populations indicates that the selective circumstance of an effectively polygynous breeding system persists. Polygynous marriage was available to successful men the world 'round until recently. And even now, in societies with legislated monogamy, men have a longer potential reproductive life span than women, remarry and raise successive families with different mates more often than do women, and are more likely than women never to marry. Moreover, there is, in many cases, reason to suspect some degree of clandestine polygyny or reproductive concubinage. Thus, although data on men's fertility histories are sparse (and of dubious validity, thanks to uncertain paternity), it seems very likely that the variance in men's fitness must still exceed that of women.

Intrasexual Competition and Violence

Competition is a subcategory of conflict, arising when two (or more) individuals aspire to make similar use of a resource that is not sufficiently abundant to satisfy both (or all). Not all conflict is competitive. If a female spurns one suitor for another, for example, then she and the rejected male have a conflict of interest, but they are not competitors (whereas the rival suitors are).

Competition for limited resources is predominantly intrasexual: female against female, male against male. It is not *entirely* intrasexual: A female and a male might both desire the same food item, for example, and might fight or even kill over it. But competition is *predominantly* intrasexual because same-sex individuals are usually more similar in the resources they require than are opposite-sex individuals. In particular, individuals of the opposite sex are often the "resource" that same-sex individuals compete for.

According to the Bateman-Trivers theory, access to the sex that makes the greater parental investment tends to become the crucial resource limiting the fitness of individuals of the less investing sex, so that selection favors competition among the latter for access to mates. Fitness variance is a measure of the intensity of competition, and the more intense that competition—that is to say, the more disparate the outcomes—then the more likely it becomes that selection will favor a psychology prone to *risky* competitive tactics, including escalated fighting even to the point of death. This point is elaborated with a game-theoretical model in Chapter 8. Note that the Bateman-Trivers theory of sexual selection leads to predictions about sex differences, but not to the simplistic account of sex differences that is so often misattributed to biologists, namely that there is something about "maleness"—androgens, in one popular version—that leads to inevitable aggressivity and violence. On the contrary, the theory predicts that sex differences will themselves differ from one species to another in their magnitude and even in their direction, and it predicts the nature of that variability in considerable detail (Trivers, 1972).

The comparative evidence is abundant, and it is clearly supportive of the theory. In monogamous wolves or gulls or gibbons, the fitness variance of females is as great as that of males, and females are about as hostile to one another as are males. In a polyandrous species such as the spotted sandpiper of North America (Maxson & Oring, 1980), females have the greater fitness variance, and thus have more to fight over; as we would expect, the females' battles are more spectacular and evidently dangerous than those of the males. In polygynous species, it is predominantly the males who fight, and their fights are more severe the more polygynous the species. Although there are still many puzzling cases and additional complications, these general cross-species correlations are not controversial (see, for example, Daly & Wilson, 1983).

In Chapter 6, we proposed that a large proportion of the homicides in America—and in particular most of those traditionally dismissed as being the results of "trivial altercations"—have to be understood as the rare, fatal consequences of a ubiquitous competitive struggle among men for status and respect. These social "resources" have come to be valued by the male psyche because of their positive fitness consequences. Since our selective history has been one of effective polygyny (and our present circumstances apparently maintain the sex difference in fitness variance), and since differential fitness is demonstrably more strongly correlated with differential status in males than in females, we may expect men to be more inclined to risky, confrontational intrasexual interactions than women, and we may expect this difference to be much more generally manifested than in America alone. So what are the facts?

Table 7.1 presents the numbers of male–male and female–female homicides that have been recorded in various studies in a wide range of societies. *The difference between the sexes is immense, and it is universal.* There is no known human society in which the level of lethal violence among women even begins to approach that among men.

The sex differences in Table 7.1 are huge, but they indubitably *under*estimate the actual sex difference in intrasexual competitive violence. This is so because the table includes homicides that are not properly construed as the outcomes of competition, and these constitute a higher proportion of the female cases than of the male cases. The single female–female homicide in Miami in 1980, for example, was an infanticide, and so was the single case in 14th-century Oxford. As we saw in Chapters 3 and 4, killing one's own dependent offspring is a very different matter from an intrasexual, competitive altercation, and such

Table 7.1. Same-Sex Homicides in Various Studies

	References	Male killed male	Female killed female	Proportion male
Canada, 1974–1983		2965	175	.944
Miami,1925–1926	Wilbanks, 1984	111	5	.957
North Carolina, 1930–1940	Garfinkel, 1949	603	28	.956
Birmingham, 1937–1944	Harlan, 1950	277	20	.933
Cleveland, 1947–1953	Bensing & Schroeder, 1960	417	14	.968
Philadelphia, 1948–1952	Wolfgang, 1958	333	16	.954
Houston, 1958–1961	Pokorny, 1965	246	16	.939
Chicago, 1965	Voss & Hepburn, 1968	219	10	.956
Pittsburgh, 1966–1974	Costantino *et al.*, 1977	382	16	.960
Detroit, 1972	Wilson & Daly, 1985	345	16	.956
St. Louis, 1973	Herjanic & Meyer, 1976	135	2	.985
Miami, 1980	Wilbanks, 1984	369	1	.997
Gros Ventre (USA) 1850–1885	Flannery, 1953	13	0	1.000
Tzeltal Mayans (Mexico) 1938–1965	Nash, 1967	37	0	1.000
Belo Horizonte (Brazil) 1961–1965	Yearwood, 1974	228	6	.974
New South Wales (Australia 1968–1981)	Wallace, 1986	675	46	.936
Oxford (England), 1296–1398	Hammer, 1978	105	1	.991
England, 13th century	Given, 1977	1409	73	.951
England and Wales, 1982	Edwards, 1985	241	22	.916
Scotland, 1953–1974	Gillies, 1976	172	12	.935
Iceland, 1946–1970	Hansen & Bjarnason, 1974	10	0	1.000
Denmark, 1933–1961	Siciliano, 1965	87	15	.853

(*continued*)

Table 7.1. (*Continued*)

	References	Male killed male	Female killed female	Proportion male
Baden-Wurttemburg (Germany) 1970–1971	Sessar, 1975	94	4	.959
Bison-Horn Maria (India), 1920–1941	Elwin, 1950	69	2	.972
Munda (India)	Saran, 1974	43	0	1.000
Oraon (India)	Saran, 1974	40	0	1.000
Bhil (India), 1971–1975	Varma, 1978	85	1	.988
!Kung San (Botswana), 1920–1955	Lee, 1979	19	0	1.000
Congo (now Zaire), 1948–1957	Sohier, 1959	156	4	.975
Tiv (Nigeria), 1931–1949	Bohannan, 1960b	96	3	.970
BaSoga (Uganda), 1952–1954	Fallers & Fallers 1960	46	1	.979
Gisu (Uganda), 1948–1954	LaFontaine, 1960	72	3	.960
BaLuyia (Kenya), 1949–1954	Bohannan, 1960	88	5	.946
JoLuo (Kenya)	Wilson, 1960	31	2	.939
Alur (Uganda), 1945–1954	Southall, 1960	37	1	.974

cases weigh heavily in Table 7.1. The Danish data set, for example, exhibits the smallest ratio of male–male to female–female cases ("only" 5.8 to 1), but *all* 15 of the latter were cases in which mothers killed dependent children. Similarly, the second smallest ratio ("only" 11 to 1) is that for England and Wales in 1982, but there were 27 father-son cases among the 241 male–male killings, and 18 mother–daughters among the 22 female–female; so between unrelated men, lethal same-sex violence was more than 50 times as numerous as between unrelated women.

In our 10-year Canadian sample, the tabulated data indicate 16.9 times as many male–male cases as female–female ones. However, more than half of the latter were cases in which mothers killed preschool-age daughters, whereas only 3% of male–male cases were father–son cases (still a larger *absolute* number than mother–daughter cases). If we remove these parental homicides from the comparison, there remain 2861 male–male cases and just 84 female–female cases; the former are now 34.1 times as numerous as the latter. To slice the pie yet another way, we might propose that competition tends to occur primarily between peers, and hence that the competitive element is probably greater in cases where the ages of victim and killer are not very different. If we therefore select those Canadian cases in which the parties' ages differed by no more than 10 years, we find 1519 male–male cases and a mere 39 female–female cases, the former being 38.9 times as numerous. All in all, it appears that *the sex difference in intrasexual competitive homicides is even more extreme than the data in Table 7.1 would suggest.*

In the United States, a great deal of publicity has recently been granted to allegations of an alarming rise in female criminality. It is widely believed that behavioral differences between American women and men are on the wane as a result of "women's liberation." This belief is exploited by conservative critics of feminism, who cite rising female crime statistics as the "dark side" of progress toward equality. But the bogeyman of violent crime by women is a fiction. The statistics in question are the Federal Bureau of Investigation's national arrest data for "serious crimes," and while the proportion of arrestees that are women has indeed increased more or less continuously over the past 30 years, this is *entirely* because of an increased representation of women among those arrested for "larceny-theft" (and even this difference may not represent a change in the behavior of women, but rather a change in the willingness of police to arrest them). The female proportion among arrestees for *violent* crimes—and in particular for homicide—has in fact declined slightly over the same period. There is no evidence that women in modern America are approaching the level of violent conflict prevailing among men. Indeed there is no evidence that the women in *any* society have *ever* approached the level of violent conflict prevailing among men in the same society.

Margaret Mead and New Guinea

The sex difference that is illustrated in Table 7.1 is so universally an aspect of human experience that it should surprise no one. Yet it is part of the mythology of the social sciences, particularly as they have developed in North America, that any such differences between women and men are culturally arbitrary and easily reversed. "In our culture," writes Marvin Wolfgang, trying to explain the enormous sex difference in his study of Philadelphia homicides, the female is "less given to or expected to engage in physical violence than the male" (1958, p. 163). In other writings, he has attributed the same phenomenon to "socialization" and "the theme of masculinity in American culture" (1978, p. 87). The clear implication is that things are otherwise in other cultures. But they are not.

The myth that the familiar sex difference in violence is reversed in other societies can be laid at the door of the famous anthropologist and popular writer Margaret Mead. Her study of three New Guinea tribes, published in 1935 under the title *Sex and Temperament in Three Primitive Societies*, has been presented to literally millions of college undergraduates as a demonstration that differences in the traits of men and women are arbitrary and reversible cultural artifacts. As she summed up the matter in her preface to the 1950 edition,

> Here, admittedly looking for light on the subject of sex differences, I found three tribes all conveniently within a hundred mile area. In one, both men and women act as we expect women to act—in a mild parental responsive way; in the second, both act as we expect men to act—in a fierce initiating fashion; and in the third, the men act according to our stereotype for women—are catty, wear curls and go shopping, while the women are energetic, managerial, unadorned partners.

These peoples were the "gentle Arapesh," the "violent, cannibalistic Mundugumor," and the sex-reversed Tschambuli, respectively.

Imagine a 2 × 2 matrix: aggressivity vs. passivity in males times the same alternatives in females. The dark forces of ethnocentrism and sexism would have had us believe that aggressive-male/passive-female constituted the only possible combination. Suddenly, Mead had demolished that claim by filling in the other three cells of the matrix at a single stroke! What could be neater?

Mead was a major public figure and propagandist for humane causes. For over a decade, *Redbook* magazine ran a popular monthly column called "Margaret Mead answers." The reading public could ask her anything from "Do primitive people keep pets?" to "Is the U.S. State Department right to forbid Americans to travel to Cuba?," and could count on a thoughtful answer. By 1975, 3 years after her death, Mead's bibliography of publications—the books, scientific papers, book reviews, interviews, letters, columns—ran to 1397 items (Gordon, 1976). But Mead's ideological and popularizing goals seriously compromised her ethnographic research, as has recently been made painfully clear by Derek Freeman's (1983) surgical exposé of the fantastic misrepresentation of Samoan culture that constituted Mead's doctoral thesis and made her famous. What then, of her later work in New Guinea? What *did* Margaret Mead observe in those three tribes?

As it happens, Mead published extensively only on the "gentle" Arapesh. She never provided details on who her informants were in the other cultures, nor what they actually told her, let alone present any behavioral data. The bases for the wonderful story of sex-role arbitrariness are entirely contained in the two popular books *Sex and Temperament* and *Male and Female*. Mead's goal, following the "culture and personality" program of her friend and mentor Ruth Benedict, was to characterize each society's "temperament" in broad, artistic strokes. And that she certainly did. Let us consider the three societies, one by one.

Mead insisted that the Arapesh of both sexes were "gentle" and "passive," but whatever these terms were intended to convey, nonviolence was not the point. Mead herself described homicides and spear-throwing battles ("mainly over women"), and somehow the participants in such violence were exclusively male. Subsequent ethnographers, especially Donald Tuzin (1977, 1980), have documented the bloody preoccupations of Arapesh men, and in particular the *obligation* that a young man must commit homicide in order to be initiated into adulthood. Four years after *Sex and Temperament* appeared, Mead's former husband and collaborator, Reo Fortune (1939), published a paper on "Arapesh Warfare" in the *American Anthropologist*. Fortune dramatically illustrated the chronic violence among these "gentle" men, and explicitly contradicted Mead's claim that the Arapesh idealize an identical temperament for men and women. Mead neither changed her story nor refuted Fortune's paper; she simply added it to her reference list.

Enough said about the gentle Arapesh. What about the Mundugumor, of whom Mead (1935) claimed, "Both men and women are expected to be violent, competitive, aggressively sexed, jealous and ready to see and avenge insult, delighting in display, in action, in fighting" (p. 225)? Alas, this is a society much less well documented than the others, and on a return visit in 1973, Mead concluded that the traditional culture had been completely extinguished by missionaries and other modern influences. Neither Mead nor Fortune ever got around to working up their Mundugumor materials for scholarly publication, but there are hints about the nature of male and female violence in Mead's popular books. The men, it seems, were avid polygynists, raiding neighboring tribes for wives, and for heads. Women, of course, did not raid, neither for heads nor for husbands. A young man, but not a woman, was again evidently obliged to kill an enemy before achieving fully adult status.

Though both sexes were "violent in their love-making," Mundugumor women otherwise manifested their violence differently than did men. Mead (1949) writes, for example, that they "express their active aggressive impulses by fishing and eating better than men, or serving dishes tastier than their co-wives [sic] to a common husband" (p. 122). Some further insight into the nature of female violence comes from Mead's (1935) allusion to

> aberrant personalities who are so violent that even Mundugumor standards have no place for them. A man of this sort becomes too continuously embroiled with his fellows, until he may be finally killed. . . . A woman of equal violence, who continually tries to attach new lovers and is insatiable in her demands, may in the end be handed over to another community to be communally raped. (p. 232)

These quotes exhaust the available material on the "violence" of Mundugumor women.

And what, finally, can be said about the "Tschambuli," the remarkable society in which, in Mead's words, "we found a genuine reversal of the sex-attitudes of our culture"? Well, whatever is meant by "sex-attitudes," they do not extend to violent conflict. Like the Arapesh, the Tschambuli (called Chambri in recent literature) have been studied further. Like the other Sepik River societies, they have a long history of warfare, in which they have totally annihilated certain neighboring tribes (Gewertz, 1983). As in all tribal societies, warfare is a male monopoly. As in the Arapesh and the Mundugumor, killing his first enemy is an important milestone in a young man's life. In fact, it entitles him to wear the make-up that Mead found so feminine. So wherein lies the famous sex-reversal? Well, the Tschambuli women are "dominant," insisted Mead (1935), "And yet the men are after all stronger, and a man can beat his wife, and this possibility serves to confuse the whole issue of female dominance" (p. 264).

Indeed.

Biophobia

The "culture and personality" program to which Margaret Mead subscribed is anthropological history. It failed—like so many other failed perspectives in the social sciences—because it overextended a weak analogy between societies and individuals. "A people" does not have "a personality."

Today, Mead's descriptions of the various tribal peoples she studied appear quaintly typological, as must any attempt to characterize the "temperament" of an entire society. Indeed, Mead asserted, without evident awareness of her own ethnocentrism, that the cultural differences between any two neighboring American families were as large as those "between New Guinea tribes." Her research is scarcely cited in anthropological texts nowadays, with the result that many of her professional colleagues considered Freeman's (1983) debunking of her Samoan story to be gratuitous viciousness.

But the myths that Margaret Mead gave us live on, in adjacent disciplines, in journals of opinion, in the American world view. According to a recent survey of 61 current psychology textbooks (Minderhout, 1986), Mead is the most frequently cited anthropologist, and *Sex and Temperament* is her most frequently cited work. She is also the most cited anthropologist in 51 sociology texts (tied with Ruth Benedict).

Mead's "discovery" that differences between the sexes are reversed in other societies created a sensation, and it is impossible to exaggerate its impact upon the attitudes of the educated public. It has been retold in print many hundreds of times, and, like any good tale, it has frequently been embellished in the retelling. Here, for example, is an excerpt from a page-long version, collected from a recent popular book (Nowak, 1980):

> Human nature, the Arapesh believe, is basically peaceful, but people can be taught to be aggressive in the defense of others. When to the wonderment of the Arapesh, some men or women do become violent, the Arapesh resign themselves and try not to provoke these unfortunate souls. (p. 34)

And here (in its entirety) is a short, punchy version, collected from a recent introductory psychology textbook (multiauthored, in the current fashion, so that each section has been written by a specialist in the relevant field) (Schlenker & Severy, 1979):

> Margaret Mead (1949) in her classic work *Males and Females* [sic], describes various New Guinea cultures wherein it is the female who is responsible, makes all the decisions, and is aggressive—with the males being docile, submissive, and homebodies. (p. 518)

"Makes all the decisions" and "homebodies" are timely little touches for the contemporary American scene. Does it really matter that Mead herself made no such claims?

Our point is not to blame the late Dr. Mead for the liberties that others have taken with the myth she created. What is of interest is how *the myth fills a need* for social scientists and commentators. It seems to demonstrate that our social natures are pure cultural artifacts, as arbitrary as the name of the rose, and that we can therefore create any world we want, simply by changing our "socialization practices." (This may sound a remarkably totalitarian vision, but it's not, you see, because the new, improved socialization practices will be designed by *nice* people with everyone's best interests at heart, and not by nasty, self-interested despots.) The social science that is used to legitimize this ideology can only be described as *biophobic*.

We wish we were exaggerating, but we are not. American social scientists fear and despise biology, although few of them have troubled to learn any. We can get a hint about the sources of their biophobia from the following words of Marvin Wolfgang (1978), dean of American criminologists, boosting a sociological approach by disparaging other disciplines:

> Biological needs and psychological drives may be declared uniformly distributed and hence of no utility in explaining one form of behavior relative to another. . . . Neither biology . . . or psychology . . . helps to explain the overwhelming involvement in crime of men over women, slums over suburbs, youth over age, urban over rural life. (p. 87)

Psychologists will take vigorous exception to Wolfgang's caricature of their discipline, and rightly so. "Uniformly distributed drives"? Why, the entire subject matter of psychology has to do with the multitudinous causes of behavioral variation! But will the same psychologists recognize that biology is no less caricatured?

Again and again in the writings of social scientists, we find "biological" equated with "invariant" or "genetic" or "instinctive," and contrasted with "social," with "cultural," with "learned." This usage betrays an incomprehension of the domain of biology. Theoretical and empirical work on social behavior abounds in biological research journals, for example. Developmental biologists are engaged in elucidating how environmental variations interact with and influence the organism as it grows. Behavioral ecologists are concerned with the strategies by which creatures acquire information, that is to say, how they learn, and how they utilize what they have learnt.

Here is a dictionary definition of biology (Morris, 1969):

> The science of life and life processes, including the structure, functioning, growth, origin, evolution, and distribution of living organisms.

That is pretty well what biologists mean by it, too. By this definition, the social sciences are branches of biology, and we think that they would profit by considering themselves to be just that. Our point has nothing to do with interdisciplinary imperialism, nor is it a mere quibble about definitions. The important point is not simply that biology *definitionally* encompasses all the life sciences, but that it provides an encompassing *conceptual* framework, which the social sciences ignore to their disadvantage. Progress in every subfield of what is usually called biology is predicated upon evolutionary insights, and most of it upon an understanding of selection. Little wonder, since selection is the creative process that "designed" organisms and all their constituent parts from cell membranes to minds. As George Williams (1966) has written, "Is it not reasonable to anticipate that our understanding of the human mind would be aided greatly by knowing the purpose for which it was designed?" (p. 16).

Suppose that an archaeologist were advised to study the processes of sedimentation, but refused, scorning geology as "reductionism." The archaeologist's research could, of course, proceed, and some valid conclusions might be attained. But the risk of wasted efforts and nonsensical interpretations would be higher than necessary. The phenomena that archaeologists study are partly the products of well-understood geological processes, and the archaeologist who does not want to know about those processes operates under a self-imposed handicap. Of course, no archaeologist would be so foolish. But the biophobic social scientist is in an analogous position.

Consider the following argument, advanced by an eminent anthropologist (Harris, 1974):

> Knowing only the facts of human anatomy and biology, one could not predict that females would be the socially subordinate sex. . . . If I had knowledge only of the anatomy and cultural capacities of men and women, I would predict that women rather than men would be more likely to gain control over the technology of defense and aggression. . . . I would expect women to concentrate their efforts on rearing solidary and aggressive females rather than males. . . . I would predict that women would monopolize the headship of local groups. . . . Finally, I would expect that the ideal and most prestigious form of marriage would be polyandry—one woman controlling the sexual and economic services of several men. (pp. 84–85)

In this passage, Marvin Harris, leader of the "cultural materialist" school of American anthropology, clearly imagines that he has demonstrated the futility of biologizing. Instead, he has demonstrated his ignorance of evolutionary theory. Armed with the theory of sexual selection that is outlined in this chapter, and with no more knowledge of *Homo sapiens* than that provided by a few skeletons, a biologist from outer space would guess right about every aspect of male–female relations that Harris would get wrong.

Harris's playful "predictions" are indeed in never-never land, but not because of biology's impotence, as he implies; the "predictions" follow not from "anatomy" but from Harris's incomprehension of what the male–female phenomenon is fundamentally about. Why assume, for example, that women should be much *interested* in controlling "the technology of aggression" or "the sexual services of several men"? (A widespread and ironically sexist presumption is that "liberated" women will think and act like men.) Marvin Harris is by no means the only outstanding social scientist suffering from biophobia. What a waste.

On the Causes of Sex Differences

It is our conviction that the biophobia that is rampant in the social sciences is founded more in ignorance than in a reasoned critique of evolutionary theory. But that is not to say that there are no substantive points of contention. There appears to be a genuine difference of opinion about why sex differences like that in Table 7.1 exist.

A popular explanation for sex differences is "culture." A sociologist studying spousal homicide in Canada, for example, echoes Marvin Wolfgang (Chimbos, 1978):

> The marked differences of violent crimes . . . between the sexes . . . can be partly explained in terms of cultural conditioning. For example, in North America, aggressiveness and physical prowess are important to male development while softness and gentleness are emphasized in female development. (p. 21)

But why invoke North American culture to explain a sex difference that is universal? The clear implication of this paragraph is that men would not be more violent than women if "conditioned" by some other culture. No such culture has ever been discovered. It is particularly ironic that both Wolfgang and Chimbos should attribute to North American culture a sex difference (rates of violent crime) that is apparently smaller in modern North America than in any other human society, present or past.

When the same universal sex difference is observed in other societies, it is again likely to be attributed to cultural peculiarities. *Amok,* for example, is a regularly recurring phenomenon in several southeast Asian societies, in which a young man embarks on a frenzied homicidal rampage until killed or subdued. And why don't women do the same? Well, here is the explanation offered by a psychiatrist (Westermeyer, 1973):

> The total absence of amok women from all studies over the last century and a half can perhaps also be understood from the psychosocial perspective. By virtue of their socially subordinate status to men, they have not been so

vulnerable to social upheaval; prestige and a reliable social role are available to them in the home. Where stress does mount, their cultures offer behavioral alternatives which channel anger into nondestructive syndromes such as *latah*. In Laos, where men are expected to keep a "cool heart" in public, women can loudly vent their feelings at home. Thus, women in these cultures appear more able to show hostility in their arena (the home); where they cannot do so, the socially prescribed syndromes do not lead to irremediable violence. (p. 875)

Fine, but homicidal rampages analogous to the amok syndrome are not peculiar to southeast Asia, and mass murderers are invariably men, never women. Have women but not men "socially prescribed" means to "vent their hostile feelings" in *all* societies? Westermeyer's proposed explanation is vacuous.

One more example. An historian encounters the familiar sex difference in homicidal violence in records from 13th-century England, and seeks an explanation in terms of contemporary social practices (Given, 1977):

To an extent, the low level of female participation in homicide, both as killers and victims, may be explained by the different social roles that contemporaries expected the sexes to play. The use of violence was regarded as inappropriate for women. . . . The strong social and cultural inhibitions against the use of force by women as a means of settling disputes is [sic] reflected in the verdicts handed down on women accused of homicides. . . . Women . . . stood a greater chance of being executed. (pp. 134–137)

The trouble with this "explanation" is that women continue to behave far less violently than men when they are the sex that is penalized less severely, as for example in contemporary North America. More generally, the basic strategy of attempting to explain cross-culturally universal phenomena in terms of culturally and historically peculiar causes is surely futile.

In Chapter 1, we briefly outlined Donald Symons's useful analysis of what is at issue beneath the polemics and mutual misunderstandings of the "sociobiology debate." Symons (1987) suggested that "imaginations informed by Darwinism" tend generally to expect that the human brain/mind will comprise a large and complex set of special-purpose behavioral control mechanisms that have been shaped by natural and sexual selection. The alternative view is that the brain/mind is a general-purpose machine guided in its development by the principles of learning and by a few "primary reinforcers." (That, at least, has been the mainstream view within psychology, which is the only social science to have addressed the question of the explicit nature of "socialization" and other ontogenetic processes. Recently, psychologists themselves have become increasingly inclined to postulate a complex repertoire of evolved mental mechanisms; see, for example, Fodor, 1984; Shepherd, 1984; Cosmides, 1985.)

For the case of sex differences, the issue may be stated as follows. Are behavioral sex differences entirely the products of differential personal histories of socially administered reinforcement and sex-role socialization? Or has selection differentially shaped the psyches of males and females by enlisting a variety of sexually differentiated developmental processes other than those that are usually encompassed by the term "socialization"?

Note that this issue has nothing to do with greater or lesser roles of genes or environments as causal agents in development. *All* developmental processes from the single-cell stage to death are *entirely* dependent upon both gene action and environmental influence. Another thing that is not the issue is whether sex-typical behavior happens to be learned. Those phenotypic attributes that arise as a result of "learning" are every bit as susceptible to modification by natural and sexual selection as are those phenotypic attributes that arise by developmental processes that do not happen to include "learning." And finally, it is not the issue whether the causal sequence leading to any particular behavioral difference between women and men can be traced back to a genetic difference, for it always can. It is, after all, a genetic difference between the sexes that is causally antecedent to fetal gonadal differentiation, which is, in turn, causally antecedent to the structural differentiation that allows parents to identify the sex of their child and to socialize it accordingly. It follows that even those sex differences that are induced by arbitrary culture-specific sex-role socialization are nevertheless "traceable to genetic differences." No doubt some readers will think this argument is a semantic trick, but in fact, this is all that is *ever* meant by the claim that some trait is "genetic": There is some sort of chain of causal links from the alternative traits back to alternative genotypes.

Let us approach sex differences in another way. If, for some reason, it were our ambition to eliminate the behavioral differences between women and men, what sort of ontogenetic engineering would be likely to achieve the desired end? Would treating girls and boys alike make them similar in adulthood, or would we have to treat them differently?

The conventional wisdom in the social sciences is the former: that men and women are not psychologically different except by virtue of having been treated differently. However, several lines of evidence suggest that this is unlikely to be true. We know, for example, that males and females behave differently in ways that are not merely cross-culturally consistent, but are furthermore just as one would predict from sexual selection theory and from the morphological dimorphism of our particular species. These sex differences include not only the violence illustrated in Table 7.1, but various aspects of interactions between the sexes as well (see, e.g., Symons, 1979; Daly & Wilson, 1983). We also know that gonadal hormones are secreted according to different schedules in young males and females, and that such patterns of secretion influence the developing brain in every animal in which the matter has been studied experimentally (e.g., MacLusky & Naftolin, 1981); of course, such experiments have not been done on people. We know that the sexes differ in a number of perceptual and information-processing domains that are difficult to attribute to sex-role socialization. Little boys exhibit significantly longer postrotatory nystagmus than little girls (Crowe, Deitz, & Siegner, 1984), to take a recent, arbitrary example; men process materials presented to their left versus right visual half-fields at different speeds whereas women do not, for another (Heister, 1984). We do not know much about the functional significance of these differences, if any, nor much about their implications for sex-typical cognitive styles, but it would be rash to assume that there are *no* such implications.

Moreover, people have begun to discover anatomical differences between the brains of women and men, too (e.g., Swaab & Fliers, 1985). The most dramatic such difference to date is the much larger posterior corpus callosum in females (Lacoste-Utamsing & Holloway, 1982), a morphological difference that is apparent before birth, and that might well have been predicted from the mounting evidence that women have superior interhemispheric communication while men's cortical functions are more lateralized (see McGlone, 1980).

On the other side of the issue, the direct evidence for an important influence of sex-role socialization upon sexually differentiated behavior is astonishingly thin (see, e.g., Pleck, 1981). In fairness, it must be remarked that the problem is one of exceptional methodological difficulty. If parents punish boys more than girls, for example, or assign more child-care duties to girls, it may be that the parents are reacting to behavioral sex differences at least as much as they are creating them. Indeed, in these particular examples, there is evidence that boys are punished more because they transgress more, and that boys are less likely than girls to comply with parental requests to mind younger siblings, so that parents eventually prefer to assign such tasks to the more willing daughters (see, e.g., Maccoby & Jacklin, 1974).

A recent study of parental behavior and later intellectual skills of the children (Bee *et al.*, 1984) speaks directly to the issue as we stated it above. In this study, individual differences in early parental behavior were found to be predictive of individual differences in the children's later performance, with the child's sex proving to be an important variable in a possibly surprising way. Parents did not treat the sexes differently, but within sexes, the ways in which measures of parental behavior were predictive of the child's subsequent performance were different for girls than for boys. As the authors of this study (Bee *et al.*, 1984) conclude, "The combination of these two groups of findings—lack of difference on measures of environment and parent-child interaction, and the presence of differences in prediction—suggest that the same experiences produce different effects for boys and girls" (p. 783).

The last four paragraphs have outlined a number of empirical reasons why it would be very surprising to discover that men's and women's psyches develop similarly except as a result of differential sex-role socialization. But there is a still more powerful reason to doubt this conventional wisdom. The fitness of males and females is differentially affected by numerous variables. (One obvious example is what Bateman, 1948, called "the greater dependence of males for their fertility on frequency of insemination.") If the conventional wisdom were true— that is, if the psyches of women and men have *not* been differentially shaped by selection—then someone has to explain *why* not. Why should patterns of differential reproduction have been without selective consequences in this one sphere, namely behavioral sex differences, when they have so clearly been effective in shaping morphological sex differences, and in shaping those aspects of behavioral control systems that are not sexually differentiated?

So the problem with the conventional wisdom as a scientific theory is not just that there is little evidence in favor of it and much that speaks against it. The even bigger problem is that no theoretical framework has yet been proposed within which a sexually *un*differentiated psychology would be anticipated, or even explicable. Why, then, is this incoherent and unsupported theory still popular? A partial answer is the biological illiteracy of most social scientists, which interacts with an ideological reason: By virtue of their equating biology with "determinism," many social scientists are motivated to denigrate all biologically informed approaches to the study of sex differences. Fortunately, this biophobia is on the wane, but the improbable idea of a sexually undifferentiated psychology is still textbook fare, where it is regularly asserted not as hypothesis but as dogma. We believe that such assertions are motivated not by scientific reasoning, good or bad, but by good intentions and bad philosophy combining to produce the conviction that human equality (a moral objective) somehow rests upon human equipotentiality.

The developmental causes of sex differences may be legitimately controversial, but the fact of difference is not. Whatever is eventually discovered about the sources of sex differences—and whatever it would take to engineer a rearing environment in which behavioral sex differences were abolished—this much is clear: *Intrasexual competition is far more violent among men than among women in every human society for which information exists.*

The Logic of
Same-Sex Conflict

— 8 —

Men become embroiled in dangerous competitive interactions far more often than do women. This is a sex difference that we share with other effectively polygynous mammals, and there is no mystery about why this should be so: As we saw in Chapter 7, the sex difference in fitness variance means that mammalian males typically compete for bigger prizes than do females. Bigger prizes warrant bigger gambles.

As the variance in individual fitness associated with competitive success or failure increases—as the outcomes for winners and losers become more disparate—the temptation to resort to dangerous competitive tactics is also likely to increase. A simulation model may clarify this point for some readers, and so we present such a model in the following box. The simulation, with its arbitrary parameters, is not a realistic description of a competitive situation. Rather, it is intended to demonstrate in principle that the competitive strategy that is favored by natural selection can vary according to the exact relationship between competitive success and fitness. In particular, selection may favor behavior that is increasingly dangerous, both to one's opponent and to one's self, as fitness differentials increase.

Throughout human history, the winners have got the women, and the biggest winners—Moulay Ismael the Bloodthirsty is an extreme case—have got the most women. But when we consider the psychology of dangerous risk-taking, what is possibly even more crucial than the chance of winning big is the high probability of losing totally. Any creature that is recognizably on track toward complete reproductive failure must somehow expend effort, often at risk of death, to try to improve its present life trajectory. If, for example, the energetic return from foraging in a predator-free area is sufficient to maintain oneself but insufficient to breed, then the only foragers to leave descendants will be those willing to forage outside the predator-free area, even though they must therefore incur some predation risk. If one's present status guarantees lifelong exclusion from mating opportunities, then one must strive to raise that status. Wilson and Herrnstein (1985) have suggested

Box 8.1
Fitness Payoffs of Risky Competition: A Simulation

This simulation illustrates the increasing utility of dangerous competitive tactics as the prize for victory increases. The parameters have no real-life significance, but were chosen for expository convenience.

In the simulation, each individual possesses one of three possible competitive strategies: *high-risk, medium-risk, low-risk*. Competitive interactions take the form of fights between two individuals. In every fight, there is one winner. The other contestant may simply lose, or may be killed.

When two low-risk individuals fight, each has a 0.5 probability of winning and there is no risk of death. A riskier strategy raises its practitioner's chance of winning, but also raises both contestants' chances of being killed. Thus, for example, a medium-risk individual has a 0.6 probability of winning a fight with a low-risk individual, but each contestant also has a 0.05 probability of death. The complete matrix of outcome probabilities is this:

—continued—

Risk type		A's outcome			B's outcome		
A	B	Win	Lose	Die	Win	Lose	Die
High	High	.50	.10	.40	.50	.10	.40
High	Med.	.60	.10	.30	.40	.30	.30
High	Low	.70	.10	.20	.30	.50	.20
Med.	High	.40	.30	.30	.60	.10	.30
Med.	Med.	.50	.40	.10	.50	.40	.10
Med.	Low	.60	.35	.05	.40	.55	.05
Low	High	.30	.50	.20	.70	.10	.20
Low	Med.	.40	.55	.05	.60	.35	.05
Low	Low	.50	.50	.00	.50	.50	.00

The simulation begins with a first generation of 60 individuals: 20 of each risk-type. Everyone starts with a score of 0. Pairs of surviving individuals are randomly selected to fight, and the fight's result is generated randomly according to the probabilities in the above matrix. The winner gets one point added to his score, and the loser gets one subtracted. This process continues until either 90 fights have been completed or only 10 survivors remain. The survivors are then the parents of the next generation of 60 individuals, according to a rule relating competitive success to fitness. This rule is what is varied below.

—continued—

Offspring inherit the parental risk-type (as in asexual reproduction, or a trait carried on a Y chromosome). Any risk-type may thus gain or lose in numerical representation from one generation to the next. The entire process is repeated, generation after generation, until the population consists entirely of a single risk-type ("fixation") and the other two are extinct.

Rule 1. Survivors: All surviving individuals have equal fitness.

Twenty simulations were run with this rule and the low-risk strategy went to fixation every time (requiring anywhere from 18 to 57 generations to do so). This result should not be surprising. The only objective under this rule is survival. A loss is as good as a win. There is therefore no utility in taking risks in order to win.

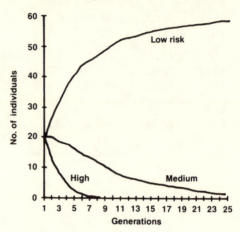

Rule 2. Winning survivors: All survivors with a positive score (i.e., wins exceed losses) have equal fitness.

This rule is perhaps analogous to a territorial system, in which some individuals hold a resource that permits monogamous breeding status, and others do not. There is no premium on running up a large positive score, but one must win at least one more contest than one loses. Twenty simulations were run with this rule and the medium-risk strategy went to fixation 18 times, with each of the others going to fixation once.

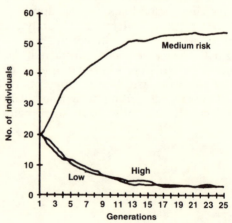

—continued—

Rule 3. <u>Linear</u>: Survivors with a positive score have fitness proportional to that score.

This rule is more like a dominance hierarchy with greater fitness the reward for a higher
aggressive ranking. Twenty simulations were run with this rule.
The high-risk strategy went to
fixation 9 times, and the medium-risk strategy 11 times.

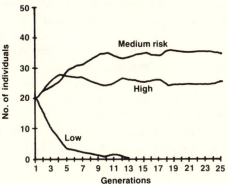

Rule 4. <u>Squared</u>: Survivors with a positive score have fitness proportional to the square of that score.

This rule raises the premium
on victory still higher, producing
the greatest fitness variance yet.
Twenty simulations were run
with this rule, and the high-risk
strategy went to fixation 16
times, the medium-risk strategy 4
times.

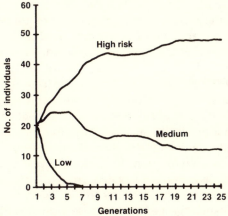

What this simulation shows is that selection can favor relatively
risky competitive strategies despite substantial mortality costs.
Under all four rules, high-risk individuals experienced the highest
mortality during the fighting phase, and low-risk individuals
experienced the lowest mortality. But surviving the fighting phase
is only the first step to fitness, and the payoffs for high positive
scores can offset the mortality risks. The same principle applies to
competition in the real world.

that men who engage in predatory violence and other risky criminal activity have different "time-horizons" than law-abiding men, weighing the near future relatively heavily against the long term. Several lines of evidence support this idea. What Wilson and Herrnstein do not emphasize is that such adjustment of one's personal time-horizons is probably an adaptive response to predictive information about one's prospects for longevity and eventual success.

Natural selection will especially tend to favor risk-proneness in circumstances where one's anticipated life trajectory, in the absence of risk, is so poor that one has little or no expected fitness to lose. As a particular example of this general proposition, dangerous competitive tactics are predicted to be especially prevalent within those demographic categories in which the probability of reproductive failure is high.

The Demography of Homicide

Figure 8.1 presents the risk of becoming involved in a homicide in Canada, either as killer or victim, as a function of age and sex. The sex difference in homicidal violence requires no further discussion, but what about age? Killing is concentrated among young men, and so, to a lesser extent, is the risk of *being* killed. Men appear to be most conflictual in late adolescence and young adulthood, a life stage at which competitive striving to achieve status, resources, and marriageability has surely been essential in historical societies, and probably still is. It may be argued, then, that a willingness to resort to violence has been most strongly favored in the age–sex class that has historically experienced the most intense sexual selection. Conversely, however, one might argue that where two men find themselves similarly disenfranchised—unemployed, broke, isolated from relatives—that it is the *older*, not the younger, who has less to lose and should therefore be readier to resort to such dangerous tactics as armed robbery or violent confrontation.

An empirically based choice between these alternative Darwinian models is not so easily achieved as one might initially suppose. It is clear that young men are more *often* violent than their elders, and many writers have implied that this difference reflects a maturational change in inclinations and attitudes. But of course *circumstances* change over the life span, too. If celibacy and childlessness, for example, are circumstantial factors contributing to risk-proneness, then the proportion of men who are risk-prone will decline with age simply because the proportions unwed and childless decline. Whether there is a significant aging effect upon risk-proneness and violence, over and above the effects of

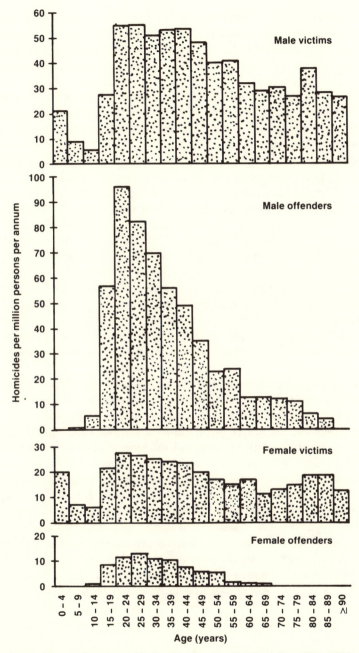

Figure 8.1. Age- and sex-specific homicide rates in Canada, 1974–1983.

circumstantial variables associated with age, is a question that is wide open for future research and well worth pursuing.

It would be extremely interesting to know to what extent a man's risk-proneness declines when he becomes a father, if at all. Unfortunately, information on the incidence of fatherhood—either in the population-at-large or in such criterion groups as homicide offenders— is nonexistent. Some other demographic variables that may be related to present and expected fitness can be assessed, however, namely employment status and marital status.

Our study of homicide in Detroit in 1972 provides the best available information on the relationships of various demographic factors to the chance of becoming involved in a homicide. The age- and sex-specific rates of such involvement are shown in Figure 8.2. The distributions are roughly similar in shape to those for Canada (Figure 8.1), but note that the rates are substantially higher. Note too that the Detroit male victimization rate is more conspicuously age-dependent than the Canadian male victimization rate. Indeed, Detroit victim and offender distributions look very similar to one another, a fact that reflects the prevalence of "trivial altercations" (see Chapter 6) in this sample. In Detroit in 1972, 43% of adult male homicide victims and 41% of adult male offenders were unemployed, compared to 11.2% of all adult men in the city (Figure 8.3). Sixty-nine percent of adult male victims and 73% of adult male offenders were unmarried, compared to 43% of all adult men in the city (Figure 8.4). Thus, it is indeed the case that circumstantial variables are related to the probability of becoming involved in lethal violence, even in comparisons within an age–sex class.

The victim and offender populations are remarkably alike, and this similarity extends to other variables too. Among both male victims and male offenders, 36% had previous criminal records (excluding convictions for motor vehicle violations, drunkenness, and narcotics offenses). The high proportion of altercations among these homicides is largely responsible for this similarity between killers and victims: In this most prevalent type of conflict leading to homicide in Detroit, the hostilities are reciprocal, and it is often an open question which party will end up dead. But of course not all homicides involve such reciprocity, and further analysis of the factors associated with becoming a "participant" in homicide will require some differentiation of motive categories.

The Problem of "Motive"

"Altercation of relatively trivial origin; insult, curse, jostling, etc." That was Wolfgang's (1958) characterization of the predominant "mo-

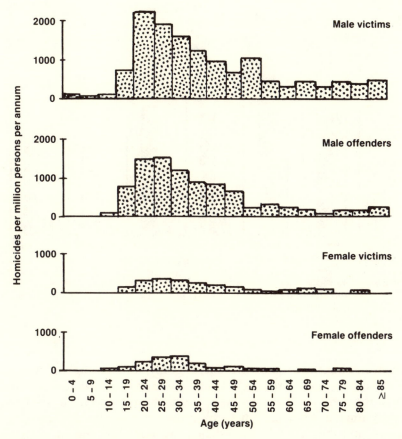

Figure 8.2. Age- and sex-specific rates of homicide in Detroit, 1972. (From Wilson & Daly, 1985.)

tive" in American homicide, and all subsequent students of the subject have been influenced by his categories. The description of altercations and the recognition of their prevalence were important insights, but it is debatable whether they have truly illuminated the question of motive, or have instead deflected attention away from that question.

The essence of the "altercation" category is the spontaneity of the dispute, its interactive face-to-face character, and its uninterrupted development to a dénouement. These elements are crucial to police and prosecutors, because of the paramount issues of "premeditation" and "provocation" in determining the charge under which a homicide can be successfully prosecuted. If a verbal insult provokes a direct violent

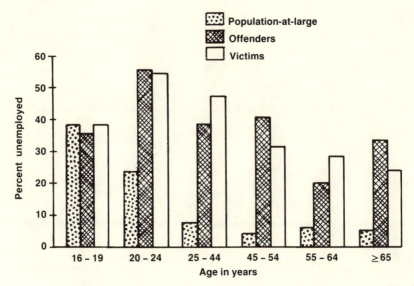

Figure 8.3. Unemployment rates among male homicide offenders, male victims, and the male population-at-large in Detroit, 1972. (From Wilson & Daly, 1985.)

response, for example, then the killer is guilty of manslaughter at most, and the motive will be recorded as an "argument" or "altercation." But should the identical insult inspire its recipient to brood for a week and then to ambush his antagonist, the prosecutor can bring a charge of murder, and the case will be assigned to some other motive category such as "revenge." Thus, the category of "altercations" cuts across more substantive issues.

The motive categories that Wolfgang invented for his Philadelphia study are listed in Table 8.1. His list has certain virtues: The categories are broad enough to encompass most cases, and they have a certain face validity, corresponding roughly to the recurring "types" of cases that experienced homicide detectives recognize as familiar. But Wolfgang's list is a conceptual hodgepodge. His two leading categories do not refer to the substantive issues at all, and "domestic quarrel" is the only "motive" on the list that is *defined* by the particular relationship between killer and victim. Even the more substantive issues are problematic because of the way they cross-cut other motives. Sexual rivalry and/or infidelity are apparently at issue in all 68 "jealousy" cases, for example, but this same substantive issue could also be the point in a case

Figure 8.4. Proportions unmarried among male homicide offenders, male victims, and the male population-at-large in Detroit, 1972. (From Wilson & Daly, 1985.)

categorized as a "domestic quarrel" or an "altercation of relatively trivial origin."

Wolfgang's unsatisfactory taxonomy of motives remains pretty much the state of the art. Most subsequent students of homicide have adopted his categories, have modified them slightly, or have ignored the question altogether. The upshot is that the prevailing criminological conception of motives in homicide is a woolly amalgam of several potentially independent dimensions: spontaneity versus premeditation, the victim–offender relationship, and only a relatively small dose of those substantive issues that murder mystery writers and ordinary speakers of English mean when they speak of "the motive." This unsatisfactory state of affairs exists partly because the popular conception of a motive is primarily appropriate to premeditated murders, and not to the sort of reactive, unplanned assaults that produce most homicides. In a murder mystery, the question of motive is "Why did Killer want Victim dead?" In real life, Killer often did not especially want Victim dead at all, or at least did not approach the conflict in those terms. Nevertheless, simply because a homicide occurs spontaneously

Table 8.1. Motive Categories and the Number of Cases (Victims)
Within Each, for 588 Criminal Homicides in the City of
Philadelphia, 1948–1952[a]

"Motive"	Number of cases	Percentage of total
Altercation of relatively trivial origin; insult, curse, jostling, etc.	206	35.0
Domestic quarrel	83	14.1
Jealousy	68	11.6
Altercation over money	62	10.5
Robbery	40	6.8
Revenge	31	5.3
Accidental	23	3.9
Self-defense	8	1.4
Halting of felon	7	1.2
Escaping arrest	6	1.0
Concealing birth	6	1.0
Other	20	3.4
Unknown	28	4.8

[a]From Wolfgang (1958).

and with questionable intent to kill, it does not follow that "altercation"
or "domestic quarrel" is an adequate characterization of the dispute.
Violence arises from conflicts *about something*, difficult though it may be
to pinpoint exactly what, and notwithstanding the fact that the bones of
contention may be multiple.

Insult and Redress

The last sentence requires a minor qualification. Some homicides are
so impersonal that there can hardly be said to have been a "conflict"
between the parties. The clearest such example is the robbery–murder in
which the killer and the victim are complete strangers. If we wish to
examine the substance of dangerous interpersonal conflicts and the
characteristics of those who become embroiled in them, then it is
appropriate to separate out these impersonal, nonconflictual cases, that
is to say those cases in which the victim played no active interpersonal
role in precipitating his own demise. This objective is hard to achieve in
practice, but it has been approximated where a dichotomous classifica-

Table 8.2. Five Hundred Twelve Closed Homicide Cases in the City of Detroit, 1972, Classified by the Type of Case and by the Victim-Offender Relationship[a]

Victim-offender relationship	Type of case		
	Crime-specific	Social conflict	Unknown
Genealogical relatives	1	31	0
Spouses	1	79	0
Marital relatives (affine, step)	0	15	0
Friends or acquaintances	47	193	3
Strangers	119	19	0
Unknown	0	2	2
Total	168	339	5

[a]From Wilson and Daly (1985), Table 1.

tion has been drawn between "social conflict" cases and those incidental to the commission of another crime (which usually means robbery).

Just such a classification—"social conflict" versus "crime-specific"—was employed by sociologist Marie Wilt (1974) in her study of the 690 homicides that occurred in Detroit in 1972, a study that preceded our own research on the same cases. Out of 512 solved cases, about one-third were adjudged to have been crime-specific, and about two-thirds to have been social conflicts (Table 8.2).

Wilt originally classified the Detroit social conflict cases into four categories, which she had derived not from any particular theory but simply from a preliminary reading of 100 cases. These four types she referred to as "jealousy conflicts," "business conflicts," "family conflicts," and "arguments between friends, acquaintances, or neighbors." Like Wolfgang's categories, then, Wilt's were an uneasy mixture: partly defined by the substance of the dispute, and partly by the relationship between the parties. For that reason, we retained her substantive categories of "jealousy" and "business," but then tried to classify the remaining cases under similarly substantive issues. The resulting classification is shown in Table 8.3.

More than half of the cases summarized in Table 8.3 (124 of 212) fall into one of the first two categories, both of which may be considered matters of status competition and the maintenance of face. These are homicide motives that we discussed at some length in Chapter 6. Most

Table 8.3. Two Hundred Twelve Closed Social Conflict Homicides in
Detroit, 1972, in Which Victim and Offender Were Unre-
lated (Friends, Acquaintances or Strangers), Classified by
Conflict Typology and by the Sexes of the Principals[a]

Conflict typology	Male killed male	Male killed female	Female killed male	Female killed female
Escalated showing-off contests	26	0	2	1
Retaliation for previous verbal or physical abuse	75	9	6	5
Jealousy conflicts	20	5	6	3
Business conflicts	10	1	2	0
Intervention in family dispute	5	0	0	0
Miscellaneous unique disputes	2	0	1	1
Insufficient information	26	4	1	1
Total social conflicts among nonrelatives	164	19	18	11

[a]From Wilson and Daly (1985), Table 3.

of these 124 cases would probably have been categorized by Wolfgang
and other criminologists influenced by him as "altercations of relatively
trivial origin," although a few would certainly have been labeled
"revenge." The flavor of these quarrels can best be captured by a few
brief synopses.

What we have called an "escalated showing-off contest" involves two
or more individuals trying to best one another before an audience of
mutual acquaintances. There were no such cases in which the dispu-
tants were related to one another. Here are two illustrative synopses,
based on Wilt's summaries of the police documentation:

> Case 121: The victim (a male, age 19), the offender (male, 23), and others
> were drinking and bantering together at an acquaintance's home. The
> victim was a boxer, and was talking about his fights. The offender was
> carrying a night stick, which he placed between the victim's legs, and
> then lifted the latter off the ground. The victim, embarrassed, had to ask
> to be let down, then accused the offender of tearing his pants and
> demanded that the offender pay for them. The latter laughed at this
> demand, and so did some of the other men in the room, whereupon the
> victim struck the offender, and both were asked to leave. The victim left
> first, and waited on the porch, where the offender maintains that he was

again struck as he exited, whereupon he produced a gun and killed the
teen-age boxer.

> Case 185: The victim (male, age 22) and the offender (male, age 41) were in
> a bar when a mutual acquaintance walked in. The older man began to
> brag about the newcomer's fighting ability and, by implication, his own.
> The victim picked up on this implication, and turned the discussion into
> an argument about which of the two was the better man. When the
> argument became heated, the victim was reported by witnesses to have
> pointed to the gun in his pocket and said "I got mine," whereupon the
> offender indicated his own pocket and replied "I got mine too." To that,
> the victim reportedly said, "I don't want to die and I know you don't
> want to die. Let's forget about it." But the offender produced a small
> automatic, shot the younger man dead, and left the bar.

Such escalated showing-off disputes as these are overwhelmingly a
male affair, as one would expect from Chapter 7's discussion of sex
differences in the intensity of intrasexual competition. The two cases in
which a woman killed a man (Table 8.3) both occurred as a result of the
woman's intervening in a heated showing-off dispute between two
men, killing one in defense of the other. Thus, 28 cases involved
escalated showing-off contests between men, a single case involved
such a contest between two women, and no cases involved showing-off
contests between people of opposite sex.

The category that accounts for the largest number of cases in Table
8.3, namely "retaliation for previous verbal or physical abuse," is a little
more heterogeneous. It includes retaliation for insults, for accusations of
cheating or theft, and for physical attacks at some time past. The
unifying feature of these cases is the affront or public humiliation that
seems to demand redress if face is to be maintained. One such example
is this brief synopsis:

> Case 79: The victim (a male, age 23) accused the offender (male, age 17) of
> having broken into his home, and then gave the teenager a beating. The
> latter left, got a gun from a friend, returned and killed his assailant before
> several witnesses.

A somewhat similar case, though with a merely verbal provocation,
involved two pairs of brothers:

> Case 324: The victim (a male, age 25), walking along a street with his
> brother, directed an insulting remark at a pair of brothers (ages 20 & 22).
> When the latter pair responded aggressively, the victim and his brother
> withdrew and went home. The insulted parties got guns and waited in
> ambush for the other pair to re-emerge, whereupon the victim was killed
> and his brother wounded.

Clearly, there is every intermediate gradation between the impulsive rage reaction of an "altercation" and the "cold-blooded revenge murder," although the classification as one or the other can have enormous impact upon the legal penalty that is imposed. Revenge is a topic to which we shall return in Chapter 10.

Robbery Homicides

The fact that men are prepared to compete dangerously for intangible social resources like status and face has puzzled many commentators. But the fact that men use violence to acquire more tangible *material* resources apparently surprises no one. In fact, robbery homicide is widely construed as such a temptation to the reasoning man that it requires especially severe penalties to deter it. (Whether this oft-stated rationale is the real reason or not, robbery homicides are indeed punished much more severely than altercations and other less overtly utilitarian homicides.) Yet without a Darwinian framework, the facts about robbery homicides are really no more intelligible than the facts about "trivial altercations."

The reason for this claim is the enormous sex difference in robbery homicides, and indeed in robbery generally. If theft were related simply to penury, then the majority of thieves would be women. But that is nowhere the case. In the United States in 1985, according to the FBI's most recent Uniform Crime Reports, 92.3% of robberies were committed by males, as were 92.3% of burglaries (U.S. Department of Justice, 1986). American men are certainly not poorer than American women, but they help themselves to other people's property more often. This sex difference in property crime is evidently a cross-cultural universal (Bacon, Child, & Barry, 1963).

In our Detroit sample, the killers in "crime-specific" homicides were even more often male (95% of 134 cases) than were "social conflict" offenders (75% of 337 cases). Moreover, the seven crime-specific homicides committed by women included four in self-defense against male burglars or attempted rapists, leaving just three cases in which the woman was the party engaged in criminal activity. Similarly, in our 10-year Canadian sample, men were the killers in 96% of 454 solved cases in which the motive was reported to Statistics Canada as "robbery, theft."

Not only were the crime-specific offenders in Detroit more often male than the social conflict offenders, but they also matched the demographic profile of a typical risk-taker more closely: The crime-specific male killers were younger (mean = 27.8 years) than their social conflict counterparts (mean = 34.2), were more often unemployed (43.6 vs. 38.9%), and were more often unmarried (73.8 vs. 57.8%).

What are we to make of the fact that robbery homicide is even more male-dominated than homicide generally, indeed that it is a male monopoly? Men's minimum needs for survival and sustenance are hardly greater than those of women, and the men of Detroit are certainly no more likely to be desperately poor than their female counterparts. But in a paternally investing species such as our own, males gain reproductive success by commanding and displaying resources that exceed their own subsistence needs. We suggest that the chronic competitive situation among males is ultimately responsible for that sex's greater felt need for surplus resources with which to quell rivals and attract mates.

It is also noteworthy how few of the *victims* of robbery homicide are women. In Canada, for example, only 20.3% of 626 murdered robbery victims between 1974 and 1983 were females. If these cases were simply to be understood as the violent appropriation of other people's money, then we might expect male offenders to pick on women fairly often. In fact, women *are* frequent robbery victims. Although only 7 of Detroit's 49 *murdered* robbery victims in 1972 were female, Detroit women were victims of *non*homicidal theft exactly as often as men (Wilson & Daly, 1985). There are several possible reasons for this. Perhaps men are more often killed because they resist robbery more strenuously than women, either because of the same "felt need" that motivates the robber, or because men typically carry larger sums. But at least part of the explanation for the much greater number of male victims seems to lie in the fact that robbery homicides contain some of the same confrontational elements of face and male rivalry that characterize "trivial altercations": Male robbery victims sometimes resist recklessly because they cannot tolerate the affront of being dominated and humiliated by another man (e.g., Toch, 1969).

Sexual Rivalry

In any sexually reproducing species in which the females make a large investment of time and energy in the welfare of their offspring, the males inevitably compete for the opportunity to fertilize females and thus to profit (in fitness) from those maternal efforts. Because of the phenomena of internal gestation, placentation, and lactation, male sexual rivalry is endemic to the 4000 or so species of the class Mammalia, including ourselves.

In most mammalian species, males make no conspicuous contribution to the welfare or development of their offspring after conception. Whereas the reproductive efforts of females are overwhelmingly concentrated upon the rearing of young, males put their reproductive effort into mating competition, status competition, and courtship (not to mention harassment!) of females. However, in a substantial minority of mammals—scattered across the various orders from rodents to primates—females and males cooperate in parental care. *Homo sapiens* is one such species.

Mammalian fathers who are about to make paternal contributions confront a problem that mothers are spared, a problem so serious that it largely explains why most mammalian fathers opt out of paternal investment altogether. That problem is the uncertainty of paternity. Wherever fertilization occurs inside the female's body and is therefore cryptic, a paternally investing male is at risk of *cuckoldry:* the fertilization of his mate by a rival and the consequent squandering of his paternal efforts to the benefit of some other male's fitness and not his own. As we saw in Chapter 3, the suspicion or knowledge of nonpaternity is considered grounds for infanticide in a number of societies. And as we saw in Chapter 4, children with men other than their natural fathers *in loco paternis* experience a greatly elevated risk of abuse and death in our own society, even though there is no articulated norm justifying or demanding such discrimination against stepchildren.

The fact of paternal investment has a complicated influence upon male sexual rivalry. On the one hand, those mammals in which males play a major parental role—wolves, marmosets, and beavers are all examples—tend generally to form monogamous pairs. In the absence of a highly polygynous breeding system, the variance in male fitness is not extreme, approximating that of females, and the intensity of face-to-face mating competition is therefore reduced. One result is that the males are not morphologically specialized for combat in these monogamous, paternally investing species, and are in fact hardly discriminable in basic body plan from the females. (*Homo sapiens* is clearly not an exemplary monogamist, but we lie closer to that end of a monogamy-polygyny dimension than to such polygynous, dimorphic creatures as baboons, say, or bison.) The practice of paternal investment, by reapportioning male reproductive effort away from mating competition, tends to reduce both the fitness prize for high rank and the risk of total reproductive failure. Biparental care of the young thus softens male–male conflict and selects for less dangerous competitive tactics. That is one side of the story.

On the other hand, the fact of paternal investment makes cuckoldry a much more serious matter than simply losing a particular fertilization to a competitor. In a promiscuous mating system without paternal investment, a male tries to maximize potentially fertile matings, and he may also try to interfere directly with those of his rivals. Some he wins and some he loses, but it is seldom worth his while to *completely* guarantee his paternity of a particular female's young by guarding her throughout her potentially fertile period, or at least it will not be worth his while if such guarding can only be achieved by neglecting other potentially receptive females. Nor is the male in such a mating system likely to be unresponsive to a female who has just mated with another male and may already have been fertilized: Although he might prefer an unmated female with a higher expected return for his courtship and copulatory efforts, there is no huge selective premium upon discriminating the one female from the other. (Indeed the fact that a female has mated with another male can actually be sexually arousing, probably because the male who is thus aroused has a better chance in sperm competition with his predecessor; see Smith, 1984.) But the situation is quite different in those species in which the male will later behave paternally, eventually investing far more of his time and energy in the care of his presumed offspring than he did in conceiving them. For such a male, maximizing the number of progeny is no longer the only objective; if his later parental efforts are to be deployed to his own advantage, he must also be concerned to correctly identify those progeny. It follows that *paternal investment places a selective premium upon male sexual jealousy*, that is to say a concern that his sexual access to his mate be *exclusive*.

Investing fathers have evolved various behavioral inclinations that have the effect of reducing the risk of cuckoldry and misdirected paternal investment. (Most relevant research has been conducted on birds, among whom biparental care is much more common than among mammals.) Females betraying the possibility of prior fertilization may be discriminated against as potential mates, for example, as has been demonstrated in doves (Erickson & Zenone, 1976). More commonly, the male guards his mate closely throughout the period in which she is potentially fertile. A male starling never lets his mate out of his sight during those few days of the nesting cycle when a copulation might bear fruit, even though his guarding of the female means both that the initiation of incubation is delayed and that the nest is left unguarded and vulnerable to egg-dumping by brood parasites; both before and after the female's fertile period, the nesting pair divides the task of nest attendance and spends many hours apart (Power, Litovich, & Lombardo, 1981).

Homo sapiens exhibits a complex of psychological propensities that achieve the same end, namely improving the probability that a man's putative offspring are indeed his own. We have referred to this motivational–emotional–behavioral complex as "male sexual jealousy" (Daly, Wilson, & Weghorst, 1982), but a better label might be *male sexual proprietariness*. It is manifested in the dogged inclination of men to control the activities of women, and in the male perspective according to which sexual access and woman's reproductive capacity are *commodities* that men can "own" and exchange. This proprietary point of view is furthermore inextricably bound up with the use or threat of violence in order to achieve and maintain sexual exclusivity and control. Although many authors have argued that sexual jealousy is an artifact of particular cultures and is absent from at least a few, the ethnographic evidence supports the alternative view, namely that the complex described above is cross-culturally universal; we shall consider the evidence on this point at some length in Chapter 9, when we examine spousal violence.

"Fearful or wary of being supplanted; apprehensive of loss of position or affection." That is a dictionary definition of "jealous" (Morris, 1969). Behavioral manifestations of jealousy vary from violence to vigilance, and the emotional content of jealousy ranges from anger to fear to depression. Thus, jealousy can be defined neither as a specific emotion, nor by specific acts. The word refers to an internal *state* that is aroused by a perceived threat to a valued relationship, and motivates behavior aimed at countering the threat. Jealousy is "sexual" if the valued relationship is sexual.

A Darwinian perspective upon sexual jealousy suggests the hypothesis that it will prove to be a *sexually differentiated* state in people and other biparental mammals because of the asymmetrical risk of cuckoldry. While women may be expected to be jealous of their mates' allocation of attention and resources, for example, they do not have the same rationale as men have for being concerned with specifically *sexual* fidelity.

So is jealousy indeed sexually differentiated as theory leads us to expect? Well, *violent* manifestations of jealousy exhibit an enormous sex difference—indeed, male sexual jealousy far surpasses female sexual jealousy as a homicide motive the world 'round, and is by far the leading motive in spousal homicides, as we shall see in Chapter 9. But of course men are more violent than women generally, and so their greater violence in this sphere does not necessarily imply a sex difference in jealousy. Studies that have attempted to characterize the *quality* of women's and men's jealousy are more to the point. Unfortunately, these are few, and are confined primarily to the western world.

American men and women do not appear to differ in their likelihood of admitting to jealousy. Among 66 male and 102 female college students in a study by Bryson (1976), for example, only one subject reported that she had never felt jealous. But although both sexes experience jealousy, just what they experience evidently differs. Bryson (1976, 1977) found several sex differences in subjects' descriptions of the feelings associated with jealousy. Shettel-Neuber, Bryson, and Young (1978) had students describe their own probable behavior in a jealousy-inducing situation portrayed on videotape. Men considered themselves more likely to become angry, drunk, threatening, and aroused than did women, and more likely to start going out with others. Women, on the other hand, were more likely to anticipate crying, feigning indifference, or striving to increase their attractiveness.

Among these American social psychological studies of jealousy, the one most relevant to a Darwinian analysis of jealousy was an unpublished Ph.D. thesis by Mark Teismann (1975) at the University of Connecticut. Teismann had his subjects—young American couples who were unmarried but were dating one another—"role-play" a hypothetical jealousy-inducing situation in one of two sexually symmetrical forms, namely a confrontation between the couple over a possible infidelity of one partner or the other. The subjects were asked to report the feelings that this pretense aroused. The most striking result was a large sex difference in the reported substance of the jealous experience. The men found themselves afflicted with fantasies of sexual contact between partner and rival, whereas the women were primarily concerned with their boyfriends' expending time, money, and attention upon the rival female. This is, of course, just the sort of sex difference that an evolutionist would predict, and we should like to know whether this result would hold with other populations.

Sexual Rivalry Homicides

Jealousy ranks third in Wolfgang's Philadelphia homicide "motive" list (Table 8.1), and is, as we noted earlier, the first truly substantive issue on his list. It is likely that many "altercations" (motive 1) were matters of male sexual rivalry, and it is extremely likely that many "domestic quarrels" (motive 2) concerned male accusations of female infidelity, as we shall see in Chapter 9.

Unfortunately, it is far from clear just what sort of cases are subsumed by Wolfgang's (1958) "jealousy" category. He writes "These cases invariably involved a victim and offender of opposite sex" (p. 193), apparently indicating that *no* cases in which the jealous individual killed the same-sex rival were included in this category. A few paragraphs earlier, however, we read

> Some overlapping probably occurs in the "jealousy" and "revenge" categories. A jealous suitor seeking revenge for his having been emotionally rejected is difficult to classify, but full description of such cases has usually led to a "revenge" classification. An offender motivated by jealousy and seeking to resolve an emotional problem by means of a physical assault usually attacks his rival. A jealous offender who kills his love object is most often motivated by revenge for the alienation he has had to suffer. (pp. 189–190)

This passage seems to imply that killing the same-sex rival *was* classified as a jealousy case, while killing the unfaithful partner was not. The two quotes are hard to reconcile, and Wolfgang's tables do not help us. What is clear is that Wolfgang's attribution of the "jealousy" motive to 68 of his cases surely underestimates the importance of the general issue of sexual rivalry/jealousy within his sample, perhaps substantially.

In our Detroit homicide sample for 1972, Wilt classified 58 cases as being due to sexual jealousy. Table 8.3 includes 34 of these; an additional 23 involved spouses, and one involved an inlaw. Men were the killers in 40 cases (22 male victims, 18 female victims) and women in 18 (15 male victims, 3 female victims), but this comparison is deceptive, since the jealous, accusatory partner was sometimes the eventual victim; the sex difference in violent jealousy was in fact even larger (Table 8.4). Wilbanks' (1984) capsule descriptions of all homicides in Miami in 1980

Table 8.4. Sexual Jealousy Conflicts Leading to Homicide, Detroit, 1972[a]

47 Cases precipitated by jealous males	11 Cases precipitated by jealous females
16 Killed female for infidelity	6 Killed male for infidelity
17 Killed rival male	3 Killed rival female
9 Were killed by accused female	2 Were killed by accused male
2 Were killed by accused female's kin	
2 Killed homosexual male for infidelity	
1 Killed bystander accidentally	

[a]From Daly, Wilson, and Weghorst (1982).

Table 8.5. Sexual Jealousy Conflicts Leading to Homicide, Miami, 1980[a]

48 Cases precipitated by jealous males	4 Cases precipitated by jealous females
18 Killed female of whom jealous	2 Killed male for infidelity
23 Killed rival male	1 Killled homosexual male for pass at her man
4 Were killed by the accused female (self-defense)	1 Was killed by the accused male (self-defense)
2 Killed estranged wife's father for harboring her	
1 Killed female friend of female over whom jealous	

[a]Data from Wilbanks, 1984.

permit a comparable breakdown (Table 8.5), and in this case, we find a still larger sex difference. Considering only those "triangle" cases in which victim and offender were same-sex rivals, the Detroit sample includes 17 involving men and 3 involving women, whereas the Miami sample includes 23 male–male cases and no cases of female sexual rivalry. Some additional examples of sexual rivalry homicides are presented in Table 8.6.

Table 8.6. "Love Triangle" Homicides in Which the Victim Was the Killer's Same-Sex Rival

	Male killed male	Female killed female	Proportion male
Detroit, 1972	17	3	.850
Miami, 1980 (Wilbanks, 1984)	23	0	1.000
Birmingham (Harlan, 1950)	42	8	.840
Bhil (Varma, 1978)	12	0	1.000
Bison-horn Maria (Elwin, 1950)	5	0	1.000
Munda (Saran, 1974	7	0	1.000
Oraon (Saran, 1974)	3	0	1.000
Basoga (Fallers & Fallers, 1960)	26	1	.964

Sexual jealousy and rivalry have been prominent in virtually every study of homicide motives. As in the Detroit and Miami studies, West's (1968) study of homicides in Manhattan found sexual jealousy to be the third-ranking motive after "unrestrained rage in the course of quarrels" and crime-related murders. Jealousy ranked second to trivial altercations in a Baltimore study (Criminal Justice Commission of Baltimore, 1967), and second to domestic quarrels in a study of modern Navajo cases in Arizona (Levy, Kunitz, and Everett, 1969). Similarly, jealousy has ranked third as a homicide motive behind "quarrels" and "robbery" in studies in England and Wales (Gibson & Klein, 1961) and Scotland (Gillies, 1976). This motive seems to be no less prevalent in other cultures. Lobban (1972), for example, read court records of homicide cases in the Sudan, and reported that sexual jealousy was the leading motive category, accounting for 74 of the 300 male-offender cases (24.7%).

Sexual jealousy is dangerous, then, but just how dangerous we have yet to see. All of these studies greatly underestimate the role of male sexual proprietariness in homicidal violence, as we shall see in the next chapter.

Till Death
Us Do Part

— 9 —

In all known human societies, extant or historical, men and women have entered into formal reproductive alliances between individuals of opposite sex. In other words, they have *married*. Marriage is a special kind of relationship. By engaging in sexual reproduction and by the cooperative rearing of offspring, couples forge a powerful commonality of interest at the fundamental level of fitness. This shared interest is analogous to that existing between blood relatives, but it is more easily shaken or betrayed.

What is the essence of the marital relationship? It cannot be the marriage license: People were marrying long before there were any civil or religious authorities to claim jurisdiction over the union. The beginning of a marriage is not necessarily demarcated by a public ceremony, and the couple, once married, do not invariably dwell under the same roof. Some have questioned whether there really is a cross-cultural phenomenon of marital alliance at all, since it is difficult to pinpoint one or a few simple criteria that will define the institution of marriage. And yet the following features characterize marriages in all or virtually all societies. There is some degree of mutual obligation between wife and husband. There is a right of sexual access (often but not invariably exclusive). There is an expectation that the relationship will persist through pregnancy, lactation, and child rearing. And there is some sort of legitimization of the status of the couple's children. These species-typical features of human marriage seem so commonplace as to hardly warrant enumeration, but it is worth remarking that they represent a radical departure from the mating practices of most other mammals. The typical mammalian alliance is an ephemeral affair, with the father playing little or no parental role. Marital alliance and biparental care are part of the human adaptation.

Many writers have suggested that the marital relationship in *Homo sapiens* is unique by virtue of being an economic union, and is therefore only weakly analogous to the merely reproductive mateships of other animal species. This argument just won't wash. A tern feeds his mate

187

during courtship and nest-building. A pair of beavers maintain their dams and domicile through the winter. We can call these unions, with their divisions of labor and exchanges of benefits, "economic," if it pleases us to do so. *All* animals accumulate and allocate resources, "economic" activity if you like, but economic activity that has evolved because of its reproductive consequences. In nonhuman animals, as in women and men, the mundane interactions of a mated pair seldom serve immediate reproductive purposes. Yet the union itself can only be understood as ultimately reproductive.

Wives as Commodities?

Human marriage *has* added a novel twist to the mating game, but it is neither economic alliance nor division of labor. The novel twist in human courtship and mating is the degree and complexity of involvement of parties other than the mates themselves. The French anthropologist Claude Lévi-Strauss (1969) has argued that marriage is a contract not between husband and wife, but between *men*, a formalized transfer of a woman as a commodity. And indeed when one examines the material and labor exchanges that surround marriage, it does begin to look like a trafficking in women. In our society, as in many, a father *gives* his daughter in marriage. Men *purchase* wives in the majority of human societies (Figure 9.1), and they often demand a refund if the bargain proves disappointing. Although the relatively rare practice of dowry might be construed to mean that who pays whom is arbitrary and reversible, dowry and bride-price are not in fact opposites: A bride-price is given as compensation to the bride's kin, whereas a dowry typically remains with the newlyweds.

What the groom and his kin pay to acquire is the bride's productive and reproductive capacity. Wives are supposed to reproduce. In a number of societies, such as the Tiv (pp. 32–33), only a small down payment is made at betrothal or marriage, with subsequent bride-price installments then being paid for each birth. But even where a full and supposedly invariant bride-price is paid before the wedding, the bride's reproductive value may be a significant determinant of the actual price paid, as anthropologist Monique Borgerhoff Mulder (1988) has shown for the Kipsigis of Kenya. That reproduction is the point of marriage is also revealed by the fact that the failure to conceive is widely considered a grounds for divorce; if a bride-price has been paid, the disgruntled purchaser may demand its return or the replacement of the barren woman with a younger sister. (And of course in modern industrial societies, infertility remains a major reason for marital dissolution.) In

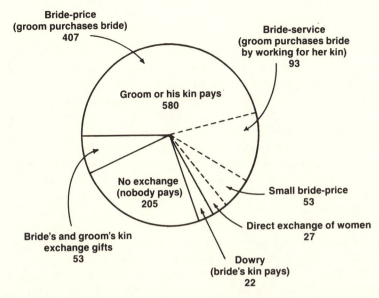

Figure 9.1. Exchange of considerations at marriage in a sample of 860 societies. (Reproduced from Daly & Wilson, 1983; data from Murdock, 1967.)

view of these facts, several anthropologists, with no Darwinian axe to grind, have suggested that "bride-price" should properly be labeled "child-price."

The exchange of women as commodities has probably become exaggerated since the invention of agriculture. In foraging societies, women seem often to have been more autonomous, perhaps entering a first arranged marriage but later leaving it to make a match of their own choice (see, for example, Shostak, 1981). And of course, even where men appear to be running the show, as for example among most nomadic herding peoples, the role of mature women as matchmakers and political forces has probably been underreported (Brown, 1982). Men, with their passion for public display and the acquisition of prestige, may be less in control than first appearances would suggest (see also Irons, 1983). Nevertheless, although Lévi-Strauss's view of marriage as an exercise in male politics may be somewhat biased, we find it highly significant that *men the world around think and talk about women and marriage in proprietary terms.* Men *strive* to control women and to traffic in their reproductive capacities (Paige & Paige, 1981), with varying degrees of success.

Adultery Law

From the husband's perspective, then, marriage entails the acquisition of proprietary rights to a woman's reproductive capacity. Nothing reflects this attitude more clearly than the concept of adultery.

It is a remarkable fact that wherever people have codified law, they have legislated restrictions (over and above the incest prohibitions) on who may have sexual contact with whom. It is not an obvious or trivial fact of social existence that sexual access should be considered an appropriate subject for legislation by all peoples, whatever their mode of existence. Many social theorists have supposed to the contrary that ancient people practiced "free love": that women and men in a state of nature coupled whenever they were moved by the whim of mutual attraction, and that sexual exclusion and jealousy are recent "cultural inventions." This free-love-as-primitive-and-natural hypothesis is, of course, naive. Aggressive competition for females and the sequestering of mates from rival males are conspicuous male preoccupations in innumerable animals, including mammals ranging from our nearest anthropoid relatives to housemice. Legal restrictions on sexual access, invented independently and repeatedly the world around, owe their striking similarities to a ubiquitous state of affairs that has characterized our societies since long before we became human: the fundamental conflict of interest that inevitably exists among male reproductive competitors.

If we undertake a cross-cultural and historical review of adultery law, we encounter this single idea again and again: *Sexual intercourse between a married woman and a man other than her husband is a crime.* The victim is the husband, and his grievance is typically stated in the language of property violations. Having been deprived of that which is rightfully his, or having had the value of his property irreparably and wrongfully diminished, the husband is commonly entitled to damages, to violent revenge, or to divorce with refund of bride-price. On the Micronesian island of Yap, for example, Hunt, Schneider, Kidder, & Stevens (1949) note that "Adultery is spoken of and may be dealt with as a 'theft'; it is classified along with the theft of personal goods, coconuts and so forth" (p. 92). In the Ashanti kingdom of Ghana, a more explicit and elaborate legal code also categorized adultery as a theft from the husband, and specifically as a theft of the sexual prerogative that the husband purchased when he paid the bride-price (Rattray, 1929). Among various cattle-herding peoples in Africa, a man acquires rights to his wife's reproductive capacities by the payment of cattle, and he is entitled to compensation in the same currency from any man caught in adultery with that wife (e.g., Howell, 1954; Schapera, 1938).

Are double standards of marital fidelity universal in the customary law of "primitive" societies? This is an issue that has been badly muddled in the literature. In a much-cited work on *The Status of Women in Preindustrial Societies*, Martin Whyte (1978) reviewed Human Relations Area Files information for a sample of 93 societies, 75 of which he was able to code for the existence of an extramarital double standard. Whyte reported that only 32 of these 75 societies (43%) exhibited the familiar double standard, penalizing women more severely for adultery than men. Forty-one societies, more than half of the sample, allegedly maintained a single standard with respect to adultery, and two societies actually exhibited "an extramarital double standard favoring females" because "when caught in the act the male is subject to a more severe penalty than the female" (Whyte, 1978, p. 80)!

Whyte's result has been heralded as proof of the cultural arbitrariness of the double standard. It is in fact nothing of the sort. His interpretation is based on a simple error, which can be seen by considering an exemplary quotation from one of Whyte's HRAF sources. The Gilyak of Siberia are one of the two societies to whom Whyte imputed a reversed double standard, on the basis of this passage (Shternberg, 1933):

> A stranger caught *in flagrante delicto* with a married woman is slain at the scene of the crime. . . . The woman suffers less in such cases. They beat her thoroughly. . . . But all this concerns only cases involving a married woman. Sexual relations with an unmarried woman or with a widow, if it is with the permission of the woman, do not provoke any reaction. . . . (pp. 227–228)

So the Gilyak man was killed and the woman only beaten, and that, for Whyte, constitutes a reversed double standard. But there is no reversal. The crime is unauthorized sexual contact with a married woman, as usual. The male adulterer's marital status is irrelevant, as usual.

Whyte's other alleged example of "an extramarital double standard favoring females" (the Gilbert Islanders) is based on the same mistake (Daly, Wilson, & Weghorst, 1982). Moreover, it appears that all his "*single* standards" are similarly miscoded. Whyte did not indicate which societies were given this code, but we have found that the familiar double standard prevailed in every society in his sample for which we have been able to find relevant HRAF materials. Whyte apparently coded each society in which the adulterous wife and her lover were punished with equal severity as maintaining a single standard. But we could find no society in his "preindustrial" sample with a genuine single standard, that is to say a society in which adultery by the wife and adultery by the husband were penalized equally.

The only human societies that have genuine single standards of adultery enshrined in law are modern industrial nations. According to our dictionaries and our laws, "adultery" encompasses the infidelities of the husband as well as those of the wife. However, the word's etymology betrays its sexually asymmetrical origin: It derives from the Latin *adulterare*, to "adulterate," i.e., "To make impure, spurious, or inferior by adding extraneous or improper ingredients" (Morris, 1969). The egalitarian definition of adultery in the law of many modern nations is a rare variant on the more usual, sexually asymmetrical definition, and is of recent origin. Placing a restriction on married men as well as women seems to be one element in an intensified enforcement of monogamy, a major trend in recent centuries, which has tempered male–male competition and thereby facilitated the growth of ever larger polities (Alexander, 1979).

The modern shift toward sexually indiscriminate adultery law does not, of course, imply that women and men have stopped reacting differently to their spouses' infidelities, nor that they are likely to do so in the foreseeable future. Where both sexes have the same legal right to divorce on the grounds of adultery, for example, men are much more likely than women to feel that spousal adultery actually *warrants* divorce, and they are much more likely to attribute their own divorces to their spouses' infidelities (Daly, Wilson, & Weghorst, 1982).

In a monograph on the history of European adultery laws, Hadjiyannakis (1969) has documented the recency (and gradualness) of the movement toward a legal equality of the sexes. Ancient Egyptians, Syrians, Hebrews, Romans, Spartans, and other Mediterranean peoples defined adultery solely in terms of the marital status of the woman, and punished both parties severely, often with death. Male infidelity was nowhere criminalized until 1810, and then in only a very limited way: A French revolutionary law made it a crime for a man to keep a concubine in his conjugal home against his wife's wishes. In 1852, Austria became the first country to explicitly treat male and female adultery as legal equivalents, although an asymmetry remained in the provision that the penalty should be especially severe when the paternity of a subsequent infant was thrown into doubt.

And there of course is the point. The "adulteration" in adultery—the "extraneous or improper ingredient"—is the risk of successful insemination. Adultery has almost invariably been defined in a sexually discriminative way because it has distinct consequences for women and men. Samuel Johnson's friend and biographer James Boswell once ventured the observation that "there is a great difference between the offence of infidelity in a man and that of his wife," with which suggestion Dr. Johnson concurred: "The difference is boundless. The man imposes no bastards upon his wife" (Boswell, 1779, p. 1035). The word "cuckold" derives from the cuckoo, a bird that surreptitiously lays its egg in another's nest and lets the duped foster parents rear the chick as their own.

Legal commentators have frequently defended a sexually discriminatory law of adultery by explicit appeal to the asymmetry invoked by Dr. Johnson. A particularly striking case comes from French revolutionary legislation. The architects of the new social order were greatly concerned to abolish the unjust inequities of the past, and yet they retained sexual discrimination in this one sphere. Here was their rationale (our translation of Fenet, 1827, as quoted by Hadjiyannakis, 1969):

> "It is not adultery *per se* that the law punishes, but only the possible introduction of alien children into the family and even the uncertainty that adultery creates in this regard. Adultery by the husband has no such consequences." (p. 502)

Paternal uncertainty is of course endemic to human reproduction, and it is therefore hardly surprising that the sexually asymmetrical definition of adultery extends far beyond European legal systems. In his massive review of *Sexual Variance in Society and History*, Vern Bullough (1976) has assembled available information on adultery law in a number of ancient societies from other parts of the world. Just as Hadjiyannakis found throughout the Mediterranean region, so too in the New World civilizations of the Incas, Mayans, and Aztecs, in the Germanic tribes of western Europe before the Roman conquest, and in the even older city states of what is now Iraq: Adultery was defined by the woman's marital status, not the man's. Precolonial African legal codes, some of which we have already illustrated, routinely exhibit the same asymmetry. And so do Chinese, Japanese, and other east Asian legal traditions, which, until the present century, typically legitimized a violent revenge by the victimized husband upon the adulterers.

Provocation and the "Reasonable Man"

This last-mentioned feature of Oriental law is by no means unusual. Many legal traditions do not just criminalize adultery, but proceed to address the question of the victimized husband's legitimate response. More than merely entitling the wronged husband to material compensation, adultery is widely construed to justify his resorting to violence that would in other circumstances be deemed criminal. Having caught his wife *in flagrante delicto*, for example, the Yapese cuckold "had the right to kill her and the adulterer or to burn them in the house" (Muller, 1917, p. 229). Among the Toba-Batak of Sumatra, "the injured husband had the right to kill the man caught in adultery as he would kill a pig in a rice-field" (Vergouwen, 1964, p. 266). Solon's law gave the same right to Greek cuckolds, while Roman law excused the homicidal cuckold only if the adultery occurred in his house; various such provisions remain in effect in continental Europe today.

Until 1974, it was the law in Texas (Texas Penal Code 1925, article 1220) that homicide is justifiable, i.e., not a criminal act, and therefore subject to no penalty whatever, "when committed by the husband upon the person of anyone taken in the act of adultery with the wife, provided the killing takes place before the parties to the act of adultery have separated."

In this, as in so many spheres, Texans are special. Killing an adulterer has remained a criminal offense in the rest of the English-speaking world, at least according to legislation. In practice—and with innumerable precedents in the common law—the courts frequently treat the cuckolded husband's jealous rage with sympathy: an understandable response that is punished relatively lightly, if at all. According to Blackstone's *Commentaries on the Laws of England*, for example, it is the common law that a man who kills upon discovering his wife *in flagrante delicto* is thus exempted from the usual criteria defining "murder," and is instead guilty of "the lowest degree" of manslaughter "because there could not be a greater provocation" (Blackstone, 1803, Book IV, pp. 191–192). This is still the law throughout the English-speaking world.

The English common law relies heavily upon a conception of the way in which a "reasonable man" could be expected to behave. This hypothetical creature embodies the judiciary's assumptions about the natural order of marital relationships and men's passions, assumptions that are laid bare in this legal scholar's summary characterization (Edwards, 1954):

> . . . the judges have gone a considerable way towards establishing—so far as the law of provocation is concerned—a standard portrayal of the make-up and reactions of the reasonable man. They say he is not impotent and he is not normally drunk. He does not lose his self-control on hearing a mere confession of adultery, but he becomes unbalanced at the sight of adultery provided, of course, that he is married to the adulteress. (p. 900)

This "reasonable man" may strike the reader as a quaintly English invention, but he is more than that. Other peoples, the world around, have similar notions of normalcy. Among the Melanesian islanders of Wogeo, for example, the principal subject of law and morality is adultery, and "the rage of the husband who has been wronged" is considered predictable and excusable; the Wogeans say "he is like a man whose pig has been stolen," only much angrier (Hogbin, 1938, pp. 236–237). Among the Nuer of east Africa, "it is commonly recognized that a man caught in adultery runs a risk of serious injury or even death at the hands of the woman's husband" (Howell, 1954, p. 156). Indeed, the ethnographic record suggests that the violent rages of cuckolds are a recognized risk everywhere.

In the United States, the principle that adultery is a provocation reducing murder to manslaughter is upheld by appellate courts several times each year. But although the common law, as manifested in the court reporters, makes such homicides "manslaughters" in most of the United States, they have in fact often been treated even less severely: Many American juries have voted to acquit homicidal cuckolds altogether, on the basis of "the unwritten law" (see, for example, Vance and Wynne, 1934). This phrase refers, according to Bouvier's Law Dictionary, to "a popular expression to designate a supposed rule of law that a man who takes the life of a wife's paramour or a daughter's seducer is not guilty of a criminal offence." Thus, although it is only in a few states such as Georgia and Texas that killing an adulterer has been legally "justified," busy prosecutors in other states often simply choose not to charge a homicidal cuckold who seems likely to be acquitted by a sympathetic jury.

The courts have differed on the question of whether homicidal wives are entitled to claim provocation on the same grounds as homicidal husbands. The point remains somewhat moot because relevant cases are few: Wives just do not seem to kill husbands discovered *in flagrante delicto* very often. One American legal scholar, for example, cites a Georgia case in which "it was held that the same standard of conduct is required of a wife as is required of a husband where a slaying growing out of the sight of adultery is concerned" (Miller, 1949). The author then asks whether this egalitarian ruling represents typical judicial practice, and can reach no conclusion, for "this is the only case found where the wife was the slayer."

More recent decisions leave the matter equivocal. In Henderson v. State (221 S.E. 2d 633), for example, a 1975 Georgia court of appeals split 4–3 in reviewing the conviction of a woman who discovered her common-law husband in the act of adultery and fatally stabbed him before he could gain his feet. All the justices seem to have agreed with the lower court that the provocation was sufficient to rule out a verdict of murder. To that degree the defense of adultery as provocation was unanimously extended to both sexes. But whereas the majority upheld a manslaughter conviction, the three dissenting judges felt that *any* conviction was too severe, and that the trial judge should have charged the jury "that one spouse has the right to kill to prevent adultery, the continuation of the act of adultery, or the completion of the act of adultery" (p. 639), as he would have done had the killer been the husband. It would seem, then, that by a narrow vote, the men but not the women of Georgia have a license to kill adulterous spouses; it is possible, however, that the minority opinion would have held sway had the couple been legally married rather than common-law.

Spousal Homicide and Sexual Jealousy in North America

The revelation of wifely infidelity is a provocation so extreme that a "reasonable man" is apt to respond with lethal violence. This impulse is so strong and so natural that the homicidal cuckold cannot be held fully responsible for his dreadful deed. So says the common law.

Other spousal misbehavior—snoring or burning supper or misman-aging the family finances—cannot be invoked as provocation. Reason-able men do not react violently to their wives' profligacy or stupidity or sloth or insults. In fact, the *only* provocations other than a wife's adultery that are invested with the same power to mitigate a killer's criminal responsibility are physical assaults upon himself or a relative (see, for example, Dressler, 1982).

There is a *theory of human nature* implicit in these laws, and it is essentially similar to the theories of human nature that are implicit in other legal traditions that have developed independently of our own. Does the reality of spousal violence conform to the implicit theory? Is the apprehension of adultery indeed a greater impetus to violence than any other source of marital conflict? As we shall see, the short answer is yes.

As we noted in Chapter 8, most studies of homicide "motives" have depended upon summary police files, and have been limited by the sparse, special-purpose information recorded there. The two leading "motive" categories in Marvin Wolfgang's trend-setting study of Phila-delphia homicides, for example, were "altercation of relatively trivial origin" and "domestic quarrel." Neither of these category labels tells us much about the sources of conflict. "Jealousy" was the leading substan-tive issue on Wolfgang's list, as it has proved to be in many studies.

The motive category of "jealousy" includes a couple of somewhat different sorts of cases, which might usefully be distinguished. On the one hand, we have what some criminologists have referred to as "love triangles": cases in which there is a known or suspected third party. In other cases, it is not clear that any particular third party was involved or even suspected by the jealous individual, who simply could not abide his partner's terminating the relationship: "If I can't have her, then no-one can." The jealous party is even more often male in such cases than in triangles. In our sample of 1972's homicides in Detroit, for example, a man was the jealous party in 30 out of 40 "triangle" murders, and in 17 out of 18 cases where the killer simply would not abide being deserted (Daly, Wilson, & Weghorst, 1982).

The distinction between a wife's adultery and her departure illustrates two separable but related considerations underlying male jealousy. Only the former places the man at risk of cuckoldry and misdirected parental investment in another man's child, but the risks are partly the same: In either case, the man is at risk of losing control of his wife's reproductive capacity and hence losing ground in the reproductive competition between men. And this "reproductive strategic" commonality between the two sorts of cases evidently imparts a psychological commonality as well: The reason why researchers have tended to lump these as "jealousy" cases is because of the aggressive proprietariness of the husband, who seems to consider adultery and desertion as equivalent violations of his rights.

Among Detroit's 690 homicides in 1972, there were 80 cases in which killer and victim were spouses (including common-law relationships). The victims were 44 husbands and 36 wives. Twenty-three of these 80 spousal homicides (29%) were "jealous conflicts" according to Wilt's (1974) classification, and in 16 of the 23 it was the husband who was the jealous party. But this is surely a serious underestimate of the role played by male sexual jealousy and proprietariness in these cases. As in Wolfgang's study, the majority of the Detroit spousal homicides could be attributed to nothing more specific than a "domestic quarrel."

Wilbanks' (1984) monograph on *Murder in Miami* includes brief synopses of 43 spousal cases that occurred in that city in 1980. The parties were legally wed and cohabitating in 19 cases, lived common-law in 14, and were estranged in 10. Victims were 23 women and 20 men. In 17 cases, the issues of contention were not stated: The dispute was described simply as a "domestic quarrel" or the like. Seventeen further cases were attributable to male sexual jealousy, and four to female sexual jealousy. Only five cases were allegedly provoked by *any* specified issue *other* than sexual jealousy, and each of these was unique: a husband who thought his wife paid the children more attention than himself; a wife defending her daughter from the abusive husband/father; a murder/suicide in an elderly, terminally ill couple; a wife

Table 9.1. Police Attribution of Motive in 1060 Spousal Homicides in
Canada, 1974–1983

	Killer is the husband	Killer is the wife	Total
Argument	353	160	513
Jealousy	195	19	214
Anger/hatred	84	22	106
Mentally ill/retarded	59	7	66
Revenge	27	7	34
Self-defense	0	10	10
Inadvertent act	6	3	9
Robbery	1	2	3
During other offense	2	1	3
Rape	1	0	1
During escape	0	0	0
Other motive	38	9	47
No motive attributed	46	8	54
Total cases	812	248	1060

ending a history of beatings; and an argument over a husband's
ransacking the house while searching for a police bug.

In Canada, the investigating police file a report on every homicide
with the federal agency Statistics Canada, using a standardized multi-
ple-choice form. The police are offered a choice of twelve "motives," one
of which is "jealousy." Between 1974 and 1983, Canadian police made
an attribution of motive for 1006 out of 1060 spousal homicides (Table
9.1). Two hundred fourteen of these (21.3%) were attributed to jealousy:
25.5% of the homicides by husbands and 7.9% of those by wives. But as
in the United States, this is surely a gross underestimate of the role
played by this issue. The most popular motive category, accounting for
513 cases (51%) was "argument or quarrel," and the next most popular
after jealousy was "anger or hatred" (106 cases, 10.5%). As we noted
earlier, such motive categories as these reflect detectives' and prosecutors' concern with the question of premeditation versus impulsive
reaction, but they tell us nothing about the substance of marital conflict.
Any of these cases might have been provoked by the suspicion or
discovery of infidelity.

Our claim that the Statistics Canada motive data underestimate the importance of adultery and jealousy in spousal conflict is more than just a conjecture. Catherine Carlson's (1984) study of the spousal homicides investigated by one Ontario police force provides clear evidence on this point. Carlson examined the police files on 36 spousal homicides for which the motive category reported to Statistics Canada was noted in the file. Only four had been labeled "jealousy" cases by the police, and yet sexual proprietariness was clearly relevant to several others. Here, for example, is a statement made to police by an unemployed 53-year-old man who shot his 42-year-old estranged wife (Carlson, 1984):

> I know she was fuckin' around. I had been waiting for approximately five minutes and seen her pull up in a taxi and I drove over and pulled up behind her car. I said "Did you enjoy your weekend?" She said "You're fuckin' right I did. I will have a lot more of them too." I said "Oh no you won't. You have been bullshitting me long enough. I can take no more." I kept asking her if she would come back to me. She told me to get out of her life. I said "No way. If I get out of this it's going to be both of us." (pp. 7–8)

In reporting to Statistics Canada, the police classified this case under the motive category "mentally ill, retarded."

In another case classified under "anger or hatred" (the most popular category with this police force, accounting for 11 of the 36 spousal homicides), a 31-year-old man stabbed his 20-year-old common-law wife after a 6-month temporary separation. In his statement to police, the accused gave this account of the fatal argument (Carlson, 1984):

> Then she said that since she came back in April she had fucked this other man about ten times. I told her how can you talk love and marriage and you been fucking with this other man. I was really mad. I went to the kitchen and got the knife. I went back to our room and said were you serious when you told me that. She said yes. We fought on the bed, I was stabbing her and her grandfather came up and tried to take the knife out of my hand. I told him to go and call the cops for me. I don't know why I killed the woman, I loved her. (p. 9)

Women who kill their husbands do not typically act out of the same proprietary inclinations as men who kill their wives. More commonly, they act in self-defense against husbands who are abusive to themselves, their children or both. Police, prosecutors, judges, and juries are regularly confronted with evidence of the man's role as initial aggressor, and the result is that husband-killers are generally penalized much less severely than wife-killers. Women who kill their spouses in North America are substantially more likely to get off scot-free than are men (Table 9.2), and if convicted they receive lighter sentences. In

Table 9.2. Dispositions of Spousal Homicides in Various Studies[a]

	N Cases	Percent suicide	Percent convicted	Percent scot-free	Percent insane
Male offenders					
Detroit, 1972	29	13.8	69.0	17.2	0
Miami, 1980	21	28.6	42.9	28.6	0
Houston, 1969	17	17.6	52.9	29.4	0
Canada, 1974–1983	644	30.3	56.2	7.1	6.4
Female offenders					
Detroit, 1972	36	0	25.0	75.0	0
Miami, 1980	20	0	40.0	60.0	0
Houston, 1969	21	0	14.3	85.7	0
Canada, 1974–1983	161	5.0	58.4	31.7	3.7

[a]Data from Canada and Detroit are from our own studies, for Miami from Wilbanks (1984), and for Houston from Lundsgaarde (1977).

Lundsgaarde's Houston study, for example, not only were just 3 of 21 homicidal wives convicted after trial, but all 3 were given probation rather than jail sentences, whereas all 9 convicted men went to jail. In Canada, 46% of convicted husbands received sentences of 10 years or more, as compared to 12% of convicted wives. It is possible that the differential sentencing of convicted men and women represents sexual discrimination by the judicial system (perhaps because men are perceived as more dangerous), but there is no question that the differential rates of conviction reflect the differential qualities of the crimes. Regardless of which spouse ends up dead, the husband is usually the instigator of violence.

The Killer's View of the Matter

Police synopses and government statistics are obviously not ideal sources of information on homicide motives. Fortunately, there have been at least a few intensive studies in which the researchers have interviewed the killers themselves about the sources of the conflicts that culminated in spousal homicide. Such studies are unanimous in suggesting that male sexual proprietariness constitutes *the* dangerous issue in marriage.

Accused killers are commonly obliged to undergo a psychiatric examination to determine whether they are "fit to stand trial." A particular forensic psychiatrist or institution usually handles all such fitness examinations for a particular court or jurisdiction. In 1955, Manfred Guttmacher, the fitness examiner for the city of Baltimore, published a report summarizing his examinations of 31 people who had killed their spouses, 24 men and 7 women. These represented all such killers among 36 consecutive Baltimore cases of intrafamilial homicide, and Guttmacher tabulated what he called "apparent motivational factors" on the basis of his personal interviews of the perpetrators. While the data are presented a little ambiguously (some cases were tabulated under more than one motive), it appears that as many as 25 (81%) of the 31 spousal homicides were motivated by sexual proprietariness. Fourteen cases were provoked by the spouse's deserting for a new partner, 5 by the spouse's "promiscuity," 4 by "pathological jealousy," 1 by the discovery of adultery *in flagrante delicto,* and 1 by a delusionary suspicion of adultery between the killer's wife and his son-in-law.

A similar report from the Forensic Psychiatry Clinic of the University of Virginia reveals a preponderance of cases of male sexual proprietariness that is even more dramatic than in the Baltimore sample. Showalter, Bonnie, and Roddy (1980) based the report on seventeen cases of "killing or seriously wounding" a legal or common-law spouse. Six were attributed to psychiatric disorders, but the authors were so impressed with the essential similarity of the remaining eleven that they called their report "The Spousal Homicide Syndrome." All eleven attackers were men, and all professed that they were deeply in love with their victims. Ten of the eleven attacks were precipitated by "an immediate threat of withdrawal," and eight of the eleven victimized wives had left the offender at least once previously, only to return. Moreover, Showalter *et al.* noted that

> "In all 11 cases, the victim was engaged in an affair with another man or had led the offender to believe that she was being unfaithful to him. In 10 of the cases, the victim made no attempt to conceal her other relationships." (p. 127)

A Canadian study of convicted spouse-killers points once again to the overwhelming predominance of male sexual jealousy and proprietariness as motives in spousal homicide. Sociologist Peter Chimbos (1978) interviewed an "availability sample" of 34 spouse killers, 29 men and 5 women. The interviews were conducted at an average interval of 3 years after the homicide; 30 interviewees were in prison, while 4 had recently been released. Seventeen had been legally married to their victims and 17 had been living common-law. In a finding reminiscent of the Virginia "syndrome," 22 of the 34 couples had previously separated due to infidelity and had later been reconciled.

The most striking result of Chimbos's interview study is the near unanimity of the killers in identifying the main source of conflict in their ill-fated marriages. Twenty-nine of the 34 (85%) pointed to "sexual matters (affairs and refusals)," 3 blamed "excessive drinking," and 2 professed that there *was* no serious conflict. And that exhausts the list. Although most of the killers were of low educational and occupational status, not a one pointed to financial problems as the primary source of marital conflict. Although 28 of the 34 couples had children, no one considered them to be the main source of conflict either. The conflicts were over sexual matters, and that mainly meant adultery.

Unfortunately, Chimbos did not break down the infidelity quarrels according to sex. Nevertheless, it is clear that the wives' adulteries were a far greater bone of contention than the husbands', no matter which party ended up dead. Scattered through the monograph are verbatim quotations from the interviewed killers. Thirteen such quotes from the male offenders included allusions to infidelity, and all thirteen were complaints about the faithlessness of the wife. By way of comparison, there were four quotes from female killers that made reference to infidelity, but these were not mirror images of the male complaints. All four of the women's allusions to adultery concerned their husbands' accusations against themselves; in one of the four, the accusations were mutual.

Chimbos chose six cases for detailed narrative description. Four were committed by men, two by women. In *every* one of these six cases— selected, according to the author, to represent the full range of conflicts in the entire sample—the husband angrily accused the wife of adultery immediately before the homicide. In three cases, the accusations were mutual.

Conjugal Jealousy and Violence Around the World

The phenomenon we have been discussing is not peculiar to North America. In every society for which we have been able to find a sample of spousal homicides, the story is basically the same: Most cases arise out of the husband's jealous, proprietary, violent response to his wife's (real or imagined) infidelity or desertion.

Several monographs have been published, for example, on the topic of homicide among various aboriginal peoples in India. These include the Bison-Horn Maria (Elwin, 1950), a society we discussed earlier (pp. 28–30), the Munda (Saran, 1974), the Oraon (Saran, 1974), and the Bhil (Varma, 1978). Rates of lethal violence among these agricultural peoples were high, and 99% of the killings were committed by men.

These homicide samples include 20 cases of Maria wives killed by their husbands, 3 such Munda cases, 3 Oraon, and 8 Bhil. In each of the four societies, the majority of spousal homicides was precipitated either by the suspicion or knowledge of wifely infidelity or by the woman's leaving or rejecting her husband. Moreover, in each of these studies, about 20% of the much more numerous male–male homicides were expressly due either to rivalry over a woman or to a man's taking offense at sexual advances made to his daughter or another female relative.

Fallers and Fallers (1960) collated information on 98 consecutive homicide cases (i.e., victims) between 1947 and 1954 among the Basoga, a patrilineal, polygynous, horticultural tribe in Uganda. Eight of these were evidently accidents, leaving 90 cases. Forty-two were cases in which a man killed a woman, usually his wife, and some sort of motive was imputed in 32 of these: 10 for adultery, 11 for desertion or for refusing sex, and 11 for a diversity of other motives. An additional 5 male–male cases were clear matters of sexual rivalry. Only 2 women were offenders, 1 taking the life of a man and 1 a woman; the latter case was the only one evidently arising out of female sexual jealousy or rivalry, as compared to 26 male cases.

Sohier (1959) reviewed court records on 275 homicides leading to convictions between 1948 and 1957 in what was then the Belgian Congo. Many cases were assigned to no particular motive category, but of those with identified motives, 59 were attributable to male jealousy and only 1 to female jealousy. Sixteen cuckolded husbands killed their adulterous wives or the male adulterer or both. Ten more killed their wives for desertion or for threatening desertion. Three killed an ex-wife after she had obtained a divorce, and three more killed an ex-wife's new husband. Another thirteen men killed faithless fiancées or mistresses. And so forth. Only 20 spousal cases were *not* attributed to male jealousy, and their motives were unspecified. The single female jealousy case was one in which a wife killed her husband's mistress.

Are there *no* exceptions to this dreary record of connubial coercion and violence? Certainly there are societies within which the homicide rate is exceptionally low. But is there even one exotic land in which the men eschew violence, take no proprietary view of their wives' sexuality, and accept consenting extramarital sex as good, clean fun? The short answer is "No," although many have sought such a society, and a few have imagined that they found it.

The most popular place to situate the mythical peaceful kingdom is a south sea island. Margaret Mead, for example, portrayed Samoa in innumerable writings as an idyllic land of free, innocent sexuality, and claimed that sexual jealousy was hardly known there. For example, she wrote (1931):

> Granting that jealousy is undesirable, a festering spot in every personality so afflicted, an ineffective negativistic attitude which is more likely to lose than gain any goal, what are the possibilities if not of eliminating it, at least of excluding it more and more from human life? Samoa has taken one road, by eliminating strong emotion, high stakes, emphasis upon personality, interest in competition. Such a cultural attitude eliminates many of the attitudes which have afflicted mankind, and perhaps jealousy most importantly of all. . . . (p. 46)

Derek Freeman finally exploded Mead's myth in 1983, showing that violent responses to adultery and sexual rivalry are *exceptionally* frequent in Samoa, and have long been endemic to the society.

The factual evidence that Margaret Mead's Samoa was a fantasy had long been available. But the facts were ignored. The reason, we believe, is the same reason why Martin Whyte's erroneous conclusions about the double standard (see p. 191) have been greeted so enthusiastically. Scholars who should have looked at the data critically *wanted* to believe in a tropical island where jealousy and violence were unknown. The prevalent ideology in the social sciences combines the premise that conflict is an evil and harmony a good—fair enough as a moral stance, although of dubious relevance to the scientific study of society—with a sort of "naturalistic fallacy" that makes goodness natural and evil artificial. The upshot is that conflict must be explained as the product of some modern, artificial nastiness (capitalism, say, or patriarchy), while the romantic ideal of the noble savage is retained, with nobility fantastically construed to mean an absence of all conflictual motives including sexual possessiveness.

Part of the confusion about the alleged existence of exotic peoples devoid of jealousy derives from a failure to distinguish between societal sanctions and the private use of force. In an influential volume entitled *The Family in Cross-Cultural Perspective*, for example, William Stephens (1963) asserted that in 4 societies out of a sample of 39, "there seems to be little if any bar to any sort of non-incestuous adultery" (p. 251). Yet here is one of Stephens's own sources (Handy, 1923) discussing the situation in one of those 4 societies, namely the Marquesa Islanders: "When a woman undertook to live with a man, she placed herself under his authority. If she cohabited with another man without his permission, she was beaten or, if her husband's jealousy was sufficiently aroused, killed . . ." (p. 100). In fact, when one consults Stephens' ethnographic sources, one finds accounts of wife-beating as punishment for adultery in every one of the four permissive societies (Daly, Wilson, & Weghorst, 1982). What Stephens evidently meant by claiming "little if any bar" to adultery was that no criminal sanctions were levied against adulterers by the larger society. Cuckolded husbands took matters into their own hands.

Ford and Beach's (1951) classic work *Patterns of Sexual Behavior* contains an assertion very like Stephens's, but even more misleading. These authors (Ford & Beach, 1951) claimed to have discovered 7 societies, out of a sample of 139, in which ". . . the customary incest prohibitions appear to be the only major barrier to sexual intercourse outside of mateship. Men and women in these societies are free to engage in sexual liaisons and indeed are expected to do so provided the incest rules are observed" (p. 113). Once again, we can make sense of these assertions only by assuming that Ford and Beach intend "barriers" to refer to legal or quasilegal sanctions by the larger society. For just as in Stephens' sample, the original ethnographies make it clear that men in every one of the seven societies were apt to respond with extreme violence to their wives' dalliances (Daly, Wilson, & Weghorst, 1982). Cuckolded men in these societies sometimes killed their adulterous wives, and they sometimes killed their rivals. If the fear of violent reprisal is not a "major barrier" to "sexual liaisons," it is hard to imagine what would be!

Violence as Coercive Control

In attempting to exert proprietary rights over the sexuality and reproduction of women, men walk a tightrope. The man who actually kills his wife has usually overstepped the bounds of utility, whether utility is assessed in fitness or in more proximal currencies. Killing provokes retribution by the criminal justice system or the victim's relatives; at the least, murdered wives are costly to replace. But killing is just the tip of the iceberg: For every murdered wife, hundreds are beaten, coerced, and intimidated. Although homicide probably does not often serve the interests of the perpetrator, it is far from clear that the same can be said of sublethal violence. Men, as we noted earlier, strive to control women, albeit with variable success; women struggle to resist coercion and to maintain their choices. There is brinksmanship and risk of disaster in any such contest, and homicides by spouses of either sex may be considered the slips in this dangerous game.

This view of spousal homicides as the slip-ups in a power struggle may explain an otherwise anomalous pattern of results in the Canadian

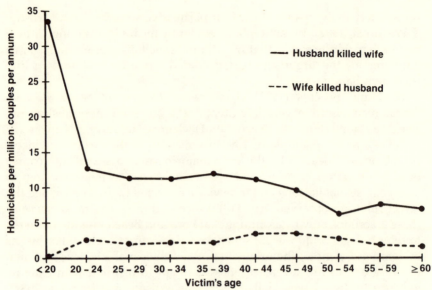

Figure 9.2. Spousal homicide victimization rates within legal marriages, as a function of age and sex. Canada, 1974–1983.

data: The risk of being killed by one's legal spouse is maximal for the youngest wives (Figure 9.2).

A Darwinian might have predicted very different effects of age. If the risk that A will kill B is affected by B's value as a potential contributor to A's fitness, might we not expect men to be especially likely to kill expendable postmenopausal wives? Men pay the highest bride-prices for the most fertile women. Should they not then be expected to cherish such wives most highly, and to be most inhibited in the use of dangerous tactics when in conflict with such wives? Well, perhaps they should, but the data in Figure 9.2 suggest that any such effect is swamped by something else. We propose that the data reflect the fact that men are most jealous of the youngest women and are therefore most inclined to behave coercively toward such wives (see Dickemann, 1981). Paradoxically, the high homicide risk incurred by young wives is indicative not of their low worth from the male perspective, but of precisely the opposite (see also Thornhill and Thornhill, 1983).

This interpretation is reinforced by simultaneous consideration of the killer's age along with the victim's. One might suppose that the high risk to the youngest wives merely reflects high risk from the youngest husbands, since the ages of spouses are highly correlated and young men are already known to be especially violent (e.g., Figure 8.1). But in spousal cases, the woman's age is a better predictor of risk than the man's, and this is true whether one is considering those cases in which she is the victim or the killer. (That is to say, one obtains a better fit to the observed numbers of spousal homicides for each combination of spousal ages if one generates expected values from the age-specific female victimization rate rather than from the age-specific male offender rate for homicides in general; *and* a better fit from the age-specific female offender rate than from the age-specific male victim rate.)

According to the argument in the preceding paragraphs, spousal homicides are the relatively rare and extreme manifestations of the same basic conflicts that inspire sublethal marital violence on a much larger scale. And indeed that is so. As in homicide, so too in wife-beating: The predominant issues are adultery, jealousy, and male proprietariness. Whitehurst (1971), for example, attended 100 Canadian court cases involving couples in litigation over the husband's use of violence upon the wife. He reported, without quantification, that ". . . at the core of nearly all the cases . . . the husband responded out of frustration at being unable to control the wife, often accusing her of being a whore or of having an affair . . ." (p. 686).

Dobash and Dobash (1984) interviewed 109 battered Scottish wives, and asked them to identify the main source of conflict in a "typical" battering incident. Forty-eight of the women pointed to possessiveness and sexual jealousy on the part of the batterer, making this far and away the leading response; arguments over money ranked second (18 women), and the husband's expectations about domestic work ranked third (17 women). A similar interview study (Rounsaville, 1978) of 31 battered American women in hostels and hospitals obtained similar results: ". . . jealousy was the most frequently mentioned topic that led to violent argument, with 52% of the women listing it as the main incitement and 94% naming it as a frequent cause" (p. 21). Battering husbands seldom make themselves available for interview, but when they do, they tell essentially the same story as their victims. Brisson (1983), for example, asked 122 wife-beaters in Denver to name the "topics around which violence occurred." Jealousy topped the list, with alcohol second, and money a distant third.

Although wife-beating is often inspired by a suspicion of infidelity, it can be the product of a more generalized proprietariness. Battered women commonly report that their husbands object violently to the continuation of old friendships, even with other women, and indeed to the wives' having any social life whatever. In a study of 60 battered wives who sought help at a clinic in rural North Carolina, Hilberman and Munson (1978) reported that the husbands exhibited "morbid jealousy," such that "leaving the house for any reason invariably resulted in accusations of infidelity which culminated in assault" (p. 461), in an astonishing 57 cases (95%)! Husbands who refuse to let their wives go to the store unescorted may run the risk, in our society, of being considered psychiatric cases. Yet there are many societies in which such constraint and confinement of women are considered normal and laudable (see, e.g., Dickemann, 1981).

It cannot be assumed that the jealous suspicions of abusive husbands are necessarily delusional. Shields and Hanneke (1983) asked a group of American battered wives and a control sample of "nonvictimized" women a number of questions, including whether the respondent had "ever had sex" with another man while living with her present husband. Of those women who had been both raped and beaten by their husbands, 47% admitted to adultery, compared to 23% of those battered but not raped, and 10% of the "nonvictimized." Shields and Hanneke evidently assume that the infidelity was a response to the husband's violence rather than a provocation thereto, but they offer their readers no reason to accept that interpretation; the women were not asked what preceded or inspired what. The adultery-as-a-response-to-violence interpretation seems especially improbable in view of the fact that increasing violence by the husband was correlated with a more negative view of men generally. Beatings do not make women feel sexy.

Obviously, wife-beating can sometimes be counterproductive. It might even provoke some wives to adultery, as Shields and Hanneke believe, whether with the aim of seeking solace, spiting the abuser, or just trying to find a better man. But by and large, men resort to violence in their efforts to control women, because—to some degree—violence works. Here, for example, is the self-report of an American Indian woman, from one of the seven societies in which Ford and Beach claimed that "men and women are free to engage in sexual liaisons and indeed are expected to do so" (Lowie, 1917): "I was never foolish or bad, my husband knew it and never got angry. Some husbands nearly killed their wives because they went with other men" (p. 47).

From May to December

In Miami's first spousal homicide of 1980, a 29-year-old woman shot and killed her 55-year-old common-law husband, for reasons not stated in the police synopsis (Wilbanks, 1984, Case 43). She shot at him twice and twice she missed, whereupon he managed to run from their house, but she finally connected on a shot through the window. The self-made widow was tried and convicted of manslaughter. Perhaps the couple's conflicts were exacerbated by a generation gap?

In December of the same year, a 27-year-old man killed his 47-year-old ex-wife when she refused to return to him (Case 538). He got a life sentence for second-degree murder. Not your typical violent marriage, of course. More often, it is the husband who is 20 years older, as in Case 319 in which a 33-year-old woman shot her 55-year-old mate during an argument as she was moving out, or Case 445 in which a 38-year-old woman shot her abusive 58-year-old husband in self-defense.

If these lethal May–December marriages are beginning to strike you as improbably frequent, you are right: They are. Wilbanks reports the ages of both parties in 42 Miami spousal homicides. The age disparity was 10 years or more in 12 of them (29%), surely far more than would be expected in a random sample of couples. In another 22 cases, the victim was the killer's "girlfriend" or "boyfriend," and the couples here are even odder: At the extremes, a 60-year-old man killed his 26-year-old girlfriend for jilting him, and a 33-year-old man killed a 65-year-old girlfriend. The age disparity was 10 years or more in 13 of the 22 "girlfriend–boyfriend" cases (59%). This remarkable prevalence of May–December couples among homicides is not peculiar to Miami. Lundsgaarde (1977), for example, gives the ages of both parties in 32 spousal homicides that occurred in Houston in 1969; the age disparity was a decade or more in 8 of them (25%).

The Canadian data are sufficient to quantify this May–December phenomenon more precisely. We know both parties' ages in all but 2 of the 1060 spousal homicides between 1974 and 1983. Figure 9.3 translates these cases into rates, as against the numbers of married couples (including common-law) in the population-at-large, according to the 1981 census. (The 1981 census was the first for which a table of spousal age differences was published; Statistics Canada 1984, Table 7. The rather curious category boundaries in Figure 9.3 are those given in that table. The use of just one census could introduce error into Figure 9.3 if the population-at-large distribution of spousal age disparities has changed radically over the decade, but this seems unlikely, since the distribution of age disparities in new marriages has fluctuated very little; Statistics Canada 1961–1985.)

Marriages with exceptionally high age disparities—in either direction—have homicide rates more than four times as high as that prevailing in marriages with the most common gap, namely those in which the husband is about 2 years older. Only about 6% of the 5,611,500 cohabiting couples in Canada in 1981 differed in age by 11 or more years, as compared to 18% of the spousal homicides between 1974 and 1983.

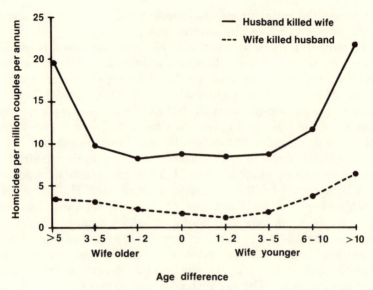

Figure 9.3. Spousal homicide rates as a function of the age difference between wife and husband. Canada, 1974–1983.

The U shape of Figure 9.3 holds up regardless of which sex has killed, and it holds up within both common-law marriages and those that have been "churched."

Although the U effect of Figure 9.3 is robust, its interpretation is nevertheless tricky. We are tempted to propose that there are legitimate grounds for heightened jealousy, and perhaps for other sorts of conflict, when one partner is a good deal older than the other. But the effect could in principle reflect nothing more than the greater risk of mutual misunderstanding across an increasing generation gap. Another possible explanation for the effects in Figure 9.3 is that the population of couples with unusual age differences, like any population defined by unusual behavior, contains a disproportionate number of eccentrics, losers, and misfits. This interpretation suggests that there is no particular risk of spousal homicide *per se* in May–December marriages; people who are married to people much older or younger than themselves may be at high risk of involvement in *all* sorts of trouble, including *non*spousal homicide. Unfortunately, the Statistics Canada data files do not include the offender's spouse's age (unless, of course, the spouse was the victim), so we cannot presently test this hypothesis.

Partners in Procreation

The panhuman institution of marriage is, we have argued, basically a reproductive union. Couples share a profound, beneficent interest in the welfare of their offspring, the vehicles of both parties' fitness prospects. It follows that children of the present marriage are likely to be sources of spousal harmony rather than discord, because they facilitate consensus on the crucial question of how the couple's resources should be allocated. Children from former mateships, on the other hand, are a source of spousal conflict, especially but not only if they reside with the married couple.

The Darwinian theory of nuclear family conflict that is outlined in the preceding paragraph is strongly supported by research. Clingempeel (1981), for example, studied two groups of American stepfather–natural-mother families that differed in whether the husband had noncustodial children of his own from a previous marriage. The current marriage was less successful for both partners if he did. Messinger (1976) asked remarried Canadians with children from former marriages to rank the areas of "overt conflict" in each of their marriages. For the failed first marriages, children and money were hardly ever mentioned as areas of conflict, but they ranked at the top of the list for the remarriages. The crux of these conflicts is clear from Messinger's report: The natural mother wanted more of the stepfather's resources invested in her children than he was inclined to volunteer.

According to Becker, Landes, and Michael's (1977) analyses of a large body of American demographic data, the presence of children of the current marriage lowers the divorce rate for first and subsequent marriages alike, whereas the presence of children of former marriages raises it. We predict that the risk of spousal homicide will be found to vary in the same way as the risk of divorce. We do not presently have the data to test this prediction: Available samples of spousal homicide cases do not include information on the reproductive histories of the protagonists.

If homicide risk parallels divorce risk, we should expect to see lower rates of homicide between couples with children than in childless couples of similar age and duration of marriage. We have no evidence at all on this question, but it is conceivable that no such effect will be found simply because childless couples in conflict are better able to walk away from the marriage before the explosion than are those with children. Moreover, putative offspring of the marriage may be worse than none at all, if the husband questions his paternity of them. To this we shall return.

The prediction of marital conflict as a result of nonconsonant reproductive interests is stronger for the case of families with broods of mixed parentage. We have already seen the huge elevation of homicide risk that is suffered by stepchildren at the hands of resentful substitute parents in Chapter 4. What we are asking now is whether the marriage partners themselves experience an increased risk of violence in stepfamilies. Some homicide studies suggest that they do.

Henry Lundsgaarde (1977) examined police files on one year's sample of Houston killings. His monograph includes brief capsule accounts of 33 conjugal cases. In 11 of these synopses, the narrative reveals that there was a stepchild in the household. One in three is certainly a much higher proportion of stephouseholds than would be expected by chance, and the situation may be even worse: One in three is a minimum estimate, since Lundsgaarde expressed no particular interest in stepfamilies. In each case, he happened to disclose the steprelationship incidentally to other details.

Peter Chimbos's (1978) Canadian interview study also suggests a link between spousal homicide and stepchildren. Three of the six "typical" cases that Chimbos described in detail were stepfamilies: one stepmother home, one stepfather home, and one family where both parties had children from previous marriages. In two of the remaining three cases, the couple had children who were allegedly sired by the husband but in both cases the wife had a long history of affairs that were known to him, and one might reasonably question his confidence of paternity.

The relationship between the suspicion or knowledge of nonpaternity and a jealous rage is deserving of study. When legal scholars discuss the doctrine of "provocation and the reasonable man," they deal at length with revelations of adultery: Should such revelations be accorded the same provocative status as direct observation of the act? But there has been little discussion of the effects of revelations of nonpaternity. It is clear that the latter revelation can have deadly consequences, too, and not just secondarily to the implicit revelation of infidelity. Consider, for example, the words of this killer in Chimbos's (1978) study (not one of the six detailed cases discussed above), recounting the events precipitating his wife's death:

> You see, we were always arguing about her extramarital affairs. That day was something more than that. I came home from work and as soon as I entered the house I picked up my little daughter and held her in my arms. Then my wife turned around and said to me: "You are so damned stupid that you don't even know she is someone else's child and not yours." I was shocked! I became so mad, I took the rifle and shot her. (p. 54)

Reproductive conflicts are probably relevant to another conspicuous phenomenon in spousal homicide: the remarkable prevalence of couples living common-law. In various samples of spousal homicide in America, a substantial proportion of the couples dwelt common-law rather than being legally married: 35% of 43 cases in Miami in 1980 (Wilbanks, 1984), for example, 31% of 45 in Houston in 1969 (Lundsgaarde, 1977), and 46% of 972 cases occurring in Detroit between 1926 and 1968 (Boudouris, 1971). Common-law unions are probably especially prevalent among the poor, the young, perhaps the city dwellers, the very groups in whom homicide rates are highest; still, they seem to be overrepresented. Perhaps the material investment of men in common-law unions is relatively low, and the women are therefore more likely to be on the lookout for alternatives, inspiring a more coercive proprietariness in their mates.

In Canada, the homicide rate is very much higher in common-law unions (Figure 9.4). And what is more intriguing than the simple rate difference is the fact that risk is a strikingly different function of age in common-law marriages than in legal marriages (compare Figure 9.5 with Figure 9.2).

In absolute numbers, there are more common-law homicides among people in their 20's and 30's than among those somewhat older. The remarkably high homicide rate among middle-aged couples represents a few dozen cases within an age group that very rarely *lives* common-law in Canada. But although that high rate represents relatively few cases, it is still of interest to inquire why this group should exhibit such exceptional risk. Our hypothesis is that middle-aged couples living common-law are exceptionally likely to have children from previous unions. (We know that about half of our middle-aged common-law homicide cases involved couples in which one or both parties were still legally married to someone other than the present mate.) Small or grown, residing with the couple or not, such children might be a major source of discord. Confirmation or refutation of this hypothesis awaits further research.

Familicide, Suicide, and Spite

As we noted in Chapter 4, there is an infrequent but regularly recurring variety of homicide in which a husband kills his wife and one or more minor children: During a 23-year period, there were 61 such cases in Canada and no equivalent massacres by wives.

In many of these cases, it may be that the perpetrator views himself as the long-suffering victim of a parasitic wife and an insatiable brood of

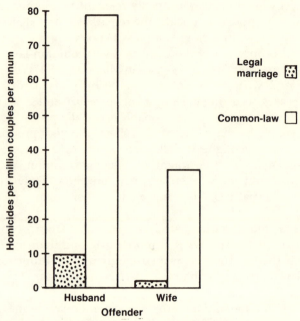

Figure 9.4. Rate of spousal homicide in legal versus common-law marriages. Canada, 1974–1983.

dubious origin. Explicit suspicion of nonpaternity is seldom noted in such cases, but wifely infidelity is often the immediate stimulus, as in this 1969 Canadian case (Greenland & Rosenblatt, 1975):

Offender: Male, age 38
Victims: Female, age 31, wife of offender
          Male, age 8, son of offender
          Female, age 11, daughter of offender
          Male, age 41, lover of offender's wife

    The wife of the offender was a secretary in a business where she met and began an affair with the marketing manager. Her husband learned of the relationship, and telephoned their employer as well as the wife of the marketing manager.

    Several days before the mass murder and suicide, he purchased a rifle from a Canadian Tire store where he had to be shown how to operate and load it. The salesman said he seemed very nervous and upset.

    His wife and her lover were found dead of rifle wounds in his automobile in a public park. Apparently the offender then returned to his home (in a car rented that day), took the children to an isolated recreation area where he shot them and himself. (p. 86)

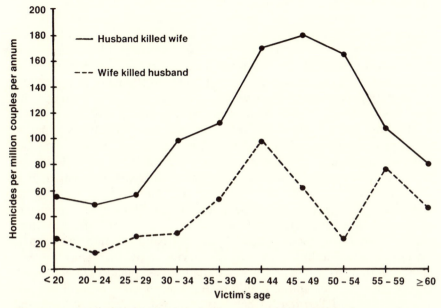

Figure 9.5. Spousal homicide victimization rates within common-law marriages, as a function of age and sex. Canada, 1974–1983.

This sort of case illustrates with particular clarity just why we insist that adaptation must be sought at a more psychological level than that of direct behavioral optimization and fitness maximization. A rational fitness-maximizer would surely let the children live, for even if he doubted their paternity, they might, after all, be his. But fitness is not the man's proximal concern. His view of his family is apparently more *proprietary* than solicitous, and this same proprietary attitude manifests itself in cases where the husband cannot tolerate his wife's impending or recent desertion of him. Such cases are extremely prevalent among wife-murders generally, and also among the suicidal and familicidal cases. The prospect of losing his family through death apparently strikes the desperate familicidal father as no more disastrous than the prospect of losing them through desertion! Better, perhaps, since at least he has called the shots and exerted his authority. Call such a killer "mentally ill" if you like—Canadian police reporting such cases to Statistics Canada routinely choose that "motive" category—but sane men, too, feel rage and despair under the same circumstances.

In Chapter 5, we discussed a recurring variety of filicide-suicide by mothers, who despair for their children as well as themselves, and resolve to "rescue" the children from a cruel world. A few familicides by men may be similar. An Australian psychiatrist has described, for example, four cases of "family murder followed by suicide," two committed by women and two by men (Goldney, 1977). One case, attributed to "morbid jealousy," was of the sort we have already seen: The husband slew his wife, three children and himself after making noisy public accusations of the wife's infidelity. But the other male killer was classified with the two women as acting out of "severe depression."

Whether the "depression" of familicidal men is truly like that of women remains questionable, however. Goldney's little Australian sample still reflects a male–female contrast: Both men methodically destroyed their wives and children before themselves, whereas neither woman made any attempt upon her husband's life. This contrast between the sexes turns out to be quite general. Women who resolve to die and to take their loved ones with them seem *never* to include their husbands in their "rescue fantasies." The husbands are more likely to be part of the problem that the women are trying to rescue themselves and their children *from*. In our 10-year Canadian sample, 15 women killed one or more of their minor children and then themselves, and not one of those 15 also killed her husband. By contrast, 12 out of 36 men who committed comparable acts of filicide-suicide also killed their wives.

Not to deny that familicidal men are "depressed"; many clearly are. But even in their depression, they betray a proprietary attitude toward the wife and children that women manifest, if at all, toward the children alone. Possibly even more common than the jealous or deserted familicidal man is the one who, depressed by his own failures, kills a family whose loyalty to himself he does not doubt. An American domestic servant who shot his wife and only son (age 14) in their beds and then botched a suicide, explained his behavior (while under "light sodium pentothal narcosis") thus (Guttmacher, 1960):

> I kept thinking this was an easy way out of everything. Everytime we planned anything there was an obstacle. The boy was part of it. We planned to buy a home and that fell through. My wife, my son, oh my wife! We struggled; everytime we think we was out of a rut, we dropped back in. Something was pulling us down all the time. (p. 105)

A 55-year-old professional man, seemingly much more successful, provides an eerily similar explanation, after he too killed his wife and son in their beds (in this case with a hammer) and then botched his suicide (MacDonald, 1961):

> I kept thinking about the bills coming, the house taxes. Piling up, piling up in my mind. I knew I couldn't keep doing that. I thought everything was

going to fall around my head. I know it could be a catastrophe in a short time. My son wouldn't be able to stand the stigma, my wife wouldn't have the things she was used to. (p. 222)

Similar cases are presented by West (1965, p. 53), by Scott (1973a, p. 122), and by Greenland and Rosenblatt (1975, p. 74), among others. If there is a standard familicidal syndrome (at least among the suicide cases), this is it.

The only homicides in which there is any substantial probability of suicide are those rare cases involving blood relatives and those much more frequent cases in which a man kills a woman. Men who kill unrelated men, whether acquaintances or strangers, hardly ever commit suicide. Suicidal killers are mainly men who have killed women, and more particularly women with whom they have (or in some cases only aspire to) a sexual relationship (Table 9.3). Indeed, romantic motives are so generally relevant to murder-suicide that if a man kills a *man* and then himself, experienced police will immediately entertain the hypothesis of a homosexual relationship.

In Canada between 1974 and 1983, just 7 of the 248 women who killed their husbands (2.8%) committed suicide at the scene of the murder, compared to 192 of the 812 men who killed their wives (23.6%). Of course the overall suicide rate in men surpasses that in women (see, e.g., deCatanzaro, 1981), but by much less than this eightfold difference in suicide rates between male and female spouse-killers. In Wolfgang's Philadelphia study, 10 of 53 spouse-killing men (19%) committed suicide, as compared to one of 47 spouse-killing women (2%). In Wilbanks' Miami study, the corresponding figures were 6 of 23 men (26%) and none of 20 women.

What on earth is a man thinking about when he kills his wife or girlfriend—perhaps their children as well—and then himself? Several writers have suggested that such suicides are remorseful reactions to having killed, and by implication were unplanned. (It was once popular to assert further that women do not commit suicide after killing, because they lack the male's highly developed moral sense, and are therefore remorseless!) However, detailed reports of particular cases often render this theory untenable: The killer leaves instructions, notes, or other evidence that the murder-suicide was a preplanned whole. In fact, unplanned suicide out of remorse for having killed appears to be an extremely rare event. (Whereas 192 homicidal Canadian husbands killed themselves immediately after the homicide, only another 3 committed suicide days or weeks later. Indeed, in the total sample of 6559 Canadian homicides, there were just 8 killers who committed suicide after a delay that might reflect remorseful brooding.)

Table 9.3. The Probability of Suicide After Homicide, in Relation to the Sexes of Killer and Victim, and Their Relationship, Canada, 1974–1983

Killer's relationship to victim	Male killer		Female killer	
	Male victim	Female victim	Male victim	Female victim
Spouse	—	.236 (192/812)	.028 (7/248)	—
Lover	—	.268 (22/82)	.000 (0/7)	—
Parent	.333 (42/126)	.380 (35/92)	.108 (11/102)	.136 (12/88)
Offspring	.009 (1/112)	.040 (2/50)	.091 (1/11)	.083 (1/12)
Other blood relative	.031 (7/225)	.092 (6/65)	.000 (0/21)	.000 (0/13)
Other marital relative	.113 (13/115)	.257 (9/35)	.000 (0/9)	.000 (0/3)
Unrelated acquaintances	.029 (45/1527)	.086 (27/314)	.011 (1/87)	.029 (1/34)
Unrelated strangers	.014 (12/860)	.034 (11/324)	.000 (0/43)	.000 (0/15)
Totals	.040 (120/2965)	.171 (304/1774)	.038 (20/528)	.080 (14/175)

Whether we conceive of a man's interests in terms of fitness or more proximal pleasures, murder-suicide seems a spectacularly futile act. It is "spiteful," as evolutionists use the concept of spite: The actor plans and carries out a course of action that is devastating to his own interests, just for the sake of inflicting damage on another. In straightforward models of the natural selection of social inclinations, spiteful urges cannot readily evolve. That a desperate man should formulate the bitter intent to kill and then to die—and should act upon that intent—must somehow be a byproduct of his more adaptive concerns with social competence, material success, fidelity, paternity, deterrent power, reputation, self-esteem, and his authority as a husband and father.

Men do not easily let women go. They search out women who have left them, to plead and threaten and sometimes to kill. As one Illinois man told his wife 6 months before she divorced him and 7 months before he killed her in her home with a shotgun, "I swear if you ever leave me, I'll follow you to the ends of the earth and kill you" (People v. Wood, 391 N.E. 2d 206). The estranged wife, hunted down and murdered, is a common item in police files; the converse case of a vengeful murder by a jilted wife is an extreme rarity, the popularity of the theme in fiction notwithstanding. Among legally married, cohabiting Canadian spouses in 1974–1983, a man was almost four times as likely to kill his wife as to be killed by her (404 cases vs. 107); among estranged couples, he was more than *nine* times as likely to kill her as she him (119 vs. 13). And whereas 43% of the 119 homicides by estranged husbands were attributed by the police to "jealousy," only 2 of the 13 by estranged wives were so attributed; the rare case of a woman killing her estranged husband is likely to be a case of self-defense against a man who will not let her be.

The man who hunts down and kills a woman who has left him has surely lapsed into futile spite, acting out his vestigial agenda of dominance to no useful end. As one might then expect, murder-suicide is even more prevalent among such men than among wife-killers generally: 42 of the 119 Canadian men who killed estranged wives (35.3%) killed themselves as well, as compared to 21.6% of other wife-killers. The fiercely proprietary jealousy of men, so useful in intimidating wives and rivals, is at best a two-edged sword.

Retaliation
and Revenge

— 10 —

"Osveta, that means . . . a kind of spiritual fulfillment. You have killed my
son, so I killed yours; I have taken revenge for that, so I now sit peacefully
in my chair. There you are.

Response of an elderly Montenegrin villager to a request for a definition of
"osveta" [vengeance].

Boehm (1984), p. 54

In preceding chapters, we have considered the circumstances in which
people kill their children, their parents, their husbands, their wives. We
have considered the status competition between men that fuels the
majority of fatal conflicts in America, and the sexual rivalry and
proprietariness that comprise the principal provocations to homicide in
the modern world. But we have hardly yet considered a homicide
motive that may well have claimed even more lives in human prehistory
than any of these: blood revenge.

Blood Revenge in Foraging Societies

For hundreds of millenia, all people lived by gathering uncultivated
plants and by hunting wild animals. The divisions of labor, of expertise,
and of authority that we take for granted were unknown. There was no
professional police force and no judiciary. Victims of injustice had to rely
upon what legal scholars refer to as "self-help"; if aggrieved parties did
not take the initiative in redressing their grievances, nobody else would.

The trouble with the term "self-help" is its seeming implication of
total individualism. To the contrary, early people—and indeed our
prehuman ancestors—were perfectly capable of cooperation in the
pursuit of shared goals. Above all, they relied upon *kin* help. Our
foraging forebears lived in bands that were based largely upon kinship
and the fundamental commonality of interest that kinship implies.
Although it must be conceded that relations between close kinsmen can
sometimes be murderously rivalrous, as we have seen, fraternal

221

solidarity is much the more dominant force. The relations between neighboring bands, by contrast, were inevitably rivalrous and frequently hostile. So while one's chances of avoiding rape, theft, displacement, exploitation, and death depended upon one's individual formidability to a degree, they depended even more upon social solidarity and the deterrent force of one's kinsmen. These surmises are verified by studies of the several and various hunting-and-gathering societies that persisted into the twentieth century. In such societies, many—perhaps most—murders were motivated by the desire to avenge prior deaths of relatives. Let us consider a few examples from modern hunter-gatherers.

Historical and ethnographic accounts of Inuit (Eskimo) life tell of frequent bloodshed from Greenland to Alaska. The Inuit's stoical acceptance of infanticide and senilicide under conditions of cold and starvation are famous. What is less well known is that Inuit men in the prime of life were also frequent murder victims. It seems that men killed other men primarily in order to abscond with their wives, and men without formidable relatives at hand were vulnerable indeed. Among the Netsilik of Pelly Bay, for example (Balikci, 1970),

> A stranger in the camp, particularly if he was travelling with his wife, could become easy prey to the local people. He might be killed by any camp fellow in need of a woman. In ancient times such assassinations led to the formation of revenge parties consisting of the relatives of the victim, resembling war expeditions. (p. 182)

This ethnography proceeds to a description of one particularly bloody such expedition, culminating in a massacre. The story was still being recounted, with extensive details of the individuals and their genealogical relationships, more than a hundred years after the event. Balikci (1970) concludes that

> The objective of the revenge party was not just to kill the original murderer but members of his kindred as well. In a sense the members of the kindred shared responsibility for the murder. (p. 184)

The acquisition of wives by murder. Vengeance by the murder victim's kin. The targeting of the original murderer's kinsmen. Occasional revenge massacres far in excess of "an eye for an eye." Each of these features of Inuit existence is echoed repeatedly in accounts of the lives of other Amerindian foraging peoples. Among the various bison-hunters of the Great Plains, for example, men raided neighboring groups for women and for horses, killing their owners if necessary or expedient. Homicides were occasions for blood revenge which might be directed at either the killer or a kinsman, and which might be carefully reciprocal or instead become the pretext for a massacre.

Feuds, in which each killing was retaliatory, graded insensibly into circumstances of chronic enmity and warfare. Warrior virtues were exalted among Plains Indians to a degree more common among horticulturalists and pastoralists than among hunter-gatherers. Full manhood often required the "counting of coup," the ceremonial scalping of a slain enemy. Scalps thus became a homicide motive in their own right; like young men in other warring societies in Amazonia, New Guinea, and elsewhere, a young brave might kill some unoffending nontribal victim simply for the glory of having killed, and by so doing might provoke further bloodshed. According to Biolsi (1984), "revenge expeditions" involving up to several hundred men were "the most common manifestation of large-scale Plains warfare" (p. 152). Truces between Plains Indian tribes with a history of mutual killings were extremely fragile, since many men on each side might still consider the entire tribe of some kinsman's killer to be appropriate targets for revenge. Chief Thunderchild of the Plains Cree tells how several chiefly efforts to forge alliances with traditional enemies during the 19th century were undermined by individual acts of violence. A Cree warrior named Pai-chuck, for example, vowed to kill a Blackfoot, any Blackfoot, in revenge for the murder of his wife; he shot an unsuspecting chief of that tribe who was visiting the Cree chief Sweet Grass in truce. Pai-chuck exultantly advertised his success in words that have been shouted in countless tongues: "Blood for blood!" (Ahenakew, 1973).

The various tribes of the Pacific northwest may also be considered hunter-gatherers, since they neither grew crops nor kept livestock. However, their fishing economy permitted degrees of social stratification, division of labor, and accumulation of wealth that were attained elsewhere only by people with agriculture. Warfare among these west coast Amerindians was likewise more elaborate than is typical among foraging peoples, involving lengthy campaigns, long-distance invasions, and major battles. The stated motive for these expeditions was again revenge, and accounts of particular wars include numerous details of individual battle decisions based on individual grievances and kinship links. Homicides within a tribe, by contrast, were avenged with attention to precise equity: an eye for an eye. Among the Bella Coola, for example (McIlwraith, 1948),

> If a person is killed or wounded, revenge is the affair of his family . . . Every effort is made to slay the murderer, but if he should escape from the country, the injured group is satisfied by killing one of his family . . . A death is answered by a death; if two persons should be slain for one murder

the family which has suffered the double loss endeavors to kill another of their enemies. (pp.147–148)

Australian aborigines constitute another major group of hunting and gathering cultures, no less renowned for their fierceness than the native Americans. Once again, blood revenge and retaliations for other slights (especially the theft of women) appear to have been the main provocations to violence. Warner (1937) collected information on 72 "battles" among the "Murngin" of Arnhem Land, during a 20-year period in the early 20th century. Ninety-six men died in these clashes, which ranged from surreptitious nocturnal stabbings to pitched battles among dozens of men. Fifty of the 72 incidents were undertaken as acts of blood vengeance for the death of a relative.

Finally, we cannot leave a discussion of hunter-gatherer practices without reference to the Kalahari San, the best studied and most famous of foraging peoples. Unlike the warrior tribes of Australia and North America, the San have been immortalized by anthropologists as "the gentle people," and indeed they have fought no wars that anyone can still recall. But this does not mean that retaliatory violence is alien to them. Richard Lee (1979) collected the accounts of 22 homicides which had taken place among the traditional foraging !Kung San during a 50-year period. (This translates to about 293 homicides per million persons per annum, a surprising rate for a society renowned for nonviolence!) Like their more warlike counterparts on other continents, these Kalahari hunter-gatherers avenged slain kinsmen. As Lee (1979) notes, "If a killing occurred it was more likely than not to be followed by a retaliatory killing; 15 of the 22 homicides were parts of blood feuds" (p. 392).

On the Cross-Cultural Ubiquity of Blood Revenge

Blood revenge is not solely a practice of hunter-gatherers. Quite the contrary, in fact: Lethal retribution and blood feuds have evidently increased in likelihood and in intensity since the invention of agriculture.

In a foraging society without strong clans or other political organization, vengeance is likely to be taken opportunistically. It may even be foregone altogether for a variety of pragmatic reasons: if the enemy is so strong that revenge will be suicidal, for example, or if pressure from third parties is sufficient to deter repeated offenses without the necessity for a retaliatory deterrent as well. Among the Inuit, the !Kung San, and many other unstratified societies, the one-time murderer sometimes remained in society unpunished, although a second killing might place him at risk of collectively sanctioned execution. (This of course refers to a homicide within a group having sufficient coherence that its members are considered worthy of moral consideration. In most tribal societies, killing an outsider was no crime at all, except insofar as it needlessly imperiled the group by inviting massive retaliation.) Such nonobligatory vengeance is repeatedly encountered in the ethnographies of unstratified foraging societies. Here, for example, is an early description (Man, 1885) of the aftermath of homicide among the Andaman Islanders of the Indian Ocean:

> Should a man kill his opponent nothing is necessarily done to him, though it is permissible for a friend or relative of the deceased to avenge his death . . . as conscience, however, makes cowards of us all, the homicide, from prudential motives, not infrequently absents himself till he is assured that the grief and indignation of his victim's friends have considerably abated. (p. 42)

The situation is quite different among settled agriculturalists with strong hierarchical clan organizations. Here, blood revenge assumes the status of a sacred obligation. A killer cannot simply take a trip and expect the matter to blow over. Tempers may cool, but duty and hatred remain.

In one of the early classics of legal anthropology, R.F. Barton (1919) tells us this about a certain tribe of Phillipine horticulturalists: "The Ifugao has one general law, which with a few notable exceptions he applies to killings, be they killings in war, murders, or executions . . . That law is: *A life must be paid by a life.*" (italics in original) (p. 69). Other tribal peoples take a similar approach to the problem of legal order. A particularly vivid account is this South American example (Karsten, 1935):

> The Jibaro Indian is wholly penetrated by the idea of retaliation; his desire for revenge is an expression of his sense of justice. His great principle is eye for eye, tooth for tooth, life for life. . . . The soul of the murdered Indian requires that his relatives shall avenge his death. The errant spirit, which gets no rest, visits his sons, his brothers, his father, in dreams, and weeping conjures them not to let the slayer escape but to wreak vengeance upon him for the life he has taken. If they omit to fulfill this duty the anger of the vengeful spirit may turn against themselves. To avenge the blood of a murdered father, brother, or son, is therefore looked upon as one of the most sacred duties of a Jibaro Indian. . . . It may happen that a Jibaro keeps the thought of revenge in his mind for years, even for decades, waiting for the opportunity to carry it out, but he never gives it up. (pp. 271–272)

In societies from every corner of the world, we can read of vows to avenge a slain father or brother, and of rituals that sanctify those vows—

of a mother raising her son to avenge a father who died in the avenger's infancy, of graveside vows, of drinking the deceased kinsman's blood as a covenant, or keeping his bloody garment as a relic.

According to the Italian proverb, revenge is a dish best eaten cold. Other peoples have parallel sayings. The icy satisfaction of revenge is as human as mother love, or so, at least, thought so astute an observer of human affairs as Shakespeare:

> If you prick us, do we not bleed? If you tickle us, do we not laugh? If you poison us, do we not die? And if you wrong us, shall we not revenge? If we are like you in the rest, we will resemble you in that. (Shylock in *The Merchant of Venice*, III, i)

Is Shylock's implicit theory of human nature correct? Do all peoples resonate to the concept of vengeance? In order to assess the cross-cultural generality of retaliatory killings, we examined relevant ethnographic materials for that same standard sample of 60 societies (the HRAF Probability Sample) that was used in Chapter 3's survey of infanticide. We sought in the ethnographies any evidence of the idea of taking a life for a life, and we found such evidence for 57 of those 60 societies: We encountered either some reference to blood feud or capital punishment as an institutionalized practice, or specific accounts of particular cases, or at the least, some articulate expression of the *desire* for blood revenge. The only three societies for which we could *not* find such evidence were Cagaba (South America), Thai, and Dogon (West Africa).

The evidence of this ethnographic survey thus confirms a conclusion that was advanced by Kelsen (1946) and many others after him, on the basis of less systematic reviews: *Lethal retribution is an ancient and cross-culturally universal recourse of those subjected to abuse.* This generalization seems to us to gibe so well with intuition and common experience as to be unexceptionable. However, some anthropologists may be startled by its apparent contradiction with the results of Keith and Charlotte Otterbein's (1965) well-known "cross-cultural study of feuding." These authors stated that "Feuding, the dependent variable, was defined as blood revenge following a homicide" (p. 1470), and then declared that such "feuding" was "absent" in 28 societies out of a sample of 50, and "infrequent" in an additional 14.

There is no genuine contradiction with the present conclusion. The Otterbeins' (1965) seeming allegation that blood revenge was "absent" in a majority of societies depends upon definitional idiosyncrasies:

> If the kin of the decreased sometimes would accept compensation in lieu of such revenge, the society was coded as having *infrequent* feuding. Feuding

was considered to be *absent* in those societies which had a formal judicial procedure for punishing the offender, which always settled such matters through compensation, or which were reported to rarely have homicide. (italics in original) (p. 1470)

Note that the Otterbeins' categories are given what seem to be at least semiquantitative labels (frequent vs. infrequent vs. absent), but that the definitions belie the labels. The occasional acceptance of blood money is surely no evidence that blood revenge was "infrequent"; in fact, the two practices are probably positively correlated. Moreover, by treating the mere availability of judicial procedure as a criterion for the "absence" of feuding, the Otterbeins show that their concern is with ideals, not behavior: They do not ask whether blood revenge in fact *occurred*, but rather whether it was legitimate and institutionalized. (And even so, their criteria of "absence" fail, for by the criterion of formal judicial procedure, feuding is absent from such notorious feuding societies as those of 19th-century Montenegro and Albania!) In simple fact, the ethnographic record is too anecdotal and impressionistic, too lacking in numerical data, for us to determine where blood revenge was rare and where it was rampant. It seems certain that there are major cross-cultural variations in the prevalence and the institutional legitimacy of the practice, but attempts to get more quantitative than this are whistling in the dark. What our survey suggests is that the inclination to blood revenge is experienced by people in all cultures, and that the act is therefore unlikely to be altogether "absent" anywhere.

Fraternal Interest Groups

Although the Otterbeins' categorization does not really concern the "absence" or "frequency" of revenge killings, it nevertheless discriminates societies with different institutions, namely the presence or absence of arbitration in homicide disputes, the acceptability of compensation in place of blood revenge, and the institutionalization of prolonged interfamilial feuds. And so, despite the seriously misleading claim that blood revenge is "absent" from a majority of societies, the Otterbeins' principal empirical result is interesting and apparently valid; this is that protracted blood feuds are particularly characteristic of societies with *patrilocal residence* and *polygynous marriage*, that is to say societies organized into rival patrilineages or "fraternal interest groups."

> Vengeance—this is a breath of life one shares from the cradle with one's fellow clansmen, in both good fortune and bad, vengeance from eternity. Vengeance was the debt we paid for the love and sacrifice our forebears and

fellow clansmen bore for us. It was the defense of our honor and good name, and the guarantee of our maidens. It was our pride before others; our blood was not water that anyone could spill. It was, moreover, our pastures and springs—more beautiful than anyone else's—our family feasts and births. It was the glow in our eyes, the flame in our cheeks, the pounding in our temples, the word that turned to stone in our throats on our hearing that our blood had been shed. It was the sacred task transmitted in the hour of death to those who had just been conceived in our blood. It was centuries of manly pride and heroism, survival, a mother's milk and a sister's vow, bereaved parents and children in black, joy and songs turned into silence and wailing. It was all, all. (Djilas, 1958, p. 107)

Milovan Djilas, the author of this paean to vengeance, bridged the gap between tribal and modern society. One of the architects of Yugoslavian communism, and a vice-president of that country between his imprisonments, Djilas was born into a feuding clan of Montenegrins for whom head-hunting raids against the neighboring Muslims were a recent memory. The Djilasi feuded with some powerful rival clans, and they only barely survived (Djilas, 1958):

Though the life of my family is not completely typical of my homeland, Montenegro, it is typical in one respect: the men of several generations have died at the hands of Montenegrins, men of the same faith and name. My father's grandfather, my own two grandfathers, my father, and my uncle were killed, as though a dread curse lay upon them. My father and his brother and my brothers were killed even though all of them yearned to die peacefully in their beds beside their wives. Generation after generation, and the blood chain was not broken. The inherited fear and hatred of feuding clans was mightier than fear and hatred of the enemy, the Turks. It seems to me that I was born with blood on my eyes. My first sight was of blood. My first words were blood and bathed in blood. (p. 8)

And the Djilasi gave as good as they received.

Where fraternal interest groups are powerful, a man without agnatic kin is fair game. Indeed, tribal people may *explain* a particular act of seemingly unprovoked homicide to an appalled missionary or anthropologist by pointing out that the victim had no relatives. In such a social milieu, one's corporate kin group becomes paramount. Djilas, for example, writes (1958)

My forebears were drummed into my head from earliest childhood, as was the case with all my countrymen. I can recite ten generations without knowing anything in particular about them. In that long line, I am but a link, inserted only that I might form another to preserve the continuity of the family. . . . (p. 6)

Since men are the principal killers in all societies, blood feud and clan warfare flourish especially where solidary male kinship groups maintain a nominal identity and a territorial integrity. The development of such fraternal interest groups, and hence of institutionalized blood feud, is to some degree predictable from the society's mode of subsistence. Foragers often reckon descent bilaterally and are opportunistic in their residence patterns, so that territorial patriclans do not develop. A force of agnatic kin is not easily mustered, and clan warfare is rare. Patrilineality is frequently stronger among slash-and-burn horticulturalists and is apparently universal and stronger still among pastoralists; the same may be said of blood feud. With more settled agriculture, where land title is the basis of wealth, ties of vassalage replace those of kinship, central authority grows and takes over the retaliatory functions of clansmen, and feud again withers. To this we shall return.

After a single homicide, it is perhaps typical that a single act of blood revenge settles the score. But if the two sides differ in their calculations, or in their views concerning the justifiability of the initial slaying, then the result may be a seemingly interminable feud. The fact that revenge is not necessarily taken against the killer himself—and moreover that the preferred target is an individual of status equal to the original victim—provides the clue to the motivation of feuding: the fragile balance of power—indeed the balance of *terror*—between rival lineages. Feuds (and small-scale warfare) ultimately have to do with material and reproductive rivalry. The constant specter confronting each fraternal interest group is defeat or extermination by rivals: the theft of one's women, the loss of one's lands, the end of one's line. In chronically feuding and warring societies, an essential manly virtue is the capacity for violence; head-hunting and coup counting may then become prestigious, and the commission of a homicide may even be an obligatory rite of passage, as in the Sepik River peoples of New Guinea (pp. 150–152). To turn the other cheek is not saintly but stupid. Or contemptibly weak.

On the Utility of the Revenge Motive

Geronimo, that great Apache thorn in the sides of the Mexican and American armies, was driven by vengeful motives. In 1858, a troop of Mexican cavalry massacred an Apache camp in peacetime, while the men were away trading. Geronimo was a young man. His mother, his wife, and his three small children were among the victims.

In the summer of 1859, a confederation of four Apache subtribes mounted a retaliatory expedition into Mexico. They encountered the perpetrators of the massacre near the Sonoran town of Arizpe, and the Apache chieftains gave Geronimo command. He later wrote (1906):

> I was no chief and never had been, but because I had been more deeply
> wronged than others, this honor was conferred upon me. . . . In all the
> battle I thought of my murdered mother, wife and babies—of my father's
> grave and my vow of vengeance, and I fought with fury. (p. 52)

The Mexican force consisted of two companies of cavalry and two of
infantry, but with numerous losses, the Apaches killed them to the last
man (Geronimo, 1906).

> Still covered with the blood of my enemies, still holding my conquering
> weapon, still hot with the joy of battle, victory, and vengeance, I was
> surrounded by the Apache braves and made war chief of all the Apaches.
> Then I gave orders for scalping the slain.
> I could not call back my loved ones, I could not bring back the dead
> Apaches, but I could rejoice in this revenge. (pp. 53–54)

Rejoice? Geronimo wrote these words in a prison cell, his Apache
nation broken and nearly extinct. The urge for vengeance seems so
futile: There's no use crying over spilt milk, and spilt blood is equally
irrevocable. Many anthropologists and other writers have marveled at
the endurance of vengeful motives and at the effort expended and
suffering endured in pursuit of their satisfaction. Avengers may exult
even in suicidal acts of retaliation. "Nothing is more costly, nothing is
more sterile, than vengeance," wrote Winston Churchill.

Churchill's complaint is readily translated into Darwinian terms. Why
should revenge be sweet? Its attainment is not obviously fitness-
promoting. To the contrary, the avenger incurs risks to his own life,
while neglecting more clearly practical pursuits, and if he succeeds, he
risks provoking further retaliations against himself and his genetic
relatives. "Spiteful" motives—those which entail the embracing of costs
to oneself (ultimately in fitness) in order to inflict costs on a rival—
cannot readily evolve by natural selection. Adaptive decisions are based
on prospective assessments of probable future costs and benefits. The
single-minded avenger therefore seems to have forsaken the pursuit of
goals that could reasonably be expected to contribute to his fitness.

The counterargument is of course the utility of vengeance in *deterrence*. In a competitive world, it is important to convince dangerous
rivals—whether individuals or lineages, and whether more or less
powerful than oneself—that one can only be exterminated at unaccept-
able cost to the exterminator. And a believable threat of retaliation must
be a genuine one. Herbert Spencer (1897) placed this deterrent function
of revenge in a Darwinian framework almost a century ago:

> Among members of the same species, those individuals which have not, in
> any considerable degree, resented aggressions, must have ever tended to

disappear, and to have left behind those which have to some effect made counter-aggressions. . . . Every fight is a succession of retaliations—bite being given for bite, and blow for blow. Usually these follow one another in quick succession, but not always. There is a postponed retaliation; and a postponed retaliation is what we call revenge. It may be postponed for so short a time as to be merely a recommencement of the fight, or it may be postponed for days, or it may be postponed for years. And hence the retaliation which constitutes what we call revenge, diverges insensibly from the retaliations which characterize a conflict.—But the practice, alike of immediate revenge and of postponed revenge, establishes itself as in some measure a check upon aggression; since the motive to aggress is checked by the consciousness that a counter-aggression will come; if not at once then after a time. (pp. 361–362)

Spencer's argument is of course concerned with competition between individuals rather than lineages, and therefore with retaliation for sublethal insults. Indeed, it is essentially the same argument that we used to account for violence motivated by considerations of "status" and "face" (Chapter 6), provided that the certainty of counteraggression is advertised not only to one's antagonist of the moment but to a larger audience as well. But the argument is easily extended to rivalries between corporate kin groups within which there is a commonality of fitness interests, and hence to blood revenge.

An Eye for an Eye, A Tooth for a Tooth

What is harder to explain than the revenge motive itself is the widespread concern with *equity* in vengeance, with "evening the score." Why not a *life* for an eye, and a massacre for a murder? Well, of course, these things *do* occur: Minor provocations have triggered painstakingly programmatic family exterminations and genocides countless times in human history. When the extermination of an irritating rival clan looks to be practical—that is to say achievable without such severe losses as to make the killers vulnerable to other rivals—then such extermination is manifestly thinkable by tribal (and not so tribal) minds. Thinkable and do-able, as well: People plan massacres and they carry out their plans.

Margaret Durham's (1928) ethnography of tribal Albania provides a good illustration. This was a society with institutionalized practices of blood feud, according to a careful calculus of reciprocity. Predatory excesses in social competition, however, could invite retaliations whose aim was not redress but extermination.

In February 1912 an amazing case of wholesale justice was reported to me which had recently taken place in Mirdita. A certain family of the Fandi bairak had long been notorious for evil-doing—robbing, shooting, and being a pest to the tribe. A gathering of all the heads condemned all the males of the family to death. Men were appointed to lay in wait for them on a certain day and pick them off; and on that day the whole seventeen of them were shot. One was but five and another but twelve years old. I protested against thus killing children who must be innocent and was told: "It was bad blood and must not be further propagated." Such was the belief in heredity that it was proposed to kill an unfortunate woman who was pregnant, lest she should bear a male and so renew the evil. (p. 75)

Is this not a smaller-scale equivalent of the genocidal massacre of a tribe or ethnic group? Among the Jibaro of South America, for example (Karsten, 1935):

Whereas the small feuds within the sub-tribes have the character of a private blood-revenge, based on the principle of just retaliation, the wars between the different tribes are in principle wars of extermination. In these there is no question of weighing life against life; the aim is to completely annihilate the enemy tribe. . . . The victorious party is all the more anxious to leave no single person of the enemy's people, not even small children, alive, as they fear lest these should later appear as avengers against the victors. (p. 277)

The Albanian killers found moral justification for their action in the provocations and heritable inferior qualities of the victims. The Jibaros were apparently more candid in acknowledging their competitive motives. But in either case, the result was the same: some inconvenient social competitors were eliminated.

Moralistic pretexts are routinely offered as justifications for such concerted acts of violence, but the self-interest of the executioners in eliminating dangerous or otherwise costly competitors is transparent. Indeed, the instigators of opportunistic genocidal massacres *have* to adopt a moralistic stance. It is essential that they advertise to other potential rivals—perhaps their temporary allies in the present action— that the act of mass murder is an exceptional response to exceptional provocation, and not simply a manifestation of an expansionist policy. Otherwise, the perpetrators of genocides place all their rivals on defensive alert, and invite a preemptive strike against themselves.

So excess in revenge is a constant temptation and a not infrequent reality. "An eye for an eye" is not so much the articulation of the revenge motive as it is a *moral injunction* to equity—an attempt to *contain* revenge. But an attempt by whom, and in whose interest?

Many anthropologists and other writers have considered the institutionalized blood feud to have a "function" for society as a whole, namely controlling and containing lethal violence. The typical version of this interpretation, like so much of anthropological "functionalism," commits the fallacy of naive group selectionism: the assumption that adaptive practices arise by some unspecified but automatic process to serve the purposes not of individuals but of societies. (Williams, 1966, demolished naive group selectionism in evolutionary biology, but it lingers among evolutionarily uninformed social scientists.) Those writers who see the blood feud as serving a function for society as a whole are then at a loss to understand why carefully reciprocal feuding exists side-by-side with the phenomenon of opportunistic and systematic exterminations, which far surpass the demands of "an eye for an eye." But of course an avenger does not act to preserve "society," he acts to preserve his *kin group,* and often, more than merely to preserve it, to increase its power and possessions. The choice between eye-for-eye retaliation and all-out war is a decision made out of self-interest. The partial truth in the "society's interest" view is that cooperative groups of powerful individuals, concerned to maintain tribal solidarity against the threat of rival tribes, may act to limit escalated conflicts within the tribe by manipulating the rewards and penalties for lawful versus unlawful retaliation.

A precise, rule-bound equity in revenge is inevitably a fragile state of affairs; one side or the other must often be tempted to seize an opportunity or advantage, and to impose a final solution to the conflict. Since leaders are concerned to limit such internecine conflicts in the interest of forging larger polities, it is little wonder that equitable vengeance so often assumes the status of a moral imperative. The Old Testament's injunctions to avenge in kind are echoed in numerous other moral codes.

Thus the moral glow of retaliatory justice derives in part from the self-interest of arbiters. But more than this, it appears that a precise equity in revenge may often be in the best interests of the avenger himself. The cold satisfaction of retaliation in kind may therefore reflect specific evolved algorithms of social transaction, after all. The grounds for this conjecture lie in recent theoretical studies by Robert Axelrod and W.D. Hamilton, addressing the question of the bases of cooperation among potential rivals.

The "problem of altruism" in a world that has been forged by natural selection was largely solved by Hamilton's (1964) "inclusive fitness" theory: Behavioral inclinations that have negative effects upon their bearers' phenotypes and reproductive prospects can nevertheless evolve if they are effectively nepotistic. But nonrelatives are capable of cooperation too, although their alliances are more fragile than those based on blood. How, in the face of opportunities for self-interested defection, is such cooperation possible? The essence of this question can be illustrated by a "game" called the "Prisoner's Dilemma."

The prototypical version of Prisoner's Dilemma goes like this. You and a partner in crime have been caught red-handed on a job. The police, interrogating the two of you in separate rooms, offer you this deal: Implicate your partner in other crimes and they will reduce the present charge. No doubt, they are making your partner the same offer. The temptation to accept is strong: If your partner betrays you and you remain silent, you'll receive the greatest penalty. Moreover, even if your partner remains silent, you can *still* reduce your expected penalty by betraying him. In either case, rational self-interest dictates accepting the police's offer. So where's the dilemma? Well, if you both talk, you'll both go to jail for longer than if you both remain silent; by making the seemingly rational choice, both prisoners do worse than they might have by cooperating! This condition defines the game.

Now consider a variant of Prisoner's Dilemma played for rewards rather than to reduce punishments. Two players, Frank and Beans, must each choose one of two alternatives ("cooperate" or "defect"), in ignorance of the other's choice. Rewards are then as follows:

Frank plays	Beans plays	Frank receives	Beans receives
Cooperate	Cooperate	$3	$3
Cooperate	Defect	0	$5
Defect	Cooperate	$5	0
Defect	Defect	$1	$1

The objective is to maximize personal profit. As in the prison version above, if Beans cooperates, Frank's best choice is defection ($5 vs. $3) and if Beans defects, Frank's best choice is *still* defection ($1 vs. nil). Beans's situation is identical to Frank's. Both players, if rationally pursuing the objective stated above, must defect, and so they get a dollar apiece. Somehow they are missing a mutually profitable outcome. Why?

Frank and Beans are unlikely to arrive at the cooperative "contract" that would profit them both because they cannot *negotiate*. The essence of this claim is not their inability to talk to one another; talk is cheap. The inopportunity to negotiate refers to the inability to *enforce* cooperation by penalizing defection once a contract has been struck. But suppose that the two players are going to play a *series* of games. Suddenly, each has a means to reach the other: By making one's own choices contingent upon the opponent's prior choices, one can reward cooperation and punish defection.

In a single game of Prisoner's Dilemma, the most profitable strategy for each player is defection. But in a series of games—a series of indeterminate length—the best strategy involves a simple contingency: *Cooperate the first time, and then match your opponent's last move.* Axelrod discovered the superiority of this "Tit for Tat" strategy by an unorthodox method of research: He invited game theorists and other mathematically minded folks to submit strategies for a computerized Prisoner's Dilemma tournament. Tit for Tat, the simplest strategy submitted, was also the best, as Axelrod and Hamilton (1981; Axelrod, 1984) were later able to prove. Analogizing the contest to competition and selection in the biological world, by bestowing fitness in proportion to rewards and reiterating over "generations," they showed that Tit for Tat will supplant and will resist invasion by any sort of more complex conditional strategy, and in particular any that involves either a greater or a lesser response to defection by the opponent.

The Tit-for-Tatter retaliates precisely in kind, no more and no less, and, at least in this simple model, that seems to be the most profitable strategy. It is a strategy that neither provokes suicidal escalating feuds nor advertises weakness which would invite exploitation. There are thus some grounds in formal theory for supposing that when one anticipates a long history of interactions with another whose prowess approximates one's own, and when those interactions may be either cooperative or rivalrous, then the best strategy may indeed be an-eye-for-an-eye. It follows that the powerful positive affect associated with measured retaliation—the sacred duty, the spiritual fulfillment, the icy satisfaction of revenge—may well represent the human psyche's evolved response to the fundamental cost–benefit structure of enduring social relations among potential rivals.

An Honorable Resolution

Sometimes a single retaliatory homicide pays the blood debt and ends the matter. In fact, many authors have maintained that the usual extent of blood revenge is thus and no more. But hard feelings are unlikely to be banished by such retaliation, and the lineages involved are likely to differ in reckoning the balance of affronts and replies. The upshot may then be feud.

It is popular to refer to feuds as "interminable" and to stress their transmission across generations. One suspects, however, that there is often an element of exaggeration here. Missionaries and other imperialists routinely overstate the destructiveness of traditional practices, including feuds (as noted, for example, by Sonne, 1982), in order to seize the moral high ground for their own "civilizing" activities. In this exaggeration they may be abetted by the members of the feuding society themselves, who tell heroic tales about gigantic feats of vengeance and about limitless patience in its pursuit. What must be recalled is that these stories of heroic action reflect ideals at least as much as they reflect history, and that a noisy, public idealization of vengeance is a cornerstone of the intimidatory rhetoric of effective deterrence. Prolonged feuding weakens both sides, and it weakens any larger polities to which the rival lineages may both belong. There are thus many individuals, both within and without the feuding lineages, with a vested interest in the arbitration of a feud. It would be surprising indeed if feuds were truly "interminable."

The trick, of course, is to negotiate a face-saving settlement. Neither party must be seen to capitulate or to acknowledge any sort of incapacity to pursue the feud indefinitely, for such an admission of weakness would invite contempt and further mistreatment. The arbitration of long-standing feuds, with many deaths and other affronts on the ledger, was a major diplomatic feat and a principal preoccupation of tribal leaders and aspiring kings in early state societies.

Even the initial act of vengeance might be averted by appropriate arbitration. And sometimes a murder would be so legitimate in the eyes of the larger community that even the victim's kinsmen would have few options but to deem it justifiable and forswear vengeance. Many ethnographies assert, for example, that wives slain for adultery were not avenged, where uxoricides for other reasons were.

When the initial killing was provoked but less than fully justified, material compensation might be negotiated. (The calculation of homicide debts, to which we shall return shortly, is a major issue in many legal codes.) Persuading the victim's kinsmen to accept blood money was a delicate task, however. To accept such compensation and forsake revenge was often shameful, implying that one's familial loyalty could be bought. "I will not carry my dead son in my pouch," was the furious retort of a father scorning blood money (Grimm, 1899, quoted by Goebel, 1937).

It is frequently a part of the ideology of stateless societies that *all* killings must be avenged. (Moreover, it is often maintained that there are no natural deaths; those which have not been inflicted by observable means must have been caused by witchcraft. There is then considerable room for creativity in the identification and punishment of witches, and although the motives here too are likely to be vengeful—that is to say retaliatory and competitive, self-interested acts of the accusers—we shall leave the subject of sorcery accusations and subsequent action to the next chapter.) But the ideology of obligate vengeance was not necessarily adhered to in practice, even when the death was unequivocally inflicted by another human being. In particular, the chroniclers of many societies have noted that material compensation in lieu of revenge is much more likely to prove acceptable to the victim's next of kin if the initial homicide were unintentional. In the event of a deliberate murder, arbitration may only be possible *after* a revenge killing. The existence of these practices and attitudes reinforces the point that the social display of one's will and ability to retaliate are very much the point. It is an act of magnanimity to accept an apology for an accidental affront, but to turn the other cheek in response to deliberate aggression is mere weakness or stupidity. He who forgives a deliberate act of violence simply invites another.

Early legal codes are largely—sometimes almost entirely—concerned with the specification of homicide debts. Howell's (1954) "Manual of Nuer Law," for example, contains more on this subject than on any other. Differential prices are prescribed for killing prepubertal boys versus men, for accidental versus deliberate killings, for immediate versus delayed death, and so forth, although it is evident that such laws did not prevent individualistic negotiation. Elaborate traditions of procedure invest the transactions with authority and solemnity; the Nuer have ritual names for the various cattle paid to close and distant kinsmen of the homicide victim (and to the arbiter), as well as for each cow slaughtered and eaten during the negotiations.

Treston (1923) found evidence in Homer's epics of an ancient confrontation between two incompatible legal traditions: individual culpability and the obligatory execution of the killer himself, on the one hand, versus a more tribal wergild, on the other. The latter practice—that in which the kindred of the killer paid compensation to the kindred of the slain man—was certainly predominant throughout Europe and the middle east for millenia after Homer. Hardy's (1963) *Blood Feuds and the Payment of Blood Money in the Middle East* traces the evolution of homicide debt in the Arab world from preIslamic practices to the rulings of Ottoman, Syrian, Lebanese, and other courts.

Quantitative analyses of the determinants of differential homicide payments, both within and between societies, would be enlightening. The stated rules are interestingly variable. The Nuer of the Sudan were apparently unusual among pastoral people, for example, in that they prescribed identical payments in cattle for victims of either sex. The "standard rate" among their Somali neighbors was 100 camels for a man and 50 for a woman (Contini, 1971), a common magnitude of difference. Hardy (1963) suggests that the wergild for a woman was one-half of that for a man throughout the Muslim world, but he presents verbatim interviews with two Bedouin judges that suggest otherwise. Can such cross-cultural variations be linked to other practices?

Variation within societies, when studied from a sample of actual cases, may well prove even more revealing. Sometimes the prescribed blood moneys are straightforwardly interpretable as, for example, when compensation is proportional to the victim's social status, as is typical in highly stratified societies. A woman's reproductive value may affect the compensation due at her death, as in this example from the Sebei of Uganda (Goldschmidt, 1967):

> There are three different compensations made when a woman is killed: (1) when a woman has just married and not yet produced children, ten cows and one sheep are paid because of her possibility for bearing many children; (2) if a woman is of middle age and has some children but is still able to produce more, payment of eight cows and one sheep would be expected; (3) if she is an old woman, five cows and one sheep would be paid. (pp. 102–103)

Moreover, the actual case settlements are likely to depart from idealized rules. Just as Borgerhoff Mulder (1988) has shown that Kipsigis bride-prices, although idealized as invariant, in fact increase with the bride's reproductive value, so too may we expect to see variable economic valuations placed upon the victims of homicide. We are not aware of any systematic studies of this phenomenon, but there are hints in the literature that they would be worthwhile. Although Contini tells us the Somali's "standard rate," for example, he also describes lengthy negotiations that include consideration of the "age, sex and social condition of the victim." The explicit objective is compensation for the loss, and it would be interesting to know both the criteria that are openly raised in such negotiations and the variables that are actually predictive of the settlement.

Vengeance Lost

The close relatives of a murder victim in modern North America confront a system that has no place for them. If they are forceful in their demands to know either the details of the homicide itself or how the police investigation is progressing, then they are treated as an embarrassment or a nuisance. When prosecutor and defense agree to a reduced charge—perhaps for considerations quite unrelated to the present homicide, such as in exchange for information about other criminal acts—the victim's relatives are not consulted and are without recourse. If they think that the prosecution is outgunned by high-powered defense attorneys, they cannot retain their own lawyers to represent their interests in the criminal courtroom. They have no claim on the killer's property unless they launch a civil suit that is independent of the criminal trial. The offender can appeal an unsatisfactory verdict; the bereaved victims cannot.

How have we come to such a remarkable state of "impersonal justice"? The surviving victims of a homicide are entitled neither to revenge nor to compensation, nor even to representation in court! How have these profoundly interested parties come to be so thoroughly disenfranchised? These questions become especially intriguing when we recognize what an exceptional state of affairs this is. In most societies—other than the most despotic, in which all crime is crime against the despot—the interests and wishes of the offended parties are of paramount importance in determining judicial response.

The answer clearly has something to do with the individualistic ideology of the modern industrial west. In tribal societies, compensation is paid by a collective of the killer's kinsmen to the kinsmen of his victim. Our modern justice entails no such concept of distributed responsibility, and just as we limit culpability to the individual killer, so too do we limit the victim role to the slain individual. Each man is an island. But of course, this is merely a description of our present legal response to homicide and its attitudinal supports, not an explanation. Individualistic ideology has not, after all, redesigned human emotions. The relatives of the slain still feel themselves victimized, still hate, still thirst for revenge.

Don Sullivan, the founder of a Canadian organization called Victims of Violence, has a recurring dream. He sees the man who raped and murdered his daughter leaving prison after completing his sentence, and he sees himself stepping forward, raising a gun, and firing. The dream is not a nightmare; it gives Sullivan peace. Nevertheless, in writing about his daughter's case to the Solicitor General of Canada, Sullivan offered a disclaimer that is almost obligatory in our culture (Amernic, 1984): "I do not want revenge. The courts and God have and will handle that for me. I want justice for my daughter Pam's sake, and satisfaction for me and my family" (p. 124).

It is a curious fact of our society that "revenge" is a dirty word. To acknowledge that motive is to acknowlege that one has an axe to grind, rather than being a dispassionate contributor to an impersonal justice. The thirst for revenge disqualifies, as self-serving and therefore suspect, the testimony of precisely those individuals most concerned to see that the guilty pay.

Susan Jacoby (1985) quotes the ritual denials of Nazi death camp survivors and other victims of violence when accused of seeking vengeance. "No," the victim must reply without visible signs of anger or hatred, "I seek only justice." Any other stance and the battle is lost. But what exactly is this disinterested "justice"? What other than *just deserts:* a measured retribution that is appropriate to the crime? Jacoby makes a powerful case for the proposition that revenge is an essential component of the very idea of justice, and that by denying and denigrating the revenge motive, we make a coherent philosophy and practice of justice impossible.

Without punishment scaled to the severity of the wrong, neither victim nor judge can feel that justice has been done. Moreover, and paradoxically, measured retribution is essential not only for the satisfaction of those wronged, but for the protection of offenders as well. Without such a conception, the dispensing of criminal justice becomes a pragmatic system of rewards and punishments for the purpose of behavior control. Predictors of the efficacy of reinforcement and deterrence, along with the detention of those likely to offend again, become the paramount criteria of appropriate punishment in such a system. Lacking any moral authority, law without just deserts can rule only by terror.

These considerations suggest that the retributive component of justice warrants acknowledgment and respect, but they offer little insight into the reasons for the revenge motive's present low repute. Somehow, revenge has declined from a sacred duty to a shameful urge! This represents a remarkable turnabout in conventional values, a turnabout that is intimately linked to the criminal justice system's gradual disenfranchisement of the victim. If we wish to understand why we now treat homicide as we do—our modern notions of responsibility, the penalties imposed, the lack of standing of the victim's kinsmen, and so forth—we will not gain that understanding by attempting to deduce present practices and values from the first principles of some coherent moral theory of the purposes of law. Rather, we must explain modern legal responses to homicide as the products of an historical succession of conflicting interests and their resolutions.

The Decline of Kin Right in English Law

The earliest English laws of which we have record are those issued by King Aethelbert I of Kent in about 602 A.D. Aethelbert's laws were almost entirely concerned with the specification of monetary compensations for various wrongs: 50 shillings for lying with a maiden belonging to the king, for example, 12 for lying with a nobleman's serving maid, 6 for a commoner's; 3 shillings for a broken rib, 20 for a severed thumb, 9 for a forefinger, 4 for a middle finger, and on and on. The *wergild* (blood money) to be paid to a homicide victim's kin varied from 6 shillings for the lowest commoner to 100 for a free man; in the latter case, another 50 went to the king for infraction of his seigneurial rights.

Aethelbert's and other early law codes recorded extant custom at least as much as they proclaimed new rules. Graded wergilds had been paid among Germanic tribes for centuries. The responsibility for raising the wergild was distributed among a wide circle of the killer's kinsmen, sometimes extending to seventh cousins, and the receipt of werglid was similarly distributed among the kinsmen of the slain. It was a feature of Anglo-Saxon and other Germanic laws that the payment and receipt of wergild involved kinsmen on both the paternal and maternal sides, the former paying and receiving two-thirds. The same provision was found in Welsh law, and although the precise 2:1 ratio may have been borrowed from the Anglo-Saxon invaders, it is clear from Ireland and elsewhere that Celtic wergild, like the Germanic, had long involved both paternal and maternal relatives. This meant that an ego-centered kindred of unique composition was constituted in each case, by contrast to the "credit union" of a named patrilineage or clan in a strictly patrilineal system (Lancaster, 1958).

Within the Germanic tradition of wergild, the remarkable feature of Aethelbert's and other 7th-century English law codes is their indirect testimony about the degree to which English society had already moved toward feudalism. The circle of kinsmen who paid or received wergild had narrowed to a degree not seen in Scandinavia, for example, until centuries later (Phillpotts, 1913). Moreover, the parties involved in compensation might include unrelated lords and owners of the protagonists as well as blood kin.

Written laws can provide much incidental insight into contemporary society. The 74th law of King Ine of Wessex (about 690 A.D.), for example, reads as follows (Attenborough, 1922):

> If a Welsh slave slays an Englishman, his owner shall hand him over to the dead man's lord or kinsmen, or purchase his life for 60 shillings.—If,

however, the lord will not pay this price for him, he must liberate him; afterwards his kinsmen must pay the wergild, if he has a free kindred; if he has not, then his enemies may deal with him.—A freeman need not associate himself with a relative who is a slave, unless he wishes to ransom him from a vendetta; nor need a slave associate himself with a relative who is a freeman. (p. 61)

Clearly, the rights and duties of vassalage were already cross-cutting the bonds of kinship, were sometimes obviating them, and were to some degree recognized as substitutes for them. People were sometimes opting out of the rights and duties of blood relationship. Also apparent from this law is the fact that the existence of specified wergilds did not necessarily make blood revenge superfluous or illegal. (The same Anglo-Saxon law codes that specified wergilds also specified circumstances, such as the killing of a thief, in which a homicide did *not* justify a retaliatory homicide; clearly, *some* homicides *did*.) But revenge killing was apparently only justified if the wergild had not been paid.

Homicide was a violation of the "king's peace." This is no empty phrase. Kings ruled by virtue of their capacity to convince rivalrous houses of the advantages of alliance under a single banner, and by their ability to guarantee their vassals' safety. To kill a free subject was particularly an offense against the king because it undermined his guarantee. Much the same contract was implicit at each hierarchical level of feudal society. Thus, there were additional fines paid to the owner of the property on which a homicide occurred, again for violation of his peace. But in Aethelbert's time and indeed long after, a homicide was still in effect a tort: A relative of the slain man (or his lord) had to act as plaintiff by "appealing" the offender.

It was after the Norman conquest of 1066 that the king's justice assumed a new and superordinate status with respect to homicide. William did not fully disenfranchise the victim's kin, but he outlawed private vengeance. In effect, revenge for a prior killing ceased to be an acceptable defense. The victim's lord or kinsmen might still negotiate monetary compensation from the killer's, but if they wished a more violent revenge, their only legal recourse was appeal. Moreover, *all* homicides, regardless of any exchange of considerations and truce between the kindred, were now treated as offenses against the crown. The incentive to reach a satisfactory concord with the victim's relatives must have been seriously compromised by the continuing likelihood that the killer might be convicted and executed anyway.

Prior to the Norman invasion, *morth* (murder) referred to a particularly heinous variety of killing, namely that committed in stealth. King Cnut (1016–1035) maintained that ordinary homicide might be settled by feud (i.e. retaliation against the killer's kinsmen) or by wergild, but that morth required the handing over of the murderer himself to the kin of the slain man. It was not merely the urge to dispatch one's enemy without a fair and open confrontation that made morth the worst sort of homicide; unlike the honest, public killer, the murderer attempted to evade the just recompense of wergild or feud by hiding his identity.

William I changed the meaning of murder, in a manner reminiscent of modern occupying armies: He held the entire local community to account for the death of any Norman. The "hundreds" constituted an administrative level of local populace (approximately a hundred households) charged to elect a "jury" that would investigate all homicides and report the facts to the king's courts. The *murdrum* was instituted as a special fine payable by the hundred in the event that they could *not* prove the victim's Englishry, that is to say that the victim was *not* a Norman. In effect, then, the murdrum was a sort of wergild, extracted from a whole ethnicity, namely the English; more precisely, it was an instrument of colonial control.

The administration of royal justice was strengthened by William's son, Henry I, who established the *eyres*. These courts traveled the realm, sitting for weeks at a time in each locale to hear all of the king's business that had transpired since their last visit. No doubt their administration of justice was both a benefit and a burden to the local communities, but perhaps more the latter, as the justices in eyre were much concerned with levying fines against all manner of transgressions, and were a significant source of the king's revenues. Homicides were a small part of the justices' mandate, but they were investigated assiduously, as the king confiscated the chattels of convicted felons. And the jurors had better remember to present each case that had occurred since the last eyre—possibly an interval of several years—under pain of fines to themselves. A local agent of the crown, the *coroner*, had the duty of investigating deaths, and the justices in eyre consulted his records; woe betide the jury that neglected to report a death which the coroner had attributed to homicide.

Gaol sentences were not routine punishments (although an accused felon might long have languished in prison awaiting trial). William's favorite punishment was not death but mutilation (Pollock & Maitland, 1895), which must often have proved fatal in any case. His successors preferred hanging. By the twelfth century, execution followed conviction in short order, often in front of the justices in eyre themselves. And all grades of homicide—indeed all felonies—were capital crimes. In principle, that is. In practice, the majority of killers escaped the gallows by one device or another. Some killers went missing before they were apprehended, and these were solemnly *outlawed* when they failed to appear at the eyre: stripped of their property and placed under sentence of death. According to Given's (1977) analysis of 13th-century eyre records, this was the most likely outcome of all: 1444 of 3492 accuseds (41%) were outlawed, 944 (27%) were acquitted, and only 247 (7%) were executed.

Some killers were recommended to mercy by the justices as a result of mitigating circumstances such as a plausible claim of self-defense, and were then likely to be pardoned by the king. Others secured the king's pardon before they were tried, often at a considerable price. But only 56 (1.6%) of Given's accuseds were pardoned. More were allowed to *abjure the realm:* These killers were escorted to a port and sent into exile (which might eventually be revoked); 258 (7%) of Given's accuseds abjured. And some (78; 2.2%) escaped the gallows through *benefit of clergy*, the right of a man of the cloth to be tried in an ecclesiastical court whose penalties did not include death. This benefit could be claimed only once, and the branding of clergied felons ensured that this limit was observed, but the qualification for benefit of clergy was often nothing more than a literacy test or recitation of a psalm, with the effect that the educated classes were entitled to one free felony. Murder with "malice prepensed" remained a clergyable offense until 1512, and manslaughter still longer. Only in 1827 was the benefit of clergy finally abolished altogether.

What then of the victim's kin? Long past the Norman conquest, they continued to negotiate settlements with the killer, at least occasionally. But the vestiges of a formalized wergild were virtually nonexistent: Recorded agreements of the 12th and 13th centuries make it clear that there was no prescribed man-value, and that the killer alone contracted to pay (although he may, of course, have sought assistance from kinsmen).

Seemingly more important than the option of negotiating a settlement was the aggrieved kinsman's continuing right to appeal. The appellor made a formal accusation at the first available county court session, between eyres. The appellee could be seized and held in gaol until the next eyre, or could be outlawed after repeated failure to answer the appeal. If he did answer the appeal, he had a choice: jury trial or combat with the appellor! Few seem to have chosen the latter, presumably because men likely to lose in combat with the appellee were unlikely to appeal him. Indeed, most appeals were lodged by women, who were not themselves obliged to offer to fight, but who could instead name a champion; this situation was so clearly inequitable that woman's right of appeal was eventually restricted to the slain man's wife. Even the king's pardon did not obviate the kinsman's right of appeal. The pardon merely withdrew the king's own suit, and explicitly stated that the accused must still "stand to right" if appealed. (The victim's lord or vassal was also entitled to lodge an appeal, but few seem to have done so; Hurnard, 1969.) In effect, the crown's suit and the victim's suit were parallel and independent proceedings against the homicide.

In practice, however, this right of appeal seems to have been of little avail (Hurnard, 1969). By 1300, most appeals were apparently being quashed on procedural grounds. Appeals were sometimes used to force a monetary settlement, but if one were reached, the parties had to buy an expensive king's license to stop the appeal and legalize the compensation; better to arrange a settlement without appealing. As we observed above, the majority of accused killers were executed or were outlawed fugitives from justice, so why appeal them? And as for those who had been acquitted of the king's charge, they would probably elect jury trial and be acquitted again, with the unsuccessful appellor liable to deterrent penalties. Finally, among the relatively few pardons, Hurnard could find just one case in which the appellee was arrested, tried, and executed despite having secured the king's pardon. In her words, "The ostensible protection of the family's ancient right to prosecute was largely illusory" (p. 213). Long before the victim's relatives were disenfranchised *de jure*, they were disenfranchised *de facto*.

Blood feud and wergild persisted much longer in Wales (Davies, 1969) and Scotland (Wormald, 1980). Edward I was appalled by the Welsh practice of homicide settlements, and made them illegal in 1284, but Davies (1969) shows that they persisted in elaborate detail until at least 1400, and vestigially for much longer still. But feudal ties vied with those of blood: The Welsh victim's lord typically received 8 of the 24 pounds paid by his killer's kinsmen. As for Scotland, feuding was robust among the clans for longer still. Many "lettres of slanis" survive from the 15th and 16th centuries, documents acknowledging the receipt of full and acceptable compensation by the slain man's kin, and therefore pledging to refrain from blood reprisal. The English kings trod softly in imposing their law upon the Scots, and the old system persisted along with the new, only gradually atrophying, just as had Anglo-Saxon law in early Norman England.

Impersonal Justice

Feuding and compensation decline everywhere as kin solidarity declines and central authority grows. Perhaps this occurred earlier in England than in much of northern Europe because the English economy was more thoroughly based in crop agriculture and land-holding than in pastoral agriculture, trade, and pillage. Because land title was the single most crucial resource, the ties of vassalage—metaphorically modeled on kinship—began to replace those of kinship itself, as the individual's most important social bonds. (Inheritance, of course, remained intrafamilial, an important point to recall lest one overstate the degree to which vassalage supplants kinship.) Primogeniture in the inheritance of lands and titles sent second sons away into careers in the army or the church; although ties of kinship were surely not forgotten, brothers were likely to live apart and to become alienated in their perceived interests. In a world of feudal hierarchy, relatives were not necessarily an asset at all. In late Scottish wergild cases, for example, those sued often denied their relationship to the killer altogether, even though the circle of responsible kinsmen had been narrowed down to those closer than fourth cousins; the issue before the court thus became that of reconstructing genealogies.

It is the conceit of men in modern state societies that their high level of civilization has liberated them from the evils of primitive lawlessness, and there is a grain of truth in this view. The principle reason why the state has been able to usurp the role of victim-avenger is that this role is often more a burden than an entitlement. People are *relieved* to relinquish the duty of vengeance, but only if they can trust the machinery of state to punish their enemies in their behalf, and thus to deter future wrongs. Like the Anglo-Saxon kings, the apparatchiks of the modern impersonal state offer the citizenry a social contract: protection in exchange for the relinquishing of some personal autonomy. From the king's or state's perspective, feud within the realm is disruptive of order, jeopardizes the tax base, and weakens the society's defensive capabilities against external threat.

Persuading men who have relied on their personal prowess to relinquish the private threat of vengeance remains a delicate task. Fears persist that one's reliance upon the punitive and deterrent powers of the state is an admission of personal impotence and an invitation to future mistreatment. The issue is perceived as one of "honor." The mother of the American president Andrew Jackson is reported to have said that "the law affords no remedy that can satisfy the feelings of a true man" (Rogin, 1975, p. 58). Jackson clearly adopted his mother's attitude as his own, for he was an accomplished duelist, and he wrote:

> To go to law for redress is to confess publicly that you have been wronged and the demonstration of your vulnerability places your honor in jeopardy, a jeopardy from which the "satisfaction" of legal compensation in the hands of secular authority hardly redeems it. (quoted by Ayers, 1984, p. 18)

These are the words of a trained lawyer and elected head of state!

A Darwinian view of the psychology of human conflict sheds considerable light on the ways in which people react to affronts: upon the revenge motive and the tit-for-tat or eye-for-eye strategies that function to deter future affronts; upon the differential valuation that is placed upon the lives of individual victims according to their reproductive value or their degree of relatedness to the actors; in short, upon all manner of responses to homicide in face-to-face societies. But it may seem less likely that this same perspective could shed any light upon the response of the impersonal machinery of modern state justice.

We believe that attention to the evolved motives of individuals may still be illuminating even here. For one thing, to whatever degree the impersonal state may have assumed the role of plaintiff and victim in criminal cases, real people are in fact the aggrieved parties. It would be naive to suppose that the machinery of state will investigate and prosecute all cases with equal vigor. The resources of police and prosecutors are limited, and they feel the heat about some unsolved homicides or ill-prepared prosecutions more than others. *Fatal Vision*, a recent, popular account of an American army doctor's gruesome murder of his pregnant wife and two children (McGinniss, 1983), provides a clear example of a case that would never have led to a conviction without dogged detective work and badgering of the authorities by the slain woman's stepfather. It is clearly the case that persistent plaintiffs at least occasionally exert major effects upon the thoroughness of homicide investigations and upon such crucial aspects of procedure as plea bargaining. It would be interesting (and perfectly possible) to investigate whether those homicide cases in which the victim has close relatives attending to the proceedings typically lead to stiffer penalties than otherwise comparable cases in which the victim is without kin. We doubt that justice would prove itself blind to such considerations.

If individual interests can still intrude, making justice inequitable, then the system will surely defend the interests of the powerful, not necessarily by punishing high-status offenders less severely than others—the publicity surrounding such cases often precludes light sentences—but by punishing in proportion to the status of the victim. In America, for example, discrimination in sentencing against black offenders has apparently waned or even disappeared in recent decades, and yet the victim's race remains relevant, with offenses against blacks being treated less harshly than those against whites (e.g., Bowers & Pierce, 1980; Jacoby & Paternoster, 1982; Paternoster, 1983; Baldus *et al.*, 1986). There can be little doubt that people who kill high-status victims are punished more severely in North America than are those whose victims are nobodies. In fact, although public opinion makes homicide a more serious offense than any property crime (e.g., Rossi *et al.*, 1974; Weiss & Perry, 1976; Evans & Scott, 1984), major thefts and robberies are commonly penalized more severely than are homicides in which the victims are of low status.

In Chapter 7, we saw that the everyday homicides of poor, urban America are not newsworthy. Everyday judicial practice seems to concur with the evaluation of the news media: Such homicides are not treated as important. In our sample of 1972 Detroit cases, for example, we know the eventual dispositions in 121 solved, garden-variety homicides: cases in which a man killed another unrelated man in a dispute arising out of some social conflict rather than during another criminal act. Fifty-seven offenders (47.1%) were not convicted of any crime in connection with the homicide (56 cases dismissed, mainly as "justifiable," "excusable," or "self-defense," and a single acquittal after trial). Of 64 convicted offenders, only two were found guilty of first-degree murder, 12 of second-degree murder, 34 of manslaughter, and 16 of lesser charges. A typical sentence for manslaughter was 3–5 years in state prison, with parole available after 18 months.

Such summary data on sentencing are seldom published, fewer still on the actual sentences served. The few summary data that do exist concern only those killers actually imprisoned. Despite ceaseless public debates about the alleged "coddling" of criminals, about capital punishment, and so forth, it is a remarkable fact that nobody in the United States or Canada knows the statistical distribution of actual penalties imposed upon apprehended killers.

Public ignorance of our justice system's response to homicide is most poignantly revealed in the occasional bursts of publicity surrounding particular cases. In 1985, for example, 76-year-old Roswell Gilbert, a retired engineer, shot his terminally ill wife, Emily, in their Fort Lauderdale, Florida, home. Gilbert's conviction for first-degree murder and his sentence to 25 years in prison without possibility of parole provoked great sympathy and great public discussion. Commentators agonized over the moral dilemma between compassion for the nonmalevolent—indeed merciful—killer and the necessity that no homicide be condoned. According to a full-page essay in *Time* magazine (Rosenblatt, 1985), for example:

> Imagine the precedent set by freeing a killer simply because he killed for love. . . . Laws are unlikely to be changed by such cases: for every modification one can think of, there are too many loopholes and snares. What Gilbert did in fact erodes the whole basis of law, which is to keep people humane and civilized. Yet Gilbert was humane, civilized and

> wrong: a riddle. In the end we want the law intact and Gilbert free, so that
> society wins on both counts. What the case proves, however, is that society
> is helpless. . . . (*Time* magazine, Aug. 26, p. 52)

Lofty sentiments indeed, and all apparently predicated upon the assumption that Gilbert's sentence was a manifestation of the judicial
system's uniform abhorrence of murder. But this is far from the truth.
What was nowhere remarked in the immense publicity surrounding this
case was how exceptional was the sentence imposed on Gilbert.

According to Wilbanks' (1984) study of 1980 Miami homicide cases,
the *majority* of *solved* homicides did not lead to any prison term at all, and
only about one in eight to a sentence as severe as Gilbert's. More than
100 identified Miami killers—2 a week—were not even charged because
the prosecutor considered their actions to be justified. Many of these
were cases in which property owners or store clerks shot and killed
unarmed shoplifters, trespassers, and petty thieves, some of whom
were attempting to flee. Several dozen more cases that *were* prosecuted
led to dismissals or acquittals on similar grounds of justification. In one
of these, a publican shot without warning an unarmed man sitting in a
car, because he feared that the victim might fetch a weapon and return
to the killer's bar, from which he had been evicted; the case was
dismissed by a judge who ruled that one need not be in fear for one's life
at the time of killing in order to claim self-defense, if a threat had earlier
been uttered (Wilbanks, 1984, case 247, p. 337). In practice, then, killing
is officially condoned in Miami in a wide variety of circumstances.
Anyone who wishes to understand the purposes of the criminal justice
system in action would do well to consider just what it is that justifies
homicide in these cases but not in Roswell Gilbert's.

Melodramatic though it may sound, there is in effect a widespread
semiofficial policy of exaggerating the gravity of the state's response to
homicide and other crimes. A "life" sentence, for example, is *not* a life
sentence; it is a nominal fiction. Lesser sentences are also deceptively
overstated. In Canada, release on "mandatory supervision" is routinely
available after two-thirds of the sentence is served. In effect, therefore,
actual sentences are nominally inflated by 50%: The judge solemnly
pronounces and the newspaper dutifully reports a sentence of "3 years"
that in fact means 2, or "15" that means 10. This has nothing to do with
parole, which usually reduces the sentence still further. In both Canada
and the United States, official statistics report that some large number of
homicides are "murders" rather than "manslaughters"; what is not
reported is that this is the initial police categorization, and that the
majority of these "murders" will be reduced to manslaughter or less
before the judicial system is through with them.

We need no Byzantine theory of conspiracy to explain this systematic distortion of information. The judicial and penal authorities are under simultaneous conflicting pressures: economic pressure to empty the jails and political pressure to punish crime more severely. What are they to do but minimize sentences while refraining from advertising the fact? According to a report prepared by the Solicitor General of Canada's office (1981),

> Parole is needed to reduce sentences because if judges were wholly responsible for determining the exact length of incarceration they would tend to respond to public pressure by increasing sentences. Parole is thus a less visible administrative means of reducing punishment. (p. 45)

Moreover, if one takes seriously the deterrent intent of punishment—and most advocates of stiffer penalties do—then what matters is the public *perception* of the severity of those penalties rather than their actual magnitude. The deceptive exaggeration of the penalties levied against criminals could thus be an effective tactic in the battle against crime. But this is at best an incidental benefit of misinformation rather than its intent. The simple fact is that nobody in the judicial or penal systems has any interest in improving the accuracy of the public's knowledge. Each little deception helps keep the heat off.

There is an immense literature on the philosophy and intent of legal punishment. Most writers discriminate the functions of public safety, retribution, deterrence, and correction. The last can be quickly dismissed as of minimal if any importance: Regardless of what one thinks about the possibility and desirability of "rehabilitating" offenders, one must concede that extant penal practices hardly ever serve this purpose and are rarely so intended. Public safety is a more serious objective, but the prediction of "dangerousness" is notoriously inept (see, e.g., Floud & Young, 1981; Monahan, 1981; Webster, Menzies, & Jackson, 1982), and few would countenance the damage to civil liberties that would be entailed by an effective system of "preventive" sentencing. Most of the discussion therefore centers on the goals of retribution and deterrence. A prevalent, modern stance seems to be that retribution is not a legitimate objective of civilized people (e.g., Gorecki, 1983), and that deterrence and the protection of public safety are the only moral grounds for punishment. (Debate therefore shifts to the more empirical questions of the *efficacy* of punishment as deterrence.)

This prevalent stance simply will not work. If our objective were deterrence and not measured retribution, then clearly those crimes that most tempt potential killers would be most in need of deterrence and should be punished most severely. Men are more likely to kill men than to kill women, for example; so should they be punished more severely for the former, more tempting crime? Mothers are far more likely to kill their infants than their older children; do infanticides therefore require heavier penalties than later filicides? We doubt that many of those who deplore retribution and grant legitimacy to deterrence would endorse these and other such proposals. Everyone's notion of "justice" seems to entail penalty scaled to the gravity of the offense. As we suggested earlier, deterrence and retribution are not simply alternative objectives: Effective deterrence is the ultimate function behind the human passion for measured retributive justice—it is the reason why that passion evolved. But our passion for evening the score has thus become an entity in its own right, an evolved aspect of the human mind. Our desire for justice fundamentally entails a desire for revenge.

Calling the
Killers to Account

— 11 —

Homicide is the most heinous and culpable of crimes. Or is it? Not every killer encounters punishment or even disapproval. Some killings are considered praiseworthy: acts of war, some acts of lethal law enforcement, even private acts of vengeance or defense of honor. There are any number of considerations that may be invoked as justification for homicide in one society or another, and many more that are recognized as extenuating circumstances. The killer may live on in his natal community, suffering neither ostracism nor reprisal; indeed he may gain the respect of his fellows by having killed. What then is culpability all about?

The issue of culpability is the moral issue of *blameworthiness* or *desert*: the culpable party *ought* to suffer (be punished) for his misdeeds. He *should* not have done as he did, and he is *responsible* for the consequences of his actions. He is *at fault,* and it is *just* that he should pay or atone for the wrong he has done. Whatever society we may consider, every normal adult understands such mundane moralizing, and engages in it routinely. But the analysis of just what such value judgments mean has filled libraries, and remains a subject of dispute.

There is an ancient philosophical debate concerning the moral justification for the use of punishment. The various stances on this issue are generally categorized as either retributive or utilitarian (see, e.g., Ezorsky, 1972). The utilitarian position is essentially that punishment is justified by net positive consequences. Although the inflicting of suffering on the miscreant is itself an evil, it is warranted because it prevents greater evil, either by protecting society from the further misdeeds of the same wrong-doer or by deterring others from similar misdeeds (or, occasionally, by virtue of benefits resulting from more complex chains of causality). According to most utilitarians, retribution for its own sake is a "primitive" or "barbaric" urge—an urge to be risen above. Retributivists reply that naked utilitarianism is monstrous, justifying excessive punishment of minor misdeeds and even the punishment of the completely innocent, whenever useful. Punishment can only be just, they maintain, if it is considered a good in itself rather than a means to other desired ends, and it can only be a good in itself if it is deserved.

There is no end to the variations that can be played on this theme. Is it the *sine qua non* of the retributivist position that the innocent must not be punished or that the guilty must? That the penalty for a given crime has a just maximum or a just minimum? What is the net good that the utilitarian would maximize: total happiness, average happiness, the happiness of the most miserable individual? Does the justification of punishment depend on the exercise of the miscreant's free well, and if so what is the criterion of a free choice? Can utilitarian arguments be undermined by empirical discoveries (for example, that deterrence does not work), and has retributivism no comparable vulnerability to refutation by factual matters? Is it possible to categorically reject punishment of the innocent on purely utilitarian grounds, and to then arrive at essentially the same prescriptions as a retributivist?

Blameworthiness in Evolutionary Perspective

We do not mock these questions, which may be profound and well worthy of the discussion they have received. But to an evolutionary psychologist, these philosophical debates seem to skirt the issues that are most susceptible to a genuine analysis. Moral sensibility is a cross-culturally universal aspect of human nature: People everywhere have the conception of wrong-doing, the powerful emotional tone of righteous indignation, the pangs of conscience, the senses of duty and indebtedness. When we consult our sense of what is right or just—and all philosophers, however analytic, concede that moral arguments ultimately rest on irreducible apprehensions of right and wrong—then we are consulting moral/emotional/cognitive mechanisms of the human mind. These mental mechanisms must surely have been shaped, like any other organized species-typical attributes of body or mind, by a history of selection. Our moralizing is too consequential to be a mere epiphenomenon of some other cognitive capacity. If conscience and empathy were impediments to the advancement of self-interest, then we would have evolved to be amoral sociopaths. Rather than representing the denial of self-interest, our moral sensibilities must be intelligible as means to the end of fitness in the social environments in which we evolved (see Alexander, 1987; Tooby & Cosmides, 1988).

Morality is the device of an animal of exceptional cognitive complexity, pursuing its interests in an exceptionally complex social universe. Creatures that resolve their social conflicts in dyadic competitive interactions have no need to take specifically *moralistic* exception to an affront; exception that is merely hostile will suffice to motivate whatever degree of deterrent retaliation is called for. Two competitors fighting in private—or indeed even those fighting before interested witnesses, like stags jousting before hinds—simply have no reason to consider the rights and wrongs of their conflict. Might will prevail in any case, and the resolution of the test of strength is usually the sole interest of the witnesses. Where appeals to morality become relevant are in more complex social universes with alliances and reputations, with social contracts and rules and the penalizing of cheaters by the cooperative action of the signatories to the social contract (see Cosmides, 1985).

Conflict of interests is a necessary condition for there to be wrongs and hence for there to be right. But there must be some partial congruence of interests, too, or moral judgment would be superfluous and moralistic manipulation impossible. Morality entails holding other people's interests, not merely one's own, to warrant consideration in the choice of one's actions. If moral sensibilities have evolved by the utilitarian criteria of natural selection, it follows that acts which appear to be motivated by deference to interests other than the actor's own have routinely rebounded to the benefit of the moral actor. This rebound depends upon shared interests, as a result either of kinship or of cooperative reciprocity.

People need complex cognitive skills to attain an adaptive evaluation of the benefits of alternative courses of action. One must often choose short-term self-denial for the sake of benefits that are distal and diffuse, benefits like the reputation for honesty that will make one an attractive exchange partner. Conscience has presumably evolved as a mechanism enabling such self-denial. Appeals to the common interest often advocate just such self-denial, and use moral language to do so. Some such appeals are sincere (i.e., advocate that which is profitable to the appellor and the appellee), while others are deceptive (i.e., advocate that which is profitable to the appellor and costly to the appellee). A clearly useful skill is that of disguising deceptive pleas as sincere: pretending to subordinate one's own self-interest to some common good and demanding, from this moral high ground, that others do the same. The fact that there are genuine overlaps of interest means that appeals to the common interest are at least potentially believable.

Given the role of morality in the regulation of social contracts, it is hardly surprising that people have invented ways to use morality itself as a weapon in pursuing competitive advantage. We use moralistic aggression to rally observers to our side in a conflict, and we incessantly strive to portray our own optima as being in "society's interest" or better still as the edicts of divine authority. The self-interest in these ploys can be ludicrously transparent, as for example when the king pronounces regicide the most heinous, "unnatural," "ungodly" crime. (It is slightly more subtle to have the pronouncement made by a lackey disguised as an independent moral authority.) It can be surprising how susceptible people are to this sort of manipulation, but of course those who embrace an imposed ideology are not necessarily utter dupes. There can be advantage in parroting the world-view of the powerful.

If these things are so, then the retributive sense of justice that makes measured retaliation a "good in itself" is ultimately "utilitarian," not for some "common good" like the total well-being of mankind or the universe, but for the moralizing individuals themselves. (This, of course, echoes our analysis of the revenge motive in Chapter 10.) The ostensibly alternative philosophical positions of retributivism and utilitarianism can be considered to constitute different levels of analysis. From the perspective of evolutionary psychology, the retributivist may be said to consult evolved moral/cognitive/emotional mechanisms to apprehend what *feels just*. Utilitarian considerations are then relevant to the task of explaining why such mental mechanisms have evolved.

A particularly esoteric element in the philosophical literature on punishment is the discussion (often with a dash of theology) of whether there is a meaningful sense in which punishment for wrong corrects some cosmic imbalance. We punish, *should* punish, *must* punish, it is maintained, because by so doing "we annihilate the wrong and manifest the right" (Bradley, 1927, p. 28). From the perspective of evolutionary psychology, this almost mystical and seemingly irreducible sort of moral imperative is the output of a mental mechanism with a straightforward adaptive function: to reckon justice and administer punishment by a calculus which ensures that violators reap no advantage from their misdeeds. The enormous volume of mystico-religious bafflegab about atonement and penance and divine justice and the like is the attribution to higher, detached authority of what is actually a mundane, pragmatic matter: discouraging self-interested competitive acts by reducing their profitability to nil.

People speak of the wrong-doer's "paying" for his crime, even of "paying his debt to society." One might imagine that this reduction of social and moral phenomena to economics reflects a bourgeois ideology, but a little anthropological knowledge puts the lie to that thesis: The notion that misdeeds create a "debt" clearly antedates capitalism. It is in fact especially characteristic of nonindustrial, face-to-face societies, where the debt is literal: The miscreant owes his victims such restitution as will most nearly obliterate the disadvantages they have incurred by his misdeed. For example, as we saw in the last chapter, a death often demands a compensatory death, and moreover one of comparable status, thus restoring the prehomicidal balance of power between rival lineages. The usual alternative to blood revenge is restitution in cash or other valuables, and there is extensive and highly explicit attention to the determination of an appropriate sum. It is only in large state societies, capitalist or otherwise, that the concept of "paying for one's crime" has lost its implication of compensating the wronged party, for the state has usurped the role of victim and plaintiff. The language of debt persists as an almost meaningless vestige. Yet it seems to us that this very persistence bespeaks a persisting sense of justice whereby the most appropriate penalty is that which most nearly offsets the wrong by restoring the prior circumstances and relative positions of malefactor and victim.

If culpability reflects the offender's debt to the victim—the quantification of the wrong done, and hence of the compensation required to set things right again—then culpability is mitigated to the degree that the victim's fate was deserved. When a victim has wronged his killer, then the killing itself is to some degree a restoration of balance. What follows is the concept of *provocation:* the universally acknowledged principle that some prior actions of the victim may justify the killer's dire response, or at least render it less blameworthy. What qualifies as provocation, and the magnitude of the justification that any particular provocation affords, are of course cross-culturally variable, but there are certain provocations that are almost universally recognized as providing at least some justification for retaliatory violence: physical assaults upon oneself or one's near relatives, theft, adultery (by the wife, not the husband), attacks upon one's honor. Each of these provocations represents a clear threat to the interests and, ultimately the fitness prospects, of the one provoked. No one should be surprised that such threats are universally resented, nor that violence inspired by such resentment is more often lauded than condemned. Where a central authority monopolizes the right of redress and criminalizes self-help, it is still common to acknowledge that these retaliatory motives are normal human passions: Homicides that are provoked are considered less blameworthy than murders of innocents even in a state society like our own, or at least they are so considered if the killing seems to have occurred in the "heat" of passion, before the "cooling of the blood."

It follows that the concept of provocation does double duty as a moral theory and a psychological theory: It is proposed both that provocation *justifies* retaliatory action and that it *causes* such action. Moreover, the causal imputation commonly carries an implication of compulsion, an implication that can be made to account (at least in part) for the justificatory element in provocation: Many would maintain that a "cold-blooded" murder is more culpable than one committed in "heat of passion" because the former was more subject to will. The cold-blooded killer "chose" to kill rather than acting "spontaneously," and that choice makes him especially blameworthy. This is essentially the distinction between a "murder of the first degree" and a lesser homicide.

The definitional criteria of a culpable crime in our English common-law system are two: There must have been a wrongful act (*actus reus*) and there must have been a wrongful intent (*mens rea*). Neither component alone can justify a punitive response. (These principles are compromised in some areas: The state need not establish *mens rea* to penalize certain "strict liability" offenses, such as parking violations, nor to penalize an *actus reus* carried out with negligent and reckless disregard for its foreseeable but unintended consequences. But the crimes of violence that are our main concern entail neither strict liability nor negligence.) It follows that there are other defenses against a criminal charge, besides denying the *actus reus* or claiming provocation: One can deny the *mens rea*.

On Malice and Magic

The *mens rea* criterion makes the wrong-doer's intent relevant to his punishment, and jurists and moral philosophers are virtually unanimous in insisting that it must be so. We blame people for wrongs inflicted deliberately or recklessly. In essence, we are blaming them for overvaluing their own interests and undervaluing those of others. Morality and the law are both concerned with the restraint of selfishness in the interest of social harmony. The allocation of blame without reference to intent would be both futile and a moral outrage. Or would it? Are there legal and moral systems that operate by other principles?

In arguing that moral sensibilities are evolved characteristics of the human animal, we have presumed that they have cross-cultural generality. This presumption may strike some readers as ethnocentric. We believe that it is not. There is no question that the consensual view of a particular moral issue in one society may differ radically from that in another, as witness attitudes to infanticide. Moreover, moral judgments change within societies, sometimes swiftly. We have no quarrel with the proposition that moral systems are "cultural," but it does not follow that they are boundlessly variable.

The question is at what level of abstraction we can discern the cross-culturally general psychological underpinnings of different moral systems. It is difficult, for example, even to imagine a culture in which affronts would not inspire resentment and retaliatory inclinations, and Chapter 10's review of the revenge motive confirms the intuition that here indeed is a trait that is cross-culturally general. But intuition is more tentative as regards the attention that we might expect people to pay to intent when they allocate responsibility. *We* may consider it gross injustice to disregard intent and simply punish, but it is by no means clear that an adaptive moral sensibility must share that judgment. If the point of punitiveness is to deter future willful wrongs, then retaliating for *all* wrongs may be no less effective than a discriminative response. It could be even more effective, by destroying the utility of even those willful wrongs that were successfully disguised as accidents. As Mario Puzo's fictitious "godfather" put it, "Accidents don't happen to people who take accidents as a personal insult." On the other hand, taking exception to imaginary slights can be counterproductive; retaliation for unintended wrongs can embroil one in feuds that might have been avoided without incurring any risk of inviting further mistreatment. So we cannot deduce from first principles how the human mind should have evolved to weigh intent. Whether people everywhere consider it relevant in allocating responsibility is an empirical question.

Several anthropologists have suggested that intent is not taken into account in "primitive" legal systems. According to an early ethnographer of the Ifugao, for example, "For every murder committed, although it be involuntary, inexorable vengeance follows" (Villaverde, 1909, p. 246). Barton (1919), however, in his more thorough analysis of Ifugao law, described a much more flexible system, such that death in a hunting accident, for example, would not be avenged, provided that the victim's kinsmen were convinced of the absence of malice. Intent is only irrelevant in the sense that advantage to the killer is taken as presumptive evidence of malevolence. (And whether that malevolence was conscious, or the act preplanned, who can say?) Many similar examples could be cited, in which a seemingly inflexible rule of law is belied by the pragmatic treatment of actual cases (as of course is true of our own system, too). The notion that other peoples are impervious to the concept of intent has been pretty thoroughly refuted within anthropology itself (e.g., Gluckman, 1972; Moore, 1978).

Intent may be ignored as a matter of procedure when the issue is not punishment but restitution. In this case, the logic is that the victims' kinsmen have been deprived through no fault of their own, and are entitled to compensation. Although the death be accidental, someone will have to be held responsible, and who else but he whose actions caused the mishap. The responsibility here incurred is not culpability (moral fault) but liability (moral obligation). There may be no completely fair solution to a truly accidental death: Some faultless person will be out of pocket. Certain legal remedies recognize this dilemma and distribute the loss; among the Nuer, for example, an accidental homicide is compensated at one-half the rate of an intentional one (Howell, 1954).

Rather than ignoring intent, many tribal peoples might be said to impute intent where we see none. A common allegation of ethnographers is that the particular people under study do not believe in "accident," all misfortunes, and, in particular, all deaths being attributed to human malice. When the culprit is unknown, as for example in the case of disease, some sort of divination is undertaken to identify the witch or sorcerer who is responsible.

Those who make accusations of sorcery and witchcraft often exploit ignorance about causal processes in order to pursue their hostile agendas under the guise of legitimate retaliation. In what is perhaps the most thorough study of who accuses whom, Knauft (1985) has shown that the Gebusi of lowland New Guinea disproportionately often accuse their in-laws, and more particularly those in-laws against whom they have a grievance concerning unfulfilled obligations of marital exchange. These accusations are by no means mere ritual complaints; accused Gebusi sorcerers are frequently executed. Ethnographers working in other parts of the world have also noted a link between affinal kinship and accusations of witchcraft (e.g., various chapters in Middleton & Winter, 1963).

No doubt these accusations are often made with righteous conviction of their veracity; if one subscribes to a belief in malicious magic, who better to suspect than those who have genuine conflicts with the victim? When we say that sorcery accusations "exploit ignorance," we do not imply Machiavellian scheming, but simply that the accusers are swayed by their own interests. *Some* accusations, however, are knowingly false, as for example in the Gisu (East Africa) case described by LaFontaine (1963, p. 210), in which a man with a sick daughter "alleged witchcraft by his affines and in his allegations he was supported by his agnates, although privately they admitted that he had brought it on himself."

Divination is a delicate political exercise like the arbitration of disputes: One cannot transparently serve one's own interests, but must nurture a reputation for disinterest and justice while garnering the indirect benefits of political influence. It is undoubtedly incumbent upon the diviner to know or discover who are the enemies of those consulting him as well as who can safely be accused. Accused witches are often eccentric, cantankerous or elderly individuals without supportive relatives (see, e.g., Kluckhohn, 1944; Whiting, 1950; Middleton & Winter, 1963); such people are often perceived as expendable, and can be abused or killed with minimal risk of inspiring vengeance. But in some societies, accusations may also be made against those more prosperous, polygynous, or otherwise successful than their jealous neighbors (e.g., Beidelman, 1963); in such a society, sorcery accusations become a deterrent force against personal ambition and ostentation. Nor is it invariably disadvantageous to be believed a competent sorcerer; chiefs and others often derive advantage from being known as potent magicians.

As Michael Ghiselin (1974) has written, the human brain/mind is "anything but a mechanism set up to perceive the truth for its own sake." People's incessant attributions of supernatural causality certainly bear him out. But why is the human animal so quick to make such attributions? Ghiselin's next claim is that "we have evolved a nervous system that acts in the interest of our gonads," but inept causal attributions are of no more obvious utility in the pursuit of fitness than in the pursuit of truth. There *is* clear utility in our empathic capacity to analogize other minds to our own and to thereby anticipate others' actions. Could our tendency to anthropomorphize nature—to see intention everywhere—be a useless epiphenomenon of this skill? We do not find this suggestion particularly plausible; we wish merely to draw attention to the task of developing an evolutionary cognitive psychology (see Cosmides, 1985). Accounting for our human fondness for supernatural explanations is a problem akin to that of accounting for the apparent ineptness of human inferential algorithms or "heuristics" (see Nisbett & Ross, 1980). We do not pretend to know just why it is that people entertain bizarre beliefs, but we expect that a truly satisfactory answer will have to make reference to the goals that the human mind has evolved to accomplish.

The Insanity Defense

Attributions about the wrong-doer's intent seem everywhere to be relevant to the allocation of blame and responsibility. We consider the most culpable wrong to be the willful wrong, the malicious "choice" of a "free" person. Indeed, with the exception of provocation (the victim's deservingness of his fate), almost every argument for the mitigation of blameworthiness seems to entail some denial of malevolent will. Either the act was accidental and hence the product of no intention at all, or the offender's capacity to act as a free moral agent was somehow compromised: The culprit was insane, feeble-minded, bewitched, drugged, coerced, a mere child, a mere woman. Any of these attributions may be used to deny that the offender is a morally responsible person, hence blameworthy. This notion that some wrongs are the culpable acts of free agents while others are not raises several problems—not the least of these is the appropriate response to "insanity."

In 1843, one Daniel M'Naghten, the disinherited, illegitimate son of a Glasgow woodworker, shot and killed the private secretary of the English prime minister Sir Robert Peel, apparently mistaking his victim for Peel himself. Upon arrest, M'Naghten explained his crime as follows:

> The Tories in my native city have compelled me to do this. They follow and persecute me wherever I go, and have entirely destroyed my peace of mind. They followed me to France, into Scotland and all over England; in fact they follow me wherever I go. . . . (Quoted by Walker, 1968, p. 91)

A jury of his peers agreed that M'Naghten was not guilty by reason of insanity. He was committed to Bethlem hospital, and was later transferred to Broadmoor, where he eventually died of tuberculosis.

M'Naghten's escape from the gallows provoked an outcry. Journalists and politicians of every stripe made hay with demands for reform, and there were debates in both houses of parliament about how best to avoid any such leniency in future. Eventually, rather than introduce new legislation, the House of Lords settled upon demanding that the judges clarify the principles governing the insanity defense. It was this demand that produced the famous M'Naghten Rules, which governed insanity verdicts throughout the English-speaking world for the next century. The pith of the Rules is this substantial test of sanity or its absence:

> . . . to establish a defence on the ground of insanity, it must be clearly proved that, at the time of committing the act, the party accused was labouring under such a defect of reason, from disease of the mind, as not to know the nature and quality of the act he was doing; or, if he did know it, that he did not know he was doing what was wrong. (Quoted by Walker, 1968, p. 100)

This fallible human statement, produced under the duress of hostile public sentiment, has since been dissected as if it represented divine revelation. For every word in the Rules, thousands more have been written in analysis of their intent and implications. Lives have hung in the balance of these disputations. What on earth is the point?

The idea of irresponsibility due to madness did not, of course, originate with the M'Naghten Rules, which were more an attempt to articulate and justify practice than to introduce radical change. The classic treatise "Pleas of the Crown" (Hawkins, 1724, quoted by Dickens, 1981) began with this proposition:

> The guilt of offending against any law whatsoever, necessarily supposing a wilful disobedience, can never justly be imputed to those who are either incapable of understanding it, or of conforming themselves to it. (p. 36)

If culpability is to rest upon *mens rea,* as it must do to discriminate willful wrongs from those that are the unintended consequences of acceptable (even benevolent) motives, then the defense of insanity seems to follow as a corollary. There really are deranged people who seem incapable of forming a recognizable malevolent intent.

That there are lunatics from whom the public should be protected, but who are not deserving of punishment in the same way as normal wrong-doers, it is a widespread and ancient perception. An Anglo-Saxon text possibly attributable to Egbert, an 8th-century Archbishop of York, deals with the problem pragmatically:

> If a man falls out of his senses or wits, and it come to pass that he kill someone, let his kinsmen pay for the victim, and preserve the slayer against aught else of that kind. (Quoted by Walker, 1968, p. 15)

The essence of responsibility was the obligation to make restitution; if the lunatic could not be held responsible for his actions, then someone else would have to be. It is only in state societies in which the victims of crime have been disenfranchised that concepts of responsibility and culpability lose this pragmatic essence.

But how are we to identify those who are not responsible by virtue of madness? Psychiatrists are commonly presumed to be the experts on this question, but their expertise has little or nothing to do with the usual legal definitions of insanity, namely freedom of the will and the capacity to distinguish right from wrong. The more candid psychiatrists readily admit their inability to provide expert testimony on insanity as the law would define it, and have therefore joined forces with lawyers in various efforts to change the law. Revisions of the M'Naghten Rules have been legion in common law systems descended from the English. In the 1950's, for example, the American Law Institute (ALI) proposed a model penal code that was gradually adopted in all federal courts and most states over the next 20 years. Under the ALI test, rather than lacking knowledge of wrongfulness, the insane criminal had to lack either "substantial capacity to appreciate the criminality of his conduct" or "substantial capacity to conform his conduct to the requirements of law." The latter criterion (which harks back to Hawkins, 1724) represents a clear attempt to distinguish nonculpable acts of compulsion from culpable acts of will. But the psychiatrists could find no more basis for judging "substantial capacity to conform" than for judging the defendant's knowledge of wrongfulness. Both the American Psychiatric Association and the American Medical Association eventually repudiated the ALI test in the furor following would-be presidential assassin John Hinckley's 1982 acquittal by reason of insanity.

Since Hinckley, American psychiatrists have advocated what is in effect a return to the M'Naghten rules, claiming that psychiatric testimony about whether a malefactor understood the wrongfulness of his act "is more reliable and has a stronger scientific basis" than psychiatric testimony about whether he was capable of controlling his behavior (see Johnson, 1985). The advocates of these and other changes in legal tests of insanity always claim that their goal is to bring the tests into line with modern psychiatric knowledge. And yet the reforms go in circles. It is hard to point to any cumulative progress in legal definitions of insanity or to any impact of new scientific knowledge. The behavioral sciences, with their fundamentally deterministic assumptions, simply do not address the moral distinctions that are at issue in courts of law. As one critic of the ALI test (Bonnie, 1983) has said,

> There is, in short, no objective basis for distinguishing between offenders who were undeterrable and those who were merely undeterred, between the impulse that was irresistable and the impulse not resisted, or between substantial impairment of capacity and some lesser impairment. (p. 196)

Psychiatry aspires to the respectable status of a "science." To realize that aspiration, psychiatrists are obliged to adopt a deterministic stance on the question of the causation of behavior: All acts have causes that are (at least in principle) knowable; indeterminacy is simply the product of (present) ignorance. The American Psychiatric Association's (1982) position statement on the insanity defense (quoted by Johnson, 1985) embraces this scientific world view. What the profession has been more reluctant to acknowledge is that there is simply no place within such a world view for the question of whether the individual "might have done otherwise." To both ordinary people and to jurists, "responsibility" entails the choice of one's actions and the capacity to have done otherwise. The point is blameworthiness, a moral concept. If the psychiatrists' claim to be "scientists" is to be respected, then they have nothing privileged to say about blameworthiness—hence, nothing expert to say about the actor's "responsibility" for his actions; at best, they can say something about the causation of those actions, which is another matter. For these and related reasons, many psychiatrists themselves maintain that their profession has no business in the courtroom (see Coleman, 1984; Stone, 1984; Szasz, 1961; Winslade & Ross, 1983).

Who Gets Acquitted by Reason of Insanity?

A successful insanity plea leads, in most jurisdictions of the English-speaking world, to a nominal "acquittal." The defendant is "not guilty by reason of insanity" (NGRI), although he is rarely released upon that verdict and may well be detained longer than the maximum prison term he could have received if sane and convicted. NGRI is not a frequent verdict in the United States. According to a 1983 National Commission on the Insanity Defense, for example, only about 1 in 600 or 700 people accused of a serious crime in New York State pleads insanity, and only about a quarter of those pleas are successful (p. 153). In Miami in 1980, 454 of a total of 569 homicides were "solved" (although only 149 led to convictions); 6 killers were found NGRI and 2 more were detained as unfit for trial (Wilbanks, 1984, Figure 8.1).

In Canada between 1974 and 1983, 6559 people were slain in 5994 homicidal incidents. 4973 of these incidents were solved, the killer committing suicide or otherwise dying before adjudication in 361 of them. According to presently available information (incomplete for the most recent years), the remaining 4612 solved homicides have led to 2892 convictions and a total of 263 killers being found either unfit to stand trial or NGRI.

Table 11.1 presents the percentage of Canadian victims in various categories of relationship to their killers, within all homicides, within those followed by suicide, and within those in which the killer was found insane (either unfit for trial or NGRI). We have noted earlier the disproportionate number of killers deemed insane among those who have killed close relatives, and a similar disproportion is seen in studies of insane or "abnormal" homicides in other countries (e.g., Gibbens, 1958; Wong & Singer, 1973; Gillies, 1976; Gudjonsson & Petursson, 1982). This prevalence of close relatives among the victims of madmen supports the Darwinian interpretation of madness that we proposed in Chapter 4: Insanity is the loss of normal perceptions of one's interests and/or of the inclination to pursue them.

Now, of course, it could be that the act of killing a close relative inspires the attribution of insanity; that is to say, the killers of close kin might not be relatively often mad in any objective sense, but simply more often so labeled. Such labeling may indeed contribute to the association between insanity and the killing of relatives, but several facts indicate that labeling cannot be the whole story. For example, there is the parallel between cases in which the killer is judged insane and those in which he commits suicide. Homicide-suicide is a futile act which seems to reflect the same sort of loss of reason or abjuration of self-interest that is diagnostic of insanity (see pp. 213–219). The police recognize this commonality, by favoring "mentally ill/retarded" as a motive category in reporting these cases to Statistics Canada. But suicide is an unequivocal act, not a subjective label, and it is striking how the

Table 11.1. The Relationship between Killer and Victim in Canadian Homicides Generally (1974–1983), and in Those Subsets of Cases in Which the Killer Committed Suicide or Was Found Insane (Either Unfit for Trial or Not Guilty by Reason of Insanity), as Compared to the Expected Frequencies If Suicide and Insanity Were Equally Prevalent in All Relationship Categories

Relationship between killer and victim	Proportion in relationship category for all solved cases (N = 5443)	Suicides (N = 776)		Insane (N = 308)	
		Actual	Expected	Actual	Expected
Blood relative	.158	239	123	127	49
Spouse	.195	343	151	47	60
Other marital relative	.038	20	30	14	12
Not related	.608	174	472	120	187
		$\chi^2_{3df} = 545$ $p < .0001$		$\chi^2_{3df} = 151$ $p < .0001$	

incidence of suicide in particular types of cases parallels the incidence of insanity verdicts (Table 11.1 and below). Moreover, it is not just insanity attributions *after* the homicide has occurred that are exceptionally prevalent among killers of close kin, but also *previous* psychiatric difficulties and committals (e.g., Green, 1981; Husain & Daniel, 1984; Cheung, 1986). We must stress that our point is not that people suffering from diagnosed psychiatric syndromes are especially likely to kill; on the contrary, some studies suggest that even diagnosed psychotics are not an exceptionally violent group (Monahan & Steadman, 1983). Rather, the point of these comparisons is that *when* the insane kill, they do not manifest the nepotistic discrimination that is characteristic of sane killers. The lunatic seems not to recognize where his interests lie.

This evolutionary psychological view of the disordered mind can be used to predict the sorts of cases in which the killer is especially likely to commit suicide or to be found insane. Whichever category of homicides is most clearly contrary to the killer's fitness interests is the madder act; it should be relatively unlikely to occur at all, and when it *does* occur, it should be relatively likely to be followed by suicide or an insanity verdict. The obvious example is killing kinfolks: To kill one's relative is madder than to kill one's nonrelative, and is, as expected, both relatively rare (see Chapter 2) and relatively likely to be followed by suicide or an insanity verdict (Table 11.1). Other comparisons reveal the same pattern. Killing one's natural child is madder than killing a stepchild, for example, and is indeed rare relative to opportunity (Figure 4.9). Among 322 Canadian killers of natural children, 20% committed suicide and 11% were found insane (NGRI or unfit for trial); among 59 killers of stepchildren, only 10% committed suicide and a single individual was found insane. Killing one's older natural child is madder than killing one's infant child, and is indeed less frequent (Figure 4.4). Among 126 infanticidal Canadian parents, just 5% committed suicide and 6% were found insane, whereas among 196 who killed older children, the corresponding percentages were 30% suicide and 15% insane.

In Great Britain in recent years, slightly over half of *all* killers have been found insane (Judicial Statistics), an enormously higher proportion than in North America. Several commentators have suggested that this difference must reflect differences in psychiatric diagnosis or judicial behavior, but there is a more likely alternative. The overall homicide rate in Great Britain is substantially lower than that in America, so that the higher proportion of insanity cases does not reflect a higher per capita rate of insane murders, but simply a very much lower rate of sane ones. And indeed in cross-national comparisons, we generally find that a relatively high proportion of insanity verdicts is associated with a relatively low homicide rate and vice versa. The implication is that the per capita rate of insane murder is relatively invariant as compared to the more culturally labile rate of killing by the sane.

Diminished Responsibility

When we conflate the issue of the causation of behavior with that of volition and responsibility, we open the moral and philosophical Pandora's box of "diminished responsibility."

Jurists may find it a useful legal fiction to dichotomize acts into those freely chosen versus those compelled. Moralizers, too, may be attracted to black and white standards of right versus wrong. But these binary classifications do not correspond to anyone's understanding of responsibility. Instead, people everywhere understand blameworthiness as a matter of degree, and perceive free volition versus compulsion as a continuum, with any number of factors having some power to diminish a malefactor's culpability.

The binary classification of guilt versus innocence notwithstanding, the criminal law frequently has recourse to the notion that a variety of things can cloud one's moral judgment or impair volition, diminishing responsibility. This device is used, for example, to justify policies that appeal to our evolved sense of justice and yet conflict with currently fashionable moral absolutes. The fiction of a lactational incapacity that makes infanticide by the mother a lesser crime than other homicides is a prime example (see Chapter 4).

Diminution of responsibility can be claimed on numerous grounds (besides "provocation," which we discussed earlier). Impairment of judgment by alcohol has frequently been invoked to justify reduced penalties for crime, for example, although there are also precedents for insisting that people retain their responsibility for the actions they perform under the influence of self-administered drugs. But what if the drug in question—make it a legal drug like alcohol or caffeine, if you like—were to produce an effect that could not reasonably have been anticipated? Or how about the infamous "Twinky defense," the claim by lawyers acting for San Francisco killer Dan White that he was unbalanced by chemical additives in junk food? A ludicrous defense, perhaps, but what if it's true?

The more we understand about risk factors for homicide or any other sort of activity—as we identify more partial causes and better understand their impacts—the more "extenuation" we are likely to perceive in these predictors. After all, if "responsibility" is construed as that part of causality attributable to "will" (the free choice of evil, to put the matter moralistically and melodramatically), then each new predictor leaves less and less to blame the will *for*. But if we let our growing knowledge of causation erode the realm of responsibility, we confuse two universes of discourse, with results that are ludicrously unjust. "Premenstrual syndrome," for example, may truly be a cause of violence by some women, but that no more makes it a "defense" than can a man plead his maleness. And as many critics of pleas of insanity and diminished responsibility have demanded, why should not poverty or other social disadvantage afford the same mitigation of responsibility as mental disorder or junk food? The answer cannot invoke the known causal impacts of chemistry upon behavior; we have a great deal more evidence that poverty causes violence than that Twinkies or psychoses do so.

Whether the scientific world view precludes any concept of "free will" is a philosophical dilemma that we are not about to resolve. (As practicing scientists, we embrace determinism; in our other roles as human protagonists, we simply switch to the contrary and seemingly incompatible world view.) As we noted earlier, it is not within the domain of deterministic behavioral science to say whether an actor might have done otherwise in the past. However, it may be within that domain to say whether his future actions are modifiable by reward or punishment. One might, in other words, be able to say that this behavior pattern can be changed or this person can be made to behave differently whereas that one cannot.

People tend to conflate these judgments of the accessibility of action to modification with the concept of responsibility: That which is deterrable by the threat of punishment is therefore under no compulsion, hence is a free act of the will, hence blameworthy if wrongful. We have just argued that such a conflation of causal and moral judgments constitutes a categorical error, but it may be a practical way to deal with our fellows nonetheless. We punish (hold responsible) those whom we believe corrigible (manipulable). We simply restrain without moralistic rhetoric those whom we know not how to reach.

A Penalty to Fit the Crime?

Scientists have nothing prescriptive to say about morality and blameworthiness. But we can study them as phenomena—as aspects of human affairs and (evolutionary) psychology. If morality is to be understood in terms of its uses in social transactions—both in terms of its reciprocally beneficial role in the social regulation of conflicts of interest and as a weapon of social competition—then we may expect that blameworthiness will accrue especially to those breaches of morality that are manifestly to the offender's advantage. It may be stupid or tragic to engage in behavior that is destructive to the interests of others and of no use to oneself, but it is not *cheating*. When an Ifugao hunter was accidentally slain by a companion's errant arrow, the victim's relatives determined whether revenge was in order by considering whether their kinsman's death held any advantage for the killer (Barton, 1919). And who would not?

We follow a similar logic in finding the insane killer "not guilty." Where is the "guilt" in an act divorced from self-interest? We may confine or even kill the madman for pragmatic reasons, but we do not blame him. Should we discover, however, that the killing had an intelligible motive—that it was indeed to the killer's advantage as we understand advantage—then we are likely to become suspicious of his insanity plea and to adopt a more retributive frame of mind.

Culpability and responsibility encounter special complications when killer and victim are genealogical relatives. Among the Ifugao, for example, patricide, matricide, fratricide, and other "treason against one's family" incur no penalty (Barton, 1919). Wherever wergild is paid or blood revenge taken, it is apparently typical to forswear these remedies in the case of killing close kinsmen (see, e.g., Phillpotts, 1913; Bloch, 1961; Moore, 1978; Hardy, 1963). It is not difficult to see why these cases should be exempt from the usual penalties. The man who kills his kinsman wrongs himself. Restitution is problematic: Who should pay whom? Regardless of whether the killer alone is held to account or his kinsmen too, those victimized by the original killing would have to be further penalized in order to be compensated. The culpability of the killer of a close relative is therefore moot, and it is by no means unusual for him to remain in the community, unpunished, perhaps pitied, the victim-perpetrator of a tragedy.

From the perspective of evolutionary psychology, the point is that the interests of close kinsmen are fundamentally intertwined. This fact has several implications. The parties who would ordinarily be the plaintiffs, namely the victim's relatives, are kinsmen to the killer, too, and may either share his perception of the victim's expendability or feel obliged to swallow their resentment and forgive him rather than incur a double loss. He who kills a still robust and useful kinsman in a dispute has destroyed a vehicle of fitness, and is unlikely to profit. His lack of culpability is then analogous to that of other profitless homicides: Where there is no advantage to the killer, nor pursuit of his own interests with reckless disregard for those of others—where the victim's death is itself costly and rueful to the killer—then we are dealing with a variety of homicide that does not tempt by its benefits and therefore need not be deterred by the imposition of additional costs. There is no point to punishing and hence no point to blame.

The exceptions to this general rule of nonculpability are precisely those in which it is perceived that there *are* serious temptations to kill, the fact of kinship notwithstanding. For example, killings of close agnates are exceedingly rare and are not punished among hunter-gatherers and itinerant slash-and-burn horticulturalists, where there is little competition for familial property and fierce kinsmen are a man's principal assets; they are much more common and may be punished harshly among settled agriculturalists with valuable family property to compete over.

If the ultimate function of retributive urges is deterrence, then we might expect people to feel a greater urge to blame and to punish, the more tempting the crime. Kinsmen have a natural commonality of interest that makes killing them relatively unappealing. Potential killers presumably have the fewest compunctions about murdering those with whom their interests do not overlap at all. It follows that we might expect punitiveness to *increase* as the shared interests of the antagonists *decrease* across a series of victim–killer relationship categories. And indeed, the psychology of those levying sentence in Canada seems to comply with this model of punitiveness. Consider just those cases in which one man, acting alone, slew another, and take, as our measure of punitiveness, the percentage of all adjudicated cases in which the killer was sentenced to more than 10 years in jail. What we find is that this percentage increases as the relationship between the antagonists becomes more distant and their presumptive commonality of interest fades: 13.6% of those who killed father or son got more than 10 years, 15.2% of brothers, 20.0% of the killers of more distant blood kin, 29.6% of relatives by marriage, 34.9% of "friends" and "acquaintances," and 50.4% of strangers. The relatively heavy penalties imposed on those who killed strangers might be supposed to reflect the influence of "crime-specific" homicides (see p. 175), but in fact such cases were only slightly more likely to earn over 10 years (53.7%) than stranger homicides not involving another crime (47.2%).

Asymmetry of punishment within a single relationship may also be intelligible in terms of asymmetrical temptation to kill. We discussed in Chapter 5 the asymmetry of mutual valuation between father and son: The son may be more tempted to kill his aging father, who clings to familial resources for his own purposes and thus delays his son's career, than the reverse. We might then predict an asymmetry of penalties, and indeed such asymmetry is common. In Roman law, for example, filicide by the father was his right and no offense at all, whereas patricide by the son was capital treason (Jolowicz, 1932). Of course, we might have predicted the same from the fact that the older men make the rules, but the fact remains that the man who kills his son is a tragic figure, more pitied than blamed. It is interesting that in our own society, where the law makes no explicit provision for reduced penalties due to kinship, the same sympathies are sometimes expressed. When soul singer Marvin Gaye was shot dead by his father, for example, the trial judge suspended sentence on the grounds that the killer had "suffered enough."

As we saw in Chapter 10, a cross-culturally prevalent consideration in the determination of appropriate restitution for homicide is the "value" of the victim, and hence the magnitude of the loss to the bereaved relatives. The wergild depends upon the slain person's sex, status, and usefulness. In modern state societies, compensating the victims for their loss is an almost forgotten aspect of justice. Nevertheless, "impersonal" justice is still administered by real people, who might therefore be expected to judge culpability by the magnitude of the harm done. Does the trial judge's disinterested assessment of harm and culpability still entail a valuation of the victim?

High-minded moral philosophies maintain that we should love our enemies as we love our brothers, but of course no one does. Nobody values all human lives equally. As we have argued repeatedly, the relatedness of others to oneself is one important ego-centered criterion of differential valuation. Other criteria of human value are more consensual. Killing a child is more culpable than killing a zygote, and killing a saint is more heinous than killing a sinner (hence the well-known defense attorney's ploy of "putting the victim on trial"). Men might be expected to agree that a nubile woman is more valuable than one past her menopause, and indeed, some traditional codes of homicide compensation prescribe differential payments for the deaths of women of different reproductive values (see p. 238). One must wonder, then, whether the dispensers of justice in the impersonal state continue to value the lives of victims differentially in this way. The data in Figure 11.1 suggest that they may: In Canada, the penalty for killing one's wife is a declining function of her age, whereas that for killing one's husband is an increasing function of his.

Of course, the phenomena in Figure 11.1 could have any number of other explanations. One obvious possibility is that the character of the crimes is systematically different among the different age groups in some way that justifies the different penalties. The brutality of young husbands, for example, might explain both the harsh sentences for killing young wives and the light sentences for killing young husbands. And as for the harsh sentences for killing middle-aged men, it may be

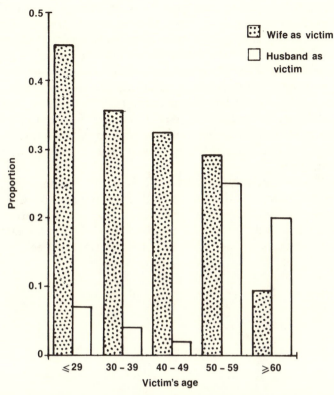

Figure 11.1. The proportion of (nonsuicidal) spouse-killers receiving sentences of 10 years or more in prison. Canada, 1974–1983.

relevant that the judges are themselves senior males! Nevertheless, the results in Figure 11.1 at least suggest that the evolutionary psychology of victim valuation deserves exploration.

But why should members of the faceless society hold strong opinions about the appropriate penalties to be imposed upon killers anyway? Whence our moral outrage about events we never witnessed, affecting people we never met? Surely the answer is that we all have a vested interest in the maintenance of the social contract: a commitment to pursue our individual interests with restraint and to punish those who cheat. From the perspective of the general public, unacquainted with either victim or killer, the homicides that deserve the most severe penalties are transparently predatory attacks upon strangers. It makes good sense that people should react most punitively to such unprovoked killings, mainly because they perceive themselves as potential victims, and perhaps also because such killings are perceived as volitional and deterrable. A homicide in the course of rape or robbery by a stranger is clearly not the resolution of an individualized conflict, but a pure victimization of the innocent, and is therefore especially culpable. The criminal justice system behaves pretty much in accordance with this popular view of culpability. In single-victim–single-offender cases in Canada between 1974 and 1983, for example, 77% of those accused of raping and killing a stranger received sentences of more than 10 years in jail, as did 56% of those accused of robbing and killing a stranger, but only 29% of those accused of killing people they already knew in social conflict situations.

Killing those outside the social contract is likely to be no offense at all: In most human societies throughout history, foreigners have been fair game. And of course war is a socially sanctioned cooperative act in which killing (the right targets) is not culpable at all, but laudable. The trick is that the rules can get changed retrospectively, especially if your side loses.

On Cultural
Variation

— 12 —

In November of 1913, a 47-year-old Icelandic woman poisoned her brother for financial gain; she was convicted of murder, but her death sentence was commuted to a prison term by the Danish king. It was dark November again, 16 years later, when a 19-year-old burglar was surprised at his work, and beat to death the man who interrupted him. The reason why these two cases are noteworthy is that they are the only two homicides known to have taken place in the little island nation of Iceland in the first 40 years of this century (G.H. Gudjonsson, 1986, personal communication).

Homicide rates are enormously variable between countries. The two Icelandic cases between 1900 and 1939 represent a rate of 0.5 homicides per million persons per annum (Gudjonsson & Petursson, 1982). In the 1980's, most European nations have experienced homicide rates on the order of 10 per million persons per annum, while Canada's rate has been over 25. In the United States and Brasil, recent homicide rates have exceeded 100 deaths per million persons per annum, and some Central American countries have experienced rates several times higher again. Knauft (1985, p. 379) summarizes data from several New Guinea tribal groups in which homicide rates are in the range of 5 to 8 *thousand* deaths per million persons per annum. (Some, though by no means all, of this New Guinea mortality could be attributed to "warfare" rather than "homicide." But the distinction becomes rather a fine one: The state of war is chronic, deaths are singular events, and killers are likely to be acquainted with their victims.)

Homicide rates also vary dramatically within countries over time. Murder seems to have been rare for centuries in Iceland, for example, but it was not always so (Hansen & Bjarnason, 1974). Before the Norwegian conquest of Iceland in 1262, local warlords pursued bloody rivalries and vendettas. These exploits are the content of the famous Icelandic sagas. Since about 1950, homicides in Iceland have shot up to a frequency of about one case a year, a per capita rate far below that of most nations, but about ten times higher than that of a few decades ago.

275

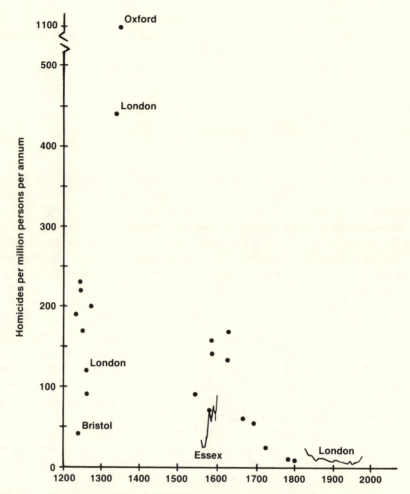

Figure 12.1. Historical changes in the homicide rate in England. Each point represents an estimated homicide rate for a city or county over a few years or decades. (Modified from Gurr, 1981.)

In England, too, the homicide rate was enormously higher in the distant past than it is today. English murders appear to have declined more or less steadily over some 700 years or more, so that the modern Englishman faces a risk of murder not 5% of that which confronted his mediaeval counterparts (Figure 12.1).

Why is one's risk of being murdered so different between societies and from one era to another? This question is obviously one of great practical importance: If criminologists could answer it, they might discover how the homicide rate could be reduced in exceptionally murderous nations like Colombia and the United States. It is presumably because of this practical importance that the analysis of differential rates of homicide has dominated the criminological literature (see reviews by Wolfgang & Ferracuti, 1967; Archer & Gartner, 1984; Huff-Corzine *et al.*, 1986).

Criminologists have collated data on differential homicide rates between nations and between regions within a nation, between cities and between subgroups within a city, between seasons, between years, between days of the week; and they have sought explanations of these variations in terms of correlated variables like average income, gun ownership, unemployment rate, housing density, city size, population structure, capital punishment, fertility rate, latitude, temperature, and ethnicity.

A review of this voluminous literature is beyond our present scope, nor have we a theory of differential homicide rates to offer. Our limited aim in this concluding chapter is to suggest that even here, in the study of populational rate data, some attention to the evolved psychology of the individual protagonists of violence might be enlightening.

On the Annual Homicide Rates of Nations

In a volume entitled *Violence and Crime in Cross-National Perspective,* Dane Archer and Rosemary Gartner (1984) amassed data on the annual rates of homicide and other crimes from some 110 nations. They used this data set to assess a wide range of theories that have been proposed to account for the variability from country to country and from year to year, subjecting those theories to a number of sophisticated and imaginative tests. The book is an exemplary piece of sociological criminology, providing several fresh insights. Despite its strengths, however, Archer and Gartner's analysis suffers from inattention to the self-interested agendas of the individual protagonists of violence.

A question of perennial interest to criminologists has been that of the impact of recent involvement in a war upon the crime rate. Some have claimed that postwar periods are especially violent, others that they are especially pacific. Using a large set of data on homicide rates in various countries before, during, and after various wars, Archer and Gartner provide the first truly convincing demonstration that a postwar increase in the homicide rate is by far the more prevalent pattern. They then proceed to a consideration of various candidate explanations, and they find reasons to reject all but one. For example, they dispose of the theory that postwar crime waves are the consequence either of sociopolitical disintegration in defeated nations or of devastated economies, by demonstrating that homicide rates increase (i.e. postwar minus prewar) by at least as much in victorious as in defeated nations and by at least as much in nations with improved postwar economies as in those with worsened economies. After several such tests, the surviving explanation is something that Archer and Gartner call the "legitimation of violence model": When acts of violence occur, and more particularly when at least some such acts seen to be socially acceptable or even lauded, then general attitudes toward the use of violence shift in the direction of acceptance, and thresholds for resorting to violence fall.

This concept of "legitimation" is appealing, but the logic by which Archer and Gartner dismiss all alternatives is flawed. One of the explanations for postwar murder waves that they reject, for example, is the "violent veteran model." This is the notion that "the experience of war resocializes soldiers to be more accepting of violence and more proficient at it," with the result that nations participating in wars experience a postwar increase in violent crimes "as a result of the actions of returning war veterans" (p. 75). The evidence that Archer and Gartner deploy against this model is the fact that there is a postwar increase in killings both by veterans and by nonveterans, and in particular that killings by women and by men increase by comparable factors. But when women kill, their victims are usually men, and most typically men who have assaulted them; these men may or may not include disproportionate numbers of combat veterans (nor need combat *per se* be a necessary element of the "resocializing" of men in the army). Archer and Gartner claim to test the proposition that "postwar increases in homicide would be due to the acts of veterans" (p. 91), but by overlooking the possibility of victim precipitation, they actually test a much narrower claim, namely that the prewar–postwar differential must consist of cases in which veterans are themselves the killers.

This sort of inattention to the social psychological context of homicide bedevils many sociological studies of murder rates. The question of the impact of the population's age structure upon such rates provides a classic example. It so happens that variations in homicide rates can sometimes be related to demographic variations. Many authors, including Archer and Gartner, have noted increases in the overall homicide rate occurring contemporaneously with the maturation of a "baby boom" cohort and hence an increase in that proportion of the total population that consists of young men. The demographic shift seems to "explain" the change in homicide rates: A change in the proportion of the population falling within the most homicidal age-sex class will change the overall homicide rate even if age-sex-class-specific rates remain constant. However, the magnitude of the increase in homicide often seems to exceed the magnitude of the demographic shift; in other words, age-sex-class-specific rates do *not* remain constant. For this reason, Archer and Gartner, in analyzing the rapidly rising American homicide rate between 1963 and 1972, conclude that, "there were homicide rate increases during this period that cannot be explained by demography alone" (p. 144).

The assumption behind this conclusion is that "demography" would constitute an "explanation" only if age- and sex-specific rates of homicide were invariant, such that all change were attributable to changing proportions of these demographic classes. But by what theory may we expect age-sex-class-specific homicide rates to be unaffected by the demographic mix? Violence is not simply a "trait" of individuals, but a product of social interactions. The interpersonal violence of young men is a manifestation of competitiveness; if the proportional representation of young men in a population increases, might not the level of competition experienced by *all* men increase? Moreover, if the proportion of men who are in a violence-prone age-class doubles (for example), then even by a simplistic random model, the proportion of all dyadic encounters that will involve *two* such men will *quadruple;* might we not expect a greater than linear increase in violence with each increment in the numbers of violence-prone persons? And how does the number of men in other age classes affect the perceived marital and economic prospects of young men, and hence their risk-prone, violent tendencies? Our point is simply that "demography alone" actually "explains" nothing without some individual-level specification of how demographic and other effects upon violence are mediated.

On Culture and Imitative Violence

The variation in homicide rates between nations and between years represents enormous differences in the aggregate behavior of large numbers of individuals. If Americans kill one another at thirty times the rate of Icelanders, it is inevitable and appropriate that we should attribute this difference to a difference between the American and Icelandic "cultures." By itself, however, the appeal to culture is little more than a relabeling of the phenomenon to be explained.

"Culture" is manifested by the relative homogeneity of behavior within societies, as compared to cross-cultural and historical variation. In order to understand cultural differences, it would seem that we must first understand how and why people are influenced by their fellows so as to behave like them. Theory here is underdeveloped: Most social scientists treat culture as an irreducible "independent variable"—as an explanation rather than an entity to be explained. However, by maintaining that appeals to "culture" commonly amount to pseudo-explanatory labeling, we do not mean to imply that cultural influence is illusory or nonexistent. People undeniably acquire ideas about what to do from instruction and from the observation of other people.

Southeast Asian men sometimes run "amok." Amok is a state of homicidal rampage that entails the apparently random killing of anyone who has the misfortune of crossing the amok man's path. Eventually, he is overwhelmed, kills himself, or collapses in exhaustion.

The amok man is manifestly out of his mind, inaccessible to any sort of appeal, seemingly in a state of "automatism." If he lives to emerge from the amok state, he generally claims total amnesia. And yet amok is a cultural construct. A well-publicized or highly successful amok rampage leads to a rash of imitations. In 1959, a Laotian man invented the new amok technique of lobbing a grenade into a city crowd. Similar grenade attacks followed in increasing numbers until there were twenty in 1966, and then the fad gradually abated (Westermeyer, 1973).

Although amok is indubitably a cultural phenomenon, it does not follow that it is arbitrary in all its details, that it is without parallel in other cultures, or that it is exempt from scrutiny in terms of evolutionary psychology. Amok rampages, complete with automatism and amnesia, are not peculiar to Indochina. They are seen in Papua-New Guinea too, for example (Burton-Bradley, 1968). And how different are the occasional mass murders in North America? Although amok men are often described as oblivious to their surroundings and indiscriminate in their violence, they typically embark upon their rampages when surrounded by nonrelatives, and they are somehow likely to spare those relatives whom they happen to encounter (Burton-Bradley, 1968; Westermeyer, 1972). Only men younger than about 35 have been reported to run amok. The most common precipitating events are difficulties with wives or girlfriends, losses of face, and losses of money in gambling. We doubt that our readers, however unfamiliar with southeast Asian cultures, will find any of these features of amok particularly surprising.

The young man who runs amok is typically residing far from home, often for the first time in his life. He has typically been brooding over failure. One cannot but wonder if his psychology is that of a doomed warrior, surrounded by enemies and determined at least to inflict some costs upon them. A psychiatrist who interviewed seven hospitalized men after amok rampages writes (Burton-Bradley, 1968):

As the result of my discussions with those amoks who survived, their "one-talks" and other Papua-New Guineans, I am of the opinion that the individual's mode of thinking (inevitably expressed here in transcultural paraphrase) is somewhat as follows:

> I am not an important or "big man." I possess only my personal sense of dignity. My life has been reduced to nothing by an intolerable insult. Therefore, I have nothing to lose except my life, which is nothing, so I trade my life for yours, as your life is favoured. The exchange is in my favour, so I shall not only kill you, but I shall kill many of you, and at the same time rehabilitate myself in the eyes of the group of which I am a member, even though I might be killed in the process.

The evidence suggests that the killings are envisaged as a means of deliverance from an unbearable situation. No doubt much thinking precedes the nihilistic feeling of desperation—kill and be killed. At some point, however, there is a complete loss of control, when strong emotion becomes unchecked by deliberation and reflection. (p. 254)

The amok killer is a creature of his culture, but his state of mind is intelligible to creatures of other cultures too.

As we noted earlier, social scientists commonly treat "culture" as an irreducible, explanatory concept. Those few who acknowledge that the within-society homogeneity of behavior and belief constituting "culture" is itself in need of explanation have focused on the "transmission" of cultural elements, invoking concepts like "conformity" and "imitation" (e.g., Boyd & Richerson, 1985). The epidemic of grenade amok in Laos is a dramatic example of imitative violence. But like the appeal to "culture," the appeal to "imitation" can be more an exercise in labeling than in explanation.

One of the most striking aspects of the variability in homicide rates is the smoothness of the changes from year to year within a nation (Figure 12.2). Change may be rapid, but it is not erratic. In fact, if we wish to predict the present level of violence in a given society, far and away the best available predictor is the level of violence in the recent past. One plausible interpretation is that present violence is itself a causal determinant of future violence. But how might such causal influence be mediated?

If present violence is indeed a causal determinant of future violence, then some of that causal impact seems to be achieved through a short-term "contagion," "imitative," or "modeling" effect. This has long been an attractive idea to social psychologists (e.g., Berkowitz & Macauley, 1971; Bandura, 1973), but they have pursued it primarily by means of laboratory studies of questionable ecological validity. Recently, some ingenious time-series analyses by sociologist David Phillips have given the old idea a fresh empirical basis.

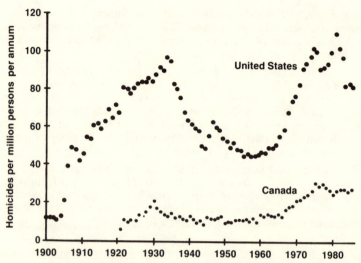

Figure 12.2. Annual homicide rates in the United States (1900–1985) and Canada (1921–1985).

Homicides in the United States are sufficiently numerous—about 60 cases per day—that one can seek transient effects of publicized events upon daily killings. Phillips (1983) reported that there is a significant increase in the number of homicides occurring a few days after a heavyweight championship boxing match. The magnitude of this increase was significantly higher for more publicized fights (those whose results were reported on network television newscasts) than for less publicized fights (those not so reported). Most remarkably, deaths of whites but not blacks increased significantly after fights with white losers, while the reverse was true after fights with black losers.

These results remain controversial. The much higher rates of homicide on weekends and holidays complicate the analyses; Phillips "controlled" these effects by statistical procedures whose assumptions were not strictly satisfied. Critics have proposed that Phillips's results are complicated artifacts (Baron & Reiss, 1985a,b) and the criticisms have been countered (Phillips & Bollen, 1985). For the present discussion, the most interesting aspect of the controversy is the conceptual vacuum pointed out by Baron and Reiss (1985a,b): No one has proposed a specific psychological theory of the alleged "imitation" that can explain what sort of publicized event will produce what sort of imitative violence, by whom, and after what delay. Truly imitative homicides are occasionally reported, cases in which American killers act out the homicidal details of some television show or news story. But these are far too few to exert a measurable impact upon national homicide rates. Phillips's explanation of his results in terms of "imitation" implies, apparently intentionally, that the influence of prizefights is somehow the same sort of phenomenon as these rare "copycat" killings. But this is just whistling in the dark.

As we have seen, most American homicides arise out of social conflicts between acquainted people, and the most common variety involves two unrelated men in a dispute over status or face. Many similar but nonfatal disputes occur for every one that ends in death. Phillips and his critics alike, operating from only the scantest statistical data, have unwittingly adopted a naive view of homicide that ignores this social context. Both sides of the controversy assume, for example, that any genuine effect of the losing fighter's race could only imply that the spectacle of a white man losing (or perhaps his being victimized in socially approved violence) specifically inspires observers to set out to kill other whites; likewise for blacks. But one can envision a completely different, and to us more plausible, process involving the well-known dynamic of victim precipitation. That is that young men who are already of a competitive, combative mindset identify with prizefighters (especially those of their own race), are rendered somewhat more belligerent by the macho banter surrounding the fight—perhaps by the defeat of a hero whose victory they had publicly predicted, perhaps by lost wagers—and are therefore a little more likely to end up dead in an escalated face dispute during those days when the fight is still a popular subject of barroom analysis. To call such a chain of causality "imitation" would stretch the word beyond recognition.

Killings by the police afford another example of the blinkering effects of the assumption that any positive feedback of violence upon further violence must be "imitative." Phillips (1983) excluded legal killings from his prizefight analysis on the assumption that they would not and should not be subject to the same imitative effects as criminal homicides. Baron & Reiss (1985b) agreed with this logic, and then gleefully pointed out that killings by the police *also* increase after fights. This they construed as evidence that any apparent effect of prizefights must be artifactual. Again, both sides in the controversy seem to have a naively idealized view of the causes of homicides, namely that whatever processes inspire criminal killings could not conceivably have a similar impact upon the police. In fact, when American policemen kill, they, like other American killers, most frequently kill belligerent antagonists in face-threatening disputes (see, e.g., Toch, 1969). Whatever psychological process mediates the prizefight effect could easily be operating in the policeman or his victim or both.

Our point is that Phillips's ingenious demonstrations of "imitative violence" explains rather less than one may at first suppose (see also Baron & Reiss, 1985a). Even if it is indeed the case that each highly publicized prizefight causes a brief flurry of homicides, the mechanism of this causal influence is simply not known.

What Sorts of Homicides Are Most Variable in Their Frequency?

In one of the first systematic examinations of homicide rate data, the Finnish criminologist Veli Verkko (1951) claimed to have discovered two "laws," which he called the *dynamic* and the *static* laws of homicide. The two were really the same: Whether one compares data between years (the dynamic law) or between locales at a single time (the static law), one tends to find that the proportion of cases involving women as victims or killers is low where the overall homicide rate is high, and vice versa. This statistical relationship is in fact no "law," but it is indeed the tendency more often than not. Exactly what this tendency means has been the subject of remarkably obtuse discussion ever since Verkko reported it.

Verkko's "laws" are actually just two of a large set of similar propositions about sex, age, and other characteristics of the protagonists in homicide. The general form of such propositions is this: One or another sort of homicide case that constitutes a small minority of all homicides where the overall rate is high, constitutes a larger proportion of all cases where the overall rate is low. This trend is often (though by no means always) seen vis-à-vis killings of blood kin, infanticides, killings of or by women, insane murders, and so forth. Table 12.1 illustrates this sort of tendency with respect to the killing of wives.

What the data in Table 12.1 indicate is that the rate of killing wives is *less variable* than the overall homicide rate. (The coefficient of variation for the overall rates in Table 12.1 is 1.31, and for the wife rates only 1.09.) The meaning of all such "Verkko's laws" comparisons is essentially similar. The rate of insane murder varies less than that of sane murder between years and between societies; hence, insane murders are likely to constitute a high proportion of all cases whenever killing is infrequent. Slayings of blood kin are less variable in their frequency than slayings of nonrelatives; hence, blood kin cases are conspicuous by virtue of their proportional representation where homicide is rare, but not where it is frequent. And so forth.

Much befuddlement has arisen from discussions of proportional data as if they represented rates. A classic example is Brearley's (1932) pointless effort to explain why "the slaying of women is much less

Table 12.1. Overall Homicide Rates and Wife-Killing Rates in Some Exemplary Studies[a]

| | Homicides per million persons per annum | | Wives as percentage of all victims |
	All cases	Wife-killings	
Iceland, 1900–1979	2.4	0.5	19.2
Denmark, 1933–1961	5.8	0.8	14.2
New South Wales, Australia, 1968–1981	16.9	2.7	15.8
Canada, 1974–1983	26.9	3.3	12.4
Philadelphia, USA, 1948–1952	56.8	4.5	8.0
Belo Horizonte, Brasil, 1961–1965	68.5	5.6	8.2
Miami, USA, 1980	353.1	14.1	4.0
Detroit, USA, 1972	456.5	23.8	5.2

[a]Data sources: Iceland (Gudjonsson & Petursson, 1982); Denmark (Siciliano, 1965); New South Wales (Wallace, 1986); Philadelphia (Wolfgang, 1958); Belo Horizonte (Yearwood, 1974); Miami (Wilbanks, 1984), Canada and Detroit (our studies).

frequent in the United States than in England" (p. 81), an assertion based on data indicating that most English homicide victims in the 1920's were women as compared to less than a fifth of American victims. In fact, according to Brearley's own data, American women in the 1920's were about four times *more* likely to be slain than English women, while the risk to American men was approximately *thirty* times that incurred by their English counterparts. We have discussed the muddles resulting from such confusion between proportions and rates before (see pp. 27–28).

So if certain classes of homicide—those involving women, madmen, and blood kin—are relatively invariant, then some other component of the overall homicide rate must be relatively volatile. By default, that must be the cases involving two unrelated men. And indeed that is so. More particularly, the most variable component of the homicide rate between industrial nations and between years is that perpetrated by (and, to a lesser degree, upon) those disadvantaged young men whose risk-proneness and violence we discussed in Chapter 8. Where rates of homicide are high, the proportion of cases that involve such young men is high. Criminologist Richard Block (1976), for example, analyzed demographic data on homicide protagonists in Chicago between 1965 and 1973, a period in which the city's homicide rate more than doubled. As the homicide rate rose, the increase was disproportionately concentrated in young, black men as offenders, and to a lesser extent as victims too. Rushforth *et al.* (1977) document a similar trend among Cleveland homicide victims: As the overall homicide rate increased, age-specific rates were increasingly peaked in young adulthood.

Why should homicides involving young men constitute an especially variable component of the overall homicide rate? One possible reason is that these are the cases most responsive to varying economic circumstances and other cues that disadvantaged young men use to predict their prospects and modulate their risk-proneness. Certainly, robbery-homicide is a significant part of this varying component in homicide rates. While the Chicago homicide rate was more than doubling between 1965 and 1973, for example, the robbery-homicide rate almost quintupled, and thus rose from 8% of all homicides to 19% (Block, 1976).

Another reason why the violence of young men might be especially variable concerns the individual's perception of the probable actions of his antagonist. As we saw in earlier chapters, most homicides involving unrelated young men are not transparently instrumental, but instead involve competition over the less tangible social resources of status and face. The assessment of risk and the choice of tactics in such a dangerous competitive milieu depends heavily upon one's estimation of the danger from others. This estimation depends in turn upon one's perception of the local, contemporary prevalence of violence. The upshot is that violence may breed more violence not by "legitimizing" violence, nor by some nonadaptive process of blind "imitation," "desensitization," or "cultural conditioning," but simply by raising the perceived risks of *non*violence. A rational man in a violent milieu will be quicker on the trigger than the same man in a more pacific setting, although he brings the same cultural baggage to both. This sort of effect of the prevailing level of violence upon individual thresholds for resorting thereto may contribute to the predictability from one year's homicide rate to the next, which was illustrated in Figure 12.2.

"Subcultures of Violence"

Closely related to the idea of violence having a greater or lesser "legitimacy" is the allegation that there are "subcultures of violence." Wolfgang and Ferracuti (1967) have promoted this concept as an explanation for regional and ethnic differences in the incidence of homicide. Within certain reference groups, violence is frequent, and the display of one's capacity for violence is admired or even obligatory; other groups within the same larger society condemn violence, and their members rarely resort to it.

No doubt there is truth to this conception, but its value as explanation is debatable. The cultural differences between groups are manifested primarily by the same behavioral differences that the culture concept is invoked to explain; it follows that culture or subculture is often little more than a pseudoexplanatory label. Moreover, this problem cannot really be solved by assessing attitudes and values independently of the violent acts themselves; although behavioral differences are indeed likely to be associated with differences in attitudes and values, there seems little basis for attributing the former to the latter rather than the reverse.

Insofar as the appeal to "culture" entails a genuine hypothesis about the causes of behavioral differences between groups and not just a pseudoexplanatory label, that hypothesis, although rarely explicit, is surely something like this: The present difference is a product of the distinct cumulative histories of the two groups *rather than* a product of present differences in the external forces acting upon the two groups. Thus, a "cultural" difference is generally assumed to be an "arbitrary" difference in the sense that there is no present utilitarian reason for either group's adoption of the one cultural alternative rather than the other.

It is this implication of the culture concept that has provoked antagonism to Wolfgang and Ferracuti's "subculture of violence" theory. Critics have maintained that the theory, by attributing violence among black Americans to a black subculture, for example, subtly implies that the social problems of disadvantaged minorities are intrinsically generated rather than being the products of exploitation and economic inopportunity, and that it is mere happenstance that the poorer classes in industrial society exhibit more face-to-face violence than the privileged, rather than the reverse. Proponents of the subculture theory can fairly protest that they have said no such thing, and yet the criticism has justice. If we think we can explain why poor young men behave violently in terms of the "transmission" of "values" within a "subculture," then we are unlikely to seek more utilitarian explanations. In fact, poor young men with dismal prospects for the future have *good reason* to escalate their tactics of social competition and become violent. Among the many social structural variables that criminologists have attempted to correlate with homicide rates, one of the more promising is *income inequality*: It is not simply poverty that seems to be associated with relatively high rates of violent crime so much as the within-society variance in material welfare (see, e.g., Krahn *et al.*, 1986). Such an association is highly compatible with our view of homicides— especially those male–male nonrelative cases that constitute the most variable component in national rates—as manifestations of an escalated social competition more rational than it may first appear.

A satisfactory theory of the causation of variable rates of violence will have to incorporate a specific account of the ways in which the effective variables influence the individual actors and interpersonal interactions that are the stuff of aggregate statistics. Such theorizing is often scorned as "psychological reductionism" by sociologists. However, without engaging in precisely such reductionism, David Phillips cannot tell whether his "imitative" theory is supported or refuted by the data on police killings; Archer and Gartner cannot tell whether their "violent veteran model" predicts elevated violence by women as well as men; and Wolfgang and Ferracuti cannot tell which groups are likely to develop violent subcultures.

On the Legitimacy of Killing

We must reiterate that by questioning the adequacy of cultural "explanations" of differential homicide rates, we do not mean to deny the reality or importance of cultural variability. People are much readier to resort to violence in some societies than in others, and this variable resort to violence seems to pervade all situations and relationships. Although we noted earlier that certain types of homicide are relatively invariant as compared to male–male nonrelative cases, nevertheless the various sorts of homicide tend to rise and fall together. Table 12.1, for example, testifies that the rate of wife-killing varies *less* than the overall homicide rate, but it also testifies that the two rates *do* covary. In Canada, the homicide rate varies substantially between provinces, and Figure 12.3 shows that where men are more likely to be killed, so too are women, where children are more likely to be killed, so too are adults. However one slices the pie, the separate components of the homicide rate seem to rise and fall together.

Moreover, it is hard to doubt that different rates of violence between nations or eras are associated with different attitudes toward violence. Homicide is much more frequent in the United States than in other industrialized nations, for example, and is also much more approved. In Canada, a verdict of self-defense is usually available only to the killer who has made every effort to withdraw from his antagonist without violence; not so in most of the United States (see Friedland, 1984). Moreover, although the American law as written would seem to restrict

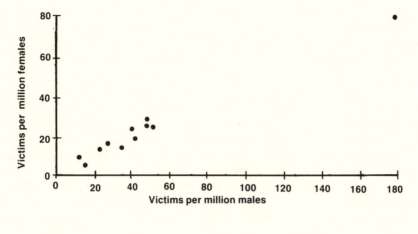

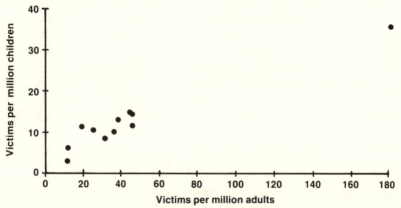

Figure 12.3. Female versus male and child versus adult homicide victimization rates in Canada by province, 1974–1983. In both cases, the cluster of ten dots represents the ten Canadian provinces, while the outlying point represents the Yukon and Northwest Territories.

legitimate violent recourse to life-threatening situations, the law as practiced is very different. The precedents from appellate courts specify that certain provocations can reduce murder to manslaughter, but in practice, prosecutors commonly allow those same provocations to reduce murder to no crime at all. We have already noted the high proportion of Miami homicides that are deemed justifiable or excusable by the criminal justice system (p. 249), and Miami is not unique in this regard. In Cleveland, Ohio, between 1947 and 1953, for example, over a quarter of all homicides in which the killer was identified and still alive

(157 out of 613) were deemed justifiable, with the result that no charge was laid, and many more led to jury acquittals on the same grounds (Bensing & Schroeder, 1960). The proportion of cases with this outcome is evidently much smaller in other industrialized nations. Trillin (1984, 1986) and Lundsgaarde (1979) provide particularly rich and insightful accounts of socially and judicially approved killings in America.

In 1984, one Bernard Goetz shot four unarmed teenagers on a New York City subway train, two of them in the back as they tried to flee. A huge debate has ensued about whether Goetz is a hero or a villain, and the most interesting aspect of this debate is the grounds on which it has been fought. Whether the teenagers behaved menacingly or were merely panhandling seems to be accepted as a relevant issue by both Goetz's boosters and his detractors. So does evidence on the subsequent criminality of his victims. Americans differ in their opinions about the justifiability of Goetz's gunplay, but the remarkable shared attitude of many commentators on both sides of the debate seems to be that he *might* be justified, if his victims were sufficiently reprehensible people.

In Archer and Gartner's terms, violence is a "legitimate" recourse of Americans with a grievance. This legitimacy is a feature of American culture, and it is widely invoked as a partial explanation for the remarkable prevalence of violence in that affluent nation. But a reverse causal arrow is equally plausible: That which is prevalent may come to be perceived as legitimate.

The same sort of indeterminacy of the direction of causality confounds attempts to assess the efficacy of stiff punishment as a deterrent. If we were to find, in some comparison across nations or eras, that murder is relatively frequent where the penalties are relatively light, it would not follow that raising the penalties will reduce the murder rate. Rather than the relatively light penalties being a cause of the high murder rate, the high rate might cause the light penalties, perhaps by creating a pressure on jail space. Or both phenomena might be manifestations of a cultural acceptance of violence, which would not necessarily change in response to a policy decision to impose stricter penalties. In fact, no very consistent association between the magnitude of penalties and the frequency of homicide is demonstrable in cross-national studies (see Archer & Gartner, 1984, Chapter 6). In a broader historical and cross-cultural sweep, the homicide rate seems to be positively related to the severity of penalty, which may indicate that both murder and hanging are manifestations of a prevailing legitimacy of violence (see, e.g., Gurr, 1981).

Violent Times?

There has always been a bull market in declamations of social disintegration and doom. Even as the English homicide rate plummetted over the last several centuries, commentators decried the rising tide of violence (see, e.g., Beattie, 1974). In fact, the rates of homicide in state societies seem to have fallen in historical times thoughout most of the world, and the data from remnant tribal societies suggest that the situation in prestate societies may have been even worse, the myth of the noble savage notwithstanding. Knauft (1985) estimates that homicide accounted for 35% of adult male mortality and 29% of adult female mortality among the Gebusi of New Guinea, and he cites evidence that homicide may account for an even higher proportion of all mortality among some Amazonian horticulturalists. Even the famous gentle !Kung San foragers of the Kalahari desert had a homicide rate approximately equivalent to that of the most violent urban American ghettos (Lee, 1979). Twentieth-century, industrial man may well have a better chance of dying peacefully in his bed than any of his predecessors.

Summary and Concluding Comments

The aim of this book has been to explore the utility of the emerging paradigm of evolutionary psychology for the study of homicide. Selection shapes behavioral control mechanisms—including the human psyche—so as to make behaving organisms effective reproductive competitors and nepotists. Species-typical motives have evolved to promote genetic posterity; it follows that our most basic human perceptions of self-interest are evolved tokens of the probable fitness consequences of alternative courses of action in historical environments. We therefore expect that two individuals will perceive themselves to be in conflict when the promotion of one's expected fitness entails the diminution of the other's. This, in brief, is the evolutionary psychological model that we have applied to the study of murder, and it has led us to a number of novel questions, hypotheses, and analyses. Although the research presented here is just a beginning, and although many of our ideas may prove wrong, we believe that the utility of the paradigm is established. Let's briefly review where that paradigm has led us.

The fundamental commonality of interest among genetic relatives makes their killing one another seem especially anomalous, so we devoted much attention to such cases. In Chapter 2, we showed that homicide is not such a family affair as is widely believed: Murders of relatives are actually rather rare in comparison to murders of nonrelatives. The difference is not simply one of absolute frequencies, but of risk in relation to opportunity. Homicidal conflicts and collaborations do not arise in proportion to mutual access; instead, the distributions of co-offender and victim–offender relationships are predictably different. It follows that feelings of solidarity among blood relatives cannot be reduced to mere familiarity and shared experience, nor to the individualized reciprocity that binds unrelated friends and allies. Familial solidarity rests on a deeper concern for one another's welfare. The perception of kinship itself apparently mediates this concern. (Witness, for example, the psychological consequences of a revelation of nonpaternity.) The psychology of perceived kinship is a topic in need of

293

much further study, and so too is the variable valuation that we place upon relatives as vehicles of our fitness.

Of course, people *do* kill blood relatives, albeit rarely. People even kill their own children, and we tested several ideas about the possible predictors of such behavior. A cross-cultural analysis of ethnographic materials (Chapter 3) showed that the circumstances in which infanticide is allegedly practiced in any particular society are almost invariably circumstances in which the child is of inappropriate paternity, is of poor phenotypic quality, or is unlikely to survive for other reasons. Parental disinclination to raise a particular child is therefore best understood as reflecting evolved motives for allocating scarce parental resources; virtually all apparent exceptions to this generalization involved coercive interventions by parties other than the new parents. In Chapter 4, we used contemporary Canadian data on infanticides and other filicides to test further hypotheses about demographic predictors of the risk that a parent will kill his or her child, predicting and verifying the relevance of maternal age, maternal marital status, and child's age. We also documented an enormously elevated risk to children residing with stepparents, and presented some evidence of this result's cross-cultural generality. Many issues demand further research, including the determinants of maternal attachment and maternal despair, the fate of adoptees in various cultural contexts, the differential risk in stepmother versus stepfather households, and the psychological nature and impact of paternity confidence.

The conflict between parents and offspring is a two-way street, as discussed in Chapter 5, which focused on parricide. There we showed the superiority of an evolutionary theoretical model of parent–offspring conflict to Freud's Oedipal theory. The evolutionary model predicts and explains detailed patterns in parent–offspring homicide data, and better accounts for the comparative and cross-cultural evidence, too.

Most murders do not, of course, occur within the family. In Chapters 6, 7, and 8, we considered the predominant variety of homicide, namely that in which the antagonists are unrelated men, especially young men whose dismal prospects make dangerous escalation of social competition attractive. Evolutionary models—especially Darwin's sexual selection theory as elaborated by Bateman and Trivers—explain and predict species differences in the prevalence of violent same-sex competition and in the sexually differentiated effects of life stage and circumstance upon such competition. We reviewed this body of theory, and showed how it predicts a sex difference in human competition and violence. We then documented the cross-cultural universality of enormous sex differences in reproductive competition and same-sex homicide, as well as the relevance of a young man's circumstances and life prospects to the probability that he will turn to violence in his pursuit of status, resources, and women. We debunked the ideologically motivated myth that such sex differences are reversed or absent in exotic cultures, and decried the biophobia that is rampant in the social sciences.

What men are competing *for*—whether immediately or more ultimately—is control over the reproductive capacities of women. This consideration led us back, in Chapter 9, to "family" murder in its predominant form: the killing of spouses. Marital violence arises out of men's efforts to exert control over women and their reproductive capacities, and women's efforts to retain some independence in the face of male coercion. This male sexual proprietariness is the principal source of conflict in the great majority of spousal homicides, regardless of whether the eventual killer is the husband or the wife, and it provides a conceptual framework for the analysis of such aspects of spousal homicide as the differential risk in legal versus commonlaw unions, the effects of age and age disparities, the relevance of separation, and the uniquely male crime of familicide.

Vengeance and blame were the subjects of Chapters 10 and 11. We argued that the revenge motive is effectively deterrent in function and has evolved for that reason. Vengeful urges are profoundly linked to familial solidarity, and are problematic for those who aspire to forge polities on other than familial bases. But revenge is also an onerous duty, and people have willingly relinquished their retaliatory rights to the state, in exchange for guarantees that justice will indeed be executed. These considerations led us to examine the anthropology, history, and ideology of state-administered justice, and the remarkable disenfranchisement of victims in modern states. We also argued that vengeful urges and attributions of blame, having evolved to be effectively deterrent, are directed against those perceived as deterrable. This accounts for our persistent uncertainty about the most appropriate response to the misdeeds of the insane, who do not respond to the sticks and carrots that move most people. We suggested that "insanity" is attributed to those who fail to perceive (or choose not to pursue) "self-interest" as an evolutionary psychologist would define it; and we supported this interpretation with analyses of insanity dispositions in homicide cases.

Finally, in Chapter 12, we reviewed some current theories addressing the important question of why there is such enormous geographic and temporal variability in homicide rates. We identified the most volatile component of these variable rates, namely those cases in which killer and victim are unrelated young men, but we also showed that the various sorts of homicides tend to covary in their frequency, lending support to the idea of local variation in the prevalence and legitimacy of violence. We do not pretend to have solved the mystery of why homicidal violence is so variable in its occurrence between times and places, but we argue that a satisfactory answer will have to include some consideration of the evolved motives of the individual protagonists of violence.

*   *   *

It is a widespread misapprehension that biological approaches to the study of violence are narrowly "deterministic" in some way that is both antithetical to the analysis of social and circumstantial influences, and pessimistic. We hope that our readers appreciate that the evolutionary psychology that we espouse is none of these things. *All* science is deterministic in its assumptions, sociology no less than chemistry, and all the adaptive characteristics of living creatures have been shaped by selection, the human mind no less than the stag's antlers.

Any biological phenomenon of interest will inevitably be misunderstood until it is scrutinized in the light of evolutionary theory. This claim applies with special force in the case of social phenomena, because selection is the fundamental interindividual process that creates and organizes social responsiveness. Far from being antithetical to the analysis of social and circumstantial influences upon human action, evolutionary biology is essential to such analysis. All of the considerable insights that an evolutionary perspective provides about familial solidarity and fratricide, sexual love and spousal violence, mother love and infanticide, rivalry, revenge, machismo, and much more—all are insights about the social and circumstantial predictors of violence. There is no more mischievous false dichotomy than "social" versus "biological"; sociality has no meaning outside of the biological world.

The muddle about "determinism" fuels another common misapprehension, namely that a Darwinian view of the human animal is "pessimistic." (As if ignorance of our natural selective history will somehow make us free!) Ironically, the model of humankind that is really pessimistic is the one that is usually stated as an alternative, namely that man *has* no nature and is therefore limitlessly malleable by the forces of "conditioning" and "behavior modification." Extreme versions of this view would deprive the individual of any stable self-interest, making him putty in the hands of "educators," a totalitarian's dream. Fortunately, this pessimistic antibiological denial of human nature and human dignity is false. The endemic fact of conflicting interests has been the selective milieu for a human psyche that is buffered against manipulation and deception—a psyche that is capable of discerning its own interests and acting both individually and collectively to advance them. Despotic tyranny seems to be inherently unstable, and the rise of democratic power-sharing in state societies has coincided with (and perhaps caused) a decline in the private use of personal violence, possibly to an all-time low. The enormous variability in national homicide rates should be grounds for optimism: There *are* social milieus where killing is exceedingly rare. With the elimination of social inequity and desperation, we may yet see homicide become an almost negligible source of human mortality.

The human psyche *has* been shaped by a history of selection. There is no serious controversy about this proposition; the only "alternatives" to selectionist explanations of adaptation are religiously motivated creation myths. The interesting question is not whether this is so (it is), but "so what?": How can students of murder (or any other social phenomenon) use evolutionary psychological ideas to stimulate their research and improve their understanding? We do not for a moment imagine that the analyses we have undertaken are the last word on this subject; quite the contrary. What we hope we have demonstrated is the potential of evolutionary ideas as metatheory for psychology and criminology, and we hope that other students of human action will be inspired to let their imaginations be informed by contemporary evolutionary thought.

References

Ahenakew, E. (1973). *In* R. M. Buck (Ed.), *Voices of the Plains Cree.* Toronto: McClelland & Stewart.

Akiga (1939). *Akiga's story: The Tiv tribe as seen by one of its members.* (R. East, Transl. and Ed.). London: International Institute of African Languages and Cultures.

Ali, Z. and Lowry, M. (1981). Early maternal-child contact: Effects on later behaviour. *Developmental Medicine and Child Neurology, 23,* 337–345.

Alexander, R. D. (1974). The evolution of social behavior. *Annual Review of Ecology and Systematics, 5,* 325–383.

Alexander, R. D. (1979). *Darwinism and human affairs.* Seattle, WA: University of Washington Press.

Alexander, R. D. (1987). *The biology of moral systems.* New York: Aldine de Gruyter.

Alexander, R. D., Hoogland, J. L., Howard, R. D., Noonan, K. M., and Sherman, P. W. (1979). Sexual dimorphisms and breeding systems in pinnipeds, ungulates, primates and humans. *In* N. A. Chagnon and W. Irons (Eds.), *Evolutionary biology and human social behavior.* North Scituate, MA: Duxbury Press.

Amernic, J. (1984). *Victims: The orphans of justice.* Toronto: Seal Books.

Andersson, M., Wiklund, C. G., and Rundgren, H. (1980). Parental defence of offspring: A model and an example. *Animal Behaviour, 28,* 536–542.

Archer, D. and Gartner, R. (1984). *Violence and crime in cross-national perspective.* New Haven, CT: Yale University Press.

Arlacchi, P. (1980). *Mafia, peasants and great estates. Society in traditional Calabria.* Cambridge: Cambridge University Press.

Attenborough, F. L. (1922/1963). *The laws of the earliest English kings.* New York: Russell & Russell Inc.

Axelrod, R. (1984). *The evolution of cooperation.* NY: Basic Books.

Axelrod, R. and Hamilton, W. D. (1981). The evolution of cooperation. *Science, 211,* 1390–1396.

Ayers, E. L. (1984). *Vengeance and justice. Crime and punishment in the 19th-century American south.* NY: Oxford University Press.

Bachrach, C. A. (1983). Children in families: Characteristics of biological, step-, and adopted children. *Journal of Marriage and the Family, 45,* 171–179.

Bacon, M. K., Child, I. L., and Barry, H. (1963). A cross-cultural study of correlates of crime. *Journal of Abnormal and Social Psychology, 66,* 291–300.

Badcock, C. R. (1983). *Madness and modernity.* Oxford: Basil Blackwell.

Baldus, D., Pulaski, C. A., and Woodworth, G. (1986). Arbitrariness and discrimination in the administration of the death penalty: a challenge to State Supreme Courts. *Stetson Law Review, 15,* 133–261.

Balikci, A. (1970). *The Netsilik Eskimo.* Garden City, NY: The Natural History Press.

Bandura, A. (1973). *Aggression: A social learning analysis.* Englewood Cliffs, NJ: Prentice-Hall.

Barash, D. P. (1975). Evolutionary aspects of parental behavior: The distraction display of the Alpine accentor, *Prunella collaris. Wilson Bulletin, 87,* 367–373.

Baron, J. N. and Reiss, P. C. (1985a). Same time, next year: aggregate analyses of the mass media and violent behavior. *American Sociological Review, 50,* 347–363.

Baron, J. N. and Reiss, P. C. (1985b). Reply to Phillips and Bollen. *American Sociological Review, 50,* 372–376.

Barton, R. (1919). *Ifugao law.* University of California Publications in Archaeology and Ethnology, Vol. 15. Berkeley, CA: University of California press (reprinted 1969).

Bateman, A. J. (1948). Intra-sexual selection in *Drosophila. Heredity, 2,* 349–368.

Bates, D. G. and Lees, S. H. (1979). The myth of population regulation. *In* N. A. Chagnon and W. Irons (Eds.), *Evolutionary biology and human social behavior.* North Scituate, MA: Duxbury.

Beattie, J. M. (1974). The pattern of crime in England 1660–1800. *Past and Present, 62,* 47–95.

Becker, G. S., Landes, E. M., and Michael, R. T. (1977). An economic analysis of marital instability. *Journal of Political Economy, 85,* 1141–1187.

Bee, H. L., Mitchell, S. K., Barnard, K. E., Eyres, S. J., and Hammond, M. A. (1984). Predicting intellectual outcomes: Sex differences in response to early environmental stimulation. *Sex Roles, 10,* 783–803.

Behlmer, G. K. (1979). Deadly motherhood: Infanticide and medical opinion in mid-Victorian England. *Journal of the History of Medicine*, 34, 403–427.

Beidelman, T. O. (1963). Witchcraft in Ukaguru. *In* J. Middleton and E. H. Winter (Eds.), *Witchcraft and sorcery in East Africa*. London: Routledge & Kegan Paul.

Bensing, R. C. and Schroeder, O. (1960). *Homicide in an urban community*. Springfield, IL: Thomas.

Berkowitz, L. and Macauley, J. (1971). The contagion of criminal violence. *Sociometry*, 34, 238–260.

Betzig, L. L. (1982). Despotism and differential reproduction: A cross-cultural correlation of conflict asymmetry, hierarchy, and degree of polygyny. *Ethology and Sociobiology*, 3, 209–221.

Betzig, L. L. (1985). *Despotism and differential reproduction: A Darwinian view of history*. NY: Aldine de Gruyter.

Biles, D. (1982). *The size of the crime problem in Australia* (2nd ed.). Canberra: Australian Institute of Criminology.

Biolsi, T. (1984). Ecological and cultural factors in Plains Indian warfare. *In* R. B. Ferguson (Ed.), *Warfare, culture, and environment*. Orlando, FL: Academic Press.

Birkhead, T. R. (1978). Behavioural adaptations to high density nesting in the common guillemot, *Uria aalge*. *Animal Behaviour*, 26, 321–331.

Blackstone, W. (1803). *Commentaries on the laws of England, in four books*. (Cited from the edition edited by St. G. Tucker.) Philadelphia, PA: William Young Birch & Abraham Small.

Bloch, D. (1978). *"So the witch won't eat me." Fantasy and the child's fear of infanticide*. NY: Grove Press Inc.

Bloch, M. (1961). *Feudal Society. Vol. 1: The growth of ties of dependence*. (Transl. by L. A. Manyon). Chicago, IL: University of Chicago Press.

Block, R. (1976). Homicide in Chicago: a nine-year study (1965–1973). *Journal of Criminal Law and Criminology*, 66, 496–510.

Boehm, C. (1984). *Blood revenge. The anthropology of feuding in Montenegro and other tribal societies*. Lawrence, KS: University Press of Kansas.

Bohannan, P. (Ed.). (1960a). *African homicide and suicide*. Princeton, NJ: Princeton University Press.

Bohannan, P. (1960b). Homicide among the Tiv of Central Nigeria. *In African homicide and suicide*, pp. 30–64. Princeton, NJ: Princeton University Press.

Bohannan, P. and Bohannan, L. (1953/1969). The Tiv of Central Nigeria. Reprinted *In* D. Forde (Ed.), *Ethnographic survey of Africa. Western Africa, Part VIII*. London: International African Institute.

Bonnie, R. J. (1983). The moral basis of the insanity defense. *American Bar Association Journal, 69,* 194–197.

Borgerhoff Mulder, M. (1988). Bridewealth variability among the Kipsigis. *In* L. Betzig, M. Borgerhoff Mulder, and P. Turke (Eds.), *Human reproductive behaviour: A Darwinian perspective.* Cambridge: Cambridge University Press, in press.

Boswell, J. (1779). *Life of Johnson.* Cited from the 1953 edition, R. W. Chapman (Ed.). Oxford: Oxford University Press.

Boudouris, J. (1971). Homicide and the family. *Journal of Marriage and the Family, 33,* 667–676.

Bowers, W. J., and Pierce, G. L. (1980). Arbitrariness and discrimination under post-*Furman* capital statutes. *Crime and Delinquency, 26,* 563–635.

Boyd, R. and Richerson, P. J. (1985). *Culture and the evolutionary process.* Chicago, IL: University of Chicago Press.

Bradley, F. H. (1927). *Ethical studies* (2nd ed.). London: Oxford University Press.

Brearley, H. C. (1932) *Homicide in the United States.* Chapel Hill, NC: University of North Carolina Press.

Brisson, N. J. (1983). Battering husbands: a survey of abusive men. *Victimology, 6,* 338–344.

British Parliamentary Papers 1871. Vol. 7. No. 372. House of Commons.

Brown, J. K. (1982). Cross-cultural perspectives on middle-aged women. *Current Anthropology, 23,* 143–156.

Bryson, J. B. (1976). The natures of sexual jealousy: An exploratory study. Paper presented to American Psychological Association, Washington, D.C., September 1976.

Bryson, J. B. (1977). Situational determinants of the expression of jealousy. Paper presented to American Psychological Association, San Francisco, August 1977.

Buechler, H. C. and Buechler, J.-M. (1971). *The Bolivian Aymara.* NY: Holt, Rinehart and Winston.

Bugos, P. E. and McCarthy, L. M. (1984). Ayoreo infanticide: A case study. *In* G. Hausfater and S. B. Hrdy (Eds.), *Infanticide: Comparative and evolutionary perspectives,* pp. 503–520. NY: Aldine de Gruyter.

Bullough, V. L. (1976). *Sexual variance in society and history.* NY: Wiley.

Burch, T. K. (1985). *Family history survey.* Ottawa: Statistics Canada.

Burton-Bradley, B. G. (1968). The amok syndrome in Papua and New Guinea. *Medical Journal of Australia, 1,* 252–256.

Busnot, F. D. (1715). *The history of the reign of Muley Ismael, the present king of Morocco, Fez, Tafilet, Sous, &c.* (Transl. from French, Original, 1714). London: A. Bell.

Campion, J., Cravens, J. M., Rotholc, A., Weinstein, H. C., Covan, F., and Alpert, M. (1985). A study of 15 matricidal men. *American Journal of Psychiatry, 142,* 312–317.

Carlson, C. A. (1984). Intrafamilial homicide. A sociobiological perspective. Unpublished B.Sc. thesis, McMaster University.

Carlsson, S. G., Fagerberg, H., Horneman, G., Hwang, C.-P., Larsson, K., Rodholm, M., Schaller, J., Danielsson, B., and Gundewall, C. (1978). Effects of amount of contact between mother and child on the mother's nursing behavior. *Developmental Psychobiology, 11,* 143–150.

Chagnon, N. A. (1967). Yanomamö warfare, social organization and marriage alliances. Ph.D. dissertation, University of Michigan.

Chagnon, N. A. (1983). *Yanomamö. The fierce people.* (3rd ed.). NY: Holt, Rinehart and Winston.

Charnov, E. L. (1982). *The theory of sex allocation.* Princeton, NJ: Princeton University Press.

Cherlin, A. (1978). Remarriage as an incomplete institution. *American Journal of Sociology, 84,* 634–650.

Cheung, P. T. K. (1986). Maternal filicide in Hong Kong, 1971–1985. *Medicine, Science and the Law, 26,* 185–192.

Chimbos, P. D. (1978): *Marital violence: A study of interspouse homicide.* San Francisco, CA: R & E Research Associates.

Chomsky, N. (1980). Rules and representations. *Behavioral and Brain Sciences, 3,* 1–15.

Clingempeel, W. G. (1981). Quasi-kin relationships and marital quality in stepfather families. *Journal of Personality and Social Psychology, 41,* 890–901.

Clutton-Brock, T. H. (Ed.) (1988). *Reproductive success.* Chicago, IL: University of Chicago Press, in press.

Coleman, L. (1984). *The reign of error. Psychiatry, authority, and law.* Boston, MA: Beacon Press.

Contini, P. (1971). The evolution of blood-money for homicide in Somalia. *Journal of African Law, 15,* 77–84.

Corder, B. F., Ball, B. C., Haizlip, T. M., Rollins, R., and Beaumont, R. (1976). Adolescent parricide: A comparison with other adolescent murder. *American Journal of Psychiatry, 133,* 957–961.

Cosmides, L. (1985). Deduction or Darwinian algorithms? An explanation of the "elusive" content effect on the Wason selection task. Unpublished Ph.D. dissertation, Harvard University.

Costantino, J. P., Kuller, L. H., Perper, J. A., and Cypess, R. H. (1977). An epidemiological study of homicides in Allegheny County, Pennsylvania. *American Journal of Epidemiology, 106,* 314–324.

Cox, M. R. (1892). *Cinderella. 345 variants.* London: The Folk-lore Society.

Criminal Justice Commission of Baltimore (1967). *Criminal homicides in Baltimore 1960–1964.* Baltimore, MD: Criminal Justice Commission.

Crowe, T. K., Deitz, J. C., and Siegner, C. B. (1984). Postrotatory nystagmus response of normal four-year-old children. *Physical and Occupational Therapy in Pediatrics, 4,* 19–28.

Daly M. and Wilson, M. (1981). Abuse and neglect of children in evolutionary perspective. *In* R. D. Alexander and D. W. Tinkle (Eds.), *Natural selection and social behavior.* NY: Chiron.

Daly, M. and Wilson, M. (1982). Homicide and kinship. *American Anthropologist, 84,* 372–378.

Daly, M. and Wilson, M. (1983). *Sex, evolution and behavior* (2nd ed.). Boston, MA: Willard Grant.

Daly, M. and Wilson, M. (1984). A sociobiological analysis of human infanticide. *In* G. Hausfater and S. B. Hrdy (Eds.), *Infanticide: Comparative and evolutionary perspectives,* pp. 487–502. NY: Aldine de Gruyter.

Daly, M. and Wilson, M. (1985). Child abuse and other risks of not living with both parents. *Ethology and Sociobiology, 6,* 197–210.

Daly, M. and Wilson, M. (1987a). Evolutionary psychology and family violence. *In* C. Crawford, M. Smith, and D. Krebs (Eds.), *Sociobiology and psychology.* Hillsdale, NJ: Erlbaum.

Daly, M. and Wilson, M. (1987b). Children as homicide victims. *In* R. Gelles and J. Lancaster (Eds.), *Child abuse and neglect: Biosocial dimensions.* NY: Aldine de Gruyter.

Daly, M. and Wilson, M. (1987c). The Darwinian psychology of discriminative parental solicitude. *Nebraska Symposium on Motivation, 35,* in press.

Daly, M., Wilson, M., and Weghorst, S. J. (1982). Male sexual jealousy. *Ethology and Sociobiology, 3,* 11–27.

Darwin, C. (1871). *The descent of man, and selection in relation to sex.* NY: D. Appleton.

Darwin, C. and Wallace, A. R. (1858). *Evolution by natural selection* (1958 edition). London: Cambridge University Press.

Davies, R. R. (1969). The survival of the bloodfeud in medieval Wales. *History, 54,* 338–357.

Davis, B. (1977). *Old Hickory.* NY: Dial.

Dawkins, R. (1982). *The extended phenotype.* San Francisco, CA: Freeman.

deCatanzaro, D. (1981). *Suicide and self-damaging behavior.* NY: Academic Press.

de Chateau, P. and Wiberg, B. (1977). Long-term effect on mother-infant behaviour of extra contact during the first hour post-partum. II. A follow-up at three months. *Acta Paediatrica Scandinavica, 66,* 145–151.

Dickemann, M. (1979a). The ecology of mating systems in hypergynous dowry societies. *Social Science Information, 18,* 163–195.

Dickemann, M. (1979b). Female infanticide, reproductive strategies, and social stratification: A preliminary model. *In* N. A. Chagnon and W. Irons (Eds.), *Evolutionary biology and human social behavior.* North Scituate, MA: Duxbury Press.

Dickemann, M. (1981). Paternal confidence and dowry competition: A biocultural analysis of purdah. *In* R. D. Alexander and D. W. Tinkle (Eds.). *Natural selection and social behavior: Recent research and new theory.* NY: Chiron Press.

Dickens, B. M. (1981). The sense of justice and criminal responsibility. *In* Hucker, S. J., Webster, C. D., and Ben-Aron, M. H. (Eds.), *Mental disorder and criminal responsibility,* pp. 33–61. Toronto: Butterworths.

Divale, W. T. and Harris, M. (1976). Population, warfare, and the male supremacist complex. *American Anthropologist, 78,* 521–538.

Djilas, M. (1958). *Land without justice.* NY: Harcourt, Brace.

Dobash, R. E. and Dobash, R. P. (1984). The nature and antecedents of violent events. *British Journal of Criminology, 24,* 269–288.

Dressler, J. (1982). Rethinking heat of passion: a defense in search of a rationale. *Journal of Criminal Law and Criminology, 73,* 421–470.

Duberman, L. (1975). *The reconstituted family: A study of remarried couples and their children.* Chicago, IL: Nelson-Hall.

Dunn, J. and Kendrick, C. (1982). *Siblings.* Cambridge, MA: Harvard University Press.

Dunning, R. W. (1959). *Social and economic change among the northern Ojibwa.* Toronto: University of Toronto Press.

Durham, M. E. (1928). *Some tribal origins laws and customs of the Balkans.* London: George Allan & Unwin.

Eagle Eye (1861–1863). *Infanticide memoranda.* (Langdell Hall, Harvard University).

Edwards, J. Ll. J. (1954). Provocation and the reasonable man: Another view. *Criminal Law Review, 1954,* 898–906.

Edwards, S. S. M. (1985). A socio-legal evaluation of gender ideologies in domestic violence assault and spousal homicides. *Victimology, 10,* 186–205.

Ellison, P. T. (1985). Lineal inheritance and lineal extinction. *Behavioral and Brain Sciences, 8,* 672.

Elwin, V. (1950). *Maria Murder and Suicide* (2nd ed.). Bombay: Oxford University Press.

Erickson, C. J. and Zenone, P. G. (1976). Courtship differences in male ring doves: Avoidance of cuckoldry? *Science, 192,* 1353–1354.

Evans, S. S. and Scott, J. E. (1984). The seriousness of crime cross-culturally. The impact of religiosity. *Criminology, 22,* 39–59.

Ezorsky, G. (1972). *Philosophical perspectives on punishment.* Albany, NY: State University of New York Press.

Fallers, L. A. and Fallers, M. C. (1960). Homicide and suicide in Busoga. *In* P. Bohannan (Ed.), *African homicide and suicide.* Princeton, NJ: Princeton University Press.

Festinger, T. (1986). *Necessary risk: A study of adoptions and disrupted adoption placements.* Washington: Child Welfare League of America.

Fisher, R. A. (1930). *The genetical theory of natural selection.* Oxford: Oxford University Press.

Flannery, R. (1953). *The Gros Ventres of Montana: Part 1, Social Life.* Washington, D.C.: Catholic University of America.

Fleagle, J. G., Kay, R. F., and Simons, E. L. (1980). Sexual dimorphism in early anthropoids. *Nature (London), 287,* 328–330.

Flinn, M. V. (1988). Daughter guarding in a Trinidadian Village. *In* L. Betzig, M. Mulder, and P. Turke (Eds.), *Human reproductive behavior.* London: Cambridge University Press, in press.

Floud, J. and Young, W. (1981). *Dangerousness and criminal justice.* London: Heinemann.

Fodor, J. (1984). *The modularity of mind.* Cambridge, MA: MIT Press.

Ford, C. S. and Beach, F. A. (1951). *Patterns of sexual behavior.* NY: Harper & Row.

Fortune, R. (1939). Arapesh warfare. *American Anthropologist, 41,* 22–41.

Freeman, D. (1983). *Margaret Mead and Samoa. The making and unmaking of an anthropological myth.* Cambridge, MA: Harvard Univ. Press.

Freud, S. (1900). *The interpretation of dreams.* (Cited from the 1953 edition, J. Strachey, Transl. and Ed.). NY: Basic Books.

Freud, S. (1909). Analysis of a phobia in a five-year-old boy. (Cited from the 1959 edition of Freud's *Collected papers,* A. Strachey and J. Strachey, Transl. and Ed.). NY: Basic Books.

Freud, S. (1913). *Totem and taboo.* (Cited from the 1950 edition, J. Strachey, Transl. and Ed.). NY: W. W. Norton.

Friedland, M. L. (1984). *A century of criminal justice.* Toronto: Carswell Legal Publications.

Garfinkel, H. (1949). Research notes on inter- and intra-racial homicides. *Social Forces, 27,* 369–381.

Gaulin, S. J. C. and Sailer, L. D. (1985). Are females the ecological sex? *American Anthropologist, 87,* 111–119.

Geertz, C. (1983). *Local knowledge: Further essays in interpretive anthropology.* NY: Basic Books.

Gelles, R. J., and Strauss, M. A. (1979). Family experience and public support for the death penalty. *In* R. J. Gelles (Ed.), *Family violence.* Beverly Hills, CA: Sage.

Geronimo (1906). *Geronimo's story of his life.* NY: Duffield.

Gewertz, D. B. (1983). *Sepik River societies.* New Haven, CT: Yale University Press.

Ghiselin, M. T. (1974). *The economy of nature and the evolution of sex.* Berkeley, CA: University of California Press.

Gibbens, T. C. N. (1958). Sane and insane homicide. *Journal of criminal Law, Criminology and Police Science, 49,* 110–115.

Gibson, E. and Klein, S. (1961). *Murder. A home office research unit report.* London: HMSO.

Giles-Sims, J. (1984). The stepparent role. Expectations, behavior and sanctions. *Journal of Family Issues, 5,* 116–130.

Gillies, H. (1976). Homicide in the West of Scotland. *British Journal of Psychiatry, 128,* 105–127.

Given, J. B. (1977). *Society and homicide in thirteenth-century England.* Stanford, CA: Stanford University Press.

Gluckman, M. (Ed.). (1972). *The allocation of responsibility.* Manchester: Manchester University Press.

Goebel, J. (1937). *Felony and misdemeanor.* Philadelphia, PA: University of Pennsylvania Press.

Goldney, R. D. (1977). Family murder followed by suicide. *Forensic Science, 9,* 219–228.

Goldschmidt, W. R. (1967). *Sebei law.* Berkeley, CA: University of California Press.

Goodall, J. (1986). *The chimpanzees of Gombe.* Cambridge, MA: Harvard University Press.

Goode, W. (1969). Violence among intimates. *In* D. J. Mulvihill and M. M. Tumin (Eds.), *Crimes of violence, report to the National Commission on the causes and prevention of violence,* Vol. 13, pp. 941–977. Washington, D.C.: U.S. Government Printing Office.

Goody, J. (Ed.). (1966). *Succession to high office.* Cambridge: Cambridge University Press.

Gordon, J. (Ed.). (1976). *Margaret Mead: The complete bibliography 1925–1975.* The Hague: Mouton.

Gorecki, J. (1983). *Capital punishment. Criminal law and social evolution.* NY: Columbia University Press.

Gould, S. J. and Lewontin, R. C. (1979). The spandrels of San Marco and the Panglossian paradigm: A critique of the adaptationist program. *Proceedings of the Royal Society of London, 205,* 581–598.

Granzberg, G. (1973). Twin infanticide—A cross-cultural test of a materialistic explanation. *Ethos, 1,* 405–412.

Green, C. M. (1981). Matricide by sons. *Medicine, Science and the Law, 21,* 207–214.

Greenland, C. and Rosenblatt, E. (1975). Murder followed by suicide in Ontario 1966 to 1970. Unpublished manuscript, School of Social Work, McMaster University.

Greig-Smith, P. W. (1980). Parental investment in nest defence by stonechats *(Saxicola torquata). Animal Behaviour, 28,* 604–619.

Gudjonsson, G. H. and Petursson, H. (1982). Some criminological and psychiatric aspects of homicide in Iceland. *Medicine, Science and the Law, 22,* 91–98.

Gurr, T. R. (1981). Historical trends in violent crime: A critical review of the evidence. *Crime and Justice: An Annual Review of Research, 3,* 295–353.

Guttmacher, M. S. (1955). Criminal responsibility in certain homicide cases involving family members. *In* P. H. Hoch and J. Zubin (Eds.), *Psychiatry and the law.* NY: Grune & Stratton.

Guttmacher, M. S. (1960). *The mind of the murderer.* NY: Strauss & Cudahy.

Hadjiyannakis, C. (1969). *Les tendences contemporaines concernant la repression du délit d'adultère.* Thessalonika: Association Internationale de Droit Pénal.

Hales, D. J., Lozoff, B., Sosa, R., and Kennell, J. H. (1977). Defining the limits of the maternal sensitive period. *Developmental Medicine and Child Neurology, 19,* 454–461.

Hamilton, W. D. (1964). The genetical evolution of social behaviour. I and II. *Journal of Theoretical Biology, 7,* 1–52.

Hammer, C. I. (1978). Patterns of homicide in a medieval university town: Fourteenth century Oxford. *Past and Present, 78,* 1–23.

Hanawalt, B. A. (1979). *Crime and conflict in English communities, 1300–1348.* Cambridge, MA: Harvard University Press.

Handy, E. S. C. (1923). *The native culture in the Marquesas.* Bernice A. Bishop Museum, Bulletin No. 9.

Hansen, J. P. H. and Bjarnason, O. (1974). Homicide in Iceland 1946–1970. *Forensic Science, 4,* 107–117.

Hardy, M. J. L. (1963). *Blood feuds and the payment of blood money in the middle east.* Beirut: Catholic Press.

Harlan, H. (1950). Five hundred homicides. *Journal of Criminal Law and Criminology, 40,* 736–752.

Harris, M. (1974). *Cows, pigs, wars and witches.* NY: Random House.

Hart, C. W. M. and Pilling, A. R. (1960). *The Tiwi of north Australia.* NY: Holt, Rinehart & Winston.

Hartung, J. (1982). Polygyny and inheritance of wealth. *Current Anthropology, 23,* 1–12.

Hartung, J. (1985). Matrilineal inheritance: new theory and analysis. *Behavioral and Brain Sciences, 8,* 661–688.

Heister, G. (1984). Sex differences and cognitive/motor interference with visual half-field stimulation. *Neuropsychologia, 22,* 205–214.

Herbert, M., Sluckin, W., and Sluckin, A. (1982). Mother-to-infant "bonding"? *Journal of Child Psychology and Psychiatry, 23,* 205–221.

Herjanic, M. and Meyer, D. A. (1976). Notes on epidemiology of homicide in an urban area. *Forensic Science, 8,* 235–245.

Hiatt, L. R. (1965). *Kinship and conflict: A study of an aboriginal community in Northern Arnhem Land.* Canberra: Australian National University Press.

Hilberman, E. and Munson, K. (1978). Sixty battered women. *Victimology, 2,* 460–470.

Hill, K. and Kaplan, H. (1988). Tradeoffs in male and female reproductive strategies among the Ache: Part 2. In L. Betzig, M. Borgerhoff Mulder, and P. Turke (Eds.), *Human reproductive behavior.* Cambridge: Cambridge University Press, in press.

Hoffer, P. C. and Hull, N. E. H. (1981). *Murdering mothers: Infanticide in England and New England 1558–1803.* NY: New York University Press.

Hogan, J. (1932). The Irish law of kingship, with special reference to Ailech and Cenél Eoghain. *Proceedings of the Royal Irish Academy, 40,* 186–254.

Hogbin, H. I. (1938). Social reaction to crime: law and morals in the Schouten Islands, New Guinea. *Journal of the Anthropological Institute of Great Britain and Ireland, 68,* 223–262.

Holmes, W. G. and Sherman, P. W. (1982). The ontogeny of kin recognition in two species of ground squirrels. *American Zoologist, 22,* 491–517.

Holmes, W. G. and Sherman, P. W. (1983). Kin recognition in animals. *American Scientist, 71,* 46–55.

Howell, N. (1979). *Demography of the Dobe !Kung.* NY: Academic Press.

Howell, P. P. (1954). *A manual of Nuer law.* London: Oxford University Press.

Hrdy, S. B. (1981). *The woman that never evolved.* Cambridge, MA: Harvard University Press.

Huff-Corzine, L., Corzine, J., and Moore, D. C. (1986). Southern exposure: deciphering the south's influence on homicide rates. *Social Forces, 64,* 906–924.

Hunt, E. E., Schneider, D. M., Kidder, N. R., and Stevens, W. D. (1949). *The Micronesians of Yap and their depopulation.* Washington, D.C.: Pacific Science Board, National Research Council.

Hurnard, N. D. (1969). *The king's pardon for homicide before A.D. 1307.* Oxford: Clarendon Press.

Husain, A. and Daniel, A. (1984). A comparative study of filicidal and abusive mothers. *Canadian Journal of Psychiatry, 29,* 596–600.

Irons, W. (1983). Human female reproductive strategies. *In* S. K. Wasser (Ed.), *Social behavior of female vertebrates.* NY: Academic Press.

Irons, W. (1986) Incest: why all the fuss? Paper presented at the Evolution and Behavior meeting, University of Michigan, April 1986.

Jacoby, J. E. and Paternoster, R. (1982). Sentencing disparity and jury packing: Further challenges to the death penalty. *Journal of Criminal Law and Criminology, 73,* 379–387.

Jacoby, S. (1985). *Wild justice: The evolution of revenge.* London: Collins.

Jarman, P. J. (1974). The social organisation of antelope in relation to their ecology. *Behaviour, 48,* 215–267.

Johnson, P. E. (1985). The turnabout in the insanity defense. *Crime and Justice: An annual Review of Research, 6,* 221–236.

Jolowicz, H. F. (1932). *Historical introduction to the study of Roman law.* Cambridge: Cambridge University Press.

Judicial Statistics. England and Wales. (1856–1938 annually). London: The Queen's Printer.

Kaplun, D. and Reich, R. (1976). The murdered child and his killers. *American Journal of Psychiatry, 133,* 809–813.

Karsten, R. (1932). *Indian tribes of the Argentine and Bolivian Chaco. Ethnological studies.* Helsingfors: Societas Scientiarum Fennica.

Karsten, R. (1935). *The head-hunters of western Amazonus.* Helsingfors: Societas Scientiarum Fennica.

Kelsen, H. (1946). *Society and nature.* Chicago, IL: University of Chicago Press (reprinted 1974).

Kennell, J. H., Jerauld, R., Wolfe, H., Chesler, D., Kreger, N. C., McAlpine, W., Steffa, M., and Klaus, M. H. (1974). Maternal behavior one year after early and extended post-partum contact. *Developmental Medicine and Child Neurology, 16,* 172–179.

Klaus, M. H. and Kennell, J. H. (1976). *Maternal-infant bonding.* St. Louis, MO: Mosby.

Klaus, M. H., Jerauld, R., Kreger, N. C., McAlpine, W., Steffa, M., and Kennell, J. H. (1972). Maternal attachment. Importance of the first post-partum days. *New England Journal of Medicine, 286,* 460–463.

Kluckhohn, C. (1944). *Navaho witchcraft.* Vol. XXII, No. 2, Papers of the Peabody Museum, Harvard University.

Knauft, B. M. (1985). *Good company and violence: Sorcery and social control in a lowland New Guinea society.* Berkeley, CA: University of California Press.

Kompara, D. R. (1980). Difficulties in the socialization process of stepparenting. *Family Relations, 29,* 69–73.

Konner, M. J. and Worthman, C. (1980). Nursing frequency, gonadal function, and birth spacing among !Kung hunter-gatherers. *Science, 207,* 788–791.

Krahn, H., Hartnagel, T. F. and Gartrell, J. W. (1986). Income inequality and homicide rates: Cross-national data and criminological theories. *Criminology, 24,* 269–295.

Kraus, J. (1978). Family structure as a factor in the adjustment of adopted children. *British Journal of Social Work, 8,* 327–337.

Kressel, G. M. (1981). Sororicide/filiacide: homicide for family honour. *Current Anthropology, 22,* 141–158.

Lacoste-Utamsing, C. de and Holloway, R. L. (1982). Sexual dimorphism in the human corpus callosum. *Science, 216,* 1431–1432.

LaFontaine, J. S. (1960). Homicide and suicide among the Gisu. *In* P. Bohannan (Ed.), *African homicide and suicide.* Princeton, NJ: Princeton University Press.

LaFontaine, J. S. (1963). Witchcraft in Bugisu. *In* J. Middleton and E. H. Winter (Eds.), *Witchcraft and sorcery in east Africa.* London: Routledge & Kegan Paul.

Lagacé, R. O. (1974). *Nature and use of the HRAF files.* New Haven, CT: HRAF.

Lamb, M. E. and Hwang, C.-P. (1982). Maternal attachment and mother-neonate bonding: A critical review. *In* M. E. Lamb and A. L. Brown (Eds.), *Advances in developmental psychology,* Vol. 2. Hillsdale, NJ: Erlbaum.

Lancaster, L. (1958). Kinship in Anglo-Saxon society, parts 1 and 2. *British Journal of Sociology, 9,* 234–248, 359–377.

Landau, S. F. and Drapkin, I. (1968). *Ethnic patterns of criminal homicide in Israel.* Jerusalem: Hebrew University of Jerusalem.

Lane, R. (1979). *Violent death in the city: Suicide, accident and murder in nineteenth century Philadelphia.* Cambridge, MA: Harvard University Press.

Leach, E. (1982). *Social anthropology.* Oxford: Oxford University Press.

Leauté, J. (Ed.). (1968). Recherches sur l'infanticide (1955–1965). *Annales de la Faculté de Droit et des Sciences Politiques et Economiques de Strasbourg. XVI*. Paris: Librairie Dalloz.

Lee, A. K., Bradley, A. J., and Braithwaite, R. W. (1977). Corticosteroid levels and male mortality in *Antechinus stuartii*. *In* B. Stonehouse and D. Gilmore (Eds.), *The biology of marsupials*. Baltimore, MD: University Park Press.

Lee, R. B. (1979). *The !Kung San: Men, women, and work in a foraging society*. Cambridge: Cambridge University Press.

Lee, R. B. and DeVore, I. (Eds.). (1976). *Kalahari hunter-gatherers*. Cambridge, MA: Harvard University Press.

LeVine, R. A. (1965). Intergenerational tensions and extended family structures in Africa. *In* E. Shanas and G. F. Streib (Eds.), *Social structure and the family generational relations*, pp. 188–204. Englewood Cliffs, NJ: Prentice-Hall.

Lévi-Strauss, C. (1969). *The elementary structures of kinship*. Boston, MA: Beacon.

Levy, J. E., Kunitz, S. J., and Everett, M. (1969). Navajo criminal homicide. *Southwestern Journal of Anthropology, 25*, 124–152.

Lewis, O. (1961). *The children of Sánchez: Autobiography of a Mexican family*. NY: Random House.

Lobban, C. F. (1972). Law and Anthropology in the Sudan (an analysis of homicide cases). *African Studies Series No. 13*. Sudan Research Unit, Khartoum University Press.

Lowie, R. H. (1917). Notes on the social organization and customs of the Mandan, Hidatsa, and Crow Indians. *Anthropological Papers of the American Museum of Natural History, 21*, 1–99.

Lozoff, B., Brittenham, G. M., Trause, M. A., Kennell, J. H., and Klaus, M. H. (1977). The mother-newborn relationship; limits of adaptability. *Journal of Pediatrics, 91*, 1–12.

Lundsgaarde, H. P. (1977). *Murder in Space City*. NY: Oxford University Press.

Lundsgaarde, H. P. (1979). Cultural sanctions of urban homicide. *In* H. M. Rose (Ed.), *Lethal aspects of urban violence*. Lexington, MA: Lexington Books.

Maccoby, E. E. and Jacklin, C. N. (1974). *The psychology of sex differences*. Palo Alto, CA: Stanford University Press.

MacDonald, J. M. (1961). *The murderer and his victim*. Springfield, IL: Thomas.

McGinniss, J. (1983). *Fatal vision*. NY: Signet.

McGlone, J. (1980). Sex difference in human brain asymmetry: A critical survey. *The Behavioral and Brain Sciences, 3*, 215–263.

McIlwraith, T. F. (1948). *The Bella Coola Indians*. Toronto: University of Toronto Press.

McKee, L. (1984). Sex differentials in survivorship and the customary treatment of infants and children. *Medical Anthropology, 8,* 91–108.

MacLusky, N. J. and Naftolin, F. (1981). Sexual differentiation of the central nervous system. *Science, 211,* 1294–1303.

McWhirter, N. and Greenberg, S. (1979). *Guinness book of records*. Edition 26. London: Guinness Superlatives Ltd.

Man, E. H. (1885). *On the aboriginal inhabitants of the Andaman Islands*. London: Royal Anthropological Institute.

Matthiessen, P. (1962). *Under the mountain wall: A chronicle of two seasons in the stone age*. NY: Viking.

Maxson, S. J. and Oring, L. W. (1980). Breeding season time and energy budget of the polyandrous spotted sandpiper. *Behaviour, 74,* 200–263.

Mayr, E. (1983). How to carry out the adaptationist program? *American Naturalist, 121,* 324–334.

Mead, M. (1931). Jealousy: primitive and civilised. *In* S. D. Schmalhausen and V. F. Calverton (Eds.), *Woman's coming of age: A symposium*, pp. 35–48. NY: Liveright.

Mead, M. (1935). *Sex and temperament in three primitive societies*. NY: William Morrow.

Mead, M. (1949). *Male and female*. NY: Morrow.

Mead, M. (1950). *Sex and temperament*, Preface. NY: Morrow.

Messinger, L. (1976). Remarriage between divorced people with children from previous marriages: A proposal for preparation for remarriage. *Journal of Marriage and Family Counseling, 2,* 193–200.

Middleton, J. and Winter, E. H. (Eds.). (1963). *Witchcraft and sorcery in East Africa*. London: Routledge & Kegan Paul.

Miller, H. B. (1949). Manslaughter—adultery as provocation. *Kentucky Law Journal, 37,* 288–293.

Minderhout, D. J. (1986). Introductory texts and social sciences stereotypes. *Anthropology Newsletter, 27*(3), 20, 14–15.

Mohr, J. W. and McKnight, C. K. (1971). Violence as a function of age and relationships with special reference to matricide. *Canadian Psychiatric Association Journal, 16,* 29–32.

Monahan, J. (1981). *The clinical prediction of violent behavior*. Rockville, MD: U.S. Department of Health & Human Services.

Monahan, J. and Steadman, H. J. (Eds.). (1983). *Mentally disordered offenders*. NY: Plenum Press.

Moore, S. F. (1978). *Law as process: An anthropological approach.* London: Routledge & Kegan Paul.

Morgan, C. L. (1894). *Introduction to comparative psychology.* NY: Scribner's.

Morris, W. (1969). *The American Heritage Dictionary of the English Language.* Boston: Houghton Mifflin.

Muller, W. (1917). *Yap.* Band 2, Halbband 1 (as translated in HRAF). Hamburg: Friederichsen.

Mulvihill, D. J., Tumin, M. M., and Curtis, L. A. (1969). *Crimes of Violence,* Vol. 11. Washington, DC: U.S. Government Printing Office.

Murdock, G. P. (1967). *Ethnographic atlas.* Pittsburgh, PA: University of Pittsburgh Press.

Nash, J. (1967). Death as a way of life: The increasing resort to homicide in a Maya Indian community. *American Anthropologist, 69,* 455–470.

National Commission on the Insanity Defense (1983). *Myths and realities.* Arlington, VA: National Mental Health Association.

Nisbett, R. and Ross, L. (1980). *Human inference: Strategies and shortcomings of social judgment.* Englewood Cliffs, NJ: Prentice-Hall.

Nowak, M. (1980). *Eve's rib.* NY: St. Martin's Press.

O'Connor, S., Vietze, P. M., Sherrod, K. B., Sandler, H. M., and Altemeier, W. A. (1980). Reduced incidence of parenting inadequacy following rooming-in. *Pediatrics, 66,* 176–182.

Otterbein, K. F. and Otterbein, C. S. (1965). An eye for an eye, a tooth for a tooth: A cross-cultural study of feuding. *American Anthropologist, 67,* 1470–1482.

Paige, K. E. and Paige, J. M. (1981). *The politics of reproductive ritual.* Berkeley, CA: University of California Press.

Paternoster, R. (1983). Race of victim and location of crime: The decision to seek the death penalty in South Carolina. *Journal of Criminal Law and Criminology, 74,* 754–785.

Patterson, T. L., Petrinovich, L., and James, D. K. (1980). Reproductive value and appropriateness of response to predators by white-crowned sparrows. *Behavioral Ecology and Sociobiology, 7,* 227–231.

Phillips, D. P. (1983). The impact of mass media violence on U.S. homicides. *American Sociological Review, 48,* 560–568.

Phillips, D. P. and Bollen, K. A. (1985). Same time, last year: Selective data dredging for negative findings. *American Sociological Review, 50,* 364–371.

Phillpotts, B. S. (1913). *Kindred and clan in the middle ages and after. A study in the sociology of the Teutonic races.* Cambridge: Cambridge University Press.

Pleck, J. H. (1981). *The myth of masculinity.* Cambridge, MA: MIT Press.

Pokorny, A. (1965). A comparison of homicides in two cities. *Journal of Criminal Law, Criminology and Police Science, 56,* 479–487.

Pollock, F. and Maitland, F. W. (1895). *The History of English law. Before the Time of Edward 1,* Vol. 2. Cambridge: Cambridge University Press (reprinted 1968).

Power, H. W., Litovich, E., and Lombardo, M. P. (1981). Male starlings delay incubation in order to avoid being cuckolded. *Auk, 98,* 386–389.

Pressley, P. H. (1981). Parental effort and the evolution of nest-guarding tactics in the threespine stickleback, *Gasterosteus aculeatus L. Evolution, 35,* 282–295.

Ramanujan, A. K. (1983). The Indian Oedipus. *In* L. Edmunds and A. Dundes (Eds.), *Oedipus: A folklore casebook, pp. 234–261.* NY: Garland.

Rattray, R. S. (1929). *Ashanti law and constitution.* Oxford: Clarendon.

Rogin, M. P. (1975). *Fathers and children: Andrew Jackson and the subjugation of the American Indian.* NY: Vintage books.

Rosenblatt, R. (1985). The quality of mercy. *Time,* 26 August, 52.

Rossi, P. H., Waite, E., Bose, C. E., and Berk, R. E. (1974). The seriousness of crimes: Normative structure and individual differences. *American Sociological Review, 39,* 224–237.

Rounsaville, B. J. (1978). Theories in marital violence: Evidence from a study of battered women. *Victimology: An International Journal, 3,* 11–31.

Rushforth, N. B., Ford, A. B., Hirsch, C. S., Rushforth, N. M., and Adelson, L. (1977). Violent death in a metropolitan county. Changing patterns in homicide (1958–1974). *New England Journal of Medicine, 297,* 531–538.

Russell, D. H. (1984). A study of juvenile murderers of family members. *International Journal of Offender Therapy and Comparative Criminology, 28,* 177–192.

Sahlins, M. (1976). *Culture and practical reason.* Chicago, IL: University of Chicago Press.

Salzano, F. M., Neel, J. V., and Maybury-Lewis, D. (1967). Further studies on the Xavante Indians. I. Demographic data on two additional villages: Genetic structure of the tribe. *American Journal of Human Genetics, 19,* 463–489.

Saran, A. B. (1974). *Murder and suicide among the Munda and the Oraon.* Delhi: National Publishing House.

Sargent, W. (1974). *People of the valley.* NY: Random House.

Schapera, I. (1938). *A handbook of Tswana law and custom.* London: Oxford University Press.

Schlenker, B. R. and Severy, L. J. (1979). Perspectives on social issues. *In* M. E. Meyer (Ed.), *Foundations of contemporary psychology.* NY: Oxford University Press.

Scott, P. D. (1973a). Parents who kill their children. *Medicine, Science and the Law, 13,* 120–126.

Scott, P. D. (1973b). Fatal battered baby cases. *Medicine, Science and the Law, 13,* 197–206.

Seaborne Davies, D. (1945). Child-killing in English law. *In The modern approach to criminal law: Collected Essays,* pp. 301–343. NY: Kraus Repr.

Sessar, K. (1975). The familial character of criminal homicide. *In* I. Drapkin and E. Viano (Eds.), *Victimology: A new focus.* Vol. IV: *Violence and its victims.* Lexington, MA: Lexington.

Sheleff, L. S. (1981). *Generations apart: Adult hostility to youth.* NY: McGraw-Hill.

Shepherd, R. N. (1984). Ecological constraints on internal representation: resonant kinematics of perceiving, imagining, thinking and dreaming. *Psychological Review, 91,* 417–447.

Shettel-Neuber, J., Bryson, J. B., and Young, L. E. (1978). Physical attractiveness of the "other person" and jealousy. *Personality and Social Psychology Bulletin, 4,* 612–615.

Shields, N. M. and Hanneke, C. R. (1983). Battered wives reactions to marital rape. *In* D. Finkelhor, R. J. Gelles, G. T. Hotaling, and M. A. Straus (Eds.), *The dark side of families,* pp. 131–148. Beverly Hills, CA: Sage.

Shostak, M. (1981). *Nisa.* Cambridge, MA: Harvard University Press.

Showalter, C. R., Bonnie, R. J., and Roddy, V. (1980). The spousal-homicide syndrome. *International Journal of Law and Psychiatry, 3,* 117–141.

Shternberg, L. I. (1933). *Giliaki, orochi, gol'dy, negidal'tsy, ainy; stat'i i materialy* (as translated in HRAF). Khabarovsk: Dal'giz.

Siciliano, S. (1965). *l'Omicidio.* Padova: Case Editrice Dott. Antonio Milani.

Siegel, E., Bauman, K. E., Schaefer, E. S., Saunders, M. M., and Ingram, D. D. (1980). Hospital and home support during infancy: Impact on maternal attachment, child abuse and neglect, and health care utilization. *Pediatrics, 66,* 183–190.

Skinner, B. F. (1957). *Verbal behavior.* NY: Appleton-Century-Crofts.

Skinner, B. F. (1971). *Beyond Freedom and Dignity.* NY: Knopf.

Slavin, M. O. (1985). The origins of psychic conflict and the adaptive function of repression: An evolutionary biological view. *Psychoanalysis and Contemporary Thought, 8,* 407–440.

Smith, J. N. M. (1974). The food searching behaviour of two European thrushes. II. The adaptiveness of the search patterns. *Behaviour, 49,* 1–61.

Smith, R. L. (1984). *Sperm competition.* NY: Academic Press.

Sohier, J. (1959). *Essai sur la criminalité dans la province de Léopoldville.* Brussels: J. Duculot.

Solicitor General of Canada (1981). *Solicitor general's study of conditional release.* Ottawa: Solicitor General's Office.

Sonne, B. (1982). The ideology and practice of blood feuds in East and West Greenland. *Études/Inuit/Studies, 6*(2), 21–49.

Sosa, R., Kennell, J. H., Klaus, M., and Urrutia, J. J. (1976). The effect of early mother-infant contact on breastfeeding, infection and growth. *CIBA Foundation Symposium No. 45. Breastfeeding and the mother.* pp. 179–204. Amsterdam: Elsevier.

Southall, A. W. (1960). Homicide and suicide among the Alur. *In* P. Bohannan (Ed.), *African homicide and suicide.* Princeton, NJ: Princeton University Press.

Southwold, M. (1966). Succession to the throne in Buganda, *In* J. Goody (Ed.), *Succession to high office,* pp. 82–126. Cambridge: Cambridge University Press.

Spencer, H. (1897). *Principles of ethics,* Vol. 1. New York: D. Appleton & Co.

Spencer, R. F. (1959). *The North Alaskan Eskimo.* Smithsonian Institution, Bureau of American Ethnology, Bulletin 171. Washington, D.C.: U.S. Government Printing Office.

Spencer, W. B. and Gillen, F. J. (1927). *The Arunta: A study of a stone age people.* London: Macmillan.

Spiro, M. E. (1982). *Oedipus in the Trobriands.* Chicago, IL: University of Chicago Press.

Statistics Canada (1984). *1981 Census of Canada. Census families in private households (92–935).* Ottawa: Statistics Canada.

Stephens, W. N. (1963). *The family in cross-cultural perspective.* NY: Holt, Rinehart & Winston.

Stone, A. A. (1984). *Law, psychiatry, and morality.* Washington, D.C.: American Psychiatric Press.

Stone, L. (1977). *The family, sex and marriage in England, 1500–1800.* NY: Harper & Row.

Svare, B. (1981). Maternal aggression in mammals. *In* P. Klopfer and D. Gubernick (Eds.), *Parental care in mammals,* pp. 179–210. NY: Plenum Press.

Svejda, M. J., Campos, J. J., and Emde, R. N. (1980). Mother-infant "bonding": Failure to generalize. *Child Development, 51,* 775–779.

Swaab, D. F. and Fliers, E. (1985). A sexually dimorphic nucleus in the human brain. *Science, 228,* 1112–1115.

Symons, D. (1979). *The evolution of human sexuality.* NY: Oxford University Press.

Symons, D. (1987). If we're all Darwinians, what's the fuss about? *In* C. Crawford, M. Smith and D. Krebs (Eds.), *Sociobiology and psychology.* Hillsdale, NJ: Erlbaum.

Szasz, T. S. (1961). *The myth of mental illness.* NY: Harper.

Teismann, M. W. (1975). Jealous conflict: A study of verbal interaction and labeling of jealousy among dating couples involved in jealousy improvisations. Unpublished Ph.D. dissertation, University of Connecticut.

Thompson, S. (1955). *Motif-index of folk-literature.* Vols. 1–6. Bloomington, IN: Indiana University Press.

Thornhill, R. and Thornhill, N. W. (1983). Human rape: An evolutionary analysis. *Ethology and Sociobiology, 4,* 137–173.

Thornhill, N. W. and Thornhill, R. (1987). Evolutionary theory and rules of mating and marriage pertaining to relatives by consanguinity and affinity. *In* C. Crawford, M. Smith, and D. Krebs (Eds.), *Sociobiology and Psychology.* Hillsdale, NJ: Erlbaum.

Toch, H. (1969). *Violent men: An inquiry into the psychology of violence.* Chicago, IL: Aldine.

Tooby, J. and Cosmides, L. (1988). Evolutionary psychology and the generation of culture, part I. Theoretical considerations. *Ethology and Sociobiology,* in press.

Treston, H. J. (1923). *Poine. A study in ancient Greek blood-vengeance.* London: Longmans, Green.

Trillin, C. (1984). *Killings.* NY: Ticknor & Fields.

Trillin, C. (1986). American chronicles: outdoor life. *The New Yorker,* 11 Aug., 63–73.

Trinkaus, E. (1980). Sexual differences in Neanderthal limb bones. *Journal of Human Evolution, 9,* 377–397.

Trinkaus, E. and Zimmerman, M. R. (1982). Trauma among the Shanidar Neandertals. *American Journal of Physical Anthropology, 57,* 61–76.

Trivers, R. L. (1972). Parental investment and sexual selection. *In* B. Campbell (Ed.), *Sexual selection and the descent of man 1871–1971.* Chicago, IL: Aldine.

Trivers, R. L. (1974). Parent-offspring conflict. *American Zoologist, 14,* 249–264.

Trivers, R. (1985). *Social evolution.* Menlo Park, CA: Benjamin/Cummings.

Trivers, R. L. and Willard, D. E. (1973). Natural selection of parental ability to vary the sex ratio of offspring. *Science, 179,* 90–92.

Tuzin, D. F. (1977). *The Ilahita Arapesh.* Berkeley, CA: University of California Press.

Tuzin, D. F. (1980). *The voice of the Tambaran.* Berkeley, CA: University of California Press.

U.S. Bureau of the Census (1978). 1976 survey of institutionalized persons: a study of persons in the United States. *Current Population Reports P-60,* No. 69. Washington, D.C.: U.S. Government Printing House.

U.S. Department of Justice (1986). *Uniform crime reports. Crime in the United States.* Washington, D.C.

Vail, P. (1973). *The great American rascal.* NY: Hawthorn.

Vance, R. B. and Wynne, W. (1934). Folk rationalizations in the "unwritten law." *American Journal of Sociology, 39,* 483–492.

van den Berghe, P. L. (1983). Human inbreeding avoidance: Culture in nature. *Behavioral and Brain Sciences, 6,* 91–123.

van den Berghe, P. L. (1985). Comment on G. E. Goodell, "Paternalism, patronage, and potlatch: The dynamics of giving and being given to." *Current Anthropology, 26,* 262–263.

Varma, S. C. (1978). *The Bhil kills.* Delhi: Kunj Publ. House.

Vergouwen, J. C. (1964). *The social organization and customary law of the Toba-Batak of northern Sumatra.* The Hague: Martinus Nijhoff.

Verkko, V. (1951). *Homicides and suicides in Finland and their dependence on national character.* Copenhagen: G. E. C. Gads Forlag.

Villaverde, J. (1909). The Ifugaos of Quiangan and vicinity (D. C. Worcester, Transl. and Ed.). *Phillipine Journal of Science, 4,* 237–262.

Voland, E. (1984). Human sex-ratio manipulation: Historical data from a German parish. *Journal of Human Evolution, 13,* 99–107.

Voss, H. L. and Hepburn, J. R. (1968). Patterns in criminal homicide in Chicago. *Journal of Criminal Law, Criminology and Police Science, 59,* 499–508.

Wadsworth, J., Burnell, I., Taylor, B., and Butler, N. (1983). Family type and accidents in preschool children. *Journal of Epidemiology and Community Health, 37,* 100–104.

Walker, N. (1968). *Crime and insanity in England.* Vol. 1: *The historical perspective.* Edinburgh: Edinburgh University Press.

Walker, P. L. (1985). Cranial injuries as evidence of violence in prehistoric southern California. Unpublished manuscript.

Wallace, A. (1986). *Homicide: The social reality.* Sydney: New South Wales Bureau of Crime Statistics and Research.

Warner, W. Ll. (1937). *A black civilisation.* NY: Harper.

Webster, C. D., Menzies, R. J., and Jackson, M. A. (1982). *Clinical assessment before trial.* Toronto: Butterworths.

Weir, R. F. (1984). *Selective nontreatment of handicapped newborns: Moral dilemmas in neonatal medicine.* NY: Oxford University Press.

Weiss, J. M. A. and Perry, M. E. (1976). Transcultural attitudes toward antisocial behavior: The 'worst' crimes. *Social Science and Medicine, 10,* 541–545.

West, D. J. (1965). *Murder followed by suicide.* London: Heinemann.

West, D. J. (1968). A note on murders in Manhattan. *Medicine, Science and the Law, 8,* 249–255.

Westermeyer, J. (1972). A comparison of amok and other homicide in Laos. *American Journal of Psychiatry, 129,* 703–709.

Westermeyer, J. (1973). On the epidemiology of amok violence. *Archives of General Psychiatry, 28,* 873–876.

Whitehurst, R. N. (1971). Violence potential in extramarital sexual responses. *Journal of Marriage and the Family, 33,* 683–691.

Whiting, B. B. (1950). *Paiute sorcery.* NY: Viking Fund Publications in Anthropology, No. 15.

Whyte, M. K. (1978). *The status of woman in preindustrial societies.* Princeton, NJ: Princeton University Press.

Wilbanks, W. (1984). *Murder in Miami.* Lanham, MD: University Press of America.

Williams, G. C. (1966). *Adaptation and natural selection.* Princeton, NJ: Princeton University Press.

Williams, G. C. (Ed.). (1971). *Group selection.* Chicago, IL: Aldine-Atherton.

Williams, J. K. (1980). *Duelling in the old south. Vignettes of social history.* College Station, TX: Texas A & M University Press.

Wilson, G. M. (1960). Homicide and suicide among the Joluo of Kenya. In P. Bohannan (Ed.), *African homicide and suicide.* Princeton, NJ: Princeton University Press.

Wilson, J. Q. and Herrnstein, R. J. (1985). *Crime and human nature.* NY: Simon and Schuster.

Wilson, M and Daly, M. (1985). Competitiveness, risk taking, and violence: The young male syndrome. *Ethology and Sociobiology, 6,* 59–73.

Wilson, M. and Daly, M. (1987). Risk of maltreatment of children living with step-parents. In R. Gelles and J. Lancaster (Eds.), *Child abuse and Neglect: Biosocial dimensions.* NY: Aldine de Gruyter.

Wilson, M., Daly, M., and Weghorst, S. J. (1980). Household composition and the risk of child abuse and neglect. *Journal of Biosocial Science, 12,* 333–340.

Wilson, M., Daly, M., and Weghorst, S. J. (1983). Differential maltreatment of girls and boys. *Victimology, 6,* 249–261.

Wilson, P. (1971). *Murderess. A study of the women executed in Britain since 1843.* London: Michael Joseph.

Wilt, G. M. (1974). *Toward an understanding of the social realities of participating in homicides.* Unpublished Ph.D. dissertation, Wayne State University.

Winslade, W. J. and Ross, J. W. (1983). *The insanity plea.* NY: Charles Scribner's & Sons.

Wolfgang, M. E. (1958). *Patterns in criminal homicide.* Philadelphia, PA: University of Pennsylvania Press.

Wolfgang, M. E. (1978). Family violence and criminal behavior. *In* R. L. Sadoff (Ed.), *Violence and responsibility.* NY: Spectrum.

Wolfgang, M. E. and Ferracuti, F. (1967). *The subculture of violence.* London: Tavistock.

Wong, M. and Singer, K. (1973). Abnormal homicide in Hong Kong. *British Journal of Psychiatry, 123,* 295–298.

Wormald, J. (1980). Bloodfeud, kindred and government in early modern Scotland. *Past and Present, 87,* 54–97.

Wright, S. (1922). Coefficients of inbreeding and relationship. *American Naturalist, 56,* 330–338.

Yearwood, J. H. E. (1974). Firearms and interpersonal relationships in homicide: Some cross-national comparisons. *In* M. Riedel and T. P. Thornberry (Eds.), *Crime and delinquency: Dimensions of deviance.* NY: Praeger.

Young, K. (1970). *Isn't one wife enough?* Newport, CT: Greenwood Press.

Zimring, F. E., Mukherjee, S. K., and van Winkle, B. (1983). Intimate violence: A study of interpersonal homicide in Chicago. *University of Chicago Law Review, 50,* 910–930.

Index